GOETHE:

The Story of A Man

OTHER WORKS OF LUDWIG LEWISOHN

Criticism
    THE MODERN DRAMA
    THE SPIRIT OF MODERN GERMAN LITERATURE
    THE POETS OF MODERN FRANCE
    THE DRAMA AND THE STAGE
    THE CREATIVE LIFE
    CITIES AND MEN
    EXPRESSION IN AMERICA
    THIRTY-ONE POEMS BY RAINER MARIA RILKE

Autobiography and Philosophy
    UPSTREAM
    ISRAEL
    MID-CHANNEL
    THE PERMANENT HORIZON
    THE ANSWER

Fiction
    THE BROKEN SNARE
    DON JUAN
    ROMAN SUMMER
    THE CASE OF MR. CRUMP
    THE ISLAND WITHIN
    STEPHEN ESCOTT (THE VEHEMENT FLAME)
    THE LAST DAYS OF SHYLOCK
    THE GOLDEN VASE
    THIS PEOPLE
    AN ALTAR IN THE FIELDS
    TRUMPET OF JUBILEE
    FOREVER WILT THOU LOVE
    RENEGADE
    BREATHE UPON THESE
    ANNIVERSARY

Drama
    ADAM: A DRAMATIC HISTORY

Goethe in Italy. Portrait in oils by Angelika Kauffmann.

GOETHE:

The Story of A Man

BEING THE LIFE OF *Johann Wolfgang Goethe*
AS TOLD IN HIS OWN WORDS AND THE WORDS
OF HIS CONTEMPORARIES

Volume One

By LUDWIG LEWISOHN

Farrar, Straus and Company

NEW YORK

Manufactured in the U.S.A. by
The Colonial Press Inc., Clinton, Massachusetts
Designed by Stefan Salter

49-8936 ✳
3/18/52

TO MY DEAR WIFE

*without whose devoted and
untiring collaboration
this book could never
have been written*

PREFATORY NOTE

Through the good offices of Dr. Milton James Ferguson, Chief Librarian of the Brooklyn Public Library, there were placed at my disposal not only books from his library but many volumes from the Goethe collections of the Library of Congress and the libraries of Harvard, Princeton and Yale Universities. To Doctor Ferguson and to the libraries in question my sincerest thanks are due. I am under obligation to Messrs. Henry Holt and Company for permission to reprint the passage from A. Rogers' version of "Reynard The Fox," quoted in P. Hume Brown's "Life of Goethe."

Ludwig Lewisohn

BRANDEIS UNIVERSITY
WALTHAM, MASSACHUSETTS
AUTUMN 1948

CONTENTS

INTRODUCTION

The year nineteen hundred and forty-nine, of which the twenty-eighth day of August marks the two hundredth anniversary of the birth of Johann Wolfgang Goethe, finds that German people, of whom he came, in a state of self-inflicted ignominy and decay. Devoid of recognizable lineaments, like men robbed of a human countenance, incapable of the contrition and expiation which alone could heal and restore them, the Germans are the despair and horror of this hour in history. Relentlessly they persisted in that course which in the forever memorable words of Thomas Mann "caused their millennial history to be invalidated, reduced to the absurd, proved by the event to have been an accursed aberration and mistake and brought it thus to issue in chaos, in despair, in an unexampled bankruptcy, in a descent into hell, around which flames of thunder danced."

In this long aberration and secular sin Goethe had no share. A moderate conservative, as became his period and his station, an aristocrat, a lover of the best, of quality, like most authentic artists, he looked with sharp distrust and prophetic shame upon even the earlier, more pardonable and more amiable manifestations of German separatism, of German arrogance, upon the whole German cult of pride and blood and death. He was accused, as will be seen, of cold indifference to his country's fate; he would not let his son engage in a duel nor volunteer in the armies which gathered to resist the domination of France. In the course of time his unrivalled greatness forced him upon a half reluctant people. German scholars, both before and during the Wilhelmian Empire, built up the image of the official national poet and froze this most variable, sensitive, anguished and visionary of men into the two rigid gestures of an Apollonian youth and of a Jovian age. It is the purpose of this work to melt the petrefact and to restore to the world the image of the man.

For the works of Goethe, like the works of Montaigne or of Johnson or of André Gide, flowed from a higher, more abundant source. The circa 3000 poems and the two parts of Faust and the Autobiography, which are as fresh as this day's dawn and as pertinent as this day's thoughts, as well as the novels and plays and treatises, which have not wholly escaped the touch of time, are all the productions of a personality greater than themselves—a personality, a human being of incomparable power, intensity and ever renewed significance.

These words must be taken quite literally. Goethe's greatest work, which includes his writings, was himself, his life, both the act and the recording of his experiences between earth and sky. He was supremely capable of experience and supremely capable of reacting to experience and learning from it. Had we but small groups of his sayings, had we of him, as we have of certain founders of religions, but scattered *logia*, pronouncements and parables, mankind would still be assured of the presence on earth of an exemplary life, exemplary not in the sense of entire virtue, but in the sense of all-inclusiveness, in the sense of that life's being the symbol of all human lives.

Quidquid agunt homines, whatever such a being as man has done, hoped, suffered, aspired to, doubted and believed is all summed up, is all suffused with the interpretative power of the spirit, within the compass of this man's faring between birth and death. And he was, in the accurate meaning of that word, a modern man. He is near us; he is ours. His experience is intensely present within our own; his passions are ours, his perplexities, his anguish, his triumph. A single example may suffice. He was, as he himself was fond of saying, no formal philosopher, not even a very attentive reader of formal philosophy. Yet it is correct to state that his final speculative conclusions coincided, while they transcended them, with the late Sir Arthur Eddington's re-confirmation of Kant according to the last implications of contemporary science.

Now the life of this man happens to be one of the most fully recorded and most richly documented of all human lives. It is from this record, this immense documentation of letters, diaries, conversations, reminiscences that the following pages are drawn. The formal works have been used but little, with the single exception of the poems. Of these Goethe himself declared that they were all "poems of occasion," immediate products of experience. As his wise and charming mother reported: "My son used to say: 'whatever oppresses a man must be wrought out in another medium' and when he himself suffered any ill, he made a poem of it." And so one hundred and five poems are set in the immediate context of the experiences which gave them birth. The result should be, according to my hope, as enchanting as a great fiction and as haunting as a legend.

By far the greater portion of the contents of this work has never before appeared in English. In certain sections I could have borrowed from existing translations of the Autobiography, the Correspondence between Goethe and Schiller and the Conversations with Eckermann. I preferred to translate anew in order that style and feeling might be poured, as it were, from a single mold.

Concerning my versions of the poems I content myself by quoting with complete agreement the excellent observations of that fine poet and translator of poetry, Dante Gabriel Rossetti: "The life-blood of rhymed translation is this—that a good poem shall not be turned into a bad one. The only true motive for putting poetry into a fresh language must be to endow a fresh nation, as far as possible, with one more possession of beauty. Poetry not being an exact science, literality of rendering is altogether secondary to this chief aim. I say *literality*—not fidelity, which is by no means the same thing."

Two additional remarks are to be made. The measures of the ancients, the hexameter, the elegiac distich, have never, despite the experiments of Longfellow and Clough and others, become acclimated in our tongue. Hence I have followed a very long tradition and rendered my selections from the Roman Elegies and the Venetian Epigrams, as well as several other epigrams in the English heroic pentameter, blank or rimed. I have borrowed, since it would have been an affectation to rewrite them, Longfellow's translation of the two Wanderer's Nightsongs.

There arose in me that inclination, from which I have not deviated throughout life, to transmute whatever caused me joy or anguish or preoccupied me at all into an image or a poem in order to settle the account with myself, to rectify my concepts of the world without, as well as to tranquilize my soul. Perhaps no one ever needed this gift more than I, whose nature constantly impelled him from one extreme to the other. Whatever of mine has become known represents, therefore, only the fragments of a great confession, which this small book ventures to attempt to complete.

POETRY AND TRUTH. *Part Two. Book Seven.*

Biography should be given a rank far above history, since it delineates the living individual as well as his century and the vital impact of the one upon the other. The story of a life is meant to portray life, as it is in its own nature and for its own sake. . . . All that has genuine biographical value, such as letters that have been preserved, diaries, memoirs or whatever else in that kind, resuscitate the life of the past with more or less reality or in pictorial fullness. One does not tire of reading biographies, for they cause us to live among the living.

POETRY AND TRUTH. *Discarded Preface to the third volume.*

BOOK ONE

Childhood and Early Youth.   *1749-1770*

FRANKFURT

(August 28, 1749 to late September, 1765)

Poetry and Truth

The formal autobiography which extends through Goethe's twenty-sixth year.

It was on August 28, 1749 that, on the stroke of noon, I saw the light of day at Frankfurt-on-the-Main. The constellations were of happy augury; the sun stood in the sign of the Virgin and culminated for the day; Jupiter and Mars were neutral; only the moon, just come to fullness, shed an unfavorable glow, all the more as its planetary hour had just set in. Thus the satellite opposed my birth, which could not take place until that hour had passed. These happy aspects, to which astrologers later gave so favorable an interpretation, may well have been the cause of my preservation. For, the mid-wife being unskillful, I was thought to have been stillborn and it took many efforts to persuade me to behold the light. This circumstance, which caused my family intense anxiety, turned out to be of benefit to my fellow citizens. My grandfather, the Magistrate Johann Wolfgang Textor, used this occasion to cause an obstetrician to be appointed and to have instruction for mid-wives inaugurated or renewed, which benefited many who came after me.

Elisabeth Goethe's Memories

Goethe's mother, Elisabeth, 1731-1808, told these anecdotes of his childhood to Bettina Brentano, 1788-1859, the daughter of early friends of the Goethe family. Bettina communicated them to him in a series of letters.

. . . Understand me when I tell you that the childbed in which your mother bore you had hangings dotted with blue cubes. She was 18 at that time and had been married just a year. She said to herself that you would always be young and that your heart would never

3

grow old, since your mother's youth was part of your birthright. You took three days till you came into the world and caused your mother difficult hours. . . . They rubbed your chest with wine, despairing of your life. Your grandmother stood behind the bed. Suddenly you opened your eyes and she cried out: "Madame, he lives!" "Then," as your mother told me in her seventy-fifth year, "then did my maternal heart awake and has lived from that hour to this continuously uplifted." . . . She put you against her breast, but you could not be persuaded to suck. A wet nurse was engaged and of her you took nourishment with great appetite and enjoyment.

Poetry and Truth

When one tries to recall what happened in one's earliest years, one is often tempted to mistake what one has heard from others for one's own actual experience. . . . I seem to be conscious of the fact that we lived in an old house which consisted of two houses thrown together. Stairs as in a tower led to originally unrelated rooms and steps were needed to connect the storeys. To us children, a younger sister and myself, the great lower hall was the favorite place. At its door there was tall grillwork, through which one had immediate access to the street and the open air. It was like a great cage, and many houses had such an one at that time. There the women sat, sewing or knitting; there the cook cleaned her salad; from there the neighbor women conversed with each other. . . .
My father's mother, in whose house we actually lived, occupied a large room in the rear, adjoining the lower hall, and we carried our games up to her very chair and, when she was ill, to her bedside. She seems a spirit, as it were, in my memory, beautiful, gaunt, in stainless white.

Supplement to Poetry and Truth

My maternal grandfather was a dreamer and an interpreter of dreams; in dreams many things concerning his family had been revealed to him. He also foretold a great conflagration and the unexpected arrival of the Emperor of the Holy Roman Empire. A year before it happened he dreamed that he would be appointed Chief

Magistrate. . . . My mother did not inherit this talent; she attributed this fact to her cheerful temperament and her healthy understanding.

Elisabeth Goethe's Memories

According to Bettina Brentano.

His father was a handsome man. She married him without much reflection. She knew how to influence him in many ways to the advantage of the children. His great passion was for travel. His room was hung with maps; in idle hours he would go over the maps and point out with his finger all notable places and relate the adventures which travelers had met in them. This entertained her delightfully.

Wolfgang was not fond of playing with little children unless they were beautiful. Once at a party he suddenly began to cry and exclaimed: "Away with that ugly child; I can't bear it!" He did not cease crying until he got home where his mother questioned him about his misbehavior. He could not get over that child's homeliness. At that time he was three.

He treated his little sister Cornelia, when she was still in her cradle, with the tenderest affection. He brought her everything he had and wanted to feed and take care of her and was jealous when she was lifted from her cradle. It seemed strange to his mother that, when his little brother Jacob, who had been his playmate, died, he shed no tear. He seemed rather to be irritated by the mourning of his parents. When, a few days later, his mother asked him whether he hadn't been fond of his little brother, he ran into his room and brought forth from under the bed many sheets of paper on which he had written lessons and little stories and he said that he had done all this in order to teach them to Jacob.

"I never tired," said his mother, "of telling him fairy tales nor did he tire of listening. There I sat and he devoured me with his great black eyes and whenever the fate of his favorite hero did not turn out according to his liking I saw a vein swell on his forehead and that he had to control his tears. 'Surely, mother, the princess is not going to marry the wretched tailor, even though he kills the giant.' "

◇◇◇◇◇

Reflections of all kinds concerning the earthquake of Lisbon were made in the presence of the children. . . . The matter absorbed Wolfgang more deeply than we suspected. . . . When he came home with his grandfather from church, where the preacher had sought to vindicate the wisdom of the Creator, and his father asked him in what sense he had understood the sermon, he answered: "In the end it may be even simpler than the preacher thinks. God is sure to know that no harm can come to the immortal soul through an evil catastrophe."

◇◇◇◇◇

Often he would gaze at the stars, of which he had been told that they had been favorable at his birth. . . . Anxiously he would say to his mother: "Surely the stars will not forget me, but will keep the promise they held out over my cradle!" His mother replied: "Why are you so eager to have the help of the stars? We others must get along without them." He said quite proudly: "I can't get along with what suffices other people." He was seven years old then. . . .

◇◇◇◇◇

He was a strange child. One day a friend stood with me at the window. Wolfgang was coming up the street with other boys and his air was grave and dignified. When he entered the room my friend teased him and asked him why he bore himself thus. He answered: "That is only a beginning; later on I will distinguish myself in quite other ways."

◇◇◇◇◇

Once at the time of the festival of the wine harvest there were observed will-o'-the-wisps in the farthest fields about the city. Now they were distant from each other, now they were close, now they moved in the rhythms of a dance. Wolfgang had caused his companions to stick lit candles into their caps and it was he who led the dancing. . . .

On a bright winter day, on which his mother had guests, Wolfgang proposed a drive to the Main. "Mother," he said, "you have never seen me skate and it's such a wonderful day." She put on her heavy scarlet velvet cloak, which had a long train and was fastened down the front with golden buckles and so they all drove to the river. There she saw him on his skates, shooting like an arrow among the others; the cold air had reddened his cheeks and the powder had been scattered from his brown locks. He came to the carriage and saw her crimson cloak and laughed. "What do you want?" she asked. "Oh Mother, you are all so cozy in the carriage; lend me your velvet cloak!" "Surely you're not going to put it on!" "I will indeed!" And so she took off that splendid cloak and he wrapped it about him and threw the train over his arm and glided gracefully away over the ice.

Supplement to Poetry and Truth

My mother was of the opinion that the heart and thus the whole destiny of a human being often develops through incidents which seem too trivial to mention and which affect one inwardly so subtly and secretly that one scarcely feels them. "Daily," she used to say, "I experience such things, which seem stupid to most people, but they are my world and the splendor and the glory thereof." . . . She would add that all her life she had not been contented with the common ways of every day; her powerful nature had desired to absorb important and powerful events and this had been granted her in fullest measure. She had not lived only for her son's sake but her son had lived for her sake and when she grasped these two confronting facts, then she knew what to think.

Poetry and Truth

My father was upon the whole of a didactic nature. Since he had withdrawn from all business affairs, he was fond of transmitting to others what he knew and could do. In the early years of their marriage he had made my mother practice her writing as well as her piano playing and her singing. In connection with this she had been forced to acquire some knowledge and skill in the use of Italian.

All fathers entertain the pious wish of seeing their own lacks realized in their sons. It is quite as though one could live for a second time and put to full use the experiences of one's first career. Conscious of his knowledge, sure of his pertinacity and filled with distrust of the teachers of that period, my father undertook to instruct his children himself and to have only a few supplementary lessons given by other teachers.

My father wanted me, upon the whole, to pursue the same path that he had trodden, but more comfortably and to farther ends. He valued my innate gifts all the more since he lacked them. . . . In earlier and later years, seriously and in jest, he assured me that, had he had my talents, he would have borne himself quite otherwise and not have been so shiftless and wasteful of them.

Through swift apprehension, assimilation and retentiveness I soon outgrew the instruction which my father and the other teachers could afford me, although I got a thorough foundation in nothing. . . . I quickly acquired the forms and turns of speech; also I clarified to myself rapidly whatever inhered in the conception of any matter. . . . My father taught my sister Italian in the same room in which I memorized my Latin. Since I finished my task very readily and yet had to go on sitting still, I would listen to the other lesson and quickly learned Italian, which struck me as an amusing deviation from Latin. . . . I shared an increasing number of private lessons with a group of neighbors' children. These lessons did me little good. . . .

It goes without saying that these children and I enjoyed a constant and continuous instruction in religion. But this ecclesiastical Protestantism, which was transmitted to us, was really only a kind of arid moralism. No one dreamed of attempting a spirited presentation; this teaching could please neither the soul nor the heart. . . . Unfortunately, too, good morals and seemly behavior were commended to us not for their own sake, but for the sake of what people would say of us. This was the constant slogan and I imagined that these people must be very weighty people and must be able to give a right value to all things. . . . In retrospect it is quite clear to me now that the germ of my indifference to and even contempt of public opinion, which characterized me for a long period of my life, arose at this time. Only much later was this attitude modified by insight and culture.

I could always make happy the friendlier among my playmates, when I told them tales of my own invention. They were especially fond of having me tell these fairy stories as though they had happened to me and were delighted that things so wondrous could happen to their playmate. . . . If one contemplates this impulse of my childhood one might well recognize in it that very presumption which the poet uses when peremptorily he expresses things most improbable and demands of his hearers that they admit the reality of what seems true in any way to the narrator.

1825

My father gave me force and frame,
The moral life's foundation;
The gay heart from my mother came,
The high imagination.
Some grandsire worshipped beauty so
That it was bound to win me;
Some grandame lured by gold and glow
Must surely stir within me!
And if these portions cannot be
In the whole wight divided,
On what originality
Could he himself have prided?

Poetry and Truth

There came New Year's Day, 1759, which seemed as desirable and agreeable to us children as previous New Year's Days. The day seemed anxious and ominous to our elders. Since the beginning of the Seven Years' War we were accustomed to the French marching

through our city, and these marches had increased in frequency
during the last days of the old year. . . . Suddenly now our peaceful streets were turned into a scene of war. On them the troops
waited and bivouacked until their housing was provided by system-
atic billeting. This unexpected burden, unheard of for many years,
was felt to be very oppressive by our comfortable citizens; by no one
was it more grievously felt than by my father. Had he been able to
face the matter in a lighter mood, he could have spared himself and
us many a dreary hour, seeing that he spoke French well and always
bore himself with dignity and charm, for we were asked to house
the Royal French Advocate General who, although he was a military officer, held court only in civil matters, such as disagreements
between soldiers and citizens, matters of indebtedness and quarrels.
The gentleman was Count Thorane, a native of Grasse in Provence,
near Antibes. He was tall and thin and serious with a face badly
marred by smallpox, with black fiery eyes and a dignified and highly
restrained demeanor. . . .

Had my father, I may repeat, been able to be more cheerful under
the circumstances, there would have been little that was oppressive
in our situation. The Count was austerely unselfish; he refused even
such gifts as were his due. . . . His inferiors were given strict orders
to cause no expense to the owner of the house. Quite the contrary.
He sent us children handsome shares of his dessert. I cannot but
take this occasion to illustrate the innocence of those days by relat-
ing how our mother grieved us by throwing out the ice cream which
the Count had sent us from his table because it seemed impossible to
her that the human stomach could digest lumps of ice even though
they had been sugared.

Although the French billeting had caused us many inconveniences,
yet we had become too accustomed to it not to miss it. Especially to
us children the house seemed dead. . . . Of course, I reoccupied my
attic room. . . . At this time the distrust of any public instruction
increased daily. Thus private tutors were engaged and since single
families could not afford the expense, several joined in this enterprise. But the children rarely agreed; the young teacher had in-

sufficient authority and repeated annoyances led to angry separations. . . .

We were almost grown now and according to a lazy tradition we were also to be taught fencing and riding in order that we might at need defend ourselves and not sit a horse too awkwardly. . . . In all these matters it happened, as it does so often, that the rudiments of a perfected skill are transmitted in a painful and repellent fashion. In recent times the conviction that this is burdensome and hurtful has led to the pedagogical principle that all things must be taught to the young in an easy, amusing and comfortable manner, from whence in their turn other evils and disadvantages have arisen. . . .

Among the mysteriously significant things which weighed upon my boyhood and my youth, not the least was the condition of the Jews' Town or, rather, the Jews' Street, because it consisted of hardly more than a few streets which in early days had been squeezed in between the wall and the moat. . . . The narrowness, the dirt, the swarming people, the accent of an undelightful dialect—all these combined to form a disagreeable impression even if one glanced in through the gate. It was long before I ventured in alone. . . . Yet these people remained the chosen of God and connected us, however it may have come to pass, with the memories of remote antiquity. Moreover they were human beings, active, kindly, and even the pertinacity with which they clung to their ways commanded one's respect. Moreover, the girls were pretty and liked it well enough when on the Sabbath a Christian boy, meeting them in the fields, bore himself in friendly and attentive fashion. I was extremely curious to become acquainted with their ceremonies. I did not desist until I had visited the synagogue several times; I was present at a circumcision, at a wedding and carried away an image of the Feast of Tabernacles. I was well received everywhere and hospitably entertained and invited to return. . . .

All this time it was undoubtedly in my mind that I was to bring forth something extraordinary; wherein it was to consist, I did not clearly know. But since everyone thinks first of the reward that he is to receive rather than of the merit which is to earn it, thus

I cannot deny that in all my thoughts of a desirable happiness, the
most delightful seemed to me that symbol of the laurel wreath which
is meant to crown the poet. . . .

It was at this time, too, that a friend urgently invited me to an evening party. . . . We met quite late; the meal was most frugal, the
wine just drinkable. . . . When at last the latter gave out someone called for a servant. Instead there appeared a girl of uncommon
and, indeed, in that environment, of incredible beauty.—"What do
you want?" she asked, after she had saluted us all in the friendliest
way. "The maid servant is ill and in bed. Perhaps I can help you."—
"There's no wine left," said one of the company. "If you were to
get us a couple of bottles, it would be very nice."—"Oh please do,
Gretchen," said another. "It's only three steps." . . . From that
moment on the image of this girl followed me wherever I went. It
was the first lasting impression which a being of the other sex had
made on me. Since I could neither find nor even seek a pretext to
see her in her house, I attended church for her sake. I soon found
out where she would sit and so I gazed my fill during the long
Protestant service. . . . The first stirrings of love of an unspoiled
youth take on a decisive spiritual coloration. Nature seems to desire that the one sex should apprehend in the other that which is
good and beautiful in sensuous form. And so to me, too, there was
revealed through the vision of this girl and through my love of her
a new world of the beautiful and the excellent. . . .

The coronation of the Roman Emperor, Joseph II, took place in
Frankfurt on April 3, 1764. The weather was favorable and the
whole population in movement. Various kinsmen and friends and
myself had been assigned a window in an upper storey from which
we had a view of the festivities. We went there almost at dawn and
had a bird's-eye view of the preparations. . . . A new fountain had
been erected with two great vats on either side. From the beak of
one of the eagles of the Imperial Standard spouted white wine; from
the beak of the other flowed the red. Yonder stood the rude hut in
which during several days one had watched a whole ox roast over
charcoal flames on an enormous spit. . . . I meant to celebrate the

radiant evening of this day in an agreeable fashion, for I had agreed
with Gretchen and some friends that we were to meet somewhere
after dark. The city was illuminated throughout when I met my
beloved. I offered Gretchen my arm and we strolled from one quarter
to another and were very happy together. . . . In many places bread
and sausages were distributed among the people, nor was free wine
lacking. . . . The four of us kept close together and strolled comfortably, and I, at Gretchen's side, seemed to myself to be traversing
those happy, fabled Elysian fields. . . . Later we all found a delightful inn and since there were no other guests, we enjoyed ourselves
all the more and passed the greater part of the night serenely and
happily. . . . When I accompanied Gretchen to her own door she
kissed me on the forehead. It was the first and the last time that she
bestowed a kiss upon me, for I was destined never to see her
again. . . .

My heart had been too deeply indulged to grow calm again. It had
known love and had been deprived of its object; it had lived and
now life seemed shriveled to it indeed. . . .
Partly through a chance suggestion and partly through acquaintances I began now to wander through the nearby mountains which
from my childhood on, had seemed so distant and so severe of aspect.
. . . From such excursions I was again and again drawn back home
by an attraction which had always affected me powerfully. That was
my sister. She was only a year younger than I; she had accompanied
me through my whole conscious existence and therefore we were
most profoundly united. These natural circumstances were intensified by our domestic situation. There was our father, loving and
well disposed but who, conscious of an extreme inner tenderness,
played the part of iron strictness with unbelievable consistency, in
order to give his children the best possible education and not only
to build, but to order and preserve his well-established house. Then
there was our mother, almost a child herself, who attained a full
consciousness of life only with and through her two oldest children.
She and we two regarded the world with a healthy look; we were
capable of life and desired an immediate fulfillment.
This contradiction which hovered over our family increased as the
years went on. Our father pursued his aim with uninterrupted de-

termination. The mother and her two children could not resign
themselves to give up their feelings, their demands, their wishes.
Under these circumstances it was but natural that brother and sister clung together and clung closely to their mother. . . . And so
during those years, since play and study, growth and development,
were the same for the brother and sister, and one might have thought
them twins, thus this unity between them and this mutual confidence remained constant during their physical and moral development. The deepest interest of youth, that astonished perception of
the awakening of sensual instincts, which clothes itself in intellectual
forms and needs but also in sensual images, as well as all the pertinent reflections concerning this matter, which serve to darken
rather than to clarify—these and many errors and confusions that
arise from them, the brother and sister shared and endured hand in
hand, the less capable of being enlightened concerning their strange
condition by virtue of the sacred shyness due to the bonds of blood.
The closer they wanted to approach each other and the more they
desired to attain clearness, the more powerfully were they sundered
from each other. . . .

When still, from time to time, the pain over the loss of Gretchen
renewed itself within me and I would suddenly weep and lament
and bear myself in an unruly fashion, my despair aroused in my
sister an equally desperate impatience over the non-fruition, the failures and the transitoriness of youthful inclinations, so that we both
felt ourselves to be immeasurably unhappy, the more so as in this
strange instance the two confidants could not be transformed into
a pair of lovers. . . .

◇◇◇◇◇

Michaelmas, the period at which I was to enter the university, approached. My soul was equally stirred by life and by learning. I felt
ever more clearly my dislike of my native city. . . . Privately I rejected the notion of studying law and meant to devote myself to
languages, to antiquities, to history. . . . Nurturing these sentiments I had in mind the University of Göttingen. But my father
was not to be moved, and so I regarded my decision to embrace my
own course of study and of life contrary to his conviction and desire
as a justified defense of myself. . . . The hidden joy of a prisoner
who has torn his chains and filed the iron bars of his cell cannot be

greater than was mine as I saw the days glide by and October draw near. . . . At last Michaelmas came and I drove off, leaving the noble city which had given me birth and which had nurtured me with an indifference as great as though I never meant to set foot in it again.

LEIPZIG

(Early September, 1765 to late August, 1768)

1765

Poetry and Truth

When I arrived in Leipzig, it happened to be the time of the great
Fair. . . . With much interest I wandered through the market place
and saw the booths, and I was especially attracted by the strange
garb of the dwellers in the Eastern parts of Europe, the Poles and
Russians and, above all, the Greeks, whose notable figures and dignified robes I went to see again and again. . . . I found quarters between the Old and New Market. There were several agreeable rooms,
giving on the court, which a bookseller inhabited during the days of
the Fair and which I was able to rent for the rest of the year at a
tolerable figure.

Leipzig, October 12, 1765

To His Sister Cornelia

Dear little sister, It would be quite unfair, if I were not to think of
you; that is, it would be the greatest injustice ever perpetrated by a
student, since the children of Adam began to attend universities,
were I to neglect to write you. What would you say, little sister, if you
were to look into my room now? In astonishment you would exclaim: So neat and orderly, brother! There! Open your eyes and
look! Here is my bed, there my books, yonder a table prettily arranged as your toilet table can never be. Oh, but I forgot. Little
girls like you haven't the vision of poets like me. So you must take
my word for it that everything in my room is in good order—the
word of a poet. Postscript to Father: I'm writing to the old Rector.
That won't be difficult. All I am doing now is grinding at Latin! One
more thing, you'll hardly believe what grand people these professors are. I've been quite charmed to see several of them in all their
splendor.

October 18, 1765

To Cornelia

I never ate so many good things as I do now and in this place. There are pheasants, partridges, grouse, larks, fishes, that is trout, in great quantities. Such is the fare at a professor's table. Sometimes there are grapes. Sixty larks cost two Rhenish thaler. But I don't like the beer. It's bitter as death. I haven't yet had a whiff of wine. I must complain of the poor pieces they put on at the theatre. . . .

October 20, 1765

To Johannes Jakob Riese

A Frankfurt playmate and fellow pupil, at this time student of law at the University of Marburg. J. C. Gottsched, 1700-1768, a then leading poet and critic and adherent of the French classical tradition in German letters.

I haven't seen Gottsched yet. He just got married again. She's the daughter of a major. You've heard about it. She is 19 and he is 65; she is 4 feet and he is 7; she's thin as a herring and he is fat as a feather-bed. I am cutting quite a figure here! I'm no Beau Brummel yet nor do I intend to be one. It takes astuteness to get time for my work. There are parties, concerts, plays, entertainments, suppers, drives the whole time. Oh, it's wonderful, but it's wonderfully expensive, too. My purse feels it, I assure you. . . . Nevertheless, one can live inexpensively here. Now that the Fair is over I intend to practice economy. I hope to get along for the year with 300 Rhenish thaler. What do I say? Even with 200. . . . And yet consider the menu here: chicken, goose, turkey, duck, partridges, snipe, hare, venison, pike, pheasants, oysters etc. Such is our daily fare. We never have such ordinary meats as beef, veal, mutton. I don't know how it tastes any more and all this grandeur is cheap enough.

December 6, 1765

To Cornelia

What would you like me to teach you? Would you like to know at
what rate the speed of falling bodies increases, or that the square root
of 16 is 4? What good would that be to you? I'll teach you something
better. We'll do it this way. Write your letters on the one half of a
sheet of paper and I will write my answer and criticism on the rest.
But don't let Father help you. That's no good. I want to see how
you can write. . . . Remember this: write only as you would speak;
then your letters will be good.

December 12, 1765

To Cornelia

Today is Grandfather's birthday and you will be sitting and feasting
while I, poor fellow, will have to content myself with the wing of a
goose and a roll. . . .
Now here is a commission for you. I am enclosing in this letter a
New Year's poem for Grandfather. Have it on you on New Year's
Day, and when they have all assembled in the evening, then hand it
to him, but not before and try to have our Uncle Textor read it
aloud. Then observe the emotional reaction of the company and
give me a faithful account. . . .
You can tell Father how many louis d'or I have left. I won't get my
new breeches until the New Year Fair. Even then my holiday will be
brief, for lectures continue through the whole time of the Fair.

Poetry and Truth

In the beginning I attended my courses busily and faithfully; philosophy, however, seemed to offer no clarification at all. . . . Of matter, of the world, of God, it seemed to me that I knew quite as much
as my teacher. . . . It was no better in the law courses. Here, too,
I knew precisely as much as the teacher chose to impart. . . . After
some time and after many struggles I conceived so great a contempt
for all that I had begun or completed, that one fine day I burned in
the kitchen stove poetry and prose, plans and sketches and outlines,

so that the smoke which filled the whole house frightened and disturbed our good old landlady not a little.

Poetry and Truth

I gave up my professorial dining club and felt all the happier in my new one, since I was much taken with the daughter of the house, a pretty, agreeable girl, and there were many opportunities to exchange friendly glances with her, a kind of delight which I had neither sought nor found since my mishap with Gretchen. . . .

It is but human to be fascinated by one's own name and, after the manner of young and untutored people I inscribed it wherever I could. I had once carved it handsomely and precisely into the smooth trunk of a linden tree. That next autumn, when my passion for Annette was at its height, I did my best to carve her name above my own. In the meantime, toward the end of the winter, I had been a moody lover and had, as it were, sought occasions to torment and grieve her. That spring I happened to visit the tree and the sap oozed through the incisions which represented her name and bedewed with its innocent botanical tears the hardened lines of my name. It seemed to me as though these were tears which she shed over my misbehavior and I was in great dismay.

1766

August 12, 1766

From J. A. Horn to W. C. L. Moors

J. A. Horn, 1750-1806, was a fellow student in Leipzig. W. C. L. Moors, 1749-1806, was a boyhood friend and later Municipal Secretary of Frankfurt.

Let me tell you about our Goethe. He is still the proud, fantastic creature which he was when he came to Leipzig. I wish you could see him. You would either be enraged or burst with laughter. I can't understand how anyone could change so quickly. All his ways and his whole behavior are infinitely different from the way he bore himself at first. He is not only proud but a Beau Brummel, and his

garments, handsome as they are, are of so bizarre a taste that they
mark him out among all the students.

October 1, 1766

To W. C. L. Moors

I have finally decided to disclose everything to you and Horn has
taken it upon himself to write you on this matter which is not the
pleasantest in the world. And so you know everything and you will
have seen that your friend is not as culpable as you may think. If
you will look upon it as a philosopher—and you must do so if you
want to be happy in this world—what is the blameworthy aspect of
my love? What is social rank? It is an empty color that man has invented in order to paint with it people who do not deserve it. And
money is an equally despicable advantage in the eyes of one who re-
flects. I love a girl who has neither standing nor wealth and for the
first time I feel the happiness which true loves brings. I have gained
the affection of my girl not through the wretched trickeries of ordinary love-making, but through my character and my heart. . . . The
excellent heart of the girl is my pledge that she will never desert me
unless duty and necessity bid us part. If you knew this admirable girl
you would forgive me the folly I commit in loving her.

October 3, 1766

J. A. Horn to W. C. L. Moors

You will be very happy when I tell you that we have not, as we mis-
takenly believed, lost a friend in Goethe. . . . He is in love, it is
true; he has confessed it to me and will to you. But his love, melancholy as it may be, is not a guilty love, as I had believed. He is not in
love with the young lady whom I suspected. He loves a girl below
him in station but one whom, take my word for it, you, too, would
love, were you to see her. . . . He loves her very tenderly with the
most correct intentions of a virtuous person, although he knows that
she can never become his wife. I do not know whether she returns
his affection. . . . He has recently given me his entire confidence;
he has initiated me into his accounts and shown me that the display
he seems to make is not as great as people think. He is more of a

philosopher and moralist than ever and, innocent as his love is, yet
he disapproves of it. . . . I pity him and his good heart. How
wretched he must be to love without hope a girl most virtuous and
perfect. And if we assume that she returns his love, how doubly
wretched must he be.

October 8, 1766

To Ernst Wolfgang Behrisch

Goethe's chief confidant in Leipzig, 1738-1809, eleven years older, private tutor in princely families.

She has gone, my dear good Behrisch, she has gone to the play with
her mother and her pretended future husband who tries to please
her by giving an hundred parties. It's a choice thing to behold,
worthy of the observation of a student of life. Here is a man doing
his best to be agreeable, inventive, careful, always under her feet,
without attaining the slightest results, one who would give gold to
the poor for a single kiss, which he'll never get. Meanwhile there am
I, very still in a corner, indulging in no gallantries, paying her no
compliments, regarded by that other as stupid and unskillful and in
the end behold this stupid fellow the recipient of gifts for which the
other would make a pilgrimage to Rome. I wanted to go out at the
same time that she did, but to keep me from doing so she gave me
the key of her desk so that I could do or write as I liked there. Before
leaving she said to me: Stay there until I come back. You always have
some mad thing in your head, whether in prose or in verse. Write it
down. . . . She also left me two beautiful apples, a present from
my rival.

October 13, 1766

To Cornelia

I am beginning to be pretty dissatisfied with Leipzig and its people.
I'm quite out of favor with the people to whom I had introductions
and that for the reason that I followed Father's advice and refused
to play at cards. I am considered a superfluous person who serves no
purpose. . . . There is another reason why I am disliked in good
society. I have more taste and knowledge than these fashionable people and I couldn't help showing them the wretchedness of their judg-
ments at a big party.

October 14, 1766

To Cornelia

The original is in English and is reprinted as he wrote.

French enough! Let us write english! I shall become haughty sister, if thou doest praise me in like a manner. Truely, my english knowledge is very little, but i'll gather all my forces, to perfection it. Visiting my letters, ye shall have found many faults, ye may pardon. The few you have marked, have been caused, by lack of attention. I've found that Adieu in many english lettres, and I did then adopt it. . . . The honnour to sit in the first paragraph, shall have Miss. B (ethmann). Ye wait, the dear father and thou, for a long description, of her beeing here; but I can't give You a complet notice thereof. I did see her, four or five times, and four or five times she was a goose. . . . That is all what I know. The companions of Miss. B (ethmann) are mediocre beauties, for her wit, I did never see it. . . .

May 11, 1767

To Cornelia

Among my vivid acquaintances little Annette does not deserve to be forgotten. She's a very good girl with a very honest heart to which she joins an agreeable simplicity, although her education has been severe rather than good. She takes care of me and tends to my laundry, for she understands such things well and takes pleasure in helping me and I love her very much for that. Am I not a funny fellow? I love all these girls. But who can help it if they are so good? As for beauty—it touches me not at all and, truly, all my girl friends are good rather than beautiful. . . .

Since I am wholly without pride I may trust that inner conviction which tells me that I possess some of the qualities which go to make a poet, and that industry may someday make me one. I started to write verses when I was 10 and thought them good; now that I am 17 I see that they are bad, but being seven years older the new ones are seven years better. . . . A year ago I lost all courage and it took six months until, at the desire of my sweetheart, I was able to write a few songs. . . . People should leave me alone. If I have the genius

I'll be a poet, even though no one tries to improve me. If I lack genius, no criticisms will do me any good.

1767

SUMMER NIGHT

I must leave the cottage lowly
Where but now my sweetheart was,
And with muffled steps and slowly
Through the sombre forest pass.
Swift the moon the bushes blanches,
Gentle winds begin to play,
And the birches from their branches
Strew their incense on my way.

Exquisite the cool about me
Of the wondrous summer night!
Peace within me and without me
To complete the soul's delight!
Rapture here past all believing!
Yet, O Heaven, I would run,
All such nights unto thee leaving,
Were my girl to grant me one.

Early October, 1767

To E. W. Behrisch

Two people have moved into the vacant room downstairs. Maybe you've seen them, but that doesn't matter. One is an older man, one a younger. . . . The thing didn't disturb me in so far. They're not only dining but supping here every night. That's more disagreeable, but that isn't all of it. You can imagine how my girl beseeches me not to let this change make any difference in my behavior or in my heart. Caressing me passionately, she besought me not to torment her with jealousy and has sworn to me that she will be forever mine. And what does not seem credible when one loves?

October 13, 1767

To Behrisch

Another night like this and all my sins will not send me to hell. You may sleep tranquilly, but consider a jealous lover who had drunk enough champagne to raise his blood to a pleasant heat and to fire his imagination in the extreme. First I couldn't sleep at all; I tossed in my bed; I leaped up and raged. When I was worn out and slept for a while I had stupid and ghastly dreams.

October 14, 1767

To Cornelia

I have wholly renounced going to concerts or plays or riding or driving and abandoned the company of any young people who might persuade me to the one or the other. This will be of great use to my purse. This week I go from my room to my meals and from my meals back to my room and will continue to do so through the winter and bad weather. . . . My studies sometimes make me feel stupid. The Pandects have plagued my memory this half year and truly I have retained no great matter. . . . I've had no better luck with the Institutes of Law and its history. . . . I'll be hanged if I know anything. If you don't understand this passage in my letter, read it to Father; it will be as disagreeable to him as it is to me.

November 2, 1767

To Behrisch

My love salutes you; I love her as always. Does she love me? I believe it for the time. . . . Love is misery, but all misery has its voluptuous element when we may moderate the oppressive sting of the heart through our complaints. And no pleasure of this kind exceeds the pains of love when a friend hears of our ill and sees our tears and heals our wound by his sympathy.

November, 1767

To Behrisch

I have trimmed me another pen in order to recover. My beloved! And she will be that always. I feel that at the very moment when she enrages me. God, why must I love her so!

Now, Behrisch, don't ask me to tell you what happened in cold blood. This evening I sent downstairs to fetch something. My maid came and brought me the news that *she* had gone to the play with her mother. A cold fever had just shaken me and now this piece of news set my blood on fire. To the play! Indeed! At the very moment that she knows her lover to be ill. God! That was miserable, but I forgave her. I didn't know what was being played. Had she met those men in the playhouse—those? That shook me to the core. I had to know. I threw on my clothes and ran like mad to the playhouse and bought me a gallery seat. I climbed up and, O horror, my eyesight did not reach the boxes. I thought I was going mad and meant to rush home to fetch my opera glasses. A simple fellow beside me saved me from utter confusion. I saw that he had two pair and begged him to lend me one. He did so. I looked down and found her box. She sat in the corner with her brother and mother. But behind her the gentleman in question, very intimate in his attitude. Think of it! Think of it! Myself in the gallery seeing this from afar. . . .

The clock strikes nine and the damned play will be at an end. A curse upon it. Let me go on with my story. I sat for a quarter of an hour and saw nothing but what I had seen the first five minutes. Suddenly the fever overcame me with full force and I thought to die on the instant. I returned the opera glasses to my neighbor and ran and have been back for two hours. . . . All this time I have wanted to weep but my teeth chatter. . . .

I have slept a little; I am very weak. What will be tomorrow? My poor head whirls. Tomorrow I'll go out and see her. Perhaps her unjust coldness will have abated. If not, I am sure that my fever will be redoubled tomorrow. Let it be. I no longer have any control over myself.

Wednesday morning, November 11, 1767

To Behrisch

The thing that made yesterday hell to me makes heaven of it today.
And this will go on until this circumstance can create neither for me
any more. We were alone for a quarter of an hour. No more was
needed to reconcile us. In vain does Shakespeare say: "Frailty, thy
name is woman"; this might rather apply to the youth in question.
She acknowledged her error, my illness touched her and she fell on
my neck and begged me to forgive her, which I did. . . .
I had strength of mind enough to conceal from her my folly at the
playhouse. "Look," she said, "we were at the play yesterday, but
you mustn't be angry at me. I went into the back of the box and,
though he kept standing behind my chair, I avoided talking to him
as much as possible. . . ." O Behrisch, it seemed to me that I had
indeed seen this and now she confirmed it. She! And with her arms
about me. One moment's delight makes up for a thousand of torment. Who would live if this were not so?

November 20, 1767

To Behrisch

For some time, since I could not see her in the evening, she has shown
me all tenderness and was restless if ever I did not come to her in the
afternoon. Only she has not tormented me with her jealousy, with
no suspicion of me, and that meant that the ardor of her passion had
greatly diminished. But for the past four weeks, since I have been
seeing something of another girl, the fire has broken out again with
all violence—a jealousy to the point of rage, a suspiciousness, a pos-
sessiveness which has reached the point that I dare not have her
know whether I have kissed a lady's hand. It makes us both wretched.
She, especially, is infinitely miserable and it is my compassion for her
that makes me exercise so much patience.

1768

To Behrisch

How is Annette? Look, is there such a girl as Annette in the world? You may know it but you seem long to have forgotten it. For at least three months you never asked after her and I thought courtesy demanded that I do not write you about her.

'Tis well that you want to know how it is with us. I'll tell you. We love each other more than ever, although we see each other more rarely. I have conquered myself to keep from seeing her and thought I had won the battle. But I am more wretched than before and perceive that love will persist even in absence. I can live without seeing her, never without loving her. I am the cause of all our distress. She is an angel and I am a fool.

Hear me, Behrisch, I cannot and I would not leave her and yet I must away, I must. Yet she must not be unhappy. . . . And yet I am forced to the cruelty of robbing her of all hope. I must. For whoever gives a girl hope has already promised. If she can marry an honorable man and live happily without me, how glad would I be. . . . Never shall she feel the pain of seeing me in the arms of another until I have felt that identical pain concerning her. . . .

Do send me by the next mail my poems to her, which you copied for me. You don't need the manuscript and I have thought of changes needed in the verses and have written new ones.

To Behrisch

Today it is two years since I first told her that I loved her, two years. We began with love, we end with friendship. Yet not I. I love her still, so much, so much. Oh that you were here to console me, to show me your affection.

Poetry and Truth

I had brought with me from home a certain hypochondriac tendency. . . . An ill-chosen diet disturbed my digestion; the heavy Merseburg beer clouded my brain, the coffee, which depressed me, especially when taken with milk after dinner, paralyzed my bowels and stopped their functioning almost entirely. . . . Moreover this was the period in which cold baths were strictly recommended. People were told to sleep on a hard couch with a light covering, so that all accustomed transpiration was suppressed. These and other follies were, according to a misinterpretation of Rousseau, to lead us back to nature out of the corruption of custom. . . .

One night I woke up with a violent hemorrhage and had just strength and sense enough to awaken my neighbor. . . . For several days I hovered between life and death and even the pleasure of a consequent improvement was embittered by an eruption, a swelling on the left side of the throat, which was observed only now after the acute danger was past.

It was in September, 1768 that, in the company of reliable people known to me, I left Leipzig in a comfortable hired coach. . . . As we approached my native city I could not but recall to myself with increasing dismay the conditions, prospects, hopes which had accompanied me when I set out from home; and it was a most depressing feeling to realize that I was returning, as it were, in the character of one who had suffered shipwreck.

Autobiographical Fragments

Thus, prior to my twentieth year, I had run through all the schools of moral philosophy. Their teachings were more often contradictory than they were capable of being harmonized. But always and everywhere the emphasis was on a certain quality of moderation of which I, according to my temperament, understood exceedingly little. Youth can not indeed grasp the necessity of moderation and, seeking to attain it, is likely to fall into awkwardness and extremity. Such thoughts and such an attitude had, however, been awakened within me, and though I lived my youthful life cheerfully and freely and vividly, yet I could not but be often reminded of the desirability of that norm unknown to me. Though I lived unfettered I soon became aware of the circumstance that the environment, do as we will, must always limit us and so I formed the conclusion that the most precious thing was to attain an inner, a spiritual independence.

FRANKFURT

(Early September, 1768 to late March, 1770)

Poetry and Truth

My sister made common cause with me at once and, as I had hitherto done from her letters, so I could now learn through her in greater detail and more exactly the conditions and the situation of our family. After my departure for Leipzig my father had concentrated his didactic hobby entirely on my sister and had cut her off from almost every opportunity of being active or of seeking refreshment outside of the house. . . . My sister's character was and remained hard to define, a curious mixture of sternness and softness, of stubbornness and yieldingness. . . . In a way that frightened me she had now turned all her hardness against our father, whom she never forgave for these three years during which he had hindered her from any innocent pleasure or embittered it for her, so that she refused utterly to acknowledge any of his good or excellent qualities. . . . She would no longer consent to anything out of affection or to be agreeable and this was one of the first things about which my mother complained to me in a confidential conversation. But since my sister needed affection as keenly as any human being, she fixed all that she had on me. She devoted all her time to my care and to my entertainment; even her girl friends, of whom she was the leader, although she did not know this, were forced to take thought how to amuse and comfort me. . . .

October 27, 1768

Cornelia Goethe

From an account she wrote of a cousin's visit to the Goethe house in Frankfurt.

"My dear girl," said the cousin, "I haven't yet told you of my pleasure at finding anyone so amiable as your brother. We must congratulate you that you have one so worthy of our love."—"I am happy, sir, to see you convinced that I was right to grieve over the absence of my beloved brother. These have been three long years and I wished for his return at every moment."—"Sister, sister," said my brother, "and yet now that I am here no one wants to see me; it is as though I were not here."—"You must not reproach me, brother; you know it isn't my fault; you're constantly busy and I dare not disturb you as often as I would like. . . ."

My brother, in order to give a different turn to the conversation, spoke of Leipzig and of the pleasant time he had passed there. At the same time he began to complain of our own city, of the bad taste prevalent here, of our stupid fellow citizens and finally, in a sort of intoxication, he went to the length of asserting that even the girls of Frankfurt were unbearable. . . . "I admit," he cried, "that they are more beautiful, but what avails beauty if it is not combined with that charm which enchants us more than beauty does itself."

October 20, 1768

Cornelia Goethe to a Friend

We are paying a number of visits, my brother and I. We are going to cross the river to see my uncle who has a garden on the other bank. Then we will take a long walk, which will be very well for our health, since I must confess to you that we're not very well, either of us. . . .

November 16, 1768

I just looked in on my brother who is working at a new comedy. He reads me all his things and you can imagine the infinite pleasure with which I listen. He has also been drawing some delightful heads, and I'll send you one of them sometime.

November 19, 1768

Yesterday we went to a concert, my brother and I. The audience was a brilliant one and the music of the choicest.

December 7, 1768

My brother is very ill. Suddenly he had a violent attack of the colic and suffers extremely. Everything is being done for his repose and respite, so far in vain. I cannot bear to see him without a breaking heart. What would I give to help him!

December 10, 1768

After two days of suffering my poor brother feels a little better. But he is still very weak and can be up only a quarter of an hour at a time. If only the pain would ease, his strength would return.

September 8, 1768

To E. T. Langer

A fellow student in Leipzig.

The news that my journey home was safe and tranquil and that my physician here diagnoses my trouble as not affecting the lung but the windpipe will be agreeable to all who care for me. . . . My love affair, that unhappy passion, which cost me far, far more than that I should ever forget it, is buried deep in memory and covered over with the cold sod of diversion. At times I think of it quite indifferently. I am no more touched by the thought of your girl than by that of Annette. . . .

Things are as I thought they would be. My mother has declared herself an open adherent of the group of Pietists; my father knows and does not object. My sister has gone to the prayer meetings. . . . And I'll probably end by going, too. . . .

Poetry and Truth

My mother with her vivid and lively nature had found the days monotonous and slow. Her small household was soon taken care of. Her admirable, ever busy soul sought some interest and the first she found was in religion, which she chose the more happily, since her most excellent friends were cultivated and sincere Christians. The chief of these was a Fräulein von Klettenberg. . . . This lady found in me what she sought, a creature young, vivid, equally desirous of an unknown salvation who, though he could not consider himself unusually sinful, was yet far from serene and healthy in either mind or body. . . .

She interpreted my restlessness, my impatience, my striving, my seeking, my searching and meditating and vacillating in her own fashion and did not conceal her conviction, nay, she assured me of its completeness, that all this was due to my lack of a conciliated Divinity. Well, I had always imagined that I was on quite good terms with God; in fact, I rather fancied after a good many experiences that He was somewhat in my debt and that it was I who had to pardon Him for several circumstances. . . .

September 13, 1768

To Adam Friedrich Oeser

> The director of the Academy of Art at Leipzig, to whom Goethe felt that he owed the foundation of his training in both drawing and the theory of aesthetics.

Dearest Professor, I have now been back in my worthy native city for twelve days, surrounded by relatives, friends and acquaintances who are partly delighted at my appearance here, partly astonished, but who all strive to be agreeable to the new arrival and the half-stranger. By their amiable society they seek to render tolerable to me a city too different from Leipzig to afford me much that is agreeable. I can't tell you yet how well they will succeed; I am still too distracted and too busy readjusting myself to have much feeling either for what I have lost or for all that I find here again. So all that I am writing you today is that my arrival after an agreeable trip has brought a much needed serenity to my family and that my physicians here have decided that my trouble is not in the lung but in the adjacent parts and seems daily to improve.

October 1, 1768

To the Family of Annette

The family's name was Schönkopf and Annette the middle name of the
daughter Käthchen.

Your servant, Herr Schönkopf; how is Madame; good evening, young
lady; Peterkin, good evening. I've been away a long time, haven't I?
It's five whole weeks and more that I haven't seen you or talked to
you. That happened only once in eighteen months and from now
on, alas, will happen oftener. How I have fared the while you would
probably like to know. Well, it's easy enough to tell you, just so-so,
just in mediocre fashion.

Apropos, surely you have forgiven me for not saying farewell. I was
in your neighborhood; I was downstairs at your door and saw the
lantern burn and went to the foot of the stairs. But I didn't have the
heart to go up. That last time, how would I ever have gotten down
again? So I do now what I should have done then. I thank you for
all the love and friendship which you showed me so constantly and
which I will never forget. I needn't beg you to remember me. A
thousand occasions will arise at which you will have to think of one
who was a member of your family for eighteen months, who often
irritated you, no doubt, but who was always a good fellow at bottom
and whom, I hope, you will miss from time to time. At least I can say
that I miss you often. Let's pass over that, for that is always a melancholy chapter to me.

November 1, 1768

To Käthchen (Annette) Schönkopf

My sweetest friend, Are you as cheerful as ever, are you as malicious
as ever—as skillful to place the good under a false aspect and as
pitiless to make fun of one who suffers and to jeer at one who la-
ments; your letter contains all these amiable cruelties. . . .

I do thank you for your unexpectedly prompt answer. I beg of you
to continue to think of me in pleasant and cheerful hours and, if you
can, to write me. To perceive your vividness, your cheerfulness, your
wit is one of my greatest pleasures; let these qualities be as frivolous,
as bitter, as they may.

No one knows better than I what a figure I cut, and I can imagine what part my letters play. When one remembers how others fared, one need be no soothsayer to guess one's own fate. I am content; 'tis the common fate of the dead that survivors and successors dance on their grave. . . .

November 9, 1768

To Oeser

. . . My health begins to improve and yet it is still bad enough. The enclosed letter, which I ventured to write to your daughter, contains more on this point and on my way of life.

Art is, as usual, almost my chief occupation, although I am reading more and thinking more on the subject than actually drawing. For now that I am on my own feet I begin to feel my weakness. . . .

How deeply in your debt I am, dearest professor. . . . My taste, my knowledge, my insight, do I not owe them all to you? How certain and luminous has that strange and at first incomprehensible maxim become to me, that the workshop of a great artist contributes more to the development of the thinker or poet than the classroom of the philosopher and the critic. Teaching can do much, but direct stimulation does everything. . . .

My parents send their greetings to you and your family with the affection and gratitude they owe to a man to whom their son is so deeply indebted.

December 30, 1768

To Käthchen (Annette) Schönkopf

My dear and anxious friend, On the occasion of the New Year you will doubtless have heard of my recovery through our friend Horn. I hasten to confirm the fact. Yes, my dear, it is over and in future you must not be disturbed if ever you are told that I have taken to my bed again. You know, my constitution makes occasional mistakes, but within a week these rectify themselves. This time it was bad and looked even worse and gave rise to dreadful pain. But misfortune has its advantages. I learned a good deal during my illness, which I would not have learned under other circumstances. . . . What a queer creature man is. Often in cheerful society I was morose; now that I am deserted and alone I am gay; even during my illness my

gaiety consoled my family, which was in no condition to console itself, let alone me. . . .

So soon as I am quite strong again I shall fare forth into foreign
parts and it will depend but upon you and one other how soon I
see Leipzig. Meanwhile I plan to go to France and observe the color
of French life. So you can imagine what a polished person I will be
when I come to see you again. Sometimes it occurs to me what a
mad stroke of fate it would be if, despite my handsome plans, I were
to die before Easter. Then I would order me a headstone in the
Leipzig cemetery, so that at least once a year, on my name's day,
you could visit my grave. How does that appeal to you?

1769

January 6, 1769

To Annette

After her betrothal to Doctor Kanne, later member of the Leipzig Municipal Council.

From your letter to Horn I got the news of your happiness, of your
joy, and my joy for you you can imagine if you are still capable of
imagining how much I love you. . . . My silence might have been
culpable, had you awaited my letters with impatience. But I knew
that this was a period when a letter from my hand meant no more
to you than the daily paper and that, all things considered, I am
no better to you than a stale plate of fish and I would swear—but
let me not swear—you might believe that I meant it. . . .

My poems aren't printed yet. Someday when they are, I'd like to
send you a copy. . . . When I wrote them I was a different fellow
from now. . . . If you were to see how I pass my time you would
think it very funny. Writing is a tough job, especially—to you.
Unless you give a special order you won't hear from me before
October. For, my dear friend, although you call me your friend and
sometimes your best friend, yet even a best friend tends to be a bore.
Who would eat preserved beans if he can have the fresh article? Fresh
pike are the best; if you're afraid they'll spoil, you pickle them in
salt, especially if you want to send them away. You must be immensely amused when you think of all the lovers whom you have

pickled away in friendship, tall ones and short ones, crooked ones
and straight ones; I myself laugh when I think of them. Yet you
mustn't break off our correspondence entirely. For a pickled fish
I'm not too bad.

1769

Dear songs I chanted, cease not flowing
To the oblivion of the main;
No lad will voice your accents glowing,
Nor lass when springtime comes again.

In every rhythm you besought her
Who pays my faithfulness with scorn.
So, seeing you were writ in water
Far on its waves may you be borne.

January 17, 1769

To Langer

Things have taken a strange turning, at least outwardly. Several
of the Pietist Brothers watched with me; my father, who was
troubled, appreciated their kindliness and was friendly and courteous. Since that time we have a freer *Exercitium Religionis.* Day
before yesterday we even had an assembly in our house on some
valid pretext, as you may imagine. It was all arranged in the manner
of a party; wine and sausages and white bread were placed on a
side table. The women sat around another table with their hymnals.
At the grand piano there was one who played the hymns accompanied by two on flutes. The rest of us sang.

February 13, 1769

To Friederike Oeser

Daughter of Goethe's teacher of art in Leipzig.

. . . Oh, my friend, the light is the truth, but the sun is not the
truth, even though the light proceeds therefrom. Night is *un*-truth.
And what is beauty? It is not the light and it is not the night. It is
twilight—a child of truth and untruth: a thing of the middle. In its

realm lies a crossroads, so equivocal, so facing both ways that a very Hercules among philosophers could take the wrong turning. I'll say no more. When I enter upon this matter I become extravagant, and yet it is my favorite subject. How dearly I would like to spend a few evenings with your dear father; I would have so much to say to him. . . . How I would love to come to you at Easter, if only I could! I'll tell you a good idea: do you come here, or send me your father. We have place for you all if you could come. I mean that seriously.

August 28, 1769

To Annette

. . . It is strange—today a year ago I saw you for the last time. A year is a curious thing; it changes the aspect of so much; I wager that if I were to see you again, I would not know you any more. Three years ago I would have sworn that all would be other than it is. I now know that one should swear by nothing. There was a time when I had so much to say to you that I could never end; now all my wit does not suffice to finish a page for you. For I can think of nothing that would be agreeable to you. If someday you write me that you are happy, unreservedly happy, that would indeed delight me. . . . Oh, could I recall those eighteen months, I swear to you I would act more wisely.

December 12, 1769

To Annette

My wretchedness has dulled me equally against any good that remains to me. My body has recovered but my soul is not yet healed. I am in a state of inactive stillness and there is no happiness in that. And in this composure my imagination is so powerless that I cannot recall even that which was once dearest to me. Only in dreams does my heart sometimes appear as it is, only in dreams can I recall those dear images in such a fashion that my feelings come to life again. You owe this letter to a dream. In it I saw you; I was with you. The thing was too strange to relate. To put it into one word: you were married. Can that be true? I looked at your letter again and the periods coincided. If it is true, may this be the beginning of your happiness. . . .

Farewell, my dearest friend. Accept this letter with love and kindness. My heart had to speak once more upon an occasion when a dream communicated to me an event, which should have bidden it be silent.

1770

January 23, 1770

To Annette

If I remember rightly my last letter to you came in a somewhat sombre guise. This one will strike a more cheerful tone, since you have given me respite until Easter. I wish you were well married and had all that goes with it, but at bottom it concerns me just the same, as you can imagine.

All I can tell you is that I live quietly and am well and strong and also industrious, seeing that no girl troubles my mind. . . .

After due consideration I know that I have had more than enough of Frankfurt and I am leaving it by the end of March. I see well that I dare not come to you, because if I came at Easter you might not yet be married. And I don't want to see you any more if I cannot see you otherwise than so. Consequently, if you are interested, as I think you are, I am going to Strassburg by the end of March. Will you write me there? . . .

You have never been other than a lovable girl, and you will be a lovable woman, too. And I, I will remain Goethe. You know what that means. When I name my name I define myself wholly. . . .

From Strassburg I'll go on to Paris and hope to be well contented there and perhaps stay quite a while. Afterwards—but God only knows how it will turn out. But I do hope that you will get married by Easter. Ah well, if it isn't Easter it will be Michaelmas and if it isn't by then, I won't hang myself either. . . .

And so, since it does seem as though you didn't care for me, pick me as wife that one among your friends who is likest you. . . . At the end of two years I'll be back. And afterwards? I have a house, I have money. Heart, what more do you want? A wife!

Farewell, dear friend. I have written merrily today and so have written ill.

February 6, 1770

To Christian Gottfried Hermann

Professor of Philology in Leipzig.

I'm flying farther at the end of March. First to Strassburg, where I would like to have my juristic merits crowned. Thence I'll march on—*salvis accidentibus*—to Paris. From there—but God only knows. . . . If any among my songs have pleased you, I am very glad. I nurse the hope that I will write better as time goes on; but with our kind one must have patience. . . .

February 20, 1770

To Philip Erasmus Reich

A Leipzig acquaintance.

. . . Remember me to dear Oeser. Next to him and Shakespeare, the poet Wieland is the only one whom I regard as having been a true teacher to me. Others showed me wherein I erred; these three showed me how I could do better.

Poetry and Truth

When, at this time, I re-read the letters, which I had written from Leipzig to my sister, it could not escape me that at the very beginning of my academic instruction I had thought myself to be very clever and very wise. So soon as I had learned anything, I substituted myself for my professor and myself became didactic on the spot. . . . The poems, too, which I had written in Leipzig, seemed trivial to me now—cold and dry and in respect of the expression of the conditions of the human heart and mind all too superficial. And so I was persuaded, being on the point of leaving the paternal roof again and going to a second university, to deliver my manuscripts once more to the flames.

Having seen so many good resolutions come to naught and so many honest hopes vanish, I made no resistance to the decision of my father to send me to Strassburg, where a gay and cheerful life was promised me and where I meant to continue my studies and in the end acquire my doctorate in law.

By the spring of 1770 I felt that not only my health but also my youthful courage were restored. Once more I yearned to be away from my paternal house, though for quite other reasons than the first time. The agreeable rooms and halls in which I had suffered so much had grown dismal to me and I had failed to establish any kind of agreeable relationship with my father. I found it hard to forgive him for the unjust impatience he had shown over my relapses into illness and the slowness of my recovery. Instead of consoling me with some degree of indulgence, he had often and cruelly blamed me as though that which is beyond man's power depended wholly on my will. Yet I did not forget that I, too, had wounded and affronted him in more ways than one.

. . . On another matter it finally came to a scene between him and me which, though it was hushed up and smoothed over, nevertheless accelerated my journey to the beautiful land of Alsace—a journey which I made without delay and in a brief time in a modern and comfortable postchaise, which had just begun to run.

Book Two

STORM AND STRESS

1770-1775

STRASSBURG

(April, 1770 to August, 1771)

1770

Poetry and Truth

In Strassburg I stopped at the inn At the Sign of the Ghost, and hastened at once to satisfy my deepest desire by seeing the Cathedral . . . Hastily I climbed to the top of the tower in order not to miss the beautiful view under a high and serene sun, which was to reveal to me this broad rich land. . . . And so from a projection like a platform I surveyed the lovely scene which was to be for a space my dwelling. . . .

A first vision of a new land, in which we are to dwell for a period, has this peculiarity, agreeable as well as ominous, that it lies before us like a virgin page. No sorrows and no joys that have any relation to us are as yet inscribed upon it. . . . Neither inclination nor passion emphasizes for us one spot above another. Yet some presage of what is to come disquiets the young heart even now, and an unsatiated need already demands that which is to come and which in any event, be it of weal or woe, will insensibly take on the character of the landscape in which we are.

◇◇◇◇◇

I left the inn and moved into well-situated and charming lodgings on the south side of the Fishmarket, a long and handsome street, of which the constant movement entertained every idle moment. . . . The dining club which was recommended to me was both agreeable and entertaining. . . . The majority of its members were men of kindness and good will; all students, they were obliged not to exceed in the indulgence of wine. That this rule was kept was the care of the presiding officer, a certain Doctor Salzmann. [*Johann Daniel Salzmann, 1722-1812, actuary.*] He was a bachelor and over 60; he

45

had been a member of this dining club for many years and had seen
to its order and good repute. . . .

Most of my fellow members there were students of medicine. These
are, as is well known, the only students who discuss their science and
their calling outside of the classrooms. . . . Thus I heard medical
conversation daily and . . . at the beginning of my second semester
took courses in chemistry and anatomy. . . .

Good Friday, 1770

To J. C. Limprecht

Student of theology in Leipzig whose lodgings had adjoined Goethe's.

I haven't any doubt that you are in need of money; for I had the
sudden impulse today to send you these several louis d'or. It's better
than nothing, I thought, even though it's not much. Do regard it at
least as a sign that the past is not forgotten.

I'm a student once more and have, thank God, as much health as I
need and gaiety to spare. . . . I would be so happy to know that
your circumstances have improved. You always had a heavy load to
bear and finally came that trouble with your eyes and with me. I
don't mean my illness. Your service to me on that account was one
of loving-kindness and that kind is never bitter. But when I consider
what an unbearable fellow I was that whole last summer, I'm amazed
that anyone could put up with me. Yet I deserved sympathy; I, too,
was bearing a heavy though dear burden . . .

April 19, 1770

To Limprecht

I've been here for fifteen days now and I find Strassburg neither a
hair's breadth better or worse than the rest of the world as I know
it, that is to say, quite mediocre, and yet with certain aspects which
may set one in motion toward either good or evil and have power
to take one out of one's accustomed way.

                                                              June 27, 1770
To Katharina Fabricius

  A friend of Cornelia's who lived in Worms.

What happiness it is to have a heart that is light and free! Courage
impels us toward difficulty and danger; great joys are won at great
cost. And this is perhaps my chief complaint against love. It is said
to inspire courage. Not at all. So soon as the heart is soft, it is weak.
When it beats warmly in our breast and the throat tightens and the
tears start and incomprehensible rapture overcomes us when they
flow—then, oh then, are we so feeble that daisy chains may fetter us,
not because any magic makes them strong, but because we tremble
to tear them asunder.

                                                              June 29, 1770
To Langer

If, beyond the mountains, beside your lake, it is as radiant as it is
here today, and if in your heart, dear friend, the springtime has
entered as it has into mine, then you have as little to complain of
concerning the world within and without as I have. . . . My little
adventures are now like raindrops falling into a pool, nor am I more
stirred than is a pool by tranquil evening rain. . . .
Your friend is just about what he always was. In moderate health
and rarely in conflict with his own heart and yet more rarely in harmony with it. . . . What am I studying? First of all the distinctions
and subtleties by means of which one has come pretty much to iden-
tify right and wrong. That is to say, I am studying toward a doctorate
in law.
In addition, quite on my own, I am trying to acquire some literary
acquaintance with those great books, which the learned mob now
admires, and now jeers at, and does both because it does not understand them. To discover the secrets of these books is a special task
of him who has both wisdom and sensibility. . . .
My address is in care of Herr Schlag, Furrier on the Fishmarket.

July 14, 1770

To Hetzler, the Younger

> An otherwise unidentified correspondent. The Mendelssohn mentioned is, of course, Moses Mendelssohn, 1729-1786, the eminent Jewish philosopher.

Mendelssohn and the others, whose adherent the rector of the university is, have sought to ensnare beauty as one would a butterfly and to fasten it down with pins for the benefit of curious observers. They have succeeded with the same result as in the case of the butterfly. The poor creature trembles in the net and loses its lovely hues; even if it is caught uninjured, yet when it is pinned down it is stiff and lifeless. The corpse is no longer the animal. Something is gone, the chief thing, the indispensable, that life, that spirit, which alone makes things beautiful. . . . I must force myself to end here. You know that on this subject I am as inexhaustible as a widow on the circumstances that attended the last hours of her lord and master.

August 26, 1770

To Susanna Katharina von Klettenberg

> His mother's pious friend in Frankfurt.

My association with the Pietist brethren here is not very active. In the beginning I counted on them a good deal; but it is as though this thing were not meant to be. They are such terrible bores, poor things—it's just too much for my temperament. They are exclusively people of moderate understanding, to whom their religious sensibility brought the first thinking they ever did. Now they think that what they know is all knowledge, because they know nothing else. . . . I'm beginning to take a liking to the study of jurisprudence. It's with everything as it is with bitter beer. The first time it makes you shudder; if you've drunk it for a week, you hate to do without it. But chemistry is still my secret love.

September, 1770

From the Autobiography of Heinrich Jung-Stilling

> Jung, 1740-1817, of humble origin, a student of medicine in Strassburg, who later became a well-known ophthalmologist and prolific author.

In Strassburg Jung-Stilling and his friend [*Jung writes of himself in the third person*] went for the first time to eat at their dining club. They were the first to arrive and their seats were assigned them. Places had been laid at the big table for about twenty persons, and so they saw the others enter one by one. Above all, there came one into the room with great, flashing eyes, a magnificent forehead and a handsome figure. He attracted the attention of the two friends, and the one said to the other that this must be an excellent man. Stilling agreed to this but imagined that all would not be smooth sailing with this young man, for he seemed to him to have a wild and unsettled air. He inferred this from the young student's uninhibited demeanor. Stilling found later that he was wrong. On that first occasion they were told that this notable person was called Herr Goethe. Next arrived a theologian named Lerse, one of the most admirable of men and Goethe's great favorite. . . . At the head of the table sat one whose modesty was such that it is not permissible to praise him. This was the actuary Salzmann. . . .

Poetry and Truth

My health was now such that I was able to undertake all that will or duty dictated. All that was left was a certain irritability which often disturbed my equilibrium. I was unduly sensitive to powerful noise. . . . What especially frightened me was a dizziness which attacked me whenever I looked downward from any elevation. I sought to correct these faults and, because I disliked wasting time, I took the most violent measures to do so. At sundown, at the hour of the tattoo, I marched with the group of drummers, whose violent drumming was calculated to burst one's very heart. Alone I climbed to the highest peak of the tower of the cathedral and sat there as long as a quarter of an hour until I ventured to step out on a platform at that elevation, which measured scarcely a square yard. . . . I inflicted this terror and torture upon myself so many times until the experience became a matter of indifference to me, so that in later years I was able to profit by it in mountain climbing, on tall buildings, even in Rome where daring of this kind gave me a closer view of certain works of art.

October 14, 1770

To Katharina Fabricius

I've spent some days in the country with extremely agreeable people.
The company of the amiable daughters of the house, the beautiful
landscape and the friendly sky awakened in my heart every dormant
feeling and every recollection of all that is dear to me.

October 15, 1770

To Friederike Brion

> 1751 to 1815, the object of Goethe's first great passion, which inspired
> many famous lyrics and contributed to the conception of the figure of
> Gretchen in *Faust*. Friederike never married.

Dear, dear Friend, That I have things to say to you is beyond all
question; but whether I know exactly why I am writing at this moment and just what I would write, that is another matter. A certain
inner restlessness tells me that I would be where you are. And that
being so, this scrap of paper consoles me truly and is to me, here, in
the midst of the noisy city, as much of a winged horse as it may be
to you out there in your tranquility, whenever you feel keenly the
absence of your friends.
The circumstances of our return you can somewhat imagine, because
you must have seen at my farewell how much it hurt me. . . .
It is a sweet and curious thing—this hopefulness of seeing someone
again. And we, who have spoiled hearts, when a small ache comes to
us, at once we have the remedy and say: Dear beating heart, be calm,
not long will you be distant from those you love; be calm, O heart!
And then, until the next meeting, we give the heart a silhouette, so
that it may have something, whereupon it is well behaved and quiet
like a child whose mother gives it a doll in place of an apple, which
it was forbidden to eat. . . .
Ah yes, Ma'm'selle, Strassburg has never seemed as empty to me as it
does just now. I hope this condition will improve, when time will
have a little dimmed the memory of our lovely and unrestrained
gaieties, when I shall no longer feel so ardently how kind and pleasant you, my friend, are to me. Yet would I ever want to forget that,
or be able to do so? Nay, rather would I keep this bit of heartache
and write to you often. . . .

December, 1770

Soon will I come, ye children golden,
In vain are we by winter holden
And in our cosy chambers pent.
Beside the chimney fires we'll ease us,
Where manifold delights will please us,
Like loving angels in content.
And many little wreaths we'll wind us,
And manicolored posies bind us
Like little children innocent.

1771

February, 1771

To His Grandmother

Anna Margaretha Textor.

Dearest Grandmama, The death of our dear grandfather, though daily feared for long, found me wholly unprepared. I feel this loss with all my heart, for what is the world about us, if we lose what we love? I write not to console you, who are now the head of our family, but myself, to ask for your affection and to assure you of my tenderest devotion. . . .

Our father is now free and our tears accompany his bliss and our sadness clings to you, dear Grandmama, in order that hearts full of love may gather about the consolation of your being with us. . . .

Poetry and Truth

Johann Gottfried Herder, 1744-1803, the highly distinguished scholar, who revived the study of the popular poetry of all peoples. His influence was decisive on the development of Goethe.

A most significant event, fraught with important consequences, was the acquaintance with Herder, which was to lead to so close an alliance . . . I happened to drop in at the inn At the Sign of the Ghost to call on some distinguished foreigner. At the foot of the stairs there was a gentleman, who was also about to mount, and whom I quite properly took to be a clergyman. . . . He asked after my name, which could mean nothing to him. But my frankness seemed to please him. He responded with great friendliness, and even as we were mounting the stairs together a vivid communication of ideas began between us. . . .

❖❖❖❖❖

Now suddenly through Herder I became acquainted with all the new literary directions and with the tendencies which these seemed to follow. . . . I became acquainted with the nature of poetry from quite another side, in quite another sense than hitherto, and both were most congenial to me. The poetry of the ancient Hebrews, which he treated so brilliantly, that popular poetry, of which he inspired us to seek the traditions here in Alsace, the oldest monuments of poetry everywhere—all these he used as evidence that the art of poetry was a gift inherent in mankind and in all peoples and not the private heritage of a few men of special culture. . . .

Most carefully I nevertheless hid from him my interest in certain subjects, which had become deeply implanted in me and which seemed gradually to become concrete in character. These were Götz von Berlichingen and Faust. The biography of the former had taken deep hold of me. The figure of a crude, well-meaning man who embraced self-help in a wild anarchic period, engaged my deepest sympathy. The significant old popular puppet play of *Faust* sang and hummed within me in many consonant tones. I, too, had taken my fill of many kinds of human knowledge and had early come upon the vanity thereof. I, too, had tried various fashions of life and had come away from each less contented and more anguished. These things, as well as many another, I carried about with me, and took delight in them in lonely hours without, however, writing down anything at this time. . . .

❖❖❖❖❖

We rode through Reichshofen . . . and through the forest of Hagenau . . . to the beloved Sesenheim [*the village in which Friederike's father's parsonage was*]. . . .

Neither the wild views of the Vosges Mountains nor the bright and fruitful plain could attract my inner vision, which was fixed upon so amiable and enchanting an object. This time, too, the road hither seemed more attractive than ever, because it brought me back to a girl to whom I was devoted from my very heart and who deserved my esteem as well as my love. Let me be permitted to mention one other circumstance which contributed to vitalize and heighten both my inclination and the satisfaction which it gave me. . . .

How backward my acquaintance with modern literature was may easily be gathered from the account of my Frankfurt life. . . . Now came Herder and, in addition to his great knowledge, brought us the means of study and, especially, the productions of contemporary literature. Among these he pointed out to us Oliver Goldsmith's *The Vicar of Wakefield* as an excellent work. He made us acquainted with it by reading us his improvised translation of the English text.

We rode along a charming path across the meadows and soon reached Sesenheim. Leaving our horses at the inn, we walked slowly to the parsonage. . . . It was *she* who appeared at the door, so that in very truth a lovely star arose on that pastoral heaven. Both she and her sister wore the traditional Alsatian peasant costume, which suited Friederike admirably well. In a short, white, circular little skirt, leaving the neatest of feet visible to the ankles, a tight, white bodice and an apron of black taffeta—thus she stood on the boundary line between the peasant maiden and the city girl. Her tread was as light as though her slender body had no weight and the magnificent blonde braids on her little head seemed almost too heavy for her neck to carry. Keenly her serene blue eyes gazed about her and her delightful little nose was raised so freely to the air about, as though there were no possible sorrow in the world. Her straw hat hung by its ribbon from her arm, and so I had the pleasure of having her reappear to my first glance in all her charm and loveliness.

During the evening meal I could not but ponder, as I had done before, over a similarity, which almost silenced me. . . . I was amazed beyond expression to see myself so vividly transferred to the Wakefield family of Goldsmith's story. The father, to be sure, was not comparable to the admirable Doctor Primrose. However, in this case moral dignity was concentrated in the parson's wife. . . .

The older daughter, to be sure, was not as great a beauty as the Olivia of the story; yet she was well built and lively and passionate. . . . It was certainly not difficult to think of Frederike as the younger daughter Sophie, since little is said of the latter except that she was truly worthy of love and admiration. And as similar occupations and conditions of life, wherever they may occur, bring forth similar if not identical effects, so many things were discussed here and much occurred that had been discussed and had occurred in the family at Wakefield.

◇◇◇◇◇

"Art thou mad?" cried my friend, seeking to restrain me. But I was already beyond the threshold, down the stairs, out of the house on my way to the inn. Instantly my horse was saddled and I raced onward at a mad gallop.

Early in 1771

WELCOME AND FAREWELL
(*To Friederike*)

To Horse! My heart brooked no delaying!
The action pressed upon the thought.
In evening's rhythm the earth was swaying,
And in the mountains night was caught.
The oak-tree from its misty veiling
A towering giant seemed to rise,
Where from the brush an all prevailing
Dark peered with myriad sombre eyes.

The moon behind its cloudy curtain
Gleamed lamentably dim and drear,
The winds on feeble wings uncertain
With ghostly whispers filled my ear;
Night's phantoms crept out to conspire,
Yet youth and joy fulfilled me so,
That in my veins was naught but fire,
And in my heart immortal glow.

I saw thee, and thy soul delighted
From thy sweet eyes upon me shone;
Doubly my heart to thee was plighted
And every breath for thee alone.
With all the hues of springtime's roses
Thy lovely countenance was fraught,
With all the ardor that most close is
To what I hoped, deserving not.

But dawn across the heaven races
And brings the parting hour, alas:
What ecstasy in thy embraces,
And in thine eyes what pain there was!
I went. With tearful glance and tender
Thou gazedst after me afar:
And yet, what bliss in love's surrender,
And to be loved our very star.

Poetry and Truth

. . . I sat down on a bench and observed a small oblong board fastened to the biggest tree and bearing the inscription "Friederike's Repose." It did not occur to me that I had come to disturb this repose, for a rising passion has this beautiful characteristic, that, as it is unconscious of its origin, so also it can have no notion of its end and in its assurance of joy and serenity can have no suspicion of its capacity to create disaster.

Friederike had foretold that I would come; who is not pleased with the fulfillment of such a presage? All prophetic feelings, which the event confirms, give man a higher conception of his being. . . .
Very early Friederike invited me to take a walk with her. By the dear girl's side I enjoyed the morning mood of that pastoral Sunday. . . .
Since the day on which that passionate girl had both cursed and hallowed my lips (for every consecration is made up of both elements), I had been careful, superstitious as I was, to kiss no other girl, for I feared to harm such another in some unheard-of, ghostly fashion.

◇◇◇◇◇

I knew neither pain nor any annoyance when I was near her. The company on this occasion consisted of young and extremely gay friends. . . . Even at breakfast the wine had been plentiful; at the well-spread dinner no enjoyment was lacking and everyone relished food and drink after dancing and walking in the warm weather. . . . I was boundlessly happy by the side of Friederike. . . . She, too, was frank and gay and communicative. . . . After the meal we sought the shade and games were played, above all, games of forfeit. . . . When the chance came of kissing her whom I loved so tenderly, I did not miss it nor did I deny myself the repetition of that joy. . . . Later we rewarded ourselves by taking a walk alone and hand in hand. In a lonely place in the forest we embraced each other with deep emotion and gave each other the most faithful assurance that each loved the other from the bottom of the heart. . . .

Under these circumstances there arose in me the impulse toward poetical composition, which I had not felt for long. I wrote for Friederike many lyrics that could be sung to well-known melodies. They could have constituted quite a little volume; but only a few are extant. . . .

Sesenheim, late May, 1771

To Salzmann

. . . Things aren't very bright here. The little girl is sadly ill and that creates a wrong atmosphere, not including the fact that the *mens conscia recti*—the mind conscious of its own rectitude—can hardly be said to be mine. Yet 'tis the country! Ah, if everything were as it should be, I'd invite you here. Let me hear from you by Friday and do have two pounds of the finest candy packed and sent here. You know better than I what girls like best. . . .

On the Monday of Pentecost I danced with the older sister from two o'clock in the afternoon until midnight, interrupted only by occasional refreshments. . . . You ought to have seen it. My whole self was lost in the act of dancing.

Sesenheim, June 5, 1771

To Salzmann

The world is so beautiful, so beautiful! Oh, that one could enjoy it!
Sometimes I am angry and sometimes I give myself edifying lectures
concerning the necessity of enjoying the day that is here—that doctrine which is so indispensable to our happiness and which few
professors of ethics grasp and none explains well. Adieu. Adieu. I
really wanted to write but a word to thank you for the sweetmeats
and to tell you how attached to you I am.

Sesenheim, middle of June, 1771

To Salzmann

I shall come or not or—I'll know all that better when it's over and
done with. It rains in the world and in my heart and the rude winds
of evening rustle in the vine leaves at my window, and my changeable soul is like the weather vane yonder on the steeple of the church.
. . . Still I'm studying Greek. I would have you know that while
I have been here I have so improved my knowledge of Greek that
I can almost read Homer without a translation. . . .

Sesenheim, late June, 1771

To Salzmann

Now the time approaches that I should come back, and I want to,
yes, I do. But what is the will against the forces that surround me?
My heart is in a strange condition and my health, as usual, is variable. . . . Here is the loveliest countryside and people who love
me and a group of friends! Doesn't it sound like the fulfillment of
one's childhood's dreams? Thus I ask myself when my eye sweeps
the horizon of all bliss. Are not these the magic gardens of one's
yearning? They are, they are! I realize it, dear friend, and realize
that one is not happier by a hair's breadth by attaining the object
of one's wishes. For there is an addition, a something extra, which
destiny insists on measuring out with every happiness it grants us.
Dear friend, it takes much courage not to grow melancholy in this
world. When I was a boy I planted a little cherry tree just for fun;

it grew and I loved its breaking into bloom. But a belated frost killed the blossoms and I had to wait another year. My cherries ripened, but the birds had nibbled at the greater part before I had tasted of the fruit. Another year caterpillars came, next a thievish neighbor, next came a blight. Yet were I master of a garden, I would plant cherry trees again. In spite of all miseries there remains fruit enough to still one's hunger. I know another charming story concerning what happened to my grandfather with a hedge of rose bushes, a more edifying story than my own. But it's too late to tell it.

Late June, 1771

Jung-Stilling

He returned to Strassburg and went straight to Goethe. That dear and noble soul leaped up when he saw him and embraced him. "Are you here again, my good friend?" he cried, "and how is your girl?" Stilling replied: "She is no longer merely my girl; she is my wife now." "You have done well," Goethe answered, "you are an excellent fellow!" And they spent the rest of the day in cordial converse and mutual communication.

Poetry and Truth

And now the love between Friederike and myself was to stand a peculiar test. I call it a test, although that is scarcely the right word. My pastoral friends had relatives in the city, people of good repute and in comfortable circumstances. The younger town cousins often visited Sesenheim. The older people, the mothers and aunts, less prone to outings, had heard a good deal about life in the country, about the increasing loveliness of the daughters, even of my influence there. Hence they wanted to make my acquaintance. I visited them a number of times and was well received. Now they wanted to see us all as their guests in the city, if only to return the hospitality received. . . .

And so it happened that I found the two girls, whom I had been wont to see amid country scenes, whose images came to me against a background of waving branches and flowing brooks and flowering fields and a broad horizon, for the first time in an urban scene, in rooms which, though large were confined, against a background of wallpaper, mirrors, grandfather's clocks and porcelain figurines. . . . In this situation Friederike bore herself quite remarkably. Strictly speaking, she did not fit in at all; it bore witness to her character that, instead of trying to adapt herself to this environment, she sought unconsciously to transform it according to her nature. . . .

◇◇◇◇◇

I cannot but remember a pilgrimage undertaken in the company of many believers to the top of the mountain of St. Ottilie. . . . From this elevation the eye commands all the lovely land of Alsace, ever the same and yet ever new, even as from any seat in an amphitheatre one has a view of the entire assembly. . . .

I devoted myself to such distractions and festivities to the point of a kind of intoxication, because my passionate relationship to Friederike began to frighten me. A youthful inclination of this kind, indulged suddenly and without judgment, is comparable to one of those nocturnal firework globes which, rising in a soft and radiant line, mingles with the stars and seems for a moment destined to remain among them. But next it retraces its course in reverse and ends by bringing destruction to the spot whence it arose. Friederike remained of an even disposition; she seemed unable or unwilling to think that our relationship might soon come to an end. Her sister, who liked me well enough, but was threatened by no such loss, showed both more foresight and more frankness. She spoke to me from time to time concerning my probable departure and sought consolation for both herself and her sister. A girl who renounces a man to whom she has not refused her affection, is not in nearly as painful a situation as a young man who has professed his love for her. He always cuts a sorry figure; for of him, about to attain masculine maturity, people expect sound judgment concerning his whole situation and out-and-out frivolousness becomes him but ill. The reasons given by a girl who withdraws her love always seem valid, those of a man never. . . .

◇◇◇◇◇

Oppressed and confused as I was, I yet could not bear not to see Friederike once again. There came days full of pain, the memory of

which has faded from me. When, already mounted, I gave her my
hand, the tears were in her eyes, nor was I in any better case. I rode
along a narrow path toward the next village and there a strange
presage came upon me. In the eye of the mind, not of the body, I
saw myself riding toward myself on horseback dressed in a costume
such as I had never worn—pike-gray edged with gold. I shook myself
free of the visionary trance; the image faded. Yet it is strange that
eight years later in the identical costume of my vision, which I had
not chosen but wore by chance, I did come riding along that road
to visit Friederike for the last time.

1771

> Grow ever nearer heaven
> O lofty tree, earth's pride.
> By raging storms unriven
> Thy sacred wood abide!
> Of graven names, O cherish
> The higher one through time!
> Well may the poet perish
> Who wrought today this rime.

Poetry and Truth

Alsace had not yet been under French domination for so long a
period but that among old and young there had remained an affectionate attachment for the constitution, the habits, the speech, the
very costumes of old. A conquered population forced to lose one
half of its accustomed existence, thinks shame to give up the other
half voluntarily. . . . At all events here, on the border of France,
we were suddenly stripped of all the characteristics of the French.
Their way of life seemed to us too definite and too much dictated by
fashion, their poetry seemed cold to us, their criticism nihilistic,
their philosophy abstruse and yet inadequate. Thus we were on the
point of yielding to the rawness of nature as at least an experiment.
We would have done so had not another influence prepared us for
a higher, freer, truer and more creative view of the world and of
spiritual delight and ruled over us ever more openly and more powerfully. I need hardly say that I am thinking of Shakespeare. Having
named that name, no further explanation is needed. . . . As there

are men who cannot be tripped up by any Biblical quotation, thus we made ourselves into complete Shakespearians. We imitated in our conversations both the virtues and the faults of his time. . . .

Minutes of the Faculty of the University of Strassburg

September 22, 1770. Master Goethe becomes a candidate. Master Johann Wolfgang Goethe, of Frankfurt-on-the-Main, having been released from a preliminary dissertation, his name was inscribed on the list of candidates.

September 25, 1770. The first examination of Master Goethe. Master Goethe having passed his first examination with high distinction, appropriate texts to be resolved are determined upon for his rigorous examination.

September 27, 1770. The later examination of Master Goethe. Master Goethe in his later examination worthily defended the questions proposed and deserves the favor of discussing his inaugural dissertation without supervision (by a presiding officer).

Poetry and Truth

My promotion to the Doctorate in Law took place on August 6, 1771.

Karl August Böttiger

1760-1835. Scholar and teacher and gatherer of anecdotes of his contemporaries.

Often Goethe and his friend Lerse would row up the Rhine and often on those occasions Goethe would become highly ecstatic, speaking words of prophecy in such a way as to cause Lerse to fear for his reason.

Middle of August, 1771

To Salzmann

Can't keep my eyes open, though it's only 9 o'clock. Not much order. Festive till all hours of the night and dragged out of my bed early by all kinds of plans. Inside of my head there is a disorder like that in my room. I can't even find paper except this bit of a blue sheet. Yet any paper will serve well to tell you of my affection. . . . I hope you'll be happy until we meet again. The weather in my soul is not too bright. I am too aware not to feel that I am grasping after shadows. And yet—tomorrow morning at 7 o'clock my horse will be saddled and ready. And so farewell.

FRANKFURT

(August, 1771 to May, 1772)

Henry Crabb Robinson

1775-1867, the well-known British diarist and friend of Wordsworth and his circle. He lived in Jena 1801-1805 and relates various anecdotes about Goethe in his diaries.

On his return from Strassburg to Frankfurt toward the end of August, 1771, he came home one evening in high spirits. "Oh Mother," he said, "I have found such a book in the public library and I will make a play of it! What great eyes the Philistines will make at the Knight with the Iron Hand. That's glorious—The Iron Hand."

Poetry and Truth

Now at last the wanderer had returned home for the first time healthier and more cheerful. Yet in his whole being there existed an extreme tension which hardly denoted perfect health of the spirit. . . .
My father, well enough contented with his old hobbies and occupations, took comfort in the fact that, despite hindrances and delays, his plans had come to fruition. I had taken my degree and thus taken the first step toward a sound and hopeful way of life. . . .
During my stay in Alsace I had composed many short poems, essays, descriptions of travel and broadsides. It entertained him to order and index these, to demand their perfection and he was happy in the expectation that my hitherto unconquered disinclination to have such things printed would be overcome. . . .
My sister had gathered about her a circle of sensible and amiable women. Of my older friends and acquaintances I found Horn unchangeable in fidelity as well as a cheerful companion.
I also soon made the acquaintance of Merck [*Johann Heinrich Merck, 1741-1791, writer, editor and public servant*] who had been

favorably recommended to me by Herder from Strassburg. This unique personality has exercised a profound influence upon my life. . . . I still possess certain of his poetical epistles of such uncommon boldness, outspokenness and Swiftian bitterness and at the same time of such wounding power that I have never dared to make them public.

I cannot tell how much these friends contributed to inspire and improve me. They were fond of hearing me read my finished or attempted works; they encouraged me when I gave them frank and long reports of my plans and reproved me when I deprecated what had already been begun in favor of some new impulse. *Faust* had made excellent progress and the play concerning Götz von Berlichingen, the Knight of the Iron Hand, gradually assumed concrete form in my mind.

September 21, 1771

To Johann Gottfried Röderer

A student of architecture in Strassburg with whom, in Goethe's own words, "it had not been given him to cultivate a closer friendship."

It is most excellent that you have the opportunity of actually practicing the art of building. If the artist is not at the same time a craftsman, he is nothing at all. But it is our misfortune that most of our artists are only craftsmen, It is tolerable as long as ordinary buildings are to be built; so soon as a palace or a monument is to arise, there is no one strong enough to wave a magic wand. Here it is that the true architect is needed. Any peasant can give a carpenter a notion for the building of his hut. Who is to make the dwelling place of Jupiter to aspire toward the clouds except it be Vulcan, himself a god?

September, 1771

To Herder

In my wanderings about Alsace I collected twelve folksongs, which I heard from the lips of ancient little mothers. A bit of luck, for their grandchildren sing contemporary trash. I meant them for you, for you alone. I haven't permitted my best friends to make copies, though they begged hard. I'll not stop to speak of their excellence, nor their varying degrees of value. I have carried them as a very treasure in my heart. Girls who wanted to find favor in my eyes had to learn to sing them. . . . And now a swift farewell that I may copy them. . . .

My sister makes me add this. I am to give you her regards and invite you to be here on October 14 when Shakespeare's Name Day will be celebrated with great splendor. At least in spirit you are to be with us and, if possible, send us a dissertation to be part of our liturgy. My parents send their best regards.

October 14, 1771

For the Celebration of Shakespeare Day

The first page of him that ever I read made me forever his, and when I finished the first play I was like one who, having been born blind, receives the gift of sight from a miraculous hand. I knew, I was vividly aware of the fact that my existence had been enlarged by an infinity. . . . I knew at once that I would renounce the so-called "regular theatre" of the French. . . . The Greek theatre which the French took as their model was so constituted that a marquis could more easily imitate an Alcibiades than Corneille could follow in the path of Sophocles. . . .

I am impelled to cry out: O nature, nature, nothing is so deeply nature as Shakespeare's men and women. . . . He rivaled Prometheus; he formed his creatures feature by feature. . . . Then he breathed into them the breathing of his spirit. . . .

How can this century of ours undertake to pass judgment on nature? Whence are we to know nature, who from our youth on have felt and seen in others only what is tightly laced and affected? I am often ashamed before Shakespeare. Often at first glance I think that I would have done something differently. Later I recognize that I am but a poor sinner, that nature's prophetic voice speaks through him and that my creatures are soap bubbles blown up by romantic whims.

November 28, 1771

To Salzmann

You know me so well and yet I wager you can't guess why I haven't written. It is on account of a passionate preoccupation, a quite unexpected one. . . . For its sake I forget the sun and the moon and the

dear stars. . . . For my whole being is absorbed by an undertaking
which has made me forget Homer and Shakespeare. I am making a
play of the history of one of the noblest of Germans; I am saving the
memory of a brave man [*Götz von Berlichingen*] and the heavy labor
involved is in a true sense a pastime, which I need, for it is sad to
live in a place where all one's activity must hum within one's own
self. . . . For Frankfurt remains a "nest." *Nidus,* if you like. Perhaps a place to breed birds, otherwise, equally figuratively, a *spe-
lunca,* a rotten hole. God help us out of this misery! Amen.

1772

February, 1772

To Herder

The result of my hermit's life here I am sending you in the form of
a sketch. The brush has touched the canvas here and there; a few
passages are painted and yet it is only a sketch. I am giving you no
further account of my work, nor am I telling you how I feel about
it, namely, that I have arisen and fared forth into the distance, for
that would look as though I wanted to guide your judgment of it.
. . . But this much I can say, that I am working with great faith,
that I am applying the best strength of my soul. I did this in order
to ask your opinion, knowing that that opinion would open my
eyes not only concerning this piece but will teach me beyond it,
regarding it as a milestone from which I may proceed upon a long,
long journey.

March 9, 1772

Karoline Flachsland to Herder

Herder's then betrothed, 1750-1809. They were married the following
year.

A few days ago I made the acquaintance of your friend Goethe. . . .
He is goodhearted and cheerful and without scholarly affectation.
He played a good deal with Merck's children; in the tone of his
conversation there is a likeness to yours; in other ways, too, so that
I followed him about. For a moment Goethe and my sister and I sat
in the sunset light; it was very beautiful and we talked about you.

He speaks with enthusiasm of the six months he lived with you in Strassburg. The second afternoon we all took a walk; later we had a glass of punch in our house. We were not at all sentimental but quite gay, and Goethe and I danced a few minuets. Later he recited to us a wonderful Scotch ballad of yours, which I had not heard either: "Thy sword why is't with blood so red, Edward, Edward?"

March 21, 1772

Herder to Karoline Flachsland

Yes, Goethe really is a good boy. We haven't been corresponding for some time, although I owe him the acknowledgment of a really fine production which he sent me.

April, 1772

Karoline Flachsland to Herder

Our friend Goethe came here from Frankfurt on foot. We have met every day and walked in the forest and got drenched, too. We took refuge under a tree and there Goethe sang us a little song of Shakespeare in your translation: "Under the Greenwood Tree," and we all sang the refrain with him: "But winter and rough weather." . . . He read us a few of the best scenes of his play, which is probably in your hands. He is bursting with song.

May 8, 1772

Karoline Flachsland to Herder

Merck and Goethe came into our garden. . . . And Goethe read us the story of poor Lefevre out of Sterne's *Tristram Shandy*. . . . And now our friend Goethe, that gift from heaven, is gone again. I parted from him with a kiss and a tear in my heart. He is going to Wetzlar and will not be back for three months.

Poetry and Truth

I had written a letter of farewell to Friederike in Strassburg. Her reply tore my heart in two. It was the same hand, the same spirit, the same feeling which had been cultivated through me and toward me. Now only did I wholly feel the loss which she had sustained and saw no possibility of offering her a substitute or an assuagement. Her very presence seemed to be about me; I felt the want of her keenly and what was the worst, I could not forgive myself for my own unhappiness. Gretchen had been snatched from me; Annette had abandoned me; here, for the first time, the guilt was mine. I had wounded the loveliest of hearts to its very depth and so this period was to me one of sombre remorse. . . .

At this time when the pain over Friederike's situation frightened me, I sought help in poetry according to my old habit. I continued the practice of indirect confession in order to become worthy of absolving myself through this self-tormenting act of expiation. The two Marys in *Götz von Berlichingen* and in the play *Clavigo* and the wretched figures cut by their respective lovers are probably the results of my rueful contemplation.

The wounds and illnesses of youth are swiftly overcome. . . . Luckily the chance of agreeable physical exercise came to me and I was inspired in manifold ways to renewed courage and to new delight and enjoyment. A good horse soon took the place of those slow, melancholy difficult and futile wanderings on foot. . . . Some younger comrades introduced the practice of fencing again; above all, as winter came, there arose a new world through my taking to ice skating in which art, after a brief period of exercise, reflection and pertinacity, I perfected myself sufficiently to enjoy the gay and peopled scene on the frozen river.

WETZLAR

Poetry and Truth

The darker centuries of our history had always employed my studies and imagination. . . . I had busily read the chief sources. . . . These efforts, inspired by moral and poetical intentions, now stood me in good stead and I was well prepared when I came to Wetzlar to practice at that Appellate Court of the Holy Roman Empire. . . . The history of this Court could well serve as a significant red thread through the confusions of history. . . . What happened to me in Wetzlar is of no great consequence. . . . But it is well to mark the character of the unfavorable moment of my arrival there. . . . There was a backlog of twenty thousand law suits; sixty could be adjudicated a year. But one hundred and twenty new ones were entered. Fifty thousand revisions were planned. In addition many kinds of malpractice obstructed the functioning of the Court, of which the most serious was the personal background malfeasance of certain assessors. . . .

At a large dining club I met all the younger delegates of the various countries at the Court, who received me cordially. . . . For myself I continued to use art as the expression of both my emotions and my whims.

◇◇◇◇◇

Among the young men who, members of a delegation at the Court, were to practice in preparation for their career, there was one whom the rest of us used to nickname "The Betrothed." He was distinguished by a calm and equable demeanor, clearness of view, decisiveness of act and speech. His serene activity and tireless industry commended him so strongly to his superiors that early appointment to a position was promised him. Justified by this fact, he was betrothed to a young woman who corresponded wholly to his disposition and desires. After the death of her mother she had been the head of a household comprising her numerous younger brothers and sisters. She had fulfilled her duties so ably and so well sustained her father in his widowerhood that her future husband could hope for equal service to himself and his posterity and securely look forward to domestic happiness. Everyone admitted that she was a very desirable young woman. She was not of the kind to arouse violent passion, but rather general liking and approbation. . . . Such was the betrothed . girl. Her promised husband, of a thoroughly honorable and therefore trustful nature, introduced everyone whom he esteemed to the girl. Since the greater part of his time was taken up by his professional obligations, he was happy to see his fiancée, her domestic duties having been fulfilled, amuse herself on walks and picnics with friends of both sexes. Lotte—for by that name she has become known—was doubly modest; firstly her temperament was such that she was more given to general good will than specific inclinations; secondly, she had chosen a man who was worthy of her and who had declared his intention of uniting his destiny to her own.

Johann Christian Kestner's Diary

Kestner, 1741-1800, was the young lawyer in the story. He married Charlotte Buff, 1753-1828, in 1773. These are the figures who were soon to be delineated in Goethe's *The Sorrows of Young Werther.*

In the spring of 1772 there arrived here a certain Goethe from Frankfurt, by profession a Doctor of Law, 23 years old, the only son of a very wealthy father. According to his father's intention he was to practice at the Court here; according to his own he was to study Homer and Pindar and whatever else his genius, his taste and his heart would inspire.

From the start the wits about here proclaimed him as their fellow as a contributor to the new *Frankfurt Scholars' Journal,* also as a philosopher, and did their best to make his acquaintance. Since I don't belong to this class and do not mingle much with people, I made Goethe's acquaintance somewhat later and quite by accident. One of the most distinguished of the local wits invited me to take a walk with him. We came upon Goethe lying on the grass under a tree on his back. He was conversing with an Epicurean philosopher, a Stoic philosopher and a cross between the two, who stood near him,

and was having a very good time. He told me later that he was glad
I had met him in this situation. . . .

Let me give a description of him as I came to know him later. He
has many talents; indeed, he has true genius and is a man of character. He possesses an imagination of extraordinary vividness and
expresses himself in images and similes. He used to tell us, however,
that his expression was not yet profoundly his own; as he grew
older he hoped to be able to think and to express his thoughts as
they truly are.

His feelings are violent, but he is usually master of them. His convictions are noble. He is quite free of prejudice and acts as he likes
quite without caring whether it pleases others or is the fashion or is
permissible. All compulsion is hateful to him.

He loves children and can play with them for hours. He is full of
oddity and both in his behavior and in his appearance there are
things that might be displeasing. But he is high in the good graces
of children, women and many other people too.

On the ninth of June, 1772, it came to pass that Goethe attended a
country dance at which my girl and I were present too. I did not
arrive till late and then on horseback. My girl drove out with others
in a carriage. Among these was Doctor Goethe, and so he made
Lotte's acquaintance. . . .

No woman having yet satisfied his ideal, his attention was attracted
by Lotte at once. She is still young; her beauty is not of a conven-
tional kind (I speak according to common usage, knowing that
beauty has no convention), but her face and features are most pleasing. Her glance is bright and springlike, especially when she dances,
which she loves to do. She was gay on that day and dressed with art-
less grace. He observed in her her perception of natural beauty and
her untutored good sense.

He did not know that she was no longer free. I arrived several hours
later and it is not her habit or mine to display anything but friendship in public. He was in exuberant high spirits on that day (as he
is at times, being quite melancholy at others), and Lotte conquered
him wholly, the more so as she took no pains to do so and simply
yielded to the gaiety of the hour. Next day he naturally came over
to ask how Lotte felt after the ball. He had first seen her as a merry

girl in love with dancing and innocent diversion; now he came to know her on her other, stronger domestic side.

July 10, 1772

To Herder

My little boat is still upon the waves and when the stars hide themselves from me I float, as it were, in the hand of destiny and courage and hope and fear and tranquility alternate in my breast. . . . Since I last heard from you the Greeks have been all my study. First I confined myself to Homer, next I pursued Socrates in the pages of both Xenophon and Plato and that caused my eyes to be opened concerning my own unworthiness. Then I came upon Theocritus and Anacreon and was finally attracted by Pindar to whom I still cling. Otherwise I have done nothing and everything within me is still horribly confused. . . .

I am tempted to pray the prayer attributed to Moses in the Koran: Lord, enlarge Thou the space within my narrow breast.

Poetry and Truth

The new arrival, namely myself, was free of all obligations and so equally free of care in the presence of a girl who, being already promised to another, could not interpret his pleasure in her service as a wooing and could therefore be the better pleased by it. So he calmly let himself go and was soon so enmeshed and fettered and at the same time treated so trustfully and kindly by the young couple that he hardly knew what was happening to him. Idle and dreamy, because no present ever sufficed him, he seemed to find what he lacked in this girl. . . . She enjoyed his companionship; he soon found her presence indispensable, for she made him acquainted with a world of everyday. The estate was extensive and the two soon became inseparable companions on the fields and meadows, in the cabbage patches as well as in the garden

Only a little but as much as is necessary I must now say of a young man, whose name was often and unhappily mentioned in the months

to come. His name was Jerusalem, the son of a liberal and delicately
minded clergyman. He, too, was attached to one of the delegations
at the Court. . . . His dress, he being from the Northwest coast, was
of the English fashion: a blue coat with tails, a leather-yellow waistcoat and breeches and boots with brown cuffs. I never went to his
lodgings nor did he come to mine. We met from time to time at the
house of friends. . . . A tale went about concerning a passion he
entertained for the wife of a friend. One never saw them together
in public. Indeed, little was known of him, except that he was greatly
interested in English literature. . . .

My friend Merck, aesthetician, writer, man of business by turns, had
encouraged the sound, well-informed, variously learned Schlosser
[*Johann Georg Schlosser, 1739-1799, jurist, editor and Goethe's future brother-in-law*] to found the *Frankfurt Scholars' Journal* this
year. . . . Schlosser confided to me that his friendship for my sister
had been transformed into a tenderer relationship and that he was
seeking an early appointment to office in order that they might
marry. This declaration on his part dismayed me somewhat, though
I ought, I suppose, to have inferred the fact from my sister's letters.
But we are prone to pass lightly over what could wound the good
opinion we entertain of ourselves and it was only now that I confessed to myself that I was really jealous of my sister. I could conceal
this emotion from myself the less because, since my return from
Strassburg, my sister and I had drawn closer to each other than
ever. . . .

Review in the Frankfurt Scholars' Journal

Written July-August 1772. Published September 1.
Poems by a Polish Jew. Mietau and Leipzig. Octavo. PP. 96.

First of all we must give the assurance that the title of this small
volume made a very favorable impression on us. Here, we thought,
a fiery spirit and a keenly aware heart, bred to maturity under a
strange rude sky, suddenly makes its entry into *our* world. What
feelings will stir him! What observations will he make, to whom all
is new! Even on the mere flat level of our social life, how many things
will arouse his attention, which custom has robbed of their effect

on us. Where we perish of boredom, he will discover sources of pleasure; he will shake us out of our habitual indifference; he will make us acquainted with our own wealth and teach us its uses. On the other hand, he will find unbearable many things which we let merely be. In brief, he will find what he has not sought and seek what he will not find. Then he will communicate his thoughts and feelings in untrammeled songs to our society, friends, young women. Even if he expresses nothing new, yet everything will have a fresh aspect to him. This we hoped and found—windy nothing! . . .

It is very praiseworthy for a Polish Jew to renounce trade, cultivate the Muses, learn German, confect lyrics; but if he achieves nothing other than could have been done as well by any Christian devotee of belles-lettres, it is not well done, it seems to us, to call such emphatic attention to one's Jewishness.

O genius of our fatherland, let a youth soon arise who, with the strength and vividness of his age . . . sings the most happy songs . . . and let him on his pilgrimage find him a girl who, with a soul all goodness and with a form all grace, has happily developed in a tranquil family circle of active and domestic love; who, the darling, the friend, the reliance of her mother, is herself the second mother of that house, whose ever active and amiable soul irresistibly draws every heart unto itself and of whom poets and sages would gladly learn as they behold with delight her inborn virtue, her instinctive goodness and grace. . . .

But are there such girls? Can there be such a youth? We started by talking about a Polish Jew. But we lost sight of him in the course of this review.

August 28, 1772

Merck to His Wife

I have seen Goethe's friend, the young woman of whom he speaks with so much enthusiasm in all his letters. She really deserves everything that he says about her. We're going to spend the evening with her. . . . Perhaps I can bring Goethe and his sister with me to Darmstadt on Monday.

To Kestner

I must tell you that Lotte is enraptured by the valley in the moon-light and wants still to say good night to you. I wanted to do the same; I went to your house but there was no light in your room and I didn't want to raise an alarm. We'll be taking our coffee tomor-row morning under the very tree where we ate tonight by moon-light. . . .

September 6, 1772
To Kestner

The morning is magnificent and my soul so tranquil that I can't stay in town; I must go out to the village. Lotte said yesterday she wanted to walk farther afield than usual today—not that I expect you two there—but do I wish for you? With all my heart. Hope is a little less than desire—just enough for the two to balance each other. So I shall pass my day in uncertainty and yet hope and hope. And if I must return alone by evening—well, you know how it be-hooves a sage to act and you know how wise I am. . . .

September 10, 1772
To Lotte

We will meet again; among all the images of men we will recognize each other. I go willingly and yet, were I to say that I go forever, I could not bear it. Farewell. We will meet again.

September 10, 1772
From Kestner's Diary

At noon Doctor Goethe ate with me in the garden. I didn't know it was to be the last time. . . . That evening he joined us in Lotte's house. He, Lotte and I had a strange conversation concerning our life in the beyond, our passing away and coming again. It was not he but Lotte who broached the subject. We came to an understand-ing that the first one of us three who died would, if he could do so, give the survivors news of the nature of that other life. Goethe was deeply depressed, for he knew that he was leaving next morning.

September 10, 1772

To Kestner

He will be gone, Kestner, when this note reaches you; he will be gone. Give Lotte the enclosed note. I was quite master of myself but your conversation tore at my very heart. All I can do at this moment is to wish you farewell. Had I stayed but a moment longer I could not have controlled myself. Now I am alone and tomorrow I leave. Oh, my poor head!

September 10, 1772

To Lotte

I do hope to come back, but God only knows when. Lotte, you can imagine the state of my heart during our conversation, knowing that it was the last time that I was to see you. Oh, not the last time, and yet I *do* leave in the morning. What inspired you to speak as you did? Oh that I could have said all that I felt; *I* was concerned over this world and over your hand which I was kissing for the last time. . . . I am alone now and may weep my fill, but I leave you two happy and will be present in your hearts. . . .

Next Morning

To Lotte

My things are packed, Lotte, and the day is breaking. In a quarter of an hour I'll be gone. . . . Be of good cheer, dear Lotte, you are happier than many, many! Be anything but indifferent and I, dear Lotte, am happy that I can read in your eyes your assurance that I will never change. A thousand times farewell!

September 11, 1772

From Kestner's Diary

This morning at 7 o'clock Goethe left without saying farewell. . . . He told us long ago that around this time he would take a trip to

Coblenz to see his friend, the military paymaster Merck, who was waiting for him, and that he would not say farewell but suddenly be gone. So I had expected the thing. Yet I felt as deeply as possible that, when it happened, I was still unprepared. . . . In order to be quite certain, Lotte sent a box of Goethe's which she had, to his house. He was no longer there. . . . At noon I spoke to a gentleman who rode with him as far as Braunfels. Goethe told him the substance of our conversation of last night. Goethe was deeply depressed. In the afternoon I gave Lotte his notes. His departure saddened her and tears came into her eyes when she read his words. Yet she was glad that he was gone, since she could not give him what he desired. We spoke of nothing but him, nor could I turn my thoughts in any other direction.

Poetry and Truth

I left Charlotte with a less troubled conscience than I had left Friederike, yet not without pain. This relationship, too, had been rendered more impassioned on my side by both habit and indulgence than was just; she and her betrothed, on the other hand, were able quite serenely to observe a restraint, which could not have been handsomer and more amiable. Yet the feeling of security which I drew from that caused me to forget all dangers. And so it came that I could not conceal from myself the fact that the end of this episode was at hand. The young man's appointment to office was imminent and on it alone depended his union with the dear girl. Since a man, if he have any resolution, can undertake to will what is necessary, I decided to take my voluntary leave before the unbearable occurred to drive me forth.

September 19, 1772

Karoline Flachsland to Herder

Goethe and Merck and the latter's wife are in Coblenz at the house of Sophie de la Roche.

FRANKFURT

(September, 1772 to November, 1775)

From Kestner's Diary

On September 21, 1772, I accompanied my friends to Frankfurt. . . .
Next day at 4 o'clock I went to see Schlosser and found Goethe and
Merck there. My joy was indescribable; he threw his arms about me
and pressed me close to him. . . . We went to the inn where we
found Madame Merck and Demoiselle Goethe. . . . We went to
Goethe's house. His mother was at home and welcomed us and me,
the stranger, too, because her son's good opinion of anyone means
everything to her. His father soon came in and was equally friendly
and so he and I conversed. . . . That evening I called for Schlosser
to go to the playhouse with me. Goethe and his sister and Madame
Merck were there too. Afterwards I supped at Goethe's house and
didn't get back to my inn till after 11.

September 25, 1772

To Kestner

So Lotte didn't dream of me. I take that quite amiss; I insist that
she dream of me tonight, this very night, and that she doesn't even
tell you about it. I reread that passage in your letter and was annoyed again. Not even to dream of me—an honor which we give to
the most indifferent things which surround us by day. And she knows
whether I didn't surround her body and soul and dreamed of her by
day and by night!

Next day, Saturday, after luncheon

To Kestner

This used to be the hour at which I went to see her. It was the little
hour when she was free and so now I have time to write. You ought
to see how very industrious I am. Ah, to have left suddenly everything that for four months was my very bliss!

I'm not afraid that you people will forget me and yet I brood about our reunion. In that case things here may go as they will. I don't want to see Lotte again until I can give her the definite assurance that I am really, truly in love with someone else.

Poetry and Truth

As Merck and I had agreed to meet at Coblenz, at the house of Frau von la Roche while the weather held, I had sent my luggage ahead to Frankfurt. We wandered along the beautiful serpentine and varied shores of the river Lahn. My decision had been free but my feelings were still clouded and I was in a condition to feel the beneficence of silent and yet living nature. . . .
Noble and majestic the famous castle of Ehrenbreitstein rose before me in its power and strength, fully armed. In exquisite contrast to it there lay at its foot the elegant little town in which it was not difficult to find the house of the Privy Councillor von la Roche.
Announced by Merck, I was most warmly welcomed by this admirable family and was soon regarded as a member of it. I was drawn to the mother through my literary and spiritual aims, to the father by a gay sense of reality, to the daughters by my youth. . . .
Although Herr von la Roche was hostile to any indulgence in sentiment . . . yet did he not deny a tender paternal affection for his older daughter, who was indeed amiable in a high degree. She was rather short than tall and delicately built; her figure was exquisite and eyes as black as possible were set off by a skin which could not be imagined purer and more blossom-like. . . .
Here I lived for a space in a wonderfully pleasant environment, until Merck and his family arrived. Now new elective affinities developed; the two women felt drawn to each other; Merck, a man of the world and of business, traveled and well informed, came to a good understanding with Herr von la Roche. The Mercks' boy took to the boys. The daughters, of whom the oldest soon attracted me especially, fell to my portion. It is a most agreeable sensation to feel a new passion stir within us before the echo of the old has fallen silent. Thus one beholds at sunset the moon arising in the opposite heaven and delights in the double radiance of the two luminaries.

Early November, 1772

To Kestner

O wretched Jerusalem! [*He had shot himself on October 30. Goethe had known him since the Leipzig days.*] The news was as terrible as it was unexpected . . . If it isn't ultimately the fault of that damned parson, his father, then God forgive me. May his neck be broken like that of Eli. The poor boy! When I used to come back from walks and meet him in the moonlight, I would say to myself: he is in love. Lotte must remember that. . . .

November 10, 1772

To Kestner

I just got a letter from my father. Dear God, will I be like that, too, when I get to be old? Will my soul too no longer cling to what is amiable and good? Strange, one would think that as a man gets older he will be freer of the weight of what is earthy and little. Instead he grows earthier and smaller. . . .

November 20, 1772

To Sophie von la Roche

Frau von la Roche, 1731-1807, a writer and early friend of Wieland, the poet, of whom more later and mother of Maximiliane Brentano.

Since those first priceless moments which brought me to you, since those scenes inspired by deepest feeling, how often has my whole soul been with you! . . .

Merck tells me that you would like to know some details concerning the death of Jerusalem. During the four months that I was in Wetzlar our paths were merely parallel; now, a week after his death, I was there again. One of the few people with whom he was at all intimate told me that, though it may seem hard to credit, it was his anxious striving after truth and moral integrity which undermined his heart; it was the failure of his attempts in life and in passion which brought about his tragic decision. A noble heart and a penetrating mind—how easy it is for such to be impelled by their extraor-

dinary sensibilities to such an end! And what life is—need I tell *you?*
I am contented to have erected in my heart a monument to our departed and unhappy friend, whose deed will be so callously analyzed
by the world. . . .

I hope that Mlle. Maxa will permit me to write her from time to
time. I promise not to abuse her kindness.

Poetry and Truth

Suddenly there came to me the news of the death of Jerusalem and
immediately the general rumor was followed by the most precise and
circumstantial description of what had come to pass. At that moment
the fable of *The Sorrows of Young Werther* was found. From all
sides the elements integrated and became a solid mass—even as water
in a vessel on the point of freezing is transformed into ice by the
smallest shock.

November 27, 1772
Karoline Flachsland to Herder

Our good Goethe lives here in Darmstadt and goes on drawing and
we sit around a table in this winter weather and watch him and
listen to him. There is a regular academy of art at Merck's house;
they draw and they engrave in copper. He drew a little landscape
for me with a castle on the top of a mountain and a village at its foot.

December 15, 1772
Karoline Flachsland to Herder

Goethe is gone, the goodhearted wanderer. He will write you from
Frankfurt.

Christmas Day, 1772
To Kestner

It is still dark, dear Kestner. I rose early in order to write by the
light of dawn which recalls to me pleasant memories of other days.
I have ordered coffee in honor of the day and will go on writing to
you until the sun has fully risen. It was the blowing of the watchman

on the tower which wakened me. . . . Now I hear him again; his melody comes to me with the north wind, as though it blew at my very window. Yesterday, dear Kestner, I was in the country with some fine fellows and we made very merry indeed with shouts and with laughter from beginning to end. . . . We had a beautiful evening and it was night when we returned. Now I must tell you that it always does my soul good when the sun has gone down and night, proceeding from the east spreads toward the north and the south and only a twilit ring remains of the evening. . . . I stopped on the bridge. The sombre city at both sides, the still gleaming horizon and its reflection in the river—these constituted a precious impression which I drew close to me. . . . Now, at this moment, the warders of the gates are coming from the burgomaster and rattle their keys. The first flush of dawn is on my neighbor's house and the bells in the churches are ringing. . . . And now the day rises in all its might. If good fortune comes to us as swiftly, there will be a wedding soon. . . .

Farewell, both of you, and think of me as a strange cross between a rich man and poor Lazarus.

1773

January 8, 1773

To Kestner

This night I dreamed of Lotte. It waked me up and so I sat on my bed and thought of all our life together from that first country visit to our moonlit midnight conversation by the wall. It was a beautiful life and I look back upon it with serenity.

January 18, 1773

Cornelia Goethe to Kestner

We live very simply and very happily here. All evening we sit together around the tile oven and chat, or else my brother reads us something, and then we often wish that you were here and could share our pleasure.

January 28, 1773

To Kestner

These last twenty-four hours were strange enough. Last night I helped my girl friends dress up for the ball, although I didn't go along. From the wealth of one of them I made up an aigrette of jewels and feathers, which adorned her well. And suddenly it occurred to me: Oh, I wish it were Lotte whom I was adorning thus. Then I went with two of them for a walk across the bridge in the dark. The water was high and had a strong tone and the ships were crowded together and the dear dim moon was saluted by us and the girls thought all this inexpressibly beautiful and thought all people very happy who live in the country and on ships and under God's sky. . . . We went home and I translated some Homer for them, who is now our favorite author. . . .

At midnight tonight there rose a horrid storm. It throbbed and howled. I thought of the ships on the river and felt comfortable in my civilized bed. Scarce had I fallen asleep when I was wakened by drum beats and alarm and cries of fire. I leaped to the window and saw the red glare. In a moment I was dressed and on the spot. A great broad house was in flames to the very roof. . . . I ran to my grandmother's house who lives close by. She was gathering up her silver. We took all her precious things to a place of safety and now await the outcome. The fire lasted from 1 o'clock till dawn. . . . It is smothered now, but not extinguished. . . . I feel as though I had danced all night. . . .

Early March, 1773

To Kestner

It is both disgusting and nasty on the part of both of you that you didn't commission me to have your rings made. As though it were not natural that I carry out the commission. And in spite of you and the devil himself, who must have inspired you to deny me this privilege, 'tis I who will order them and see to it that they are as beautiful as the crowns of the elect. . . .

Late March, 1773

To Kestner

It isn't my fault that you didn't get the rings a week ago. Here they are and may they please you. . . .
Be happy then and go to your new home. You wouldn't come to Frankfurt anyhow, and I am very glad, for if you came here I would have to go.

Late March, 1773

Enclosure to Charlotte Buff

May my memory be as constantly with you in your happiness as this ring will be. Dear Lotte, after a great space of time we will meet again and the ring will be on your finger and I shall still be yours.

Early April, 1773

To Kestner

> Kestner and Lotte were married on Palm Sunday instead of Easter Sunday, as originally planned.

God bless you, for you surprised me. On Good Friday I meant to dig a grave and bury Lotte's portrait silhouette. Now it still hangs on my wall and will do so till I die. . . . I wander in deserts where there is no water; my hair is my only shadow and my blood my only well. But I rejoice that your ship with gay flags and with laughter enters the harbor. . . .

April 10, 1773

To Kestner

Behold my bed, sterile as desert sand. And yet I had a day today so beautiful that work and joy and aspiration and relish became one. And in the evening, which was full of stars, my heart was big with memory of the marvelous moment at Lotte's feet. . . . To have left her. I don't understand how it was possible. For look, you're not just a stick yourself. Suppose somebody had said to you before or afterwards: Leave Lotte!—Well, would you have? That's quite a question. Well, I'm no stick either and I went and *you* can tell me whether it wasn't a bit heroic or not. I am satisfied with myself and yet not. It seemed to be not too difficult and yet I don't understand how it was possible.

April 14, 1773

To Kestner

O Kestner, when did I ever grudge you Lotte in the human sense, for not to grudge her to you in a higher sense, I would have had to be an angel without entrails. So I'll tell you a secret, in order that you may know and see clearly. When I began to be so powerfully attracted to her, a man came to me and spoke, even as people do. "If I were Kestner, I wouldn't like it. What is to be the end of it? Are you trying to take her away from him?" It was in the morning, and in his room I said to him these words: "I happen to be fool enough, if you like, to consider the girl quite out of the ordinary. Were I to be deceived and to discover that she let me be her friend in order to speculate with her charms and to bind Kestner to her by the device of jealousy—the moment of that discovery, though it might bring me closer to her, would mark the end of our friendship." This I asserted most solemnly. Between ourselves and without boasting, I have some understanding of the fair sex. . . . And now look in how far I envy you and must envy you, and I assure you that if it were to occur to you to nurse any jealousy of me, I reserve the right of writing a comedy with you people as its characters so markedly delineated that Jews and Christians both will laugh at you.

April 17, 1773

Karoline Flachsland to Herder

I have seen but little of Goethe. He is more reserved than ever and, especially in Merck's presence, uses a rather curious tone. . . . When I am alone with him he is as sweet as ever.

June 12, 1773

To Kestner

I had an odd dream about Lotte last night. She had taken my arm and I led her through the avenue of trees and everybody stood still and looked at us. . . . And the people kept looking at us, although we hurried. O Lotte, I said to her, Oh, I hope they don't find out that you're the wife of another man. . . .

And so I dream and amble through life and conduct beastly lawsuits and scribble plays and novels and such things and draw and flirt and make the time pass quickly. And you, you are blessed like the man who lives in fear of the Lord. People say of me that I carry the curse of Cain. But I have slain no brother! And the people are fools. There, my dear Kestner, you have a bit of imaginative work. Read it to your little wife when you gather together with her in God and close the doors behind you.

September 11, 1773

L. J. F. Hopfner to F. Nicolai

Hopfner, 1743-1797, professor of law in Giessen; F. Nicolai, 1733-1811, bookseller and writer.

Surely you have read *Götz von Berlichingen?* I wish you knew the author personally; he combines true genius with the greatest amiability and goodness of heart. I am truly proud of his friendship and of Merck's.

Poetry and Truth

My understanding stirred my friend Merck's delight in technical and business matters. Through our *Frankfurt Journal* he had established connections with both scholars and booksellers. It was his opinion that we should publish a work as strange and striking as *Götz von Berlichingen* at our own expense. We would thus profit by the undertaking. Like many others he had often reckoned up the profits of the publishers which, in the case of certain works, were very considerable, especially if one disregards the circumstance how much they lose on other books and through the various circumstances of their trade. At all events, it was decided that I was to buy the paper and he take care of the composition. Eagerly we went to work and I was thoroughly pleased gradually to see my wild dramatic sketch in neat proof-sheets. It really looked much better than I had imagined. Printing and binding were completed and many packages sent out. It did not take long for a great stir to arise; the attention which it aroused was quite general. But because, due to our practical limitations, we could not send copies quickly enough to all parts of the country, there suddenly appeared a pirated edition. Moreover since the returns from the packages we sent out were slow in coming and rarely came in cash, I, dependent on my father and constantly short of money, was most embarrassed because I couldn't pay for the paper at a moment when from all directions people paid me attention and applauded me, because I had given the world proof of my talent. Merck, who had resources of various kinds, nursed the happiest hopes that the matter would soon reach a favorable adjustment. I cannot say that his hopes were justified.

September 15, 1773
To Kestner

I got your letter on the evening of this day and I have trimmed me a new pen to write a long letter. I trust that my spirits will be worthy to reach Lotte. . . .
The relations of my sister to Schlosser are as they have been. He is stuck in Karlsruhe. . . . I don't understand it. My sister is staying with friends in Darmstadt. I shall lose much in losing her. She understands my whims and puts up with them.
Yes, my dear man, I'm letting my father have his way. Daily he seeks to enmesh me more in municipal affairs and I let him do it. . . .
But I do well by my own work too and hope to make all kinds of progress in the course of the winter. I've sent a copy of *Götz* to the old magistrate, who enjoyed it thoroughly; others have asked for copies. . . .
Another confidential word in my capacity of writer. My aims increase daily in beauty and greatness; if my good spirits do not leave me and my love does not, much will be forthcoming for those who care for me and the public will get its share, too.

October 12, 1773
G. F. E. von Schönborn to H. W. von Gerstenberg
    Two Danish diplomats and scholars.

The very evening of my arrival in Frankfurt I had an interview with Herr Goethe, the author of *Götz*. . . . He is a slender young man

of about my height. His color is pale; his nose big and aquiline; he
has a longish face and medium black eyes and black hair. (We meet
every day.) His expression is serious, even melancholy, although
comic and laughing and satiric moods gleam through. He is very
eloquent and produces a very stream of witty notions. . . . He was
thoroughly delighted at my report of your opinion of his play. . . .
He said it would inspire him to do even better, for he was well aware
of the fact that he was as yet far from having reached his ideal. . . .
He seems to produce with extraordinary ease. At present he is working
on a drama called *Prometheus*. He read me two acts full of admirable
passages derived from the very depth of nature. I give you my opinion as I formed it from his reading. He draws and paints, too. His
room is full of fine reproductions of excellent antiques. . . . He is
minded to go to Italy in order to gain a better insight into art.

                                                  October 27, 1773
To Langer

When I published *Götz* one of my pleasantest anticipations was that
my friends, of whom I have many in the wide world, would look
toward me again. . . . And it came to pass just so. My health has
improved steadily since our days together, but since it did not wholly
suffice for such a rôle in active life as I might have wished to play, I
followed my inclination to science and to art and did not cease until
I felt that I could present myself to the public. I addressed myself
to the heart of the people. . . . I must confess that the approbation
I have found surpassed my hopes.

Poetry and Truth

At that period of my youth I often found that when we need help
we are told: Physician, heal thyself. . . . Looking about for a confirmation of my independence, I found its securest basis in my productive talent. During sundry years it never left me for a moment; all
that I became aware of by day often assumed plastic shape in the
dreams of night and when I opened my eyes there appeared before
me either a whole or partial new and marvelous creative thing. Usually I wrote in the earliest hours of the day; but also late at night,

when wine and companionship had heightened the vital spirits, one could demand of me whatever one desired. . . . Reflecting on this gift of nature I found that it was all my own and could be favored or obstructed by no alien influence. Thus I was fond in my thoughts of founding my entire existence upon it. This notion was transmitted into imagery—into the ancient mythological figure of Prometheus who, divided from the gods, peopled the world from his own workshop. . . . In the strange composition which thus arose there occurred, in the form of a monologue, that poem which has since attained some significance in literature.

1773

PROMETHEUS

Oh darken thy heaven, Zeus,
With fume of cloud,
And like an unruly boy
Who thistles crops
The oaks and mountain-summits smite;
My earth which is solid
Thou must let stand,
And my low dwelling which thou didst not build,
And my own hearth
Of which the glow
Rouses thine envy.

Naught know I whose poverty
Equals yours, ye divinities!
A wretched sustenance
Of slaughtered victims
And of prayer's breath
Feeds your majesty,
And want were yours, were not
Children and beggars still
Full of hope and folly.

Still in my childhood,
Knowing not world or life,
I turned my errant glances
Sunward, as though beyond there dwelt

An ear to hear my lamentation,
A heart like mine
Which would the sore beset compassionate.

Who helped me
Face at need the Titans' arrogance?
Who saved me from the imminent death,
From slavery?
Has not thy sole self all completed,
Holy impassioned heart,
Which, cheated in thy youth,
Gave thanks for being saved
To him who snores above us.

I honor thee? Wherefor?
Hast thou assuaged the anguish
E'er of the sore oppressed?
Or hast thou eased the weeping
Of him beset by dread?
Was not my manhood forged
By omnipotent time
And by fate, the eternal,
My masters and thine own?

Canst thou be dreaming
I should my life find hateful
And flee to deserts,
Seeing not all my
Dreams grew from bloom to fruit?

Here sit I, molding creatures
In my own image,
A race to be like me,
To weep and to suffer,
To relish life and know delight,
And of thee to be heedless,
As I!

October 30, 1773

To Charlotte Kestner

I don't know, dear Lotte, whether my supposition is correct that you will soon need a negligée. It seems so to me, at least. And as I was reflecting on this important point, I said to myself: she likes to dress in white, but muslin is not proper for winter unless it be quilted and that would make her look too old. So what happened? The careful goddess of fashion came to me and handed me the material which I am sending to you; it has all good qualities, including durability. It is muslin, too, and has all the virtues of muslin, but the satin insets make it appropriate for winter. So, quickly to the dressmaker with it, that it may be neatly made. It must be lined with some white fabric; those I have seen were lined with linen.

Christmas Day, 1773

To Kestner

The passage in your letter with its hint of a possible residence nearer you struck into me. Ah, I have dreamed of that for long. But it will have to remain a dream. Nor would my father object to my taking an office elsewhere. . . . But the talents and powers which I have I need too sorely for my own purposes and I am too well accustomed to following my instincts than that I could serve any ruler. . . .
My sister is bearing herself well. She is learning to know life, and people become aware of their own capacities only when they meet complications. She is well and Schlosser is the best of husbands as he was the tenderest and most sane of lovers.
Dear Maxa de la Roche is getting married—to a highly esteemed merchant here. Fine! Very fine indeed!

December 31, 1773

To Elisabeth Jacobi

Wife of Friedrich H. Jacobi, 1743-1819, religious philosopher and in later life president of the Academy of Sciences in Munich.

My prospects for the new year look exactly like a cabinet of curiosities. Maxa de la Roche is marrying a Frankfurt man. Her future husband seems to be a man with whom one can get along. And so hurray

—once more the number of dear creatures will be increased, who are anything but intellectual, as you readily imagine. Between you and me, it's pretty bad on this earth with one's acquaintances and friends and loves. You think you have everything safely and well arranged, and what happens? The devil makes the earth quake and there are dust and ashes. . . .

1774

January 8, 1774

To Heinrich Christian Boie

Hannoverian official, writer, editor of *The Muses' Almanach*, 1744-1806.

On the return of my friend Merck from Petersburg I took upon myself the publication of *Götz*, and I beg you to give me a helping hand, for I am nothing less than a man of business. You received in all 150 copies; the retailer sold them, as he himself wrote me, and so it seems but fair that I should get something in return. If you can't let me have the whole sum or part of it in cash, do be so kind and get me some more paper. . . . I can't help laughing when I consider how well the book was received, how quickly the copies were sold and that I haven't been reimbursed for the printing costs.

January 21, 1774

To Sophie von la Roche

If you knew what went on within me before I shunned that house, you wouldn't try to lure me back. In those dreadful moments I suffered enough for the whole future. I am calm now. Leave me my calm—that I would not see you in that house and what people would say, etc. etc.—I've put all that behind me. And God keep me from the possibility of ever crossing that threshold again.

January 29, 1774

Merck to His Wife

Last week I was in Frankfurt visiting our friend Sophie de la Roche. The marriage which she persuaded her daughter to make is certainly queer enough. The man is young but he has five children. He is a merchant and, though very well off, has little intelligence beyond his station. It was pretty melancholy for me to go looking for our friend amid kegs of herrings and boxes of cheeses. . . . Goethe is already the intimate friend of the new household. He plays with the children and sings to Madame Maxa's accompaniment on the clavichord. The young husband, M. Brentano, though an Italian and jealous enough, is said to be fond of him and to insist on his continued visits.

February 12, 1774

To Gottfried August Bürger

The well-known poet, 1747-1794, whose ballad *Lenore* in Walter Scott's translation became famous in England and America.

Let me be proud of the fact that it is I who tears asunder the wall of paper which separates us. Often have our voices met and our hearts, too. Is not life brief and desolate enough? Should not they grasp each other's hands whose road is one? Send me what you produce. I will do the same with my stuff. It will be a source of encouragement. Otherwise you will show your things only to your dearest friends. I'll do the same.

February 14, 1774

Merck to His Wife

Goethe is not going to take the trip to Switzerland. The great success which his play has had has turned his head a little. He has detached himself from all his friends and lives wholly devoted to the writings which he is preparing to publish. He ought to succeed in all he undertakes and I foresee that a novel which will appear around Easter will be as well received as his drama was. On the side he consoles little Mme. Maxa Brentano and helps her bear the smell of oil and of cheese and her husband's manners.

March, 1774

To Charlotte Kestner

Dear Lotte, It occurs to me that I have long had a letter of yours by me, which I have not answered. The reason is that all this time, perhaps more than ever, you have been *in, cum et sub* (let your lord and master explain), me! Pretty soon it will appear in print for you. It's easily my best. For, of course, I feel well when I think of you two. I am the same as ever and your silhouette is still fastened to the wall of my room and I still borrow the pins that hold it fast, as I used to do. That I am a fool you cannot doubt, and I am ashamed to say more. For if you do not feel that I love you, why do I love you?—!

Poetry and Truth

A young man soon becomes aware through others, if not from within himself, that moral epochs change like the very seasons. . . . But what frightens a sensitive youth more than all else is the irrevocable reappearance of our mistakes. . . . Sombre reflections of this kind, which can easily lead to the bottomless, would not have arisen so markedly in the hearts of my generation, had this melancholy business not been inspired and nourished by a definite influence. The influence was that of English literature, especially of English poetry, of which the admirable qualities are accompanied by a sense of despondency, which is bound to communicate itself to the attentive reader. . . .

Regard from this point of view the majority of English poems, especially the moral and didactic ones, and it will be found that most of them express a sombre weariness of life. It is not true of Young's *Night Thoughts* alone. . . . Many volumes could be assembled to form a commentary on the dreadful, well-known lines:

> Then old Age and Experience, hand in hand,
> Lead him to death, and make him understand,
> After a search so painful and so long,
> That all his life he has been in the wrong.

In order that all this desolate musing should not lack a fitting landscape, Ossian led us indeed to that *ultima Thule,* where on a gray and endless heath, wandering among barren, mossy gravestones, about us the grass swept by a dreadful wind, we behold above us a heavily clouded heaven. . . . This mood was so universal that it accounts for the immense impression which my story, *The Sorrows of Young Werther,* made. It hit home everywhere because it represented publicly and tangibly the innermost state of a morbid delusion of a whole generation.

I isolated myself completely, I forbade the visits of my friends. Within me too I rejected everything that did not strictly belong to the matter. I integrated everything, on the other hand, that had bearing on my aim, and rehearsed those immediate experiences, of whose content I had as yet made no creative use. Under these circumstances, after long and many secret preparations, I wrote *Werther* in four weeks. . . . Through this composition, more than through any other, I had rescued myself from a stormy sea, upon which I had been violently driven back and forth through my own and others' guilt, through accident and choice, through purposefulness and precipitateness, through stubbornness and undue yielding. As after a general confession, I felt happy and free and justified in seeking a new life.

The effectiveness of the little book was great, indeed enormous, and, above all, for the reason that it came at the right moment. . . .
Now, you can't expect the public to accept a work of art as such. Its attention is fixed entirely upon content, substance, as I saw even in the reactions of my friends. In addition, there arose the old prejudice that a printed book should have a didactic intention. But art has none such. It neither approves nor blames; it develops attitudes and actions in their right order and only so illuminates and teaches. . . . Instead of anybody saying anything obliging about the little book as it was, they all wanted suddenly to know what facts were behind it. This made me very angry and I insulted a good many people. For, in order to answer this question, I would have had to take my little book, over which I had brooded so long in order to fuse its various elements into a poetic oneness, and tear it to bits again and destroy its form.

1774

REVIEWER

A fellow came with me to dine,
Quite welcome he, to what was mine;

The menu was my ordinary.
The man devoured all he could carry
And for dessert cleaned out my store.
Scarcely that he could gorge no more
But to my neighbor does the devil
Take him to wag his tongue uncivil:
"Indifferently the soup was spiced,
The roast not crisp, the wine not iced."
The "so-and-so" I must aver.
'Twas a reviewer. Kill the cur!

Elisabeth Goethe to Bettina Brentano

"Man is buried in consecrated earth. Thus one should take great
and strange experiences and bury them in a beautiful sarcophagus of
memory, which all can approach and help to commemorate." This is
what Wolfgang said to me after he had finished writing *Werther*.

April 26, 1774
To Johann Caspar Lavater

Lavater, 1741-1801, pastor in Zürich and theologian, best known by his
theory of the relation of physiognomy to character.

I'll see to it that a manuscript reaches you. It will take some time till
the printing. You will feel much sympathy with the sufferings of the
dear boy whom I describe. He and I went side by side for about six
years without getting nearer to each other. And now I have given my
sensibilities to him and the whole that came out is marvelous.

Early May, 1774
To Kestner

You have relieved me of an anxiety. Kiss the boy for me and eternal
Lotte. Tell her I can't imagine her in childbed. That's too impossible. I see her just as I left her—exactly as I don't know you as a
husband nor can recognize any relationship except the old one—to
which, on a certain occasion, I have fastened patches of alien passions and have executed it all and warn you now to take no umbrage
at it.

May 11, 1774

To Kestner

I was surprised; I did not expect that. I may have hoped it. But since no letter spoke of it, I resigned myself that the first-born be named after someone in the family. But now I would that Lotte may have asserted herself and may have burst through all hesitations and to have said: Wolfgang is to be his name. . . .
Farewell, my dear people, whom I love so much that I had to lend and adjust the fullness of my love even to the imagined delineation of the tragedy of our friend Jerusalem.

Late May, 1774

To Sophie von la Roche

I must hurry to get my *Werther* off to the printer. Nor did I think that you were in a position to follow my feeling or imagination or my fancies.
My sister is undergoing the discomforts of pregnancy; it's quite two months since I've heard from her.
I see dear Maxa rarely, yet when I do meet her it is always like a revelation from above. My mother sends warmest regards.

May 28, 1774

To Friedrich Gottlieb Klopstock

Klopstock, 1724-1803, earliest of the major poets of Germany, the "very German Milton" of Coleridge's famous anecdote. He had just published his chief work, *The Messiah*.

And why should I not write to Klopstock? Why should I not send him whatever I have and whatever be the sympathy with which he may regard it! Shall I not address the living man, to whose grave I would go as a pilgrim? . . . So soon as various things of mine are ready in print, I'll send them to you or at least announce them and I would have you feel the deep devotion of my soul to you.

May, 1774

Schlosser to Lavater

My only complaint against Providence has been that I have lacked
friends. . . . All that I knew were either beneath me or alien to me
in understanding and in heart. Goethe alone could have been my
friend, had his attitude to applause and to suffering been more
manly. But he has not yet reached the stage at which he can be a
friend.

June 1, 1774

To G. F. E. Schönborn

On the night between the 28th and the 29th of May a fire broke out
in our Jews' Street which spread quickly and violently. I helped to
carry the buckets of water too and was rewarded for my trouble on
the spot by the most marvelous and manifold spiritual experiences.
The occasion caused me to become better acquainted with the common people and it was borne in upon me again what excellent human beings they are. . . . I have written all kinds of things. One is a
story called *The Sorrows of Young Werther*. . . . Next I have written a tragedy called *Clavigo*. . . . I have come upon other plans for
important plays, that is, I found the significant details needed in
nature and in my own heart.

June 24, 1774

From Lavater's Diary

I was alone with Goethe in his room by night. Is it really you?—'Tis
I!—Inexpressibly thrilling meeting. He is very like and very unlike
my expectation. We spoke of a thousand things. Of dreadful things,
too. Of the problems of physiognomy. . . . Oh, I have forgotten a
hundred things, which he said to me with the intense expressiveness
of nature. His father and mother wished me an excellent, unaffected
wife and a good night. He and I embraced each other. All that he
spoke was full of spirit and of truth.

◇◇◇◇◇

June 26, 1774

I've been unpacking; I showed Goethe the drawings. Before and during dinner we spoke a good deal of Herder.. . . . That evening we were I forget where. Goethe spoke little but occasionally uttered his hearty agreement in important matters. . . . After supper Goethe read me excerpts from *Werther*, a tale of sentiment in letters with scenes full of true, the truest description of human nature. Frau Goethe thanked me for the sermons on Jonah which I had sent her.

June 28, 1774

I was awake at 3 o'clock. Gentle, beautiful dawn. Trilling of birds. I got up at once and packed and added some notations to yesterday's diary. Goethe came early to embrace me and to wish me a good morning.

At 4:30 we got into the carriage and drove through the silent, largely slumbering town illuminated by the gentle morning sun, out between beautiful fields. We feared a thunder storm was coming up. But it passed us by. . . . It rained only a little while. Goethe told me many things about Spinoza and his writings. None, he asserted, had spoken so like the Saviour concerning God as he. All modern Deists, moreover, had drawn primarily from him. He had been an extremely just, upright, poor man. He had been highly esteemed; the most eminent men of his time had consulted him on the most weighty matters and on mathematical problems and had cordially loved him for his extraordinary wisdom and veracity. He had contradicted the prophets and had yet been a prophet himself. . . . He had renounced a considerable inheritance, which was his just due but concerning which there was a dispute, for the sake of peace and had asked only for the bed on which his father had slept. His correspondence, Goethe added, was the most interesting book in the whole world in the matter of uprightness and the love of humanity.

We got out (I don't remember where) and sat under a tree. Goethe had a glass of wine, I one of raspberry juice and water. . . .

Before 11 o'clock we arrived at Wiesbaden and went to see the hot
baths, which give an impression of great desolateness. Sat next to
Goethe at the midday meal. There were Hussars and officers and a
very stupid parson. We were both struck by the gentle, young, humble physiognomy of a Jewish youth. . . . Goethe talked about his
plays. After the meàl we ate strawberries together. We also observed
the physiognomy of a Jewish juggler, who offered to teach me his
skill. . . .

❖❖❖❖❖

July 18, 1774

On a crowded ship on the river Lahn. Goethe wrote riming ends
for the company and coffee was drunk. . . . Magnificent old castle.
. . . We went on shore . . . to a house where we ate at noon, bacon
and beans. Back on board, we passed a chapel and a ruined castle.
Goethe talked about the men who lived in castles, and so from the
Lahn we entered the Rhine.

❖❖❖❖❖

July 20, 1774

Aboard again under a wet awning. Goethe romantic in a gray hat
with a half-withered bunch of flowers, a brown silk neck kerchief
and a high gray collar, eating his bread and butter like a very wolf
and peering after the as yet unpacked luncheons. . . . Goethe read
us from the text of an operetta and I took a nap. Now Goethe is nap-
ping under the linen awning next to me, as under a tent. . . . At
12 o'clock we reached Bonn. Left again at 2. Much rain. We slept a
good deal and talked little.

July 21, 1774

Lavater's Later Account

When Goethe and Lavater made their little trip along the Rhine it
happened at Elberfeld that J. G. Hasenkamp, the president of the
college in Duisburg, ate dinner (or perhaps it was supper) in a great
company with Lavater and Goethe, seated not far from the latter.
The mood of the company was gay and both Goethe and Lavater
charmed everyone by their vivid conversation. Suddenly Hasenkamp,

a God-fearing man, but one whose imperfect sense of fitness made him prone to forget the proprieties, turned to Goethe and asked in a solemn tone of voice: Are you Herr Goethe?—Yes!—And did you write that notorious book *The Sorrows of Young Werther?*—Yes.— In that case my conscience bids me to communicate to you my horror of that wicked piece of writing. May God improve your perverse heart! For woe, woe to him, who causes his brother to stumble!—A painful embarrassment stole over the company. Everyone dreaded to see what would happen to the honest but pedantic pedagogue. But Goethe soon restored the serenity of all present by replying: I quite understand that from your point of view you must judge the matter as you do and I respect the honesty of purpose which causes you to chide me. Remember me in your prayers.—

August 17, 1774

F. H. Jacobi to Christoph Martin Wieland

Wieland, 1733-1813, the very gifted poet and translator of Shakespeare, tutor of the Duke Karl August of Sachsen-Weimar and destined to become one of Goethe's closest friends.

From head to toe Goethe is all genius, a man possessed, who is destined to act according to the dictates of the indwelling spirit. You need to have been with him but a single hour to know how ridiculous it would be to ask of him that he think or act otherwise than he does. I do not mean that he may not change into something even greater and better, but the change must be like the unfoldment of a flower, the ripening of a seed, the growth and expansion of a tree.

Summer, 1774

F. M. Klinger to J. M. Lenz

Klinger, 1752-1831, dramatist, author of the famous play *Storm and Stress*, later general in the Russian army; Lenz, 1751-1792, minor poet, originally from Latvia, a fellow student of Goethe's in Strassburg.

I wanted to study at the university and I didn't have even an hundred florins. At that moment I made Goethe's acquaintance. That was the first truly happy hour of my youth. He offered me his help. I didn't tell him the whole truth, because I would rather have died than be undeserving of his help. Soon I had nothing. Goethe kept on insisting and reproached me for not letting him help me and now I have been living on his bounty for a whole year.

To F. H. Jacobi   August 21, 1774

Here I am in my room after a frugal supper over a little mug of wine. After a thin afternoon came your letter and an hundred ideas arose. Look you, all universities are alike, places where well-fed gentlemen sit who pick their teeth and wonder why no cook can prepare anything to their taste. . . . Now the beginning and end of the art of writing is the reproduction of the world about us, grasped by that inner world which grips, combines, transforms, kneads, and reconstitutes the matter according to its own manner and form. This is, thank God, an eternal mystery, which I will not reveal to the idle babblers and lookers-on.

To Charlotte Kestner   August 26, 1774

Who do you suppose is in my room at this moment? Dear Lotte, you'll never guess. You would think of anyone, known to fame or not, rather than of my old laundress from Wetzlar. You know her and know that she loves you, as do all those who have known you all your life. She couldn't get work enough in Wetzlar any more and my mother hopes to find her employment. I took her up to my room and she saw your silhouette and cried out: Oh, my dear sweet Lotte! . . .

Today two years ago I was with you almost the whole day and we cut string beans till almost midnight. My birthday, the 28th, began solemnly with tea and friendly faces all about and, O Lotte, you did assure me with that frankness and openness of soul, which were always so precious to me, that both of you still loved me, since it would be so very sad if the passing of time were to subdue our feelings too. One of these days soon I'm going to send you a prayer book or a jewel case or whatever you choose to call it, in order that morning and evening you may draw sustenance from the recollection of my friendship and my love.

September 23, 1774
To the Kestners

Did you get your copy of *Werther?* Then you will understand the other note I'm sending. I forgot to enclose it in the confusion of the moment. The Fair whirls and screams and all my friends are here and past and future falter into one. What will become of me? Oh, you well-settled people, how much better off you are! I beg of you lend the book to no one; continue to love him who is living and honor him who has died. Now you will understand the dark passages in my previous letters.

Same date
(The note that was not enclosed.)

Lotte, how dear the little book is to me you may feel as you read it, and this special copy is as precious to me as though it were the only one in the world. It is your copy, Lotte, which I have kissed an hundred times and kept under lock and key, so that no one may touch it. —And I beg of you to let no one see it now, for it will not really be published until the time of the Book Fair at Leipzig. I want each of you to read it all alone, you all alone, Kestner all alone, and I want each of you to write me a word about it.

October 17, 1774
H. C. Boie to an Unknown Correspondent

I've passed a whole day with Goethe quite undisturbed. . . . He read me several poems. . . . If he sends me copies, as he promises to do, you shall have them. . . . Next day we remained together till midnight and had to shut the doors in order to be alone. Again he read me poems. But soon we stopped reading. . . . Goethe's heart is as great as his mind.

1774

THE KING IN THULE

A king dwelt in a far land,
A true man to his grave,

To whom his dying mistress
A golden goblet gave.

Dearest of all things to him,
He drained it every bout;
Tears in his eyelids gathered,
Oft though he drank thereout.

And when he came to dying,
The tale of his towns he told,
Nothing his heirs begrudging
Save for that cup of gold.

He sate him at a banquet,
His glittering knights and he,
In high ancestral hall within
That castle by the sea.

Up stood the old carouser,
Quaffed one last living glow,
And hurled the sacred beaker
Into the flood below.

He saw it plunging, filling,
Engulfèd in the main.
His eyes were breaking, breaking,
Drank never a drop again.

October, 1774

To the Kestners

I must write you at once, my dear ones, my angry ones, in order
that I may relieve my heart. The deed is done; the book is published;
forgive me if you can.—I would not, oh I beg of you, I would not
hear another word from you until the event will have confirmed the
fact that your anxiety was pitched too high and until you yourselves
have felt purely in your hearts the book's innocent blending of truth
and falsehood. You, Kestner, an affectionate advocate, have ex-
hausted and anticipated all that I could have said in my own defense,

but it seems to me that in my heart there is still more that can be said, although it is not easily expressible today. . . . And so, my dear ones, when the sense of hurt threatens to overcome you, think, do think that your old Goethe, though a new and newer Goethe, is more than ever all your own.

November 20, 1774

To Kestner

I have your letter! At a strange desk, in a painter's studio, for I began yesterday to paint in oils, I have your letter with me and must thank you for it!—Oh, ye unbelieving ones, I would exclaim, ye of little faith! Could you but feel that thousandth part of what *Werther* means to a thousand hearts and souls, you would not so carefully count the cost that the book has been to you. Read the enclosed little letter and send it back to me. . . . Dear, dear Kestner, if you will but wait, help will come to you. Not at the cost of my very life would I recall the book and do take my word for it that your anxieties and your accusations will fade like ghosts of the night if you will have patience and then, between now and a year from now, I promise you to blow away in the loveliest and deepest and only manner, all that may yet be left of suspicion and misinterpretation among that herd of swine, which is the tongue-wagging public—even as a clean north wind sweeps aside fog and mist.—Werther *had* to be! You do not feel *him* but only *me* and *yourselves* and what you call the matter "pasted" on us—matter which, despite what you say and what others say, is woven into the texture.—If I still live, it is owing to you, and so you are not the other man in the book. . . .

Press Lotte's hand warmly for me and say to her: to know her name pronounced in reverence upon a thousand sacred lips is surely a cure of such ills as in common life one must expect from any female gossip and which would not greatly disturb anyone.

If you'll both be good and brave and not gnaw at me, I'll send you letters with their cries and sighs over *Werther,* and if you have faith, you will believe that all will be well and that the talk is as nothing. . . .

November 20, 1774
To Sophie von la Roche

I ran into your Maxa in the theatre. Her husband was with her and he had, as it were, concentrated all his friendliness between his sharp nose and his sharp chin. A time may come when I'll visit their house again.

November, 1774
Johann Georg Zimmermann to Charlotte von Stein

Zimmermann, 1728-1795, writer and physician in Hannover. Charlotte, Baroness von Stein, née von Schardt, 1742-1827, who was destined, when they met in Weimar, to become Goethe's friend and muse and beloved. She had met Doctor Zimmermann while taking the cure in Pyrmont.

Those who have told you, my dear friend, that *Werther* is a dangerous work, have not understood it. The origin and progress of an authentic love are delineated in the book with truth, with the colors of nature itself. . . .

You tell me that you would like to see the author of the book; you seem not to know to what extent this amiable and enchanting man could be a danger to you. I am sending you as a gift a cut of his aquiline physiognomy, which I have taken from my friend Lavater's treatise on that subject.

December 23, 1774
K. L. von Knebel to F. J. J. Bertuch

Knebel, 1744-1834, governor and tutor of the young Prince Constantine of Saxe-Weimar. He met Goethe in Frankfurt at this time and paved the way for Goethe's connection with the Ducal Court of Weimar. Bertuch, 1747-1822, another officer of the Weimar court.

You will have learned from Wieland that I made Goethe's acquaintance and that I regard him with a measure of enthusiasm. I can't help it, but I'm ready to swear that all you good people, who really have a head and a heart, would think equally well of him, were you to know him. I regard him as one of the most extraordinary phenomena that I have met in my life. . . .

Goethe lives in a state of constant inner conflict and rebellion, since all objects affect him most violently. Thus are to be explained the sudden gusts of temper and the self-will, which arise not from a bad heart but from the wealth of genius. . . .

So much of this aspect of Goethe, which is the least noteworthy. The serious side of his mind is worthy of reverence. I have a great mass of fragments by him, among others that of a *Doctor Faust,* in which there are scenes of an extreme magnificence. He brings out manuscripts from every corner of his room. He assured me that he had written *Werther* in a month and had not stricken out a line. *Götz* took him six weeks. He'll do another dozen—but of all that later.

December 28, 1774

To Karl von Knebel

I've got to begin, dear Knebel, to pump you, otherwise I probably won't learn any of the things I am eager to know: how you have all fared and what effect all the new acquaintances have had on you. I would like to have my share in all that I may know. To begin with myself. It was a strange moment when I saw you at the door of the inn of the Three Crowns in Mainz at dawn that day. . . . But look, I have just received your letter and you must forgive my little faith and accept my thanks.

Poetry and Truth

One day at this time as I was sitting in my room with softened light, there entered a slender man of good figure, whom I first took to be Fritz Jacobi. I soon recognized my error. His graceful demeanor did not wholly conceal a certain military bearing. He introduced himself as Karl von Knebel who, having lived some time in Berlin and Potsdam, had made the acquaintance of the local writers there and, upon the whole, was well and actively acquainted with German literature. . . . At present, he told me, he was in Weimar as the governor of Prince Constantine. Of the conditions in that city I had already heard much that was favorable. Many travelers came from there who bore witness to the fact that the Duchess Amalia had called the most eminent men to Weimar for the education of the princes of the Ducal house; we had heard how distinguished teachers, called to the

University of Jena, helped to contribute to this result and how the arts were not only protected by the Duchess but eagerly and thoroughly practiced by herself. . . .

December 29, 1774

To Sophie von la Roche

I was in Mainz! I went there to follow Wieland's prince, Karl August of Saxe-Weimar, who is an admirable person. From there I wrote to Wieland, too; I had the impulse to do so and got the kind of answer I expected. It's the damnedest thing that I seem to live at peace with everyone. . . .

1775

January 1, 1775

Karl August to Wieland

I have made the acquaintance of Goethe who esteems you highly.

January 13, 1775

To Karl von Knebel

Dear Knebel, I do beg of you to send me a word, especially about my manuscripts. Where are you? Are you thinking of me kindly? I've had a few very productive days.

Poetry and Truth

In spite of my sister's marriage and departure the company of young men and women which had gathered about her continued to exist. These people had become accustomed to each other and went on meeting on a certain evening of every week. . . . On these occasions, it happened, oddly enough, that I was always thrown together with the same girl, a very sweet creature, of the kind that one would like to imagine as one's wife. Her figure was lovely and harmonious, her countenance agreeable, her demeanor characterized by a tranquility which bore witness to a health of both body and mind. . . .

This chance situation did not displease my mother. From the beginning she favored this girl with whom I had established so strange a relationship and was inclined to believe that she would be as pleasant a daughter-in-law as she would become a wife. . . .

On a certain occasion I surprised my mother in the act of admiring the old cradles in our attic, among which was an enormous one of walnut, inlaid with ivory and ebony. This conspicuous one had been my own.

I must go on with the story of my relationship to Lili. [*Lili Schönemann, 1758-1817, married Bernhard F. von Türckheim in 1776.*] . . . A mutual need and a habit of our seeing each other ensued; but I would have had to renounce her during many a day and many an evening until late into the night, had I not been able to determine to see her in the social circles in which she moved. From this circumstance I came to suffer much pain.

1775

    How often is it, O most sweet,
    That thou a stranger art to me,
    When in the manyheaded throng we meet,
    By which my every joy is blighted.
    Only when darkness swathes us in tranquility,
    Then in our kisses are we reunited.

Poetry and Truth

My relationship to her had been from person to person. . . . It was like my previous love relations, only on a higher plane. I had, however, left out of account the external circumstances and the involvements of her social set. An unconquerable desire had taken hold of us both; I could not bear to be without her, nor she without me; yet in that environment which was subject to the influence of various members of her circle, we suffered many days and hours of disharmony. . . .

But in order to give this description a sense of the living experience and to approach it to the emotions of youth, may at least one of the songs, though destined to become well known later, be quoted here:

NEW LIFE NEW LOVE

Heart, whence comes this strange insistence?
What oppresses thee so sore?
What an alien, new existence?
Heart, I hardly know thee more.
Vanished whatsoever was dearest,
Gone the very hurts thou fearest,
Gone thy ardor and thy rest—
Heart what makes thee so unblest?

Ah, it is her youth entrances,
And her form in perfect flower,
And the kindness of her glances
Kindles her unending power.
When I seek to flee before her,
To be strong and not adore her,
Instantly the loiterer
Sees his way lead back to her.

By this thread I may not sever,
From her magic spindle spun,
Does the dear wild girl forever
Cause my will to be undone.
Strong the sorcery that holds me
And to her desires molds me.
Changed from all I used to be!
Tyrant love, oh set me free!

February 4, 1775
The Duke Karl August of Sachsen-Meiningen to His Sister

This Karl August, 1760-1782, is not to be confused with Goethe's friend,
the Duke of Sachsen-Weimar-Eisenach.

Herr Goethe dined with us. I was so glad that he was my neighbor at
table, for I could observe him better thus. He speaks a great deal

and well, in his own way with both originality and naïveté and is at moments astonishingly amusing and gay. . . . He has his own notions and opinions concerning all matters and all the people he knows and his own way of expressing himself, his very own diction. He delighted me. . . . He stayed on with us from noon until 5 o'clock, which pleased us very much.

February, 1775

To the Countess Auguste zu Stolberg-Stolberg

This young woman, 1753-1835, married to a Count Bernstorff in 1783, had written to Goethe what we now call an anonymous fan letter. He did not discover her identity until later as the sister of his friends Christian and Friedrich Leopold Stolberg, members of a group of young poets at Göttingen. Goethe and Auguste never met.

Dear One,—I will give you no other name, for what are all other names, friend, sister, beloved, bride, or what were a word which summed up all the meanings of these words, compared to the immediate feeling, which—but I cannot go on. Your letter gripped me in the strangest of hours. . . . Have patience with me; soon an answer will reach you. Meanwhile I am sending you my silhouette portrait and I beg for your own—not in miniature but one that corresponds to nature.

I've let this letter lie again. Do have patience with me. Write to me and in my best hours I will think of you. You asked me whether I am happy? Yes, my dear one, I am. When I am not, all the deep knowledge of joy and pain nevertheless dwells within me and no outer circumstance disturbs or troubles or obstructs me. And yet, God knows, I am even as a little child. Once more, farewell.

February 13, 1775

To Auguste

If you can imagine a Goethe in a coat with piping, reasonably elegant otherwise too, from tip to toe, moving about in the insignificant splendor of sconces and candelabra, involved in a crowd, riveted to the card table by a pair of beautiful eyes, absentmindedly driven from such a party to a concert and from thence to a ball, paying court with every circumstance of frivolity to a "cute" blonde [*Lili Schöne-*

mann]—if you can imagine that, you have a picture of a Goethe in his present carnival aspect—the same who stammered out to you sundry dull but deep emotions the other day, who doesn't like to write to you, who even forgets you at moments, because the sense of your spiritual presence makes him seem too unbearable to himself. . . .

One other thing makes me happy—the many noble souls who come to me from all the ends of the country, mingled to be sure with many insignificant and boring people, and who sometimes flit by and sometimes stay a little. For one does not know what one is until one finds oneself again in others.

February 17, 1775

To Bürger

It is difficult to give you an account of my present confusions. I have not been industrious recently. The air of spring which already from time to time blows from beyond the gardens, is beginning to stir my heart and I hope that the present constriction will cease and something come of its melting, and I hope that you will love whatever does come out of it.

1775

> 'Twill happen on such days as these
> That none nor thou thyself can please.
> Everything grates on mind and heart;
> Can it be otherwise in art?
> Goad thyself not when dullness broods,
> Never too far be happier moods:
> Thy patience through the evil hour
> Will lend the better double power.

From the Records of the Family of André

> Johann André, 1741-1799, musician and later music publisher in Offenbach.

In the early spring of 1775 Lili Schönemann used to pay visits at the country house of her uncle in Offenbach. Johann André who had an inexhaustible store of songs, both grave and comic, would let the two lovers keep him at the piano until the night watchman announced the midnight hour, by which device they were able to be with each other longer. . . . Goethe suffered at that time from all the lyrical confusions of youth.

Offenbach, March 7 and 8, 1775

To Auguste

Why should I not write to you? Why should I let the pen lie, after I had stretched out my hand for it so often? As always and always I have been thinking of you. And now!—I'm in the country with very dear people—in a state of expectation, dear Auguste.—God knows I'm a poor soul! The other day we ended Lent with a dance. I was among the first on the floor, went up and down, thought of you and then—oh, much joy and love surrounded me. Coming home at dawn I wanted to write to you but let it be and had a silent dialogue with you instead. What can I tell you, seeing that I can't wholly communciate to you my present condition, since you don't know me. My dear, my dear, think of me kindly still. I would that I could rest my brow on your hands and look into your eyes.

Good morning, dear one! The carpenters hammering at a new house across the way awakened me. I could not rest in bed. I'll write to my sister and then have a word with you.
It is still night. I tried to go into the garden but got no farther than the door. It rained so hard. I have thought of you so much and remembered that I hadn't thanked you for your likeness. . . .
I am so weary of people who dig poor Werther out of his grave and perform an autopsy on him. Each time I come back into my room I find more of the critical hogwash coming from Berlin. One fellow abuses the book and another praises it and a third one says that it's just tolerable and each is as annoying as the other. . . .

Frankfurt, March 10, 1775

Back in the city in my retreat. I'm writing you with the paper on my knees. Dear one, I'll mail all this today; I add that my head is reasonably clear and my heart reasonably free. What did I just say? But how find expression for what we feel? How can we communicate to each other our condition, seeing that it changes from hour to hour. I bless the impulse which causes me, instead of more words, to send you this drawing of my room. Farewell. Keep me, poor fellow, in your heart, and may our Father in Heaven give you many such brave and happy hours as I often have and then let the twilight come, tearful and blessed.

March 15, 1775

To Sophie von la Roche

God bless you in your rôle of grandmama and the little mama Maxa. I'm on my way to Brentano to offer my congratulations on the birth of the boy . . .

March 21, 1775

To Sophie

Brentano showed me your daily letters to him. The little woman is getting along nicely. I hope that the friendship and confidence, which her husband is showing me, is not hypocritical. I believe it isn't. In that case I hope in the future to be no more a source of annoyance to our little woman but perhaps to be able to give her an agreeable hour now and then.

March 28, 1775

To Sophie

I have kept the word that I gave Maxa. I promised her if her heart were to melt toward her husband, that I would return. I am here for her again and will be to the end if she will remain the wife and mother. . . .

April 14, 1775

To Karl von Knebel

I don't know where to send a word that it may reach you. I'll send the letter anyhow. Are you still fond of me? Do you still think of me? I tumble from one confusion into another and my poor heart is again unexpectedly immersed in the fate of another human being just when I thought that I had saved myself from that involvement. . . .

I've written all kinds of things and yet they amount to little. A play is almost finished and I carry on my legal business as stealthily as though I were a smuggler. But I am still he whom you know. Write me all about yourself and about the dear Duke and give him my love.

May 17, 1775

Count Christian zu Stolberg to His Sister Katharina

We are immensely delighted that Goethe is to go with us on our trip. He is wild and ungovernable but a thoroughly good boy. Full of spirit and full of fire. We're already very fond of each other. Already, I say! Our hearts were allied from the day we met. Together we are a group, such as you will seek in vain from India to Peru. . . . In Frankfurt we had a tailor make us Werther costumes—blue swallow tail with yellow waistcoat and breeches; round gray hats.

May, 1775

To Herder

Quite recently I seemed almost ready to enter the harbor of domestic bliss and so to be standing firmly within the true sorrow and joy of this earth, but a strange and painful wave cast me out again upon the wide, wide sea.

Poetry and Truth

Out of my love for Lili I sought to extend and to control a growing practice of the law. Hence my visits to Offenbach became rarer and a certain painful embarrassment set in, because it was evident that for the sake of the future the present was being subordinated and lost. As my prospects improved, although I confess that I thought them more significant than they were, I considered the necessity of an early act of decision. . . . In this strange situation there came to our aid a friend of the Schönemann house, who had a very clear insight into the whole coil of persons and of circumstances. Her name was Demoiselle Delph. She and her older sister operated a little merchandizing house in Heidelberg and had been put under real obligation on various occasions by the Schönemann brokerage business in

Frankfurt. She had known and loved Lili from childhood on. She herself was a strange enough person, mannish and serious of aspect, treading hastily with a rhythmic heavy tread. . . .

During many years she had gained the confidence of Lili's mother. Introduced into my house, she had known how to render herself agreeable to my parents. . . . She understood our wishes and our hopes; her delight in effectiveness made her assume the task of negotiating with my parents. No matter what her methods were, nor how she overcame the difficulties in her path—suffice it to say, that on a certain evening she faced Lili and myself with the parental consent. "Join your hands!" she cried with a gesture both pathetic and commanding. I stood opposite Lili and stretched out my hand; not hesitatingly and yet slowly she put her hand in mine. We took a deep breath and fell into each other's arms.

It was a strange decision of that high Providence which guides us that, in the course of my wondrous career, I was also to experience the emotions of an affianced spouse.

◇◇◇◇◇

For good and significant reasons it has been remarked long ago that there is no such thing as tarrying on the peak of a given situation. . . . Young married people who, especially in this modern period, enter upon their commitments with insufficient worldly goods, may be willing to renounce their honeymoons; on the instant they are confronted by the world with unharmonious demands which, if not met, expose a young couple to absurdity.

I had seriously striven after the means of carrying out this purpose. Not until now did I become aware of their inadequacy. They would have sufficed up to a certain point. Now that the goal was imminent, these means seemed imperfect on both sides. . . .

Nor, in spite of the parental consent, had there been even the beginning of a sound or familial relationship between the two sets of parents. They differed in religious observances and in habits of life. Had my charming betrothed desired to continue her accustomed way of life, she would have found in the house of my parents, respectable and spacious though it was, neither opportunity nor room.

◇◇◇◇◇

On earlier occasions I had found travel an effective solution. Precisely at this moment when it was a question of seeing whether I could do without Lili and when a painful disquietude made me incapable of any definite occupation, the invitation of the Stolberg brothers to accompany them to Switzerland, was doubly welcome. Supported by the persuasion of my father, who saw me depart in that direction with pleasure and who bade me, if fate and time permitted, not to neglect to proceed onward to Italy, I came to a swift decision and packed my bags. Not without a hint but without a definite farewell I left Lili. Yet had she come to be so deeply imbedded in my heart that I scarcely conceived of the distance put between us.

Strassburg, May 24, 1775

To Johanna Fahlmer

A kinswoman of the Jacobis, 1744-1821, and after the death of Cornelia Goethe in 1777 the second wife of J. G. Schlosser.

Little auntie, I'm in the open air on a walk under immemorial interlacing linden trees with meadows between, on one side the Cathedral and yonder the river Ill. . . . I've ordered my dinner to be served here. . . . How sweet you are and the sky is, too! And this old region here, now renewed again and all the past and all the future! . . . The Duke of Weimar was here too and is most fond of me.— Tell you the rest when I see you. Everything is better than I thought. Perhaps it is because I am in love that I find everything lovely and good.

June 5, 1775

To Johanna

I'm in Emmendingen with my sister. I live in the open air. Sleeping, eating, drinking, swimming, riding,—these have been for several days the happy content of my life. . . . I know well that I am a fool, but the knowledge does not prevent me from being one. And why, indeed, should one seek to extinguish the little lamp which illuminates so well one's way of life.

June 15, 1775

J. J. Bodmer to a Friend

Chief of the older Swiss school of critics and poets, 1698-1783.

Goethe is a man of few words. He takes great pleasure in my liveliness. He wanted me to have the joy of seeing him before my end. . . . I paid him the compliment of saying that he had made me wait for him for seventy-seven years.

June 16, 1775

Friedrich Stolberg to His Sister Henriette

Yesterday we started early and went to the Lake of Zürich, which is quite close to our hut. The boat arrived from the city and in it were Lavater and his brother-in-law and Goethe and two other fine chaps from Frankfurt. For two hours we rowed on the lake. It was utterly silent. Then the beautiful shores of the lake attracted us and we determined to walk.

1775

ON THE LAKE

Fresh sustenance and blood renewed
From this wide scene I wrest;
Nature is full of grace and good
And holds me to her breast.
On curving waves our boat rides high,
The oars in rhythm beat,
And mountains cloud-tipped to the sky
Bend toward our shallop fleet.

Yet my eyes to droop are fain.
Dreams of gold haunt me again.
Out on them and the gold thereof!
Here no less are life and love.

On the lake are sifted
Glittering star on star,
Softest mist is lifted

Over the mountains afar;
Dawnwind spreads its pinion
Over the shadowy bight,
In the watery dominion
The mirrored fruit is bright.

June 19, 1775

To Charlotte Kestner

I'm deep in Switzerland in the very spot where Tell shot the apple from his boy's head. Why should I not write a few words, having been silent so long? . . . I can neither relate nor describe anything. Perhaps I will be able to do so when these scenes are behind me, as has happened to me in other and dear matters. You do still love me a little, don't you? Go on doing so and kiss your husband and your little ones from me. Tomorrow I make the ascent of Mount Gotthard.

June 20, 1775

Friedrich Stolberg to His Sister Katharina

Goethe has gone off to Mt. St. Gotthard. Since he can't stay away from Frankfurt too long, he didn't want to miss the mountain. I am looking forward to his descent; they say the mountain is still deep under snow. We'll miss Goethe when he leaves. He has read us many manuscripts.

June 29, 1775

Bodmer to a Friend

Goethe called on me again after his return from the Gotthard. I am very glad that he didn't do that sinful *Prometheus*. I am still in his good graces. . . . He is very reticent. He didn't mention his own writings nor Wieland. Spoke with respect of Klopstock and of Homer and of the naturalness of the latter's characters.

Poetry and Truth

On the way to Switzerland the most significant stop for me was in Karlsruhe, whither had come the young Duke of Sachsen-Weimar with his distinguished betrothed, the Princess Louise of Hessen-Darmstadt for the purpose of getting married. . . . My conversations with the princely pair were of the most familiar character and they ended our last interview with the repeated assurance how delighted they would both be to see me in Weimar soon. . . .

I now left my companions in order to go to Emmendingen where my brother-in-law was senior judge. I looked upon this visit to my sister as a trial. I knew she wasn't happy, although no reproach could be addressed to her or to her husband or to her circumstances. . . .

Perhaps the strangest aspect of her admirable and accomplished being was the total absence of passion. She had grown up at my side and all her desire was to continue to pass her life in the harmony of her sisterly relation to me. . . . When I left for Wetzlar her loneliness was unbearable and my friend Schlosser seemed to take my place. Unfortunately his brotherly affection became what was not only a decisive but, in view of his extreme conscientiousness, probably his first passion. . . . I am bound to confess that whenever in my imagination I dwelt upon her fate, it never seemed to me either natural or pleasing to think of her as a wife; rather should she have been an abbess or the head of some distinguished order. She possessed everything which such an office would have demanded and nothing that the world is bound to demand. . . . A reader of any insight, capable of reading between the lines what is indicated here but not expressed, will easily suspect the grave feelings with which I went to Emmendingen. And this heaviness of heart was increased when, at my departure after a brief stay, my sister begged me, indeed commanded me most seriously to break with Lili, she herself having suffered so much from a long engagement. . . .

August 1, 1775

To Knebel

How are you, dear Knebel? I'd like to hear a word from you and from our Duke. I'm back home. I made a pilgrimage through dear and sacred German Switzerland and feel a great deal better, well contented with the past and hopeful of the future.

Offenbach, August 3, 1775

To Auguste

Gussie, Gussie, just a word to liberate my heart. Just a pressure of
the hand. . . . Oh, what discordances of mood. Oh that I could tell
you everything. Here I am in the very room of the girl who makes
me miserable without any fault of her own, the girl who has the soul
of an angel and whose bright days I darken—*I!* . . .
It was in vain that for three months I wandered in the free air and
absorbed a thousand new objects! Here, Angel, I sit in Offenbach
again, reduced to childlikeness, limited in my movements as a parrot
chained to his rod and you, Gussie, are so far away. . . .
My mood changes an hundred times a day. How happy I was with
your brothers. I seemed quite calm and suffered for Fritz, who
seemed more wretched than I with a less tolerable pain. Now I am
alone again. . . . I had been missed and Lili just came in, surprised
to find me in her room. She asked me to whom I had been writing.
I told her. Goodbye, Gussie.

Early August, 1775

To Jeanne Rachel D'Orville

  Wife of the pastor of the Reformed Church in Frankfurt.

I'm sending you the cheese dear lady. Into the cellar with it at once!
The cheese and I are quite alike. As long as it is not exposed to the
sun nor I to Lili, we're very firm, brave creatures. So into the cellar
with it, I tell you, just as I am staying in Frankfurt, which is my
icebox.

September 11, 1775

To Johanna Fahlmer

I'm back home! . . . Please! Please! Look about at the Fair for
something—for Lili!!!! Accessories, jewels, the latest and most elegant! . . . On your sacred word, nothing of this to my mama. And
write me, I beg of you, what you paid for it.

September 14-19, 1775

To Auguste

What you say about Lili is quite true. Unfortunately the distance between us seems only to strengthen the magic bond that holds me to her. I can and dare not say everything even to you. It touches me too closely and I don't like to nurse memories. Angel that you are, your letter sounded in my ears again as does the bugle in the ear of a warrior fallen asleep. . . . Yes, Gussie, we'd better leave that. There is nothing to be said about the heart of man except with the fiery insight of the moment. I am summoned to the table. . . .

After Dinner

Your good advice came to me and spoke in me suddenly. Is it not overweening pride in me to demand that the girl should know me utterly and love me by the light of that knowledge? Perhaps I don't know her either and, being so different from me, she is probably much better. Ah, Gussie! Let my silence tell you what no words can. . . .

Half past Three

Lili is not coming to the ball. If I only dared tell you everything. I got me my costume in her honor because I am supposed to be hers. . . . I did it half defiantly, too, because we haven't been particularly friendly this past week. . . . Look, Gussie, I wish I could represent myself to you as I really am; you'd be truly amazed. . . .

September 16, 1775

The morning was frank and good. I tried to do something to give Lili pleasure. After dinner went about sillily and jestingly among acquaintances and strangers. I'm off to Offenbach now in order not to run into Lili either at the play tonight or at the concert tomorrow.

Offenbach, Sunday, the 17th

Though the day was dull and only tolerable, I felt fresh this morning and wrote a scene of my *Faust*. . . . A week ago today Lili was here and at this hour last week I was, I might say, in the cruellest, sweetest, most solemn situation of my whole life. Oh, why can't I describe it? How I saw the world and the moon above through the most glowing tears of love and how everything about me was animated, and from the distance sounded the hunter's horn and the loud joy of wedding guests. . . .

Monday night, 11:30

I'm at Frankfurt at my desk. I want to tell you good night. Caroused and made merry until this moment. Tomorrow will be wilder still. Oh dearest one, what is the life of man! And yet I must not forget the many excellent people who gather about me and how much love surrounds me. . . .
Saw Lili after dinner today—at the play. Had nothing to say to her —and so was silent!—Oh were I rid of all this! And yet, Gussie, I tremble at the moment when she will be indifferent to me and I will have lost that hope.—But I must remain true to my heart and let it all go.

September, 1775

From Zimmermann's Reminiscences

Faust had been announced and one expected the work to appear quite soon. I asked Goethe to give me some information about the poem. He brought me a bag filled with a thousand fragments of paper. He threw it on the table: "There," he said, "is my *Faust*."

Poetry and Truth

I neither neglected nor could I have neglected to see Lili. The situation between us was a delicate one, each was careful of the other's feelings. I was informed that, during my absence, people had persuaded her that the separation was necessary, all the more so since

my quite voluntary absence had sufficiently declared my own intention. . . . Yet moments came in which the days of the recent past
seemed to reconstitute themselves, only, however, to vanish like
phantoms under lightning in the sky.

Kind friends confided to me that, on the other hand, when all the
obstacles to our union had been explained to Lili, she had declared
that, nevertheless, so great was her inclination toward me that she
would be willing to renounce all that constituted life for her and
flee with me to America. And in those days, it must be remembered,
America was considered even more than at a later period the Eldo-
rado of all who found themselves oppressed by their momentary situation in life.

Once more, therefore, I determined on flight and nothing could
have been more welcome to me than the fact that the young Ducal
couple of Weimar was to come to Frankfurt from Karlsruhe and
that I, according to earlier and later invitations, was to follow it to
Weimar.

FAREWELL

This poem, though difficult to date and probably composed much later,
evidently refers to the relationship with Lili.

> Pleasantly may a word be broken,
> And difficult is duty's part.
> Yet naught remains forever spoken
> That contradicts the heart.
>
> Intone not the old magic singing,
> Lure not thy scarce recovered friend;
> To the light shallop of that folly clinging
> Renews the peril thou shouldst end.
>
> Why seek to slip to some dim cover?
> Gaze straight, flee not nor be deterred!
> For soon or late I must discover
> And give thee back that once pledged word.
>
> That which was meant I have completed,
> No more forbidding any act or mood;

> Only forgive the parting friend who, fain to meet it,
> Returns unto his solitude.

December 3, 1830

Henriette von Beaulieu to Goethe

Frau von Beaulieu, 1773-1864, a younger member of the Egloffstein family, close friends of Goethe in later years, had met Lili Schönemann, when the latter, now Frau von Türckheim, had to abandon her Alsatian home during the Napoleonic wars.

With touching frankness the admirable Frau von Türckheim confessed to me that she had been told how close I was to Weimar and had sought my acquaintance in order to learn intimate details concerning the life and fate of Goethe, whom she called the very creator of her moral being. . . . With rare sincerity she confessed to me that her passion for Goethe had been more powerful than the demands of duty or of virtue and, had his magnanimity not steadfastly refused the sacrifice she had been willing to make for his sake, she would, in later years, devoid of self-respect and honor, have had to look sorrowfully back upon that past which was now the source to her of exquisite and blessed memories. . . . Since it would not in all probability be granted her ever to see Goethe again, she besought me to communicate the content of this confession to her unforgettable friend.

October 4, 1775

To Friedrich and Christian Stolberg

I feel the way I feel, given the situation. I am obliged to you monsters for your letters. If your sister, the nixie, doesn't write, beat her with nettles, when she comes out of her bath. . . . If I can get to Weimar, I'll go. Certainly not to do you a kindness, nor to do anyone a kindness, because I have a grudge against the whole world.

October 7, 1775

To Merck

I am expecting the Duke and Louise and I'm going on to Weimar with them. There, surely, we'll have all sorts of good and whole and even half things as God may bless us with. . . . If you can lend

me 10 ducats send them along by the next conveyance. I need them
etc. I've translated *The Song of Songs,* which is the most magnificent collection of love songs which God ever created.

                                                   October 8, 1775
To Auguste

I am expecting the Duke of Weimar who is on his way here from
Darmstadt with his wonderful new wife. I am following him to
Weimar. Your brothers are coming too and I'll certainly write you
from there. My heart is in evil case. Autumn is in it, neither warm
nor cold.

                                           Middle of October, 1775
To Knebel

Your young Ducal couple desired that I accompany it to Weimar.
I made my arrangements, packed my luggage, put on my traveling
clothes, said farewell and am still sitting here. By what turn of fate
this came about I don't know. The promised chamberlain did not
come. I would have gone on alone, if it weren't so horrible to make
the trip alone in this weather and in the state of the roads. Meanwhile, doubtless, letters for me are in the possession of both the
chamberlain and Wieland, among them such as concern me closely.
Do put them together and send them at once by a mounted courier
to my usual address in Frankfurt.

                                                   October 18, 1775
To Bürger

Let it be all the same to you where I am in the world! You must
feel, dear Bürger, that it is a moment of unquestioned inner necessity that makes me write you. Here, warmed on my right side by a
lovely chimney fire, I am sitting on a low stool, at a child's table,
writing you, having so much to say to you, yet unable to say it. But
you will understand everything. These are the first moments of concentration which a mad accident of fate have thrown me, the first,
I say, after the most distracted, confused, fullest yet emptiest, most
potent yet silliest three-quarters of a year in all my life. . . .

1775

Ah, what is it man should covet?
Is it best to be unmoving,
Cling to one safe stead and love it,
Or to be forever roving?
Shall he build a hut to bide in,
Or in fragile tents assemble?
Are the crags safe to confide in? ,
Nay, the solid crags may tremble.

One thing is not fit for all!
Let each govern his own striving,
Choose him his own plan of living,
And who stands guard lest he fall.

October 22, 1775

Zimmermann to Charlotte von Stein

Last summer in Strassburg, among hundreds of other silhouettes I
showed yours, dear lady, to Herr Goethe. I am sending you here the
words he wrote under that likeness of you with his own hand: "What
a magnificent spectacle it would be to behold the world as it is mirrored in this soul. She sees the world as it is and yet through the
medium of love." He will certainly come to see you when he arrives
in Weimar. Remember then that what I told him about you in
Strassburg cost him three sleepless nights.

Poetry and Truth

Having acceded to the kindly invitation of the Duke for very good
reasons, the following arrangements were proposed. A chamberlain
of the Duke who was expecting in Karlsruhe a carriage built in
Strassburg, was to arrive in Frankfurt on a given day. I was to hold
myself in readiness to accompany him to Weimar. . . . A week
passed and I know not how many additional days. . . . My father
shook his head, while my mother tried to console me as best she
could. She confided to me that one evening when I had gone out

my father had expressed his extreme surprise at the fact that I, commonly no fool, was unwilling to realize that those people were making game of me and seeking to put me to shame. . . .

More days passed and my father's hypothesis seemed ever more probable, since there was not even a letter from Karlsruhe to give a reason for the delay of the carriage. . . . In a state of doubt and hesitation concerning so important a matter, I finally agreed that if at a definite moment, neither the carriage nor news of it arrived, I was to proceed to Heidelberg and from there cross the Alps by way of the Tyrol.

October 30, 1775

On the Journey from Frankfurt to Heidelberg

From his bed my father sent me a farewell message for the future: "Pray that your flight never take place in winter nor on the Sabbath!"—This time, cried I, it takes place without my prayer on Monday morning at 6 o'clock. As for the rest, ask of that dear, invisible force, which guides and disciplines us; ask not after my liking. I packed to go north; I am faring to the south. I said I would come and do not; I refused and I am on the way! Onward, then! While the guardians of the gate rattle their keys and while ere dawn my neighbor, the cobbler, opens his shop and shutters. Away! Farewell, Mother!—On the Cornmarket the plumber's apprentice rattles his wares to put them in order and greets the neighbor's maid in the gray rain. In that greeting there was something pregnant with presage for the day to come. Ah, thought I, who might—nay, said I, there was a time— He who has memories, let no one envy him.—Lili, Lili, farewell for the second time! I parted from you the first time still nursing the hope that our destinies might be united. It was determined otherwise; singly must we now play our parts. At this moment I am anxious neither concerning you nor me, despite the confusion. Farewell. And you, how shall I name you, whom I carry in my heart like a flower of spring. Gracious as a flower shall be your name!— How shall I say farewell to you?—Be of good cheer! It is still time; it *was* still time.—Had it been a few days later—a very few—farewell! Am I in the world to writhe forever in the throes of guiltless guilt—

Poetry and Truth

There were several good reasons why I went to Heidelberg. . . .
Demoiselle Delph, who had been the confidential friend of Lili and
myself, and, as will be recalled, the intermediary between her parents
and mine, lived in Heidelberg and I esteemed it a happy thing to
talk over once more those lovely days with a patient and indulgent
friend before leaving Germany. . . .
Demoiselle Delph was one of those persons who, though not exactly
given to intrigue, always make other people's business their own and
always have a rather particular axe to grind. . . . Full of plans as
she always was, she had formed one for my future settlement in life,
and it was perfectly clear that her invitation had not been as uncom-
plicated as I had thought.
It appeared, according to her, that the Electoral Prince Karl Theo-
dore, whose residence was in Mannheim, was a great patron of the
arts and sciences. Just because his Court was Catholic while the
people of the country were Protestant, the latter faction had every
reason to strengthen its influence by the appointment of strong and
promising people. I was, in God's name, to go to Italy and to cultivate my artistic understanding. Meanwhile influences would be at
work in my behalf. On my return it would be seen, whether the
burgeoning inclination of Fräulein von W. for me had grown or
been quenched and whether then a connection with so highly esteemed a family would not firmly found my happiness in a new
fatherland. She unfolded her plans to me until late at night. . . .
We did not separate until 1 o'clock. I had slept deeply but not long,
when I was awakened by the horn of a courier on horseback who
stopped in front of the house. Almost immediately Demoiselle Delph
came to my bedside with a candle and a letter in her hands. "There
we have it!" she cried. "Read it; tell me its content. It is doubtless
from Weimar. If it is the expected invitation, do not accept it. Remember what I told you." I begged her for the candle and for a
quarter of an hour. She left me reluctantly. . . . The seal and the
handwriting were the familiar ones. The courier came from Frankfurt. My friend had arrived belatedly. Distrust and uncertainty had
confused me. . . .
I dressed myself fully and walked up and down in my room. My

eager hostess entered. "What am I to hope?" she cried. . . . I was
deeply moved, and so was she. A scene of some violence ensued,
which ended by my sending my valet to order the postchaise. In vain
I begged my hostess to calm herself and to transmute the gay farewell I had bidden her at a party the night before into a real and
serious one. . . . The chaise was at the door; my luggage had been
put in; the postillion blew his horn to mark his impatience. I tore
myself away; she would not let me go at once and sought to rehearse
her arguments once again, so that at last in a kind of passionate
exaltation I cried out to her the words I had put into the mouth of
my own Egmont:

"Child, child, no more! As though under the sting of invisible
spirits, the solar horses of time run wildly away with the light chariot
of our destiny. Nothing remains for us to do but with firm courage
to grasp the reins and seek to guide the wheels, now to the right,
now to the left, to avoid a stone here, a declivity yonder. Who knows
whither we are being driven? We do not even remember whence we
came!"

Book Three

MASTER AND MUSE

1775-1786

WEIMAR

(November, 1775 to July, 1786)

November 13, 1775

Wieland to Lavater

I must tell you that Goethe has been with us since Tuesday last and that within three days I have conceived such a deep affection for this magnificent person, that I so thoroughly see into him, feel him, understand him, am fulfilled by him—as you can far better imagine than I can describe.

November 22, 1775

To Johanna Fahlmer

My life is like a skating party—swift and resonant and gliding up and down. God knows what my destiny is, seeing the many schools through which I pass. This new one gives my life new impulse, and all will be well. I can't tell you anything about my business here; it's too complicated, but everything goes as we would have it and, as is natural, arouses a good deal of amazement. Write me a word. Wieland is a dear fellow; we stick together and I love to be with his children. His wife is also a dear, good woman and reminds me of Sophie La Roche. Ask Mother to open all letters from French territory to me. One had been sent back. Give this one to Papa with the request to undertake what is necessary and to collect the money in my name. . . . No, on second thoughts, don't bother. I'll write to Papa myself.

November, 1775

From a Weimar Chamberlain to Goethe's Parents

Conceive of your son then as the most intimate friend of our dear Duke, without whom he can't live for a moment, loved to adoration, too, by all the good lads hereabout.

Late November, 1775
Count Christian Stolberg to His Sister

Our Goethe is here. I am fonder of him than ever. The Ducal family
is like no other princely family anywhere. We associate with them
as though we were all on the same level. You know Louischen from
my description. As angelic as ever. The old Duchess is the very
personification of good sense and yet most agreeable and natural.
The Duke is a wonderful lad and full of promise; so is his brother.
And many other excellent people. . . .
One evening we were having supper at the Duke's brother's house.
Suddenly the door opened and there entered the old Duchess and
with her the wife of the Master of the Horse, the admirable, good,
lovely Frau von Stein. The two ladies had in their hands two antique swords from the military museum, each sword a yard longer
than I am tall. With these swords they knighted us. We retained our
places at table and the two ladies went about and themselves filled
our glasses with champagne. After supper we played a game of for-
feits and had a chance to kiss Frau von Stein, who stood next to the
Duchess. At what other Court will you find such informality?

November 25, 1775
Zimmermann to Lavater

The Baroness von Stein, wife of the Chamberlain and Master of the
Horse in Weimar, has extraordinarily large black eyes of the highest
beauty. Her voice is gentle and repressed. No one can fail to mark
upon her face at the first glance seriousness, gentleness, kindliness,
the suffering of virtue and a subtle and profound sensibility. The
manners of the Court, which she possesses to perfection, have been
transformed in her case into a rare and high simplicity. She is very
pious with a touching and almost ecstatic elevation of soul. From
her exquisite carriage and her almost professional skill in dancing
one would hardly infer the tranquil moonlight and midnight which
fill her heart with peace. She is thirty-odd years old; she has many
children and weak nerves. Her cheeks are quite red, her hair quite
black, her complexion, like her eyes, of an Italian hue. She is slim
and of an elegant simplicity.

December 12, 1775

To Herder

Dearest Friend, The Duke needs a General Superintendent for the Duchy. [*An office equivalent to the Episcopal one in the German Protestant Churches.*] If your plan in regard to Göttingen has changed by this time, something very real could be done here. Write me a word. In any event, since the future is changeable, turn your glance hither. Regards to the little wife. I feel fine here—in every respect. Wieland is a wonderful soul and the princes noble, dear and charming.

December 23, 1775

To Karl August

Duke of Sachsen-Weimar-Eisenach, 1757-1828, Grand Duke after the Congress of Vienna, Goethe's lifelong friend and patron.

Wind and rough weather have driven us to the forest village here and rain and all that goes with it. The mountain chasm that leads to Jena smiled at me with its spare magnificence under a happy afterglow. The situation of the town of Jena is admirable; the town I found depressing. Not much sightseeing between there and here on account of the rains which, as an old man trundling a wheelbarrow assured us, sweep hither from Italy. . . . My companion has gone to bed. His stomach gave him trouble. Neither coffee nor brandy seemed to help. I am going to bed myself. A hearty good night. Yet one more word before I sleep. As I was riding along through the pine-clad mountains there came over me the feeling of my past and of my fate and of my love:

> Lovely Lili, thou wert long
> All my delight and all my song,
> Now art thou my pain and still
> All my singing dost thou fill.

December 24, 1775

To Karl August

Horrible thaw and so the tone of the whole day ruined. I'll try to re-establish it. But high in the heaven stands the radiant morning star, which from now on I choose as my escutcheon. . . . Services in church are beginning. I'm not going. But I sent to ask the parson whether he can lend me a copy of the *Odyssey*. If he hasn't it, I'll send for one to Jena. Because it's impossible to do without it in this simple, Homeric mountain world. This morning a few verses from the *Odyssey* popped into my mind when, after a long sleep, day seemed to be delayed. They read something like this: "Wrapped in their skins they lay about the glimmering hearth. Above them blew the moist stormwind through the unending night and they lay and slept a refreshing sleep until the dawning of the morn."

December 29, 1775

Zimmermann to Charlotte von Stein

If Herr Goethe found, now that he has the advantage of really knowing you, that your silhouette does not bring out the most characteristic traits of your nature, he will doubtless by now have discovered in you new virtues and beauties, such as a mere silhouette cannot render. I am not at all surprised that Herr Goethe has pleased everyone in Weimar. Announced by a reputation so distinguished and general, attracting everyone at once by the very glow of his eyes, he could not but engage all hearts by his extreme goodness and amiability.

1776

January 2, 1776

To Herder

I can give you real hope today, which I could not do day before yesterday. And I do that at once, not so much for your sake as for your wife's. . . . I hope that you'll get the job through me and the Duke's free choice. The Governor of Erfurt said the handsomest things about you and commends your spirit and your power to our young Prince. I vouched for your political wisdom in the spiritual realm, for the Duke simply won't be annoyed by parsons on such questions as orthodoxy and the devil, which have made the clergy to stink throughout the land.

January 7, 1776

To Charlotte von Stein

I have been plagued and so good night. I have received dear letters, which plague me because they *are* dear. And all that is dear plagues me except yourself, dear as you are. Therefore this one-eyed scribbling in the night.

January 15, 1776

To Charlotte

I'm glad to get away to wean myself from you. I would my heart were bright enough to make you laugh. But all my folly and my wit seem to have fled. I'm taking Homer with me to see what he'll do for me.

January 16, 1776

To Charlotte

So here we go through frost and snow at night. Our vocation toward a life of adventure confirms itself. 'Twas hard to rise this morning after getting to bed at midnight. But it seems to waken me to write you—I've eaten my wine soup. Ah, my dear, there were times when I got up early, when waking and leaping up were one! But if there's nothing in the whole wide world to do except go rabbit hunting!— But I must dress.

January 22, 1776

To Merck

I am completely enmeshed in all matters of the Court and of politics and almost believe I'll not get away again. My situation is sufficiently advantageous and the duchies of Weimar and Eisenach are, after all, a scene on which one can try to see how a rôle in the world may become one. . .

January 24, 1776

To Herder

There won't be much more delay about your being called hither. I'm determined to sweep a little place for you, so that you can take the reins in hand at once. I may stay here for a while. So soon as this matter is cleared up, I'll feel truly well. . . . Our Duke is a splendid lad; the Duchesses want you too.

January 27, 1776

To Charlotte

I was in a devil of a mood this evening. Both Louise and I felt your absence. . . . My feet burned to run to you. Finally I began to flirt, which is the tried and true remedy in such cases. I lied and dissembled to all the pretty faces round about and, at the moment, believed what I said. . . . The Dowager Duchess was dear and kind and Louise angelic. . . . At a certain moment she contradicted the Duke violently on a trifling matter, but afterwards I made her laugh. . . .

January 28, 1776

To Charlotte

Dear Angel, I'm not coming to the concert. I feel too happy to stand the crowd. I sent for my letters and it dismayed me that there wasn't even a penciled word from you. Suffer me to love you as I do. If ever I can love anyone else, I'll let you know and quit tormenting you.

February 5, 1776

Wieland to Lavater

Goethe will probably stay here for long. He is in the web of that adventure, which I refused, so soon as I saw that it was meant for another. Since Saturday morning Goethe has been in Erfurt with the Duke. He does all that is possible. . . . But how much more he could do, magnificent spirit that he is, if he hadn't sunk into our chaos here out of which, with the best will and all his power, he will not be able to create a tolerable world. . . . But look, he's 26. How, feeling his power as he does, could he have resisted an even greater temptation? For his influence upon all members of the princely family, old and young, is incredible. In spite of all, let's wait and see. If only things here don't get as bad as they might have done; if some slight good comes to pass that would *not* have come about—it was worth all the trouble.

February, 1776

Siegmund von Seckendorff to His Brother

Seckendorff, 1744-1785, had just been called from an office in the King-
dom of Sardinia to be a chamberlain at the Ducal Court.

His Serene Highness engages constantly in the noisiest gaieties, and
never emerges from that circle of persons who have known how to
enthrall him. Every day there are new and uncommon entertainments, without any consideration of public opinion. According to
the system of his new advisors which, unfortunately, he follows very
exactly, there is no such thing in the world as conventions or de-
cencies. Those which exist, we are told, are the products of mere
whim, which the head of a state can and may sweep aside. . . .

February 12, 1776

WANDERER'S NIGHT-SONG I

(Inscribed on the wall of a sylvan hut on the slope of the
Ettersberg Mountain.)

> Thou that from the heavens art,
> Every pain and sorrow stillest,
> And the doubly wretched heart
> Doubly with refreshment fillest,
> I am weary with contending!
> Why this rapture and unrest?
> Peace descending,
> Come, ah, come into my breast!

Henry Wadsworth Longfellow

February 16, 1776

Elisabeth Goethe to Zimmermann

The testimony of Wieland's affection for my son, which you had the
kindness to communicate to me, made me truly happy. But it just
happens to be the good fortune of our Doctor Wolf that everybody

who knows him loves him and that, of course, is perfectly natural. He loves his fellow men and tries to spread happiness wherever he goes. Face to face with him you see only the friend of man and are glad to forget the writer of satire.

To Charlotte

I have slept well and my soul is clean and full of happy presage. Are you coming to Court today? Louise was pleasant yesterday. Good God, I don't see what makes her heart contract so. I seem to peer into her soul and if I didn't like her so much, I would have been chilled. Also, she obviously showed her annoyance at the Duke's dog. The fact is they're always both in the wrong. He should have left the dog outside. . . . God bless you. . . .

To Charlotte

Slept tranquilly and lightly and rose and greeted the lovely sun for the first time in two weeks with an untroubled heart. . . . I must tell you, O you chosen among women, that you have placed a love in my heart which makes me happy. I won't see you again until the party tonight.

To Charlotte

I had to leave but I must tell you good night. . . . You have all my trust and gradually, God willing, you shall have all my confidence. Oh that my sister had a brother as I have a sister in you. . . . All through the party I saw nothing but your eyes. . . . In the morning to horse!

To Johanna Fahlmer

I am adjusting myself to life here and the life is adjusting itself to me. I'd like to write you intimate details, but it can't be done. . . . Herder has accepted the call as General Superintendent here.

I shall probably stay and play my part as well as I can and as long as it pleases fate and myself. Were it but for a few years, 'tis better than the inactive existence at home where, though I had the desire to do much, nothing ever got done. Here I have a couple of duchies. I am employed in getting to know the land, which amuses me greatly. And that inspires in the Duke a love for work, and because I know him thoroughly I am not troubled by certain circumstances. I'm really a part of dear Wieland's household and dine and sup with him when I am not summoned to Court. The girls here are good-looking and well behaved and I am on good terms with them all. A magnificent soul is Frau von Stein to whom, so to speak, I have attached myself very closely. Louise and I communicate only by glances and syllables. She is and stays angelic. I have very good times with the Dowager Duchess; we go in for all sorts of escapades and harmless mischief. You'll hardly believe how many good fellows and good minds are gathered together here.

Late February, 1776

To Johanna Fahlmer

Draw what I write here to my mother's very particular attention. Within the next few days the Ducal Master of the Horse, von Stein, is passing through Frankfurt and will call on Father and Mother. He is an excellent man who is to be well received. But no one must appear to be too much pleased with my situation here! Furthermore, he is not altogether satisfied with the Duke, as is true of nearly the whole Court, because he refuses to dance to their tune, and both privately and publicly I am made responsible for this fact. If he were to hint anything of the kind, it is to be passed over lightly. In general, ask more than you say, let him talk more than you do. The rest I leave to your discretion.

February 28, 1776

Charlotte to Goethe

The only one of Charlotte's earlier letters to Goethe that has been preserved.

I had so detached myself from the world, but now it grows dear to me again, dear through you. My heart reproaches me; I feel that

I torment both myself and you. Six months ago I was so ready to die and I am ready no longer.

February 28, 1776

To Charlotte

Through snow and frost I send you a flower, even as through ice and storm my love goes out to you. Perhaps I'll see you later today.

March 6, 1776

Charlotte to Zimmermann

Goethe is both loved and hated here. One feels that many stupid people don't understand him. Louise's friendship for me grows daily, but there is much coldness between the Ducal couple, though I don't despair. Two such kind and reasonable beings must in the end understand each other. . . . Goethe was with me a few hours ago. I confessed to him that I wished he would not assume that wild demeanor, which makes people misjudge him so. At bottom it's nothing except that he hunts hard and rides hard and cracks a great whip hard—all, of course, in the company of the Duke. All this is not to his taste. But for a while he must do these things in order to win over the Duke and then begin to build toward a better future. That's my opinion. . . . He was sweet to me and in his trustfulness of heart called me *thou*. I begged of him as gently as I could not to fall into the habit, seeing that no one but myself would understand and that, in addition, he is careless of many considerations. Wildly he jumped from the sofa and said he had to go. He ran up and down the room looking for his stick without finding it and ran out without farewell, without good night.

March 6, 1776

To Johanna Fahlmer

I beg of you, all of you, once and for all, to be calm. Father may cook up what he likes; I can't always answer in detail and untangle his whims. This is the way it is: I'm staying here and have rented handsome lodgings, but Father *owes* me *furnishings* and a *settlement*. Let Mother take this matter up with him, but let her not be childish. After all, I am the best friend and reliance of a reigning prince. He made me another present of 100 ducats. All right, if you'll have it so, he gave me the money. I'm doing everything I can for him and he's doing the same for me. Now this may go on as and how long it can. Meanwhile I owe all sorts of debts, though that troubles me little. I just want Mother to do what's right and see what is to be gotten out of Father without too much trouble.—If it should happen that she needs cash and can't get it out of Father, I'll send her some.

March 8, 1776

Charlotte to Zimmermann

I was to accompany the Dowager Duchess to Wieland's house yesterday, but since I was afraid Goethe might be there, I didn't go. My heart is just bursting with matters which I must tell that monster. It isn't possible to get along in the world with such behavior! Why does he insist on making fun of everybody? They're all God's children Who suffers them. Not to mention his indecent behavior, his cursing and swearing, his vulgar and obscene expressions. I don't suppose that these things will influence the morality of his actions, but it corrupts others. A change has come over the Duke, who came to call on me yesterday. He asserted that well-bred and well-mannered people were all hypocrites. I admitted that honor is often found under a rough exterior but, surely, equally often under one of good breeding. It has come to the point where Karl likes no one who is not rude. All that seems to come from Goethe, that is, from one whose mind and heart are above those of thousands, who sees all things so clearly and without prejudice, when he wants to do so, who can master whatever he will. I feel that Goethe and I will never be friends; his attitude to women displeases me, too; he is really a male coquette and he shows no esteem for any.
Destroy this letter. It seems to me as though writing it were an act of ingratitude to Goethe. But I shall avoid any appearance of hypocrisy by telling him all this myself at the earliest opportunity.

Naumburg, March 25, 1776, 5 a.m.

To Charlotte

I came here at dawn. A wondrous, lovely twilight floats over the world. I have suffered much from cold and, what is better, slept a lot. You are still asleep. Perhaps you'll waken for an instant and think of me. I am calm and think of you and under that aspect of all that is dear to me.—How different, dear God, how different everything is from that time, ten years ago, when I, a small, strange, bundled-up boy, entered this postchaise station.—How much was driven through my head and heart by time, and how much better and freer do I feel!

March 25, 1776

To Karl August

Here, my dear Lord, I am in Leipzig, and I feel extremely odd (of which more face to face) and can't tell you how my earthy smell and earthy feeling contrast with the black, gray, stiff-coated, bow-legged, tie-wigged-bedizened, sword-swinging Masters of Arts, the modish, festive, arrogant student mob as well as with the whorish, preening, behind-swinging females that abound. . . . All night I wound and unwound many a coil of thought until this morning the sun rose divinely for me behind Naumburg. Farewell, my dear Lord.

Leipzig, March 25, 1776
Late at night

To Charlotte

All is as it was here and only I have changed. Only that has remained of which the relationship to me was of the purest. . . . Farewell, I am stupid with sleep. The Schröter girl is an angel [*Korona Schröter, 1751-1802, appointed leading member of the Weimar Opera later in 1776*]. If God would only let me have a woman like that, I could leave you in peace—but she doesn't sufficiently resemble you.

March 31, 1776

To Charlotte

Your letter did depress me a little. If only I could understand your deep lack of faith in your own soul, that soul of yours in which thousands could have faith and be blessed.—I am coming to see more and more that we are not meant to understand anything in this world.—And your dream and your tears, my dearest! I am so made that I can bear reality quite well as a rule; dreams can move me at any time.—I've seen Annette again—my first girl. I wonder what destiny has in store for me! It caused me to see many things with most definite clarity on this trip! . . .

April 5, 1776

Charlotte to a Friend

Our Court is no longer what it was. Its head is dissatisfied with himself and with the whole world. Daily he risks his life and the small health he has in order ostensibly to improve that health. His brother is still more devoid of character; then there is the careworn mother and the unsatisfied wife. They're all perfectly nice people, but nothing seems to work out well in this wretched family.

April 10, 1776

To Johanna Fahlmer

God reward you, I'm feeling very well here now. N.B. I need a dozen Dutch handkerchiefs, real big ones, as well as a pair of quite fine cuffs. I have enough ordinary ones. . . . Never mind about Lili. I'm through with her and detest that whole crowd from the bottom of my heart. To the devil with them! I pity the poor creature for having been born of that race. You are always your sane, dear self. Next time I'll write a letter of befittingly elevated character to my father.

April 13, 1776

To Charlotte

Here's a note, since I can't come. How did you sleep after yesterday's goings on? I feel well and there is more presage of good and hope in my heart than I can well say. But I do wish that something would make me laugh again and that some sprite of tricksiness would enter into me. Addio.

April 13, 1776

To Wieland

There is no explanation for what this woman means to me—for the power that she has over me, unless you accept the theory of transmigration. Oh yes, once we were man and wife! We still know about each other—secretly, in a twilit region.—I have no words for us—the past—the future—the universe.

April 14, 1776

TO CHARLOTTE VON STEIN

Why was unto us the insight granted
And the wit our future to discern,
Never to indulge in dreams undaunted,
Never unto mortal hope to turn?
Why dared we alone to sink our glances
Deep into each other's heart and see
Through the subtle web of circumstances
What our true estate was doomed to be?

For the mass of men in their confusion
Hardly know their own hearts and in vain
Hurry from illusion to illusion,
Stumbling into unsuspected pain;
They rejoice when sudden pleasure hovers
In an unanticipated dawn descried.
Only unto us forlornest lovers
Is the changeful happiness denied
Of a passion without understanding

Which from each what he is not awaits,
Every illusory bliss demanding
And in fancied dangers fluctuates.

Happy who their empty dream can lengthen,
Leaving all their morrows undiscerned!
All our meetings, our mere looks but strengthen
What from dream and presage we have learned.
Speak! Why is it this destiny engages
Us in bonds that cannot broken be?
Surely once in unremembered ages
Thou wert sister or wert wife to me!

Then thou knewest all that forms my being,
Every nerve's vibration thou couldst mark,
Sawest with thy visionary seeing
What to other mortal eyes was dark;
Thou didst soothe the angry blood that races
And the headlong course didst moderate;
The distracted heart from thy embraces
Rose aforetime to a new estate.
Mild the magic by which he was holden,
Fair and fleet to him the faery day
Through whose hours ecstatical and golden
At thy feet thy grateful lover lay;
Felt his heart against thy grave heart heighten,
In thine eyes recovering to good,
Felt his very senses clear and brighten,
Tranquilizing his tumultuous blood.

And these things forever recollected
Haunt unceasingly the uncertain heart
Which by that immortal truth affected,
Doubly feels the present's wound and smart.
And we seem like ghosts half-animated,
Twilit even when the night is far.
Glad alone that grief to which we are fated
Cannot alter what we are.

April 21, 1776
From the Diaries

> From this date on to six days before his death Goethe made brief en-
> tries in a diary. This first entry is headed "Garden House" by which he
> meant the rustic cottage set in a spacious garden surrounded by trees
> which Karl August had just given him.

Took possession of my garden this day.

April 25, 1776
To Charlotte

In all likelihood I'll dine with you today. Unless rivers or mountains
stop me I'll be with you at 1 o'clock. I had a good day yesterday.

May 1, 1776
Late
To Charlotte

You're right to try to make a saint of me, that is, to put me out of
your heart. Saintly as you are, I cannot make a saint of you, and
nothing is left me but to torment myself with the desire not to torment myself. Do you appreciate the play on words? Not tomorrow
either then? Very well, I don't want to see you.

May 2, 1776
To Charlotte

Good morning. It was a bitter thing to have to keep my vow yesterday, and so it won't be easier for me today to submit to your
wishes. But since my love for you is a matter of perpetual resignation—why let it be! Think of me.

Spring, 1776
From Herder's Reminiscences

One of the most absurd phases of this early Weimar period was the
mineralogical, when the mines at Ilmenau were to be reopened.
Suddenly man was nothing and the stone everything. Goethe dis-

covered the Divine Trinity in the forms of the crystallization of granite, so that one mystery was to be explained by another.

Ilmenau, May 4, 1776

To Karl August

I've got to read you a lecture. On my way here I reflected on the excessive heat with which you are ever in danger of doing something which, if not wrong, is certainly unnecessary, and to exert your own strength and that of others futilely. . . . Remember that I am with you in order to render you a report of the entire situation and to learn all I can rather than to be practically useful. I am getting all the information I can; I have seen the old ovens myself, and they are in a sad condition. . . . Be as tranquil as possible, cultivate your private tastes and spare your bad hip in this weather. . . .

May 10, 1776

Karl August to the Minister of State, Jakob F. von Fritsch

Karl August, nineteen years old at this time, addressed this letter to Fritsch, 1731-1814, who was hostile to Goethe. But Fritsch yielded, especially at the persuasion of the Dowager Duchess. Hence on June 11, 1776, Goethe was appointed a member of the Privy Council at an annual salary of 1200 thaler. In monetary terms this sum was the equivalent of $900; its purchasing power was incalculably greater.

Your letter of April 24, my dear Councilor, was duly received. In it you expressed to me your opinion with that degree of frankness, which I expect from so upright a man as yourself. You demand your release from my service because, as you say, you can no longer sit in a Council, of which Doctor Goethe is a member. This reason seems wholly inadequate to explain your decision. Were Doctor Goethe a man of equivocal character, everyone would approve your decision. But Goethe is upright as well as of an extraordinarily good and feeling heart. This is not only my opinion; men full of insight have congratulated me on having this man in my service. His mind and genius are well known. You ought to see for yourself that a man like that would not be able to bear the boring and mechanical task of serving from the bottom up. Not to use a man of genius in the place in which his extraordinary talents can be made to count, would plainly be to misuse him. I hope you will become as convinced of this truth as I am. . . . As far as public opinion is concerned, which would disapprove of my appointing Doctor Goethe to the highest Council of the State without his having first been a magistrate, a professor, a chamberlain or a minor councilor, I cannot see that that changes anything. The world judges according to its prejudices, but I and everyone who seeks to do his duty, does not act to gain the world's approval but in order to justify himself before God and his own conscience. . . .

May 19, 1776

To Charlotte

Slept for the first time in my garden. . . . I am sending you some asparagus just gathered. Don't mix them with any others and eat them all by yourself, since you share my happy delight in them. . . . How are things for this noon? When may I come? The tranquility out here is infinite.

Middle of May, 1776

Charlotte to Zimmermann

Strange experience with Goethe. He stormed away from me a week ago and then returned with overflowing love. He forces me to reflect that, the higher a man's grasp, the darker and more shocking is the whole of life to him and the more easily will he fail to take the tranquil path. Assuredly the fallen angels were more intelligent than the rest. . . . What will he end by making of me? For when he is here he is about me all the time. . . . I've had coffee in his garden and eaten of his asparagus which he took out of the ground himself and rinsed in his own well.

May 21, 1776

To Klopstock

The author of *The Messiah* had written a chiding letter based on rumors concerning the goings-on at the Weimar Court.

Spare us such letters in future, dear Klopstock! You don't help us and only give us a couple of nasty hours.

You must yourself feel that there's no way of answering. Either I play the part of a schoolboy and say: *pater peccavi,* or I offer sophistical excuses or else I defend myself like an honest fellow and so write you with a mixture of all three attitudes. And to what good?

So let there be no further word of this matter between us. You may believe that I'd have no moment of life left if I were to answer all such letters and all such remonstrances.—It hurt the Duke for a moment that this thing came from you. He loves and respects you. That I do, too, you ought to know and feel.

May 23, 1776

To Charlotte

Here's a letter from my sister. You can understand how it tears at my heart. I kept a couple of previous ones from you to spare you pain. But I do beseech you to pay some attention to her; write her and nag me into sending her something. . . .

May 24, 1776

To Charlotte

And so this relationship, too, is to be disturbed—the purest, loveliest, truest that ever I had with a woman, except my sister.—I was prepared for it, only I suffered infinitely both for the past and for the future. . . . I don't want to see you; it would sadden me too much. If I am not to live with you, your love avails me no more than that of others who are absent. . . . It is the presence of the beloved at the moment of need which decides, heals, fortifies. He who is absent comes to quench the flame when it is all but out. And all this for the sake of the world! This world which is nothing to me demands that you be nothing to me either.

May 25, 1776

To Charlotte

. . . Forgive me that I make you suffer. I'll try hereafter to learn to bear it alone.

The last days of May, 1776

To Auguste

. . . Morning in my garden. I have a lovely garden beyond the
gates in a valley of beautiful meadows beside the river. There's an
old cottage, which I'm having repaired. All is in bloom and the
birds are singing. . . . We took a walk in my garden—*she,* her husband, her children, her brother. Others joined us and we met the
Dowager Duchess and the Prince. . . . I left the company and went
for a moment to the Duke and supped with Frau von Stein. . . .
. . . Night in my garden. I've sent my valet home and will sleep
here alone for the first time. I'll consecrate my sleep by writing to
you first. The masons have been working here all day. . . .
. . . It is a wonderful sensation to sit alone in the field and be at
home. . . . All is silent. I hear the ticking of my clock and the sound
of the wind and the millstream from afar. . . .
I know not what will be. I will still have much to bear. I felt that
throughout all the difficulties of my youth, but I am well fortified,
too, and shall last through to the end. . . .

May 30, 1776

Elisabeth Goethe to a Friend of Goethe's Boyhood

My son, the doctor, is merry and well in his Weimar. He has moved
into a lovely garden outside the town, belonging to the Duke. There
my poet sits as though nailed to the spot. Weimar must be a dangerous place, when it comes to leaving. Everybody gets stuck there.
Well, if the little crew is so well pleased—God bless them.

Garden House, June 5, 1776

From the Diaries

Aequam memento [*The opening words of the famous Horatian ode,
II, 3: "Remember in arduous affairs to maintain a well-balanced
mind."*]

Garden House, June 7, 1776

Forenoon. Long explanation and complicated political discussion with the Duke.

June 18, 1776

To Charlotte

So yesterday Heaven was adverse. I had a bad day. Couldn't sleep last night between hope and fear. The steady rain maddened me and I was dull and empty. But, surely, you're coming with your sister today.

June 22, 1776

To Charlotte

I dare not think of your going to Pyrmont for the cure for six whole months. For your presence alone is effective to console and uplift me. Oh, sometimes it plagues me, but that plaguing is the summer shower of love. I love you much more since the other day, and much dearer and more precious is your goodness to me. But, indeed, the relationship, that one tries to pass over lightly, concerning which one is fond of deluding oneself, is clearer and deeper. It did not escape the Dowager Duchess that a sudden change had come over me. Herewith a rose from my garden. Adieu.

June 24, 1776

Wieland to Merck

It's true that during the first months here, Goethe often acted in such a way as to scandalize most people (never myself) and so to give the devil an advantage. But for long now, from the moment on that he decided to devote himself to the Duke and the Duke's affairs, he has behaved with faultless wisdom and worldly circumspection. In brief, you may be sure and assert it against all comers that the cabals against Goethe and his friends derive from nothing but envy, jealousy and thwarted ambition. And so Weimar is likely to become a Mount Ararat on which the good can set their feet, the while the general flood covers the rest of the world.

Garden House, June 25, 1776
From the Diaries

Officially instated today. Took the oath of loyalty. Ate at Court.

June 28, 1776, Morning!
To Charlotte

Already in full dress on the way to the Council's sublime session. Thereafter dinner at Court. Your drawing delightful. . . . I'm not doing a thing, alas, but maybe I'll manage to finish something for you.

June 28, 1776, Same hour
Karl August to Charlotte
  Enclosed with the above.

Good morning, dear lady! May all the spirits of mountains, castles, and of dawn and twilight be your companions. Think of me! I'm trundling along with Goethe to the Council. Drinking your waters in Pyrmont, lift the first morning glass to Goethe's health and mine.

July 2, 1776
To Charlotte

Yes, it's your presence that makes the difference! What good is it to me that you're in the world and that you think of me? I miss you in every corner and creep through my day most woefully.

July 9, 1776
To Charlotte

In bed last night and half asleep, my lad brings me a letter. Dully I take in from it that Lili is married! I turned on my other side and went back to sleep.—How I adore that destiny which orders things for me! Everything at its proper time. Good night, angel.

July 16, 1776

To Charlotte

I haven't a thing to soothe me. Wieland is the best of the lot. The
Duke and I at least share our dullness; everything else annoys me
and I can't flee to you. . . . Send me something! Regards to Zimmermann.

Ilmenau, July 20, 1776

To Charlotte

Sharp rains in the deep forest here. If you could see it; 'tis beyond
all description or delineation. . . . It remains eternally true: one
must limit oneself to one object or to a few at most; one must need
these and love them and cling to them and contemplate them from
all sides and to become one with them—'tis that which makes the
poet, the artist, the human being.—The rain goes on and on.

July 24, 1776

Elisabeth Goethe to Salzmann

That our son has been appointed a Privy Councillor in the services
of the Duke of Weimar must long have been known to you. Yesterday we heard much that was handsome and good concerning him. A
courier of the Duke's on his way to Karlsruhe stopped at our house.
I am persuaded that, as so old a friend of the doctor's, you rejoice
in our joys and share our happiness and repeat with us the words
of the Psalmist: "Well is it with him who lives to take joy in his
children!" How lovely this is for parents. May God guide him farther and let him establish much that is good in the land of Weimar.

Ilmenau, August 7, 1776

From the Diaries

Climbed up to the Castle at 9. Ate. Flirted with girls. Upland walk
after dinner. All alone. The Duke came and we clambered around
through the chasm. Made the observation to each other that he and
I, though not wholly free from ostentation toward ourselves and
others, never became guilty of that fault to each other.

August 8, 1776

To Charlotte

She had visited Goethe in Ilmenau during the 5th and 6th of August.

Your presence has had a wondrous effect upon me. I can't quite describe my state, so happy yet so lost in dreams. . . . When I think that you were here in my cave with me and that I held your hand, the while you leaned over and with the other wrote a symbol in the dust!!! It is as though it were a world of spirits and I were in this world. . . . Your relationship to me is both sacred and strange. I felt that so truly on this occasion. There are no words for it and the eyes of men cannot perceive it.

August 9, 1776

From the Diaries

Dreamy, drowsy morning—waiting, drawing a little.

August 9, 1776

To Herder

Here we are, dear friend, in Ilmenau and have been dwelling for three weeks in the Thuringian forest and I lead my life in chasms and caves and woods, beside pools and waterfalls, among subterranean spirits, sinking myself into God's world. I answer your questions concerning your arrival. You have nothing to worry about. Everything is being done for your comfort and the smell of paint has faded in your house. . . . That angel, Charlotte, was with me again. She returned to Weimar by way of Meiningen and Ilmenau. A whole day my glances blended with hers and thaw came back into my strangely frozen heart.

September 3, 1776

To Charlotte

Why should I torment you? Why fool myself and plague you to boot? We can't be anything to each other and yet are too much to each other.—You know very well that when I see things as clearly as the day, you agree with me. But just because I see things exactly as they are, I am driven into a rage. . . . I don't want to see you again. . . . In future I'll look at you as one looks at the stars.

September 8, 1776

To Charlotte

I was very melancholy yesterday and I didn't know why. It seemed to me as though I were not to see you today. I summoned the clarinetists; they played till eight, while I walked about in my garden. It was very beautiful, but my heart did not melt. With the pure morning came your note. An hour before I sent to invite Wieland here; I had the feeling that I would need someone. I owe fate too much to complain and yet I cannot help my feelings. Farewell. I'll not come to Kochberg [*the Stein chateau not far from Weimar*]. I understood both word and glance.

Garden House, September 13, 1776

From the Diaries

The Duke came in the morning, very dear and kind; next Wieland. Ate with the Duke. Both princes after dinner. A ball tonight. Unable to *feel* nature—

October 7, 1776

To Charlotte

Farewell, my dearest. Go on to Kochberg! God knows what will be. I should have been grateful to fate that permitted me during the first moments of seeing you again to realize quite purely how dear you are to me. I should have let it go at that and not have seen you again. Forgive me. I see how my presence tortures you. So I'm glad that you're going, for I couldn't stand not seeing you here in town. . . .

October, 1776

If wrong, this feeling unto which I own,
And if for this dear sin I must some day atone—

My conscience to instruct doth still refuse me.
Destroy it, Heaven, if ever it could accuse me.

Charlotte von Stein

Garden House, October 13, 1776

From the Diaries

For days a feeling of great purity and veracity in all things. . . . A great sense of hope. At Court last night. Coming back in the dark ran into the turnpike and had rather a fall.

Emmendingen, October 20, 1776

Cornelia Schlosser to Charlotte

I cannot tell you the strange effect upon me of the news that you would come here next summer. I had thought it quite impossible ever to see you in this world; I thought the remotest hope of it improbable. And now suddenly you say: I'm coming. I've read your letter over and over and over to be sure that I'm not deceived. . . . I can't thank you enough for the music you sent, though it's far above my power of execution. The recitative from the *Orpheus* of Glück must be astonishing in its effect. Oh, I believe I would faint, if ever I heard anything like that again, for here we are cut off from all the beauty in the world.

November 3, 1776

To Charlotte

I must beg you to send me the ointment for sore lips, so that I find it here tonight when I get home. You see, I'm obliged to beg you for something again—for something healing. Last night the town and the region seemed to look at me suddenly in an estranged way. It was as though I were not destined to stay here. So I swam in the river and drowned the fantasies of the old Adam.

November 6, 1776

To Elisabeth Goethe and Johanna Fahlmer

I'm sitting in my garden and the weather is still beautiful and I am planting and doing all kinds of things against the coming year. I

have just had a new path made and I would add in few words that
I am as gay and happy as a man can be. Business does not depress
me, but I am plagued by what is at the foundation of all life's business, namely, by the mad whims and passions and follies and weaknesses of man, wherein I have this advantage that I haven't time
enough to think too much about myself. Mother will remember how
insufferable I was when I had nothing to plague me and so being
plagued is rather a protection. . . . I enclose a forget-me-not. Let
Father read this letter and send it on to my sister.

Garden House, November 7, 1776

From the Diaries

Took care of my bees and brought them to their winter rest. . . .
What is man, that Thou art mindful of him? And the son of man,
that Thou visitest him?

November 8, 1776

To Charlotte

I was puzzled as to which day was the anniversary of my arrival in
Weimar. It was yesterday. And how you did help me to celebrate it!
You seemed to have saved up all your scruples to pour them out to
me at the moment when I could feel the whole thing most keenly. I
had to look into my diary in order to understand certain passages
in your note. I found everything. How much came to life again! Ah,
these past eight weeks have buried much in me, and yet I remain
the wholly sensual creature.

From the Supplementary Confessions

In his later years Goethe dictated notebooks as a "supplement to my
other confessions." He summarized the years by groups up to 1789. From
then on he devoted a separate section to each year through 1822.

There was no way of continuing work on the incompleted creations
brought along to Weimar. Since the poet anticipates reality through
his imaginative vision of it, the concrete world, when it thrusts its
realities upon him, robs him of ease and disturbs him. It seeks to

give him what he already has, though in a different form, and he must now seek to assimilate it for a second time.

December 1, 1776

To Charlotte

I shouldn't write anything, for I don't know how I feel. The trip we're taking is probably good for me, because it lifts me out of the deepest inner confusion.

December 2, 1776
6:30 in the morning

Karl August to Charlotte

Farewell, dear lady! We're off! The moon, beautifully above us, is still our companion. Live right merrily and receive this comradely farewell from us both.

Garden House, December 25, 1776

From the Diaries

With C. Suffered much. Ate alone. Then in the garden. Put things in order. Evening at the Herders', gay enough.

Garden House, December 31, 1776

From the Diaries

In the evening drove all alone to Tiefurt and smashed the sleigh. . . . Feverish with melancholy.

1777

January 3, 1777

To Charlotte

J. F. Hufeland, physician to the Weimar Court.

Last night I began to feel very queer. I told Hufeland and he gave me some medicine. I'll stay at home and hardly come to the party.

Thank you for your word of last night. I have the feeling that I won't be separated from people for quite a while yet. Remember me to the Duchess.

January 8, 1777

To Lavater

My present life is such that all my distant friends seem to melt into mist. However long it lasts, I will have heartily enjoyed a specimen of the gay goings on of the world. Dismay, hope, love, work, need, adventure, boredom, hatred, frivolousness, folly, joy, the expected and the unexpected, the shallow and the deep, quite as the dice happen to fall, tricked out with dances, cymbals, silk and spangles— 'tis a marvelous set-up and with all this, dear friend, within myself and in relation to my true purposes, quite happy, God be thanked.

February 1, 1777

Elisabeth Goethe to a Friend

I want you to remember what your friend the doctor had to go through in the way of evil gossip and lying imputations, just because people couldn't understand how you could have a real mind without belonging to the nobility. So discipline your soul to patience, see to it that you order your business well, and then hasten to us here.

February 7, 1777

To Charlotte

I've had a beautiful day today and made the test how I manage without seeing you. Instead I've sent you two embassies in the course of the day: in the morning one with flowers; in the evening one with sausages. Philip [*Seidel, 1755-1820, Goethe's valet and secretary at this time*] will confer with the cook. I sit by my lonely fire and love you very much.

February 20, 1777

To Charlotte

I have advised the Duke to have dinner at your house today. He is not in a very happy condition and if you can stand us, we'll come around 1 o'clock. But don't go to any great trouble. I am sending a good old vintage herewith.

March 11, 1777

To Charlotte

You can imagine how happy I am over this brilliant morning after yesterday's fog. And I'd like to know whether that rotten headache has left you. Council in session today, yet I hope to be through before 1. There isn't much business. So I'll come. Busy again this afternoon. Tonight, on the contrary, the little monkeys [*Charlotte's children*] are invited to fireworks.

March 18, 1777

To Charlotte

May I come to dinner today? I've got to stay in my garden till noon. By 1 o'clock, however, I'll be with you. Winter seems to be coming again and I feel as though I had to go through it once more.

Good Friday, 1777

To Charlotte

I hoped to spend a quiet morning over my documents and then to come over to you and do some drawing. Now I discover that the workmen made a very bad mistake in my renovation here and I'm very much annoyed. I've got to stay home, because I'm afraid this thing will get more and more stupid.

Early April, 1777

To Charlotte

Would you send me the books and a word as to how you slept? Infinite sleep seems to have swathed me, so that I lay happy and in dull forgetfulness, unplagued even in dreams by the affairs of the day.

Garden House, April 4, 1777

From the Diaries

Meeting of Council. Ate with the Duke.

◇◇◇◇◇

April 5, 1777

When myth arises the images grow great through the objects; when mythology develops, the objects grow great through the images.

◇◇◇◇◇

April 6, 1777

Heavy is the hand of the gods upon me.

◇◇◇◇◇

April 13, 1777

Much in my soul lies shattered.

April 16, 1777

Elisabeth Goethe to a Friend

The little brother in Weimar is, thank God, well and builds and plants and digs in his garden, so that it's a joy to see. The Schlosser's baby hasn't come yet; by Pentecost we may have good news of her.

May 3, 1777

To Charlotte

Let this bunch of asparagus say good morning to you. How did you manage yesterday? After I left, Philip prepared an omelet for me. Thereafter I wrapped myself in a blue cloak and lay on the ground in a dry garden corner and slept so well through lightning, thunder and rain, that my bed seemed wretched to me afterwards. If Stein is still at home tell him that I'd like to take out the new little horse for a training ride. So, if he doesn't mind, let him have it saddled, send it to me and come and fetch me. I'll probably come to dinner. my dearest.

May 26, 1777

To Charlotte

Just to tell you that I'm coming to dinner and bringing the Duke with me. How much I loved you last night, I dared not say. You

reproach me that my love rises and declines; it is not so, but it is
well that I do not always wholly grasp the depth of my own feeling.

                                                        June 12, 1777

To Charlotte

In my garden under the open sky. Since you went to Kochberg I feel
more truly what I possess and what my obligation is. My other little
passions and diversions and flirtations are but hung on the thread
of my feeling for you. Now that you're not here they all fall, as it
were, into a well. . . . I'm polishing armor and making all kinds of
new arrangements and taking care of my trees and the mosquitoes
have stung me badly.

                                                        June 15, 1777

To Charlotte

At 8 in the morning I was in my garden and all was well with me
and I walked up and down glancing at a book. At 9 o'clock I received letters telling me that my sister had died.—I can say no
more.—

                                        Garden House, June 16, 1777

From the Diaries

Letter concerning the death of my sister. A dark distracted day.

                                                        June 23, 1777

Elisabeth Goethe to Lavater

He gives the weary strength and power to the feeble and what He
has promised He will surely keep. We are a new and living witness
thereunto now that we have our only daughter Cornelia in the
grave—altogether unexpectedly, too; the lightning and the stroke
were one. O dear Lavater, the poor mother has much to bear. My
husband was ill all winter; the harsh banging of a door had given
him a fearful shock and to this man I had to be the messenger con-
veying the death of his daughter, whom he loved beyond every-

thing. . . . Our son Schlosser has written me twice. He is bearing his cross like a man and a Christian.

June 28, 1777

To Elisabeth Goethe

All I can tell you is that fate seems so equably kind to me, that the death of my sister seems the more painful in that it strikes upon me in so fortunate a period. I am but human and will seek to yield to nature, which appoints but a short period to sharp anguish, though a long one to grief. Live as happily as you can and nurse Father; we are still together. Farewell, dear Mother. Convey my greetings to poor Schlosser, too.

Dornburg, July 4, 1777

From the Diaries

On the River Saale, at the head of a valley, the Ducal family possessed three small chateaux. One of them and the village of Dornburg served Goethe as refuge from time to time to the end of his life.

Early to Dornburg in the dim dawn. Felt wonderful there. Climbed a dangerous path up to the chateau. Back home in the rain.

July 5, 1777, 9:30 p.m.

To Charlotte

Here I am at Kochberg in your own bedroom. Still time to say good night. I came from Dornburg today and am in your house with your family. It's a woeful feeling that you're not here. Good night. . . . Sunday morning: Good morning, my sweet. How astonished and gay I was to wake up here. I had been dreaming of Weimar. A year ago you were here and I couldn't be. Thus my life and hopes seem always suspended between heaven and earth. I hear the children singing and playing; I'll join them.

Kochberg, July 12, 1777

To Charlotte

I had a very strange week in town and therefore fled here yesterday. Started from Weimar on foot at 5:30 in the afternoon and arrived at 10. The place was locked up and everybody ready to go to bed. I called out and your old Dorothy recognized my voice and she and the cook welcomed me with many exclamations.

Weimar, July 17, 1777

To Charlotte

The first good day since I came back from Kochberg. I send you a couple of letters from the monkeys. I hear that Stein is better and am very glad of it. Nothing to say of myself, except that the weather is keeping us prisoner with catarrh, toothache and general discomfort. Nevertheless, I'm writing this under the trees in my garden, where it is warm and humid. The Duke is well; he's the only person I see.

July 17, 1777

To Auguste

Thank you, Gussie, that out of the tranquility of your life you send a sound into the disquietude of mine.

> All things do the immortals, the infinite,
> Give their chosen entire,
> All joys, the poignant and infinite,
> All infinite sorrows entire.

Thus did I chant the other day when, steeped in radiant moonlight, I arose from the river which flows through meadows by the side of my garden. The truth of the verses is proved daily in my life. Good fortune is my true love; well, so it torments me like a beloved woman. You will have heard of my sister's death. All my wishes seem realized and I suffer exclusively for the sake of others.

August 11, 1777

To Charlotte

You see from the enclosed drawings that, as in a state of dream, I steep myself in the appearances of nature and in my love for you. I've got to hold on to myself and often keep the thought of you at a distance. . . . The package from you has just come. You send me nourishment in exchange for shadows.

Kochberg and Ilmenau, August 27-28, 1777

From the Diaries

Rode after dinner from Weimar in a dark mood. Kept looking back at my garden and considered all that must needs pass through my soul until I see my poor roof again. Slowly I rode to Kochberg, found her happy and tranquil and so I felt well and free that evening. Awakened on my birthday morning so serenely that everything which confronts me looked easier. Rode away at 8 in the morning on my way to Ilmenau.

August 29-31, 1777

To Charlotte

Sat this evening between mountains and pine forests. . . . Found my way from you here yesterday without difficulty. So glad I saw you before I left. . . . Enjoyed the luncheon that you wrapped up for me! God knows what annoyances await me in Ilmenau. . . .
I am sending you this Sunday. You can write me by the same messenger who is returning. I'm all alone and letting the others climb up and down the mountains. . . . I still have some of the cake you gave me and I hope that you're abstaining from coffee.

In the mountains, September 5, 1777

From the Diaries

Nursing my swollen cheeks and reading the Book of Job.

Eisenach, September 6, 1777

To Charlotte

Everything is all right except that, contrary to my lean constitution, I've acquired a monstrously swollen cheek. Down in the village I danced in the fog until 1 o'clock in the morning with all the peasant girls and carried on like mad, and that started it all. It got worse as

snow flurries came down and now I must sit inside and keep warm
milk brewed with herbs in my mouth. No more flirting! It will be the
damnedest thing to try to flatter the wenches with a crooked face.
. . . Yes, darling, I quite believe that your love of me increases in
absence. When I'm away from you, you can love the ideal of me
which, when I am with you, is often disturbed by my folly and madness. . . . I have wound your neck kerchief about me. The blue
color faded in the wash. . . . Remember me to the children. A long
way lies between us and the straight path is more burdensome than
the crooked one.

September 12, 1777

To Charlotte

From hour to hour I see more clearly that one must gain the shore
from out of this torrent of life; one must swim to the shore with all
one's might or else go under.

Wartburg, September 13-16, 1777

To Charlotte

> The castle near Eisenach which was the scene in 1207 of the minstrels'
> war commemorated in Wagner's *Tannhäuser*. It was here, too, that
> Luther completed his translation of the Bible and had his altercation
> with the Devil in 1521. The castle belonged to the Ducal family.

Here I dwell, dearest, singing Psalms to the Lord who brought me
out of the pains of narrowness to this height and magnificence. 'Tis
the Duke who persuaded me to move up here. I have nothing in common with the people in the valley, though they may be good enough
people, nor have they anything in common with me, though some of
them even imagine that they love me. But it is not so at all. I think
of you this evening in your valley by your moat in the moonshine
and having a watch fire, since it is so cool. . . . Ah, if I could but
magically communicate to you the view from my window in the
castle. . . . I take a great joy in it, although I must confess that a
truly animating relish is absent from me today. Like one who has
long been in fetters, I stretch my limbs. . . . Oh, one should fundamentally neither draw nor write. . . . Farewell. I know that you're
thinking of me, for otherwise I would not be thinking so much of
you.

Wartburg, September 28, 1777

To Kestner

Dear Kestner, It isn't as though I had forgotten you two, but I find myself in a state of silence toward all the world, such as even the sages of antiquity recommended. It suits me extremely well, although, as I know, people are entertained by fairy tales about me even as they were, in other days, by those I told them. . . . You ask for my advice. It is difficult to advise from so far away. But the safest, truest, best tested advice is: *stay where you are!* Bear whatever there is of discomfort, annoyance, humiliation, because you will find no improvement through a mere change of place. Remain steadfastly and faithfully in your office. Pursue steadfastly and faithfully your purpose, as it is your character to do, and you will make progress through that very steadfastness, while others will weaken and give way. He who changes his situation always loses the expenses of travel and re-establishment, both morally and materially, and so suffers a setback. I tell you that as one not ignorant of the world and who is gradually learning to know how things are. But write me more. . . . Remember me to Lotte. God preserve you both and the little ones.

Wartburg, October 4, 1777

From the Diaries

A deep feeling of isolation. Even Knebel's arrival disturbed me, though he brought me greetings, in my feeling of complete isolation. His anecdotes, his very presence, tugged me back into old and past situations.

◇◇◇◇◇

October 7, 1777

Magnificent morning. No fogs at all. The Duke has gone a-hunting. Knebel and I took a walk. I did some sketching on the way. We chatted at length concerning the poverty of life at Court, of all that is known as society.

◇◇◇◇◇

October 8, 1777

My tooth is beginning again and keeps me from dancing. The abyss
between me and all the people about was so intensely obvious! I had
to get away, because it was clear that I was a nuisance to them, too.
Retired to the Duke's room and saw the moon rise over the castle.
Here now for the last time on this pure height, in the soughing of
the autumnal winds. In the valley today I was homesick for Weimar
and my garden; on this height the feeling fades. Yet I am happy to
return to my little refuge, which soon the storms will surround and
the snows cover. And, please God, I will have peace from people,
with whom I have nothing in common. I suffered less here than I
feared, yet saw the necessity of alienation, where I thought some
bonds still held. Only the Duke and I grow closer to each other and
huddle together like sheep in the rain and cold wind.

October 10, 1777. Back in my garden

To Charlotte

Just two words since I hear a messenger is riding. It hurt me to leave
the Wartburg, yet I saw Weimar again with childlike joy. I mounted
at 5 o'clock this morning and arrived here at 11:30. The Duke follows tomorrow. I am estranged from nearly everyone but not from
you.

October 10, 1777

Elisabeth Goethe to Philip Seidel

Your letter of October 5 gave us great pleasure, especially the news
that the doctor is well and in good spirits. If you go on writing us
thus now and in future, all your little tricks will be forgiven you,
especially since Herr Merck has told us so much that is good of you,
how nicely you take care of your master's affairs and supervise them.
Let him travel wherever he would, but do you always let us know in
confidence where he is; for one never knows what might happen and
letters ought to be able to reach him. . . . My husband, the Councilor, is far from well. We buy a lot of medicine and take long walks.

Yet the years are coming, of which the Scripture says, that man can
take no pleasure in them. As far as I am concerned, I am, thanks be
to God, very well and in good spirits, especially when I get good news
written by you.

Garden House, October 23, 1777

From the Diaries

Hurried about all day like the Wandering Jew. The Duke's hand
gave him much pain and I felt harried, too, because I had been repressed and driven hither and yon the whole day.

October 31, 1777

To Charlotte

I don't understand why the chief ingredient of your feelings recently
has been doubt and distrust. But it's quite true that by doubts and
dreams you could repel a lover of but moderate fidelity, even as you
can make someone believe that he looks pale and ill. Last night I
made a mortal leap and got at the three troublesome chapters of my
novel [*the earliest reference to* Wilhelm Meister] which I had long
shied away from. Now that they are behind me I hope to be able to
complete the first part.

November 7, 1777

To Charlotte

Today is Council meeting and I don't know when I'll see you. Two
years ago I arrived here. Would I live them over again!? In the end
—maybe.

November 8, 1777

To Charlotte

The trees have arrived, thirty of them, excellent cherry trees, as well
as some others of good varieties. How and when are they to be shipped
to Kochberg? They must be set and protected with powerful thorn
bushes against the rabbits.
Leaving you last night I had very curious thoughts. Among them this
one: whether I really love you or whether I delight in you only as

one does in the presence of a perfect mirror in which one's image comes out well and pure. Afterwards I concluded that fate, by transplanting me here, dealt with me entirely as one deals with linden trees: one cuts off their tops and prunes their branches, so that they get a new impulse to grow and do not wither from the top down.

November 10, 1777

To Charlotte

Last night the world was so infinitely beautiful as it seemed not to be all summer long. Doubtless it is the contrast which makes one feel greatness and beauty more intensely. I am sending you grapes.

November 16, 1777

To Elisabeth Goethe

Schlosser and Johanna Fahlmer had become engaged.

I really have no words for the strange news in your letter. My heart and mind are so accustomed from of old to have destiny play at ball with them, that I scarcely react to new happenings, be they well or ill. It is as though a tree had been planted in autumn. May God give it His blessing, so that some day we may be able to enjoy its shade and fruit. With the death of my sister there was hewn away a root of mine that went so deeply into the earth that the branches which drew nourishment therefrom had to wither and die. If, in the person of dear Johanna, a new root is to grow in sympathetic firmness, I, too, am ready to join you in gratitude. . . . My tooth and swollen cheek had no significance whatever. A little knot seemed to grow in the jaw. But it gave no pain and is disappearing. My household begins to assume order. In the little hut in my garden I often feel as though I were on a ship at sea.

Garden House, November 18, 1777

From the Diaries

Holy Destiny, you have built me a house and furnished it beyond my prayers and I was gay in my poverty under my half-rotted roof. I begged you to leave me that. Now you have stripped me of roof and narrowness as one strips a head of its nightcap. Now let me enjoy spontaneously and earnestly the cleanness. . . . Regard no crack in your household as too small for your attention. A mouse can slip in through it.

Goslar, December 4, 1777

To Charlotte

Here I am once more surrounded by the walls and gables of antiquity. The patron of the inn is a fatherly sort of person and makes one feel comfortable. On this dark journey I have again fallen in love with that class of people which is called the lower class, but which may be the highest in God's sight. It seems to combine all virtues—a limitation of desire, contentment in frugality, straight thinking, loyalty, delight in merely tolerable possessions, harmlessness, long-suffering, steadfastness—let me not lose myself in extravagance. My wet things are being dried. They're hanging by the oven. How little man needs and how precious that little becomes when he feels how much he needs it. If ever you give me a present again, let it be something that is useful on a trip like this.—You can't imagine to how many uses I've put the paper in which you wrapped the biscuits for me.

December 6, 1777

To Charlotte

It's a curious sensation to travel about the world unknown. It seems to me that one's relationship to people and to things is a far more genuine one. I say my name is Weber and that I'm a painter, or that I've studied law or simply that I'm a traveler. I'm very courteous to everyone and am well received wherever I go. So far I've had nothing to do with women. A great sense of tranquility and security surrounds me and hitherto, as luck would have it, the weather has been bright, though it will freeze hard tonight. The moon is in its first quarter. What I wish for is a full moon. But I'll compromise on a half. It's incomprehensible to me that there are moments when I can produce nothing.

December 9, 1777

To Charlotte

The reason for my inner restlessness I would not inquire into, nor
have others do. All alone like this, I remind myself of how I was in
my earliest youth. . . .
I find no repose anywhere. Deeper and deeper I penetrate the Harz
Mountains; tomorrow I'll attempt remote regions, if I can find a
guide through the snow. . . .
It was around this time nine years ago that I was sick even unto
death. In the extreme anguish of her heart my mother opened the
Bible and, as she told me later, her eye hit upon these words: "Vine-
yards will be planted again on the hills of Samaria, they will be
planted and there will be piping." She was comforted on the instant
and found joy in the saying through the years to come.
You have already guessed, no doubt, that I am living in and for the
sake of the mines.

December 10, 1777

To Charlotte

I reveal to you the fact—tell it to no one—that I penetrated into the
Harz Mountains in order to climb the Brocken [*place of a scene in
Faust*]. Well, I managed to get to the top today quite naturally, although for a week everybody had been telling me that it can't be
done. How I did it and, above all, why, I shall keep to tell you face
to face.
I said that I was praying for a full moon! Well, I have just stepped
into the open and there lies the Brocken above the pines in magnificent moonlight and I was on its peak today and rendered thanks to
God upon the Devil's altar there.

Harz Mountains, December 10, 1777

From the Diaries

Started out at 10:15 to climb the Brocken. The snow was a yard deep
but firm. Reached the top at 1:15. Magnificent and serene outlook.
Beneath me the world of clouds and mist. What is man that Thou art

mindful of him? Back by 4 o'clock. The forester gave me lodging in the peat house.

December 19, 1777

Elisabeth Goethe to a Friend

I would write you a long letter, were my house not filled to the brim with the gentlemen known as wits. Wieland has been here sundry days and so has friend Merck. So everything is topsy-turvy from early morning to late at night but since you, dear gossip, are yourself married to a poet, you must know by experience that gentlemen of this character will do more mischief in a day than we, poor common earthworms, in a year.

1778

January 1, 1778

To Charlotte

I thought a great deal about you last night as I was packing up letters and, as it were, the whole past year. I'd like so well to send you something for the New Year and find nothing. I was tempted to send you a lock of my hair; I had already loosened it, when I considered that there would be no magic in it for you. Surely I'll see you today.

January 9, 1778

Merck to Lavater

Last autumn I mounted my horse and made a pilgrimage to Eisenach where I spent a couple of weeks with Goethe in the Wartburg. His situation is the best imaginable. He lives quite as he pleases and the Duke's house is as though it were his own. Whatever asses pretend, he has lost none of his creative individuality, but has grown in his hunger and thirst for a knowledge of humanity and of affairs and has thus increased in wisdom. Goethe loves the Duke as he does none of us, because the Duke needs him as no one else does and therefore the relationship is certain to be permanent.

Garden House, January 17, 1778

From the Diaries

The girl, a member of the Court, drowned herself because her fiancé, a young Swedish nobleman, had abandoned her. A copy of *Werther* was found in her pocket.

My men found Christel von Lasberg beside the bridge under the weir. She must have been drowned last night. I had been skating with the Duke. In the afternoon busy with the poor dead girl whom they had carried to Charlotte's house. Called on her parents that evening.

January 19, 1778

To Charlotte

Instead of me this note. I had workmen here and found a private little place where the memorial to poor Christel may stand unseen. What displeased me in my notion at first was that it stood too close to the road, so that one could not step aside to pray and to remember. Thus I have caused a piece of crag to be hollowed out. From this isolated spot one can survey her last path and the place of her death. We worked till late into the night; I worked on after the others left, even to the hour in which she had died. Orion was brilliant in the sky. I am too full of memories and thoughts to leave the house again.

January 21, 1778

To Charlotte

I'm invited to dinner at the Dowager Duchess', otherwise I would have come to dinner with you. I dare not be alone yet and really want to see no one but you. I ran away last night because I couldn't stand it any longer. You observe that you exist to be tormented by me. I hope you don't get too tired of it.

Garden House, January 29, 1778

From the Diaries

Passed several days in quiet mourning about the scene of the girl's death. Thereafter forced again into the life of theatrical frivolity.

February 1, 1778

To Charlotte

Since you love me no longer, it's really nice of you that you want to feed me with preserved fruits. I thank you for them, although it looks as if you sent them to me, so that I might not be tempted to come and eat them at your house.

Garden House, February 9, 1778

From the Diaries

Much skating this week in a mood of great equability, almost too flawless. Excellent insights into myself and our economy. Inner stillness and presage of wisdom. Continuous delight in good management and saving money and making both ends meet. A good tranquil household compared to last year. A more certain feeling of voluntary restriction which is the truest kind of expansion.

Garden House, February 12, 1778

Continuous but quite pure isolation from mankind. Quiet decisiveness in life and action. But my imagination full of gay and brilliant fancies.

February 19, 1778

TO THE MOON

Grove and valley dost thou fill
With a radiance mild,
Melting my proud soul until
It is reconciled;

Spreadest o'er this broad expanse
Influence delicate,
Like a friendly countenance
Watchful of my fate.

Echoes murmur once again
Of days bright and dour,
Hold me between joy and pain
In my lonely hour.

Flow, belovèd river, flow!
Joy from me has gone,
Old embraces perished so,
Troth that was undone.

Once I had the better part,
Things that precious be,
And that haunt the tortured heart
Unforgettably.

River, roll the dale along
Without pause or ease,
Answering unto my song
With thy melodies,

Whether in the winter night
Storms sweep up thy strand,
Or in spring when blooms are bright
Floods make rich the land.

Blessèd he who without hate
Lets the world go by,
With one friend to meditate
On what, far or nigh,

Still by mortals unconfessed
Or not thought upon,
Through the labyrinthine breast
In the night fares on.

February 20, 1778

To Charlotte

I'm sending you something for breakfast. 'Tis for yourself and Fritz. [*Charlotte's six-year-old son who was Goethe's great favorite.*] May the gods be as kind to you as they are to me. Cold and bright is the light over my fields today.

March 1, 1778

To Charlotte

Before you indulge in the gaieties of the world tonight, here is a flower for you and a wish for a good evening.

March 20, 1778

Elisabeth Goethe to Lavater

Brother Wolf is very well, thanks be to God, and very merry in his little Garden House. He has written a beautiful masque for the birthday of the reigning Duchess—a beautiful thing. . . . He sent the manuscript to me, seeing that it will hardly be printed.

March 26, 1778

To Charlotte

Here are some flowers of friendship to make up to you for the dullness of my society. If you will send a servant with a basket you can have more of them, as well as radishes and lettuce.

March 31, 1778

To Charlotte

Although the banquet that awaits you this evening will quite outshine the humble morning repast of your hermit friend, yet I am sending you and Fritz this cake.

Early April, 1778

To Charlotte

I know very well how you treat my irritations. That I am quite serious you see from the fact that I'm not coming to you, though I'd like to come. Goodbye, dear angel, I send you flowers again. If I can bear to do it, I'm going away over Monday.

Garden House, April 12, 1778

From the Diaries

An unexpected spell of fair weather. Everything has turned green within a few days. I, myself, in a state of vegetation, tranquil and pure. . . . Brooding over a thousand thoughts of our relationships and our destiny. The Duke disturbed; he hankers after war. . . .

May 12, 1778

To Charlotte

> Goethe accompanied the Duke to Berlin, where the latter went in con-
> nection with a military alliance among the smaller German states. It
> was Goethe's only visit to the Prussian capital.

Dearest Lady, Just a word before our departure from Leipzig. Tomorrow we proceed to Dessau. If you hear strange rumors, be surprised, if you like, but don't be afraid on our account. . . . I am
very tranquil and straightforward. Everything is in motion and the
choice between war and peace a doubtful one. I am sending cloth
for some bodices for you. Remember me to the Duchess and to Stein
and let Philip give you the chapters I have finished. We're stopping
at the Hôtel de Bavière.

Wörlitz. Thursday, Middle of May, 1778

To Charlotte

After dinner we're going to Berlin by way of Potsdam. It's extremely
beautiful around here. As we passed by the lakes and canals and
groves last night, it moved me to think how the gods had permitted
the King to realize a veritable dream about him. It is like going
through a fairy tale. . . . I have less traffic with people than I used
to have. I seem to see all things under their dramatic and historic
aspect, observing how the great of this world play with mankind
and how the gods make sport of the great.

Berlin, Sunday, May 17, 1778

To Charlotte

How different my situation from last winter when I wrote you from
the Harz Mountains. A few words now from your friend. Dining
with Prince Heinrich of Prussia today, I thought that I must write
to you. It's a wondrous situation strangely and providentially
brought about, that we are here. I have wandered through the city
and seen many kinds of people and many trades plied. I'll tell you
more about that later. I am preserving my equanimity and inner
clearness well; but my trustfulness and openness of heart and outgo-
ing affection wither daily. . . .

It is a fine feeling to be present at the source of war at the very moment when it may overflow the banks. Here is this splendid royal
city with its life and order and superfluity in all things; yet it were
nothing if these thousands and thousands of people were not ready
to die to defend it. People and horses and wagons and artillery and
equipment throng the place. I hope I'll be able to tell you about this
great clockwork here. The movement of the puppets points clearly
to the position of the hidden wheels and especially to that central
spring F. R. [*Fridericus Rex, that is, Frederick the Great*] which
makes the melodies one hears.

Berlin, May 19, 1778

I do hope it will be given me to tell you about all this when I return.
But the iron rings that seem to surround my heart are drawn daily
tighter. . . . Thus much I will say now: as the world and life grow
in size, so grows in repulsiveness the misery of both, and I swear to
you that no ribaldry and asininity of the most vulgar farce is as revolting as what goes on among the great and the less great and the
quite small. And I have besought the gods to keep my courage and
steadfastness to the very end and rather to hasten that end than to
have me ever creep through any part of it, contaminated by the lousiness of the world. Nevertheless the value of this adventure for me
and for us all is scarcely to be overestimated.—

◇◇◇◇◇

Potsdam, May 21, 1778

A good sleep has soothed my spirits. We arrived here once more last night. We'll look about a bit and go on tomorrow. My chief desire is to get home.

June 2, 1778

To Charlotte

This is just to say good morning to you. I'd rather be in my valley and I feel better here than in the whole wide world. Last night it seemed to me that the gods must consider me a handsome picture since they have surrounded me with so precious a frame.

June 17, 1778

To Charlotte

I send you strawberries which, though they did not grow in my garden, are yet the products of our neighborhood.

June 28, 1778

To Charlotte

All I have to give you are the same fruits and flowers and feelings. Let me continue to believe that the monotony of my gifts will give you a moment's pleasure, despite your many other more entertaining circumstances.

Garden House, July 1, 1778

From the Diaries

The Duke is pulling himself together and is in a sound mood and good spirits. Knebel has a hypochondriac way of seeing things which is falsely true. It will yet cause him trouble.

July 2, 1778

To Charlotte

I woke up at 4:30 and waited for your messenger. He did not come and I had another long sleep. Here are strawberries out of my own garden, as well as flowers. We'll dine together.

August 3, 1778

To Charlotte

You were incredulous when I told you that the Duchess had a present for you. Yet she was most eager to commission me to send you the package herewith. Coming through me, it may serve to remind you of me. It came all over me again last night that there is nothing I'm fonder of seeing than your eyes and nowhere that I would rather be than with you. It is an old story by now; yet I can't help observing it anew now and then.

August 5, 1778

To Merck

It's very hard for me nowadays to communicate with others, but on this tranquil evening I'm going to write you a few words. . . . My valley grows ever more beautiful, that is to say, it becomes more homelike to me and to others, too, and more delightful in that I improve and adorn it with the very hands of love and most carefully let the gaps of art be covered and fortified by the beloved forces of nature. . . .

Last winter a trip through the Harz Mountains gave me the purest delight. . . . This spring I was in Berlin, too—a very different spectacle. We were there for sundry days and I peered like a child into that show of rarities. But you know how I live through the eye; I gained a thousand insights. It seemed to me that I drew rather near to old Fritz [*Frederick the Great*], gaining some insight into his character from his gold, silver, marble, monkeys, parrots and tattered brocades and I heard his own servile scoundrels discuss their eminent master. . . .

I had very little communication with people and uttered no word in the Prussian State which they could not have printed. Needless to say I got the reputation of being proud.

August 18, 1778

To Charlotte

Got around quite a bit yesterday and hoped to see you today. But the Duke commands a hunting party and I am off. So just a posy and a good morning.

August 27, 1778

Wieland to Merck

Last Saturday we drove to see Goethe, who had invited the Duchess to spend the evening in his garden in order to regale her with the poems he had produced in her absence on the banks of his little river. We supped in his delicious little retreat and found that, for some reason, a seventh chair was vacant at the table around which we sat. This made us wish unanimously that you could have occupied that chair. . . . We drank your health and Goethe's mother's with a bottle of Johannisberger of the year '60. Next we arose and opened the door and, behold, through an arrangement of the Divine Magician, there spread before us a view more like the creation of some great painter poet than like a mere segment of natural scenery.

Garden House, August 31, 1778

From the Diaries

A wondrous feeling to enter upon one's thirtieth year. A great change in many points of view.

September 7, 1778

Elisabeth Goethe to Philip Seidel

Your master writes me that Herr Wieland would like to have a mechanical spit, such as we call a "roaster" hereabouts, that I am to purchase one etc. I'll do it very gladly, but I must observe that a thing like that costs between 25 and 30 gulden, furthermore, that it's nobody's fault if the spring breaks. The spring on mine broke so often that I tore it out and now run the mechanism by a device of weights and pulleys. Now I don't know, of course, whether this method is known in Weimar. You'd better consult a watchmaker. . . .

My brother, Doctor Textor, has had the idea of asking your master to write some verses in celebration of Doctor Schlosser's wedding. Since I do not believe that your master will have either the time or the inclination, either give the commission to one of your local poets or do it yourself. If none of this is practicable, let me know in ample time in order that our local poets may mount their Pegasus.

Eisenach, September 13, 1778

To Charlotte

I've settled down with Prince Constantine in the Wartburg and there have been such fancy goings on that I've had no rest at all. . . . The hunt tomorrow will be a pretty swinish affair, and when you have between four and five Saxonian dukes in a single room, you can't expect any sensible conversation. . . .

You can imagine my various disappointments, since I set such hopes upon being 30, considering how childlike I still was at 29. Often I shake my head, trying to harden myself again, and finally it seems to me that I'm like that Frenchman who, having devoured the sharply roasted skin and cracklings of a pig, sent the carcass back to the kitchen in the hope that the creature would grow a second hide.

September 24, 1778

To Charlotte

I look for you everywhere, at Court and in your house and under the trees. Quite without knowing it, I walk around looking for something and in the end it turns out that what I lack is you.

October 17, 1778

To Charlotte

Your absence at Kochberg keeps me much at home. It's nice of you that you let me share in what happens around you. In exchange I send you a copy of *The Song of Songs,* sung by a wise king, with a commentary by a wise man [*namely, Herder*].

November 2, 1778

To Johann Friedrich Krafft

Nothing is known about this object of Goethe's long and patient and intense preoccupation and benevolence, not even whether this was the man's real name. At certain periods within the next few years Goethe gave Krafft as much as one-fourth to one-third of his own salary.

To him who struggles for life in the stormy waves, it is perhaps the deepest anguish that he who stands on the shore, ready and willing to help, has not the strength to rescue all those whom the storm sweeps against the coast. . . . I seem to myself to gain a very clear picture of you from your letters. What hurts me most is that I seem unable to give help or hope to one who asks so little. About this pool, which an angel so rarely stirs, hundreds wait through the years. Only a few can be healed, and I am not the man who at one of these intervals can say: Arise and walk.

Take the little that I can give you as a sort of plank which I throw you for the moment, in order to gain time. Remain where you are during this season. I will see to it that modest help reaches you. Acknowledge the receipt of the money and tell me how long it will last you. If you could use a garment, a cloak, boots, warm hose, write me, for I have more than I need.

November 11, 1778

To Krafft

A package of garments is going off to you, as well as some money. My plan for you for this winter is the following: life is cheap in Jena. I will look about there to find you a room and board etc. precisely adjusted to the needs of one who, let us say, is willing to live quietly on a modest pension, which he receives.

When that has been accomplished, I'll let you know and you can go to Jena and move in. Then I'll send you cloth and lining and money for the tailor. I'll send word to the rector of the university to say that you had been recommended to me, that you wanted quietly to study there for a period, and that you are to be registered. Then you'll have to invent some tolerable story, stick to the denomination of a secretary, for instance, and register. Then no burgomaster or other official will question you. . . . And plant your foot firmly upon earth again! We live but once. I know exactly what it means to add the responsibility for one more person to one's other burdens. But I am determined that you shall be saved.

November 23, 1778

To Krafft

No, you're not a burden to me. That isn't what I meant. This matter will teach me to manage my affairs better. I see that I have been dribbling away a good part of my income, which I had better save for those in need. And do you think that your tears and your blessing mean nothing to me? . . . Perhaps I'll find some way soon in which you can be of use to me. For not he who boasts of great projects is welcome to one who would like to achieve what is good and permanent, but rather one who modestly offers his loyal services.

November 24, 1778

Elisabeth Goethe to the Duchess Anna Amalia

Anna Amalia, often mentioned as the Dowager Duchess, 1739-1807, was the mother of Karl August. She had been Regent from the death of her husband in 1758 until 1775. It was she who had called Wieland to Weimar as the governor of her son.

A journey to dear, dear Weimar could possibly be undertaken this coming spring, and Your Highness can easily imagine that such a journey would be the highest peak of earthly happiness for me. . . . Your Highness can well see that the matter can be managed and is not wholly impossible and that, in the meantime, until the hour strikes, I will be telling myself the loveliest stories about it and will be full of the bliss of hopefulness.

December 9, 1778

To Charlotte

A year ago at this very hour I was on top of the Brocken and asked of the Spirit of Heaven much that has been fulfilled. I write you this in order that in all quietness you may share this anniversary with me.

Go on loving me in spite of this crust of ice that has formed itself about me.

Garden House, December 9, 1778
From the Diaries

Council meeting. Dinner with Charlotte. Afterwards conversation, not much but good. She seems ever more charming to me, although more like a stranger. But that's true of everybody.

December 11, 1778
To Krafft

Let me say first in order to calm you, that I'm not trying to force you into anything. You shall have the hundred thaler, wherever you may choose to live. I know very well that a man's imaginings are very real to him and, although the picture you have of Jena is quite wrong, yet I know that nothing is less subject to reason than such hypochondriac fears. But now listen to me: you would make it much easier for me to help you and I promise you that you'll be well taken care of in Jena. But if you can't bring yourself to go, stay in Gera. I'm sending you 25 thaler at New Year's; you'll get as much every quarter. That's the only way I can manage. . . . Of course, if you were in Jena, I could more easily provide you with some tasks and also make your personal acquaintance. But I want you to abide by the dictates of your heart. If my reasons do not persuade you and do not promise you repose and confidence in Jena, remain in your present quiet corner.

Garden House, December 14, 1778
From the Diaries

Conversation with the Duke about public order, police matters, laws and regulations. Difference of opinion. I mustn't put mine into definite words; it would be easily misunderstood and so become dangerous. If you try to improve irremediable evils in men and circumstances, you lose time and make matters worse. What should be done is to accept these lacks as part of the fundamental substance of life and then try to establish factors to counterbalance them.

⟡⟡⟡⟡⟡

Garden House, December 30, 1778

I'm not made for this kind of world. The minute you put your foot
out of the house it sinks into filth. Because I pay no attention to the
low actions of low people and don't gossip and don't have spies, why,
I often act stupidly.

1779

January 2, 1779

To Charlotte

Under the rising moon I took a walk around my entire place. Bitter
frost. Caught a few views of infinite beauty; would that they were
outside of your windows!

Garden House, January 10, 1779

From the Diaries

I always imagine that it's better if a man had more human passions.
I'm too remote from others to discover and put to use the right relations, which are usually made up of shabbiness and poverty, both
moral and material. I just have to do the best I can, seeing more
clearly and using more caution and often being too distrustful. But
that won't hurt.

⟡⟡⟡⟡⟡

Garden House, January 13, 1779

I've accepted the chairmanship of the Military Commission. . . .
The pressure of business is very good for the soul; when it is lifted,
the soul unfolds more freely and enjoys life. No one is more wretched
than a comfortable idle person; the handsomest gifts of fate come to
disgust him. Very difficult to put these mortal machines in motion
and to preserve them. Maxims and history are absurdly useless when
it comes to action. The proudest prayer is the prayer for wisdom, for

the gods seem to have refused wisdom to man. They give him clever-
ness, as they give the bull his horns and the cat its claws; they have
furnished their creatures with weapons.

It's very good for me to have reduced my consumption of wine by
one-half. The best dietary measure since I gave up drinking coffee.

Garden House, February 1, 1779

Council meeting. Dull air in the chamber. Fritsch's discordant humor. The Duke talked too much. The sudden warm weather was in
my bones and the room was hot. Dined with the Duke and afterwards
had an explanation with him about his talking too much, letting
things drop, guarding his dignity, moderating his way of expression
and not impulsively to discuss things, which should be passed over
in silence. . . . But I made the same mistakes in other matters. . . .
I'll look after the Military Commission well, because this business
doesn't stimulate my imagination and I won't try to produce anything, but simply get to know and put in order what exists. It's the
same with the roads.

February 8, 1779

To Charlotte

Good night, my lovely one. I've got to get used to my house again,
though I really prefer to come to you. So send me over a little something to eat.

February 19, 1779

Elisabeth Goethe to the Duchess Anna Amalia

What am I to say to begin with and what to end with! My heart is so
full that no expressions please me; they don't express what I feel.
But, dearest Princess, you know my heart and you can easily understand how I felt when I undid the package and saw your amiable and
charming and friendly countenance. . . . I can say nothing more of
the other precious gift, the splendid and beautiful snuffbox, than
that it is truly a princely gift. . . . I have had no birthday celebration like this—no, truly, not any.

February 20, 1779

To Charlotte

All day long I have been brooding over my play *Iphigenie*, so that my head is dull, although I slept ten hours last night to prepare myself for the task. Without complete concentration, with, as it were, only one foot in the stirrup of the winged horse, it will be hard enough to produce anything that is other than rags wrapped in oil cloth.

February 22, 1779

To Charlotte

The lovely tones of music are gradually liberating my soul from the bonds of protocols and legal documents. A quartet is being played in the green room next to mine and I sit here and softly summon hither far-off figures of my imagination. I think that a scene of the play will precipitate itself today, so I'll not be coming over. Had a really lovely letter from my mother.

Dornburg, March 2, 1779

To Charlotte

When I get to a place where we were together, or where I know that you have been, I feel much better. Today I thought of you in this paradise and that you walked about here before you knew me. I dislike to think that there was ever a time when you did not know me or love me. If ever I come back to earth again I'll ask the gods to let me love but once, and if you were not so hostile to the things of this world, I would beg that you be the dear companion of my life. . . . At this moment I live with these mortals here and eat and drink with them, even joke with them, and yet am hardly aware of them, for my inner life goes unimpeded on its way.

Dornburg, March 5, 1779

To Charlotte

You did well to give the messenger a note for me, for I had quite determined to be angry if no word arrived. Now the messenger is gone again. My trunk is not unpacked; therefore I write on this slip of paper.

March 6, 1779

To Charlotte

All day I was tempted to come home to Weimar; it would have been lovely had you come here to me. But such adventurousness is not in the blood of people who live around a Court. Give my regards to the Duke and tell him that I ask him for the present to be very straight in his dealings with the new recruits. Conscription is no fun; the cripples would like to serve; the handsome fellows all say they're married. . . . I make no progress with my play. I can't make the King of Tauris speak [*the scene of the play* Iphigenie] as though no textile laborers here were going hungry.

March 8, 1779

To Karl August

While the fellows are being measured and looked over I'll write you a few words. It seems most curious to me that I, who am accustomed to perceive everything in this world quite individually, am now classifying all the young lads of the country. . . . However, I let them tell me tales and then I retire into my old fortress of poetry. . . . I am having the opportunity to see that I have been treating this good gift of the gods a bit too cavalierly, and it is really time that I manage my talent with a little more care, if ever I'm to produce anything again.

March 26, 1779

To Krafft

I haven't forgotten your necessities. I've looked around in Ilmenau for room and board for you, which you will get there for the hundred thalers a quarter, which I have pledged to pay quarter by quarter. I'll dig up some pocket money for you, too. . . . One thing I will confess to you. I desire the little that I am able to give you to be spent in the territory of the Duke, since that is where I get it.

From the Diaries
Garden House, March 31, 1779

All this period I was just like the weather—clear, serene and gay.

◇◇◇◇◇

Garden House, April 6, 1779

A reading of *Iphigenie* with distributed rôles. Excellent effect, especially upon people of any inner purity.

Elisabeth Goethe to Philip Seidel
April 7, 1779

A drover on his way to Weimar will soon deliver to your master another six jugs of good old wine and a whole dozen of brand-new stockings, all knitted by a single person and certain to be very comfortable for him. Now, Philip, I have a commission for you that will make you laugh yourself sick. Imagine, in the village of Umpferstedt the position of schoolmaster is vacant. The good man who would like the job is now village teacher in Zilbach. His name is Johann Valentin Hartmann. He has friends in the city and sent them to me and they begged me so hard to get a recommendation from the doctor! I thought I'd better tell you. You can state the case to your master. I'd love to have him do it.

Elisabeth Goethe to the Duchess Anna Amalia
April 11, 1779

If Doctor Wolf could see the husband whom Sophie de la Roche is forcing on her second daughter he would certainly, according to his praiseworthy habit, grind his teeth and utter most godless oaths. Yesterday she introduced the monster to me. Good God, if I were queen of the whole earth, America included, I'd turn him down. He looks exactly like the devil in the seventh section of Luther's shorter catechism; he is as stupid as a mule; to his own misfortune he has the title of Councillor of the Court. If I understand anything of this business, may I become an oyster. A woman like Sophie, a woman of uncommon understanding, of some wealth and repute and rank who positively pushes her daughters into misery—and goes on writing novels!

Garden House, April 12, 1779

From the Diaries

One does wrong to doubt the power of people to feel and to know. In this respect one can hope for not a little. But one must not think that their actions will be of the same kind.

April 20, 1779

To Charlotte

I hid in the bushes along the road to see you drive by. I could have watched you from my hiding place quite closely. But I came too late and was far from you. If she were with me, I thought, she would enjoy the evening, which is beautiful beyond words. Now she rolls away in the dust. Yet I know that you will let the thought of me be driven from your soul neither by the rattling of your carriage wheels nor by the music you are going to hear. That I scribble on like this is a sign that I'm not feeling very well. Goodbye, dearest heart.

May 7, 1779

To Charlotte

It annoyed me that I had to have strangers tell me that you're going to Gotha and I made myself ridiculous by asserting that you were not going. Since I can't be angry with you when I see you, I'm going to hide from you and not see you and nurse my grudge until you come home.

May 12, 1779

To Charlotte

I am sending you flowers and some fruits. Knebel is reading Pindar. The Duke is riding away and I am staying behind. Eat the asparagus I send you and think of me.

May 22, 1779

To Krafft

I beg of you to try to get along with the little that I send you. By the end of June I will send you the money for your rent and board. I hope that you will feel reasonably well in the mountains. I am sending you books, too, but, since I have to borrow them myself, I must ask you to return them promptly and neatly.

May 23, 1779

To Charlotte

If only I had something different to send you than flowers, and always the same flowers. But it's like love, which is monotonous, too.

June 9, 1779

To Charlotte

Last night I plucked a rose for you which had just burst into bloom. But I met people on my way to you and had to carry the rose back home again.

Garden House, June 10, 1779

From the Diaries

The Duke will soon have left a crisis behind him and I nurse the hope that he will be able to climb to the elevation before him and tread for a while on level ground.

◇◇◇◇◇

Garden House, June 15, 1779

Council meeting in the morning. I interrupted the expert on our textile factories and expressed my doubts and criticisms. Before dinner chatted at length with Duke about the development in his ideas of things, his interest and truer grasp of them.

June 23, 1779

To Krafft

Tomorrow my messenger will leave here. I am giving him the money
for you. . . . He is to draw up some sort of contract with your landlord under which I will obligate myself to make the quarterly pay-
ments. I am adding stationery and sealing wax.

June 24, 1779

To Charlotte

You do well to have your ravens feed me mornings and evenings. 'Tis
one of the surest and most visible signs that Heaven is not forgetful
of the prophets. Last night I wrote a scene on my play *Egmont,* which
I can scarcely decipher this morning.

Garden House, July 1, 1779

From the Diaries

The Duke is having a good time studying the rôle of Pylades in my
play *Iphigenie.* He makes extraordinary efforts and improves daily
in power, grasp, pertinacity and determination.

July 4, 1779

To Charlotte

I didn't wake up till 9 o'clock yesterday. I looked for you among
the bushes and on the square and on the road to Tiefurt. Not finding
you, I went home and wrote and read and walked in the park along
the new paths. I hope to shuffle the periods of my day oftener. It's
quite delightful. Maybe you'd like to eat dinner with me today and
bring along someone—your mother or Stein or whom you like.

July 13, 1779

To Krafft

I have something to propose to you. When you are well settled in
your new quarters, I would like you to pay some attention to a boy,

for whose education I am paying and who is studying forestry in Ilmenau. He has made a start in French; perhaps you could help him a little. He draws nicely; perhaps you can encourage him. I would like to set times at which he is to come to you. . . . But it all depends upon your having a liking for such an occupation. As for myself, associating with children always makes me feel gay and young. . . . You could render me a real service in this matter and I could give you every month a small stipend out of the money set aside for the lad's education.

Garden House, July 13, 1779

From the Diaries

Merck's presence has had a good effect on me. . . . By reminiscing about the past and by his special view of things he has shown me my actions, as it were, in a mirror of wonderful clearness. Since he is the only person who quite understands what I am doing and how I do it and yet views it from another angle than my own, he gives me a very happy feeling of assurance.

Garden House, July 14, 1779

I must not deviate from the path prescribed for me. My life cannot be a simple one. Only I would that gradually everything presumptuous be eliminated. . . . Who is more enviable than the potter, bending over his wheel, and seeing issue from his hands and according to his will, now a pitcher and now a cup. It remains ever a mystery how to find the point of fusion in a multiplicity of power, wherein one's individuality must take especial thought and listen to the lure of no one.

Garden House, July 25, 1779

Meant to go on Sunday to Berka, to the mines. During the night a conflagration took place in the town of Apolda. I heard of it at once and rushed there and was roasted and cooked the whole day. The

Duke happened to be at Erfurt. Naturally my immediate plans and thoughts and schedules were burnt up, too. That's the way life goes to the end; thus will it go for those who come after us. I have a right to be grateful that on such occasions I keep my head and that my notions about our fire department are confirmed. . . .

◇◇◇◇◇

Garden House, July 30, 1779

Another fight between the Duke and Fritsch. The latter's ingratitude weighs on him and the fact that he himself is often so horribly misunderstood. Must prevent the Duke from yielding to impulses. He is still too inexperienced, especially with strangers, and has but little perception of the attitude of new acquaintances to himself. Considered the plan of a trip to Frankfurt.

◇◇◇◇◇

Garden House, August 2, 1779

The Duke came to me at 10. We spoke of things difficult to express, as we had started to do yesterday: of the governmental situation, our government's policy toward the world, my own idea of a journey which I must undertake in the same way as wine salesmen do. Of the Court, of women, of people in general and of one's knowledge of them. I explained to him why certain things were so difficult for him and told him to use less violence in trivial matters. He opened his heart to me and it was a remarkable and important discussion. . . .

◇◇◇◇◇

Garden House, August 7, 1779

Put things in order at home. Went through papers and burned the empty husks. Other times, other cares. Looked quietly back upon my life, upon the confusion, the hasty acting, the thirst after knowledge of youth which runs hither and yon to seek out something satisfactory. How I had found an almost sensual delight in hidden things and dark imaginative circumstances. . . . How shortsighted had been my attitude toward things both human and divine; how there had been so little of purposeful action, thought, creation; how so many days had been wasted in unprofitable sensibilities and shadowy passions; how little profit there had been and how, therefore, the half of my life being now practically over, there was no path to look back upon, but that I was rather like one who had saved himself from drowning and whom the beneficent sun now tries to dry. I dare not yet try to attain a clear view of the period, since October, 1775, during which I have been engaged in the business of the world. God help me to go on and give me more light, lest I stand so much in my own way. May He help us to do the appropriate from morning to evening and give us a clear comprehension of the consequences of things, so that we be not like people who complain of headaches all day and physic themselves all day and yet on every evening drink too much wine again. May the idea of pureness, which should extend to every morsel we take into our mouths, be ever brighter within me.

August 9, 1779

To Elisabeth Goethe

My desire to see you once again has always hitherto been curbed by circumstances in which I was more or less necessarily involved. At present, however, an occasion may arise, concerning which for the present I must ask you to observe the strictest discretion. The Duke is minded to enjoy the beauties of autumn on the banks of the Rhine. One chamberlain and myself would accompany him. We would be your guests for several days; we would try to avoid the hilarities of the Fair and proceed by water. Then we would return and really make your house our headquarters and from there look about in the vicinity. Whether you take this prosaically or poetically, it is on either count the dot on the i of your past life, for it is the first time that I am returning home quite well and happy and under the most honorable circumstances. But I would also like, since the wine has thriven so well on the hills of Samaria and the piping is going on, that you and Father receive us with open and happy hearts in gratitude to God Who permits you to see your son again in this fashion in his thirtieth year. I resisted all temptation to slip away from here and surprise you and so I, too, would like to enjoy this visit to my heart's content. I don't expect the impossible. God did not will

Father to enjoy the longed-for fruit in its ripeness; so be it! I will ask nothing of him but what the mood of the moment bids him. But I would like to see you in all your gaiety on these good days. Consider that I have everything a man may desire: a life in which I exercise myself toward further growth daily, that I come this time in health, without passion or confusion or blinded efforts, but as one who, by God's help, has completed the first half of his life in such a way that he may hope for future good from past suffering and for strength for such other suffering as the years may bring. If I find you happy I will return with delight to this place, where my work and the heat of the day await me.

Middle of August, 1779

To Elisabeth Goethe

That is exactly the answer I expected, dear Mother, and now I'm sure that everything will be beautiful and, indeed, splendid. We will arrive toward the middle of September and stay with you very quietly for several days. The aunts and cousins of the Duke will be at the Fair and, since he doesn't want to see them, we will swim down the Main and the Rhine after a few days. Having completed this little tour, we'll come back and take up our quarters with you in all due form. Then I'll be able to see all friends and acquaintances, while the Duke will pay some visits to Darmstadt and other places in the vicinity. Our quarters are to be arranged as follows: put up a bed for the Duke in the small bedroom and take the organ out, if it is still there. The big adjoining room will be used for callers. He sleeps on a sack of fresh straw, over which a fine linen sheet is to be spread and under one light blanket. Have mattresses placed into the little chimney room for his valets. The gray room in the rear can be prepared for the chamberlain. I'll sleep in my old room on a sack of straw etc. like the Duke's. We'll eat at 4 o'clock in the afternoon. I say—we'll eat. No banquets. The best of your habitual fare, that's all. Get all the good fruit you can for breakfast. . . . Take all the glass chandeliers out of the Duke's rooms. They would seem absurd to him. Leave the sconces. Just have everything as neat as you always do and avoid the appearance of having gone to any special trouble. Let it be as though we had been living with you for ten years. Let the Duke have your silver washbowl and candles. He doesn't take coffee or anything of the kind. Remember, strict secrecy for the present. . . . Not a syllable to Merck.

August 21, 1779

To Charlotte

This week my official burdens seemed particularly heavy. In places where the peasant women carry victuals and other things in baskets on their heads, they have what they call "rings," made of cloth and stuffed with horse hair, to prevent the basket from cutting into their head! Sometimes I feel as though such little cushions were being taken away from me. . . . Not a soul enters my house except my former flirt, Corona Schröter, and we suit each other very well, for we are in the same case. My beloved is in Kochberg and *her* friend, Karl August, has gone on other paths. . . . I call on Knebel once in a while; I hear nothing from Herder. Meanwhile I'm tinkering with a play and one of these days you'll be back.

Garden House, September 6, 1779

From the Diaries

Received the decree creating me a Privy Councillor. Seized by the whirl of mortal things but also by a number of disagreeable personal feelings. Not seemly to record them. Observe in myself a fault of policy, which will be difficult to eradicate.

September 7, 1779

To Charlotte

The Duke has created me a Privy Councillor. Strange and dreamlike to have attained at thirty the highest honor within the reach of a commoner. One never goes farther than when one does not know whither one is going—thus spoke a mighty climber upon this earth.

September 10, 1779

To Charlotte

Farewell once more. We are off for Frankfurt and I know that you rejoice in the joy of my old people there. Write me to the well-known address.

September 20, 1779

Elisabeth Goethe to the Duchess Anna Amalia

September 18 was a great day for the old Father and Mother, who were so completely happy, that one might say that rarely has mortal man tasted of greater and purer joy than we two happy parents did on this day of jubilee. . . .

Our dear and gracious Duke descended from his carriage quite a ways from our house, in order to give us a big surprise. He came quite quietly to the door and rang the bell and strolled into the blue room. Now Your Highness can imagine me sitting at my round table and seeing the door open and in the next moment Cuddly Johnny [*a pet name from Goethe's childhood*] throws his arms about my neck, the while the Duke witnesses my maternal joy from a distance. Next imagine me, as though intoxicated, hastening forward to salute our prince, half weeping, half laughing, hardly knowing how to bear myself, seeing the handsome chamberlain also moved by my extreme joy—and imagine the meeting with the Father, which cannot be described—I was afraid he would die on the spot, on this very day, but indeed he has not wholly recovered his senses yet and I'm not a whit better off than he. Your Highness can easily imagine how perfectly blissful we have been these days. Merck came, too, and behaved fairly well, though he can't quite give up his rôle of Mephistopheles [*the Devil in* Faust]. But we're used to that. All the things that happened in connection with the handsome chamberlain and with the Privy Councillor Goethe, how the noble young ladies of the city carried on and tried to make conquests, and did not succeed—all that was worthy of being put in a play. . . .

Now all our hearts are set upon the return of our guests hither. God bring them back happy and well and then there will be a mighty drinking of precious old Rhine wine from our noblest goblets.

Frankfurt, September 20, 1779

To Charlotte

We arrived on a very beautiful evening and were soon surrounded by friendly faces. My old friends and acquaintances were truly glad. I did find my father sadly changed, quieter and with failing memory; but my mother has all her old force and loving kindness.

To Charlotte

Calm as a quiet brook we flow through the world. Today is a lovely day and everything has been favorable. On this journey I am recapitulating all my previous years and see old acquaintances, and God knows what the balance will be when I make up the accounting. The trip is doing the Duke great good. Switzerland is ahead of us and we hope to look about among those great phenomena and to bathe our souls in the sublimity of nature.

September 25, 1779

Last evening I took horse and rode from Rheinzabern to Sesenheim, while the others continued on their way, and found the family there, just as I had left it eight years ago, and was received with all due kindness. The second daughter of the house loved me more than I deserved once upon a time and far more than others, to whom I have given much passion and true feeling. I was forced to leave her at a moment when it all but cost her her life. Delicately she passed over the ill-health which even today remains of that period and has behaved with extraordinary sweetness from that moment on when we almost bumped into each other on the threshold of her house. I must say of her that she did not seek even by the slightest reference to awaken the old feelings in my heart. She led me into the well-remembered arbor and sat there with me and that was all. There was a beautiful full moon above us. . . . I stayed the night and left at dawn. Friendly faces bade me farewell, so that from now on I can think with contentment of that little corner of the world and can live at peace with the reconciled spirits who dwell there.

September 26, 1779

At noon we were in Strassburg. I went to see Lili and found that pretty monkey playing with a seven-week-old baby. Her mother was there, too. Here, also, I was received with surprise and joy. I inquired after all things and sniffed around in all corners and discovered to my delight that the good creature is very happily married. From all I hear her husband is a good, sensible, busy man, very well to do, of a highly respected family and imposing social position. So that she has a handsome house and all she needs. The husband was away. I stayed for dinner. After dinner the Duke and I went to look at the Cathedral and in the evening saw a play with admirable music by Paesiello. Afterwards I dropped in to see Lili once more and left by bright moonlight.

◇◇◇◇◇

Emmendingen, September 28, 1779

Today I am near the grave of my sister. Her household is like a picture from which a beloved figure has been painted out. Johanna, who has taken her place, and my brother-in-law and various friends are as close to me as they once were. Her children are comely, cheerful and well. From here we go to Basle. No word from you yet, though other letters have been forwarded from Frankfurt.

Thun, October 8, 1779

To Lavater

The rumor will have come to you, dear friend, that I am in your vicinity. So far as the season permits, we hope to climb the glaciers. Next, though by a détour, we'll come to you. . . .
The blessings of my God, to Whom I have ever remained faithful, have been rich but in secret, for my fate is wholly hidden from the eyes of men. They see nothing of it and hear no echo of it. What can be revealed of it, I shall be happy to entrust to you.

October 8, 1779

Elisabeth Goethe to the Duchess Anna Amalia

I found Cuddly Johnny changed much to his advantage. He looks healthier and in every respect more manly. But his moral character has remained entirely the same, which delighted all his old acquaintances extremely. They found their old friend once more, and you can imagine how it charmed me to see how they all fell in love with him again, all my kith and kin and women friends and acquaintances and also my aged mother. Now everybody, of course, wanted to see Goethe's Duke and so my drawing room was constantly crowded with people who were waiting for His Serenity to come down the stairs. When he did come down, he was most affable to everyone and let them all gaze their fill and chatted with this one and that one, so that all those present were extremely pleased. I would have to write Your Highness a chronicle and no letter, were I to relate to you all that took place at our house during those five most happy days. They were indeed days of very solemn joy to us, of which may God grant us more. Keenly as I look forward to the return of our visitors, yet the fatal thought of the parting that will come flies like an arrow into my heart. But I must not think of that and darken my joy.

Lauterbrunnen, October 9, 1779

To Charlotte

Night is falling and we are at the parson's house. This is a widely spread-out village, which gets its name from the many springs which here pour down from the crags. . . .
Yesterday in Berne the hairdresser took a long time over me. I looked for some people whom I couldn't find and so had occasion to stroll through the city. It is the handsomest we have seen; the dignified, neat houses are built of a grayish white sandstone, each like the other. The cleanliness and equality of status are very pleasing. . . .
Some days ago, on board of a cantonal ship, we saw the island in the lake, to which Rousseau fled, when he was expelled from Geneva.

Thun, October 14, 1779

Our remarkable tour of the Bernese glaciers is at an end. . . . Had I been alone I would have climbed higher and descended deeper, but the Duke being with me I must set an example of moderation.

◇◇◇◇◇

Berne, October 16, 1779

Yesterday I got your letter dated September 25. That shows how far apart we are. . . . It will be some time before we see each other again.

◇◇◇◇◇

Payerne, October 20, 1779

This morning we left Berne, after a thorough view of it and after having met several interesting people. . . . We take little trips, as curious travelers are accustomed to do. . . . All through I am calm and feel right well. Whenever constant change plays a thousand varied melodies upon my psaltery, why, I am gay enough. It's all agreeing with the Duke, too.

◇◇◇◇◇

Lausanne, October 23, 1779

We drove to Vevay and I could not restrain my tears when I gazed over toward all those places which the eternal solitary Rousseau peopled with the creatures of his heart. . . . We bathed in the lake and ate dinner and drove back to town.

◇◇◇◇◇

Geneva, October 28, 1779

The past few days we made a very happy excursion, climbing to the highest peaks of the Jura.

◇◇◇◇◇

Geneva, November 2, 1779

I never suspected that the French had been so enchanted by my *Werther*. I get many compliments on all sides and I tell people that these compliments are wholly unexpected. Next they ask me: why don't I write another book just like that. I answer: God forbid that I should ever be in the situation to write such another book and so to be able to write it. Nevertheless, this echo from far places arouses my own interest in my scribblings. Perhaps I will be more industrious in future and not waste so many fruitful hours.

In the Capuchin Convent on St. Gotthard,
November 13, 1779

For the second time in my life I am in this room upon this height—let me not say with what thoughts. On this occasion, too, I will not let Italy tempt me. A journey there now would not serve the Duke well, nor were it well to stay away from home longer and not to see you again. All things cause me to avert my eye for the second time from that promised land which, nevertheless, I hope to see before I die, and lead my spirit back toward my own poor roof, under which I shall see you at my fireside more happily than ever and serve you a good roast, the while stories of brave undertakings, decisions, joys and difficulties will make brief the winter evenings.

Zürich, Middle of November, 1779

Feeling gay and well we came to Zürich several days ago. From the Gotthard we sailed across the Lake of Lucerne, went to Schwiz and the city of Lucerne, and took horse from there here. . . . I have your letter from Kochberg. By this time I hope you are back in Weimar and are preparing a friendly reception for us on the part of all good spirits, for indeed my soul longs to go home.

Zürich, November 30, 1779

To Josias von Stein

Charlotte's husband, 1735-1793, Baron Kochberg, Master of the Horse from 1764 to his death.

It's really quite handsome of you, dear Stein, to continue to give us news of the amusing conditions in our beloved city. Don't be too bored while we are away and do write us something to Frankfurt, for which city we are soon leaving. We have been in Zürich for quite a little while and have been leading an agreeable life with Lavater, seeing all the curiosities and drawings and engravings and people and animals. We are living at a very lovely inn which stands beside a bridge and has a charming view of river, lake and mountains. The food is good and so are the beds. . . . Do ask your wife to read some of my travel letters to the Duchess.

Schafhausen, December 7, 1779

To Charlotte

Lavater surprised us here. He managed to get free and arrived yesterday. Together we view the Falls of the Rhine. The weather was dark, yet one imagines the Falls to be more powerful every time one sees them. We had a mighty discussion concerning the nature of the sublime which, however, I shall neglect to record.

Karlsruhe, December 20, 1779

To Charlotte

Since our letters no longer had time to follow us to Switzerland, many of them are still waiting in Frankfurt. Here, however, I received four of your letters on the same day. . . .
In Stuttgart we witnessed the graduation exercises of the Military Academy. The Duke of Würtemberg was very handsome in the treatment of our Duke, without violating the latter's incognito, and showed him every possible attention.

Recollections of Karoline von Wolzogen

Frau von Wolzogen, née von Lengefeld, 1763-1847, the sister-in-law of Friedrich Schiller, 1759-1805, the greatest of German poetic dramatists and Goethe's closest friend and literary ally from 1794 until his own death. He was the son of a poor army barber-surgeon and in 1779 a cadet in the Military Academy at Stuttgart.

How glad he would have been to approach the celebrated man of genius and how much one glance, one word would have meant to him at that time. But Goethe could have had no faintest suspicion that a spirit was saluting him who, in a period yet far off, was to unfold itself toward him in purest friendship.

Mannheim, December 22, 1779

To Charlotte

We left Karlsruhe early yesterday. Boredom is settling down on us more heavily from hour to hour. My God, what a paradise Weimar is, to be sure.

1780

Darmstadt, January 1, 1780

To Charlotte

Since we have been wandering about from Court to Court and mingling with the so-called great of the world, there's no impulse to write. . . . The Duke is cheerful and rather in his element, behaves admirably and makes excellent remarks. I can't say as much for myself. Once and for all, there is a gap between me and this entire nation, and communion forced upon one is a crippled thing. I behave as tolerably as I can.

Homburg, January 3, 1780

We continue to trot from Court to Court, freezing, bored to death, eating ill and drinking worse. I'm really sorry for these people; they have more than a suspicion how it is with them and a stranger fills them with dread. All their arrangements are bad and they have usually surrounded themselves with fools and rogues.

Garden House, January 17, 1780

From the Diaries

Everybody very well satisfied with the Duke. They praise us now and call our trip a masterpiece, an epic undertaking! 'Tis luck that hands out names while things remain forevermore the same.

Garden House, January 18, 1780

Made the proper arrangements for Krafft. Settled other details one by one. I must not rest until I've caught up with all unfinished matters. There are always new ones. Attended the Military Commission meeting. Found things in good order.

February 13, 1780

To Jakob Friedrich, Baron von Fritsch

I am taking the liberty of addressing a request to Your Excellency. For long I have had occasion to desire that I might belong to the Society of Free Masons. This desire has become more vivid during our recent journey. It has been, at times, my lack of membership in this Society, which has prevented me from entering into closer relations with persons whom I highly esteem. It is this social motivation which prompts me to seek reception into the Society. To whom could I more properly address myself with this request than to Your Excellency?

February 29, 1780

To Charlotte

It's very nice indeed that we are exchanging our old furnishings. I thank you for what you sent. I might have come along yesterday, but when I got home sleep overwhelmed me and I could do no more.

March 6, 1780

To Lavater

Your Albrecht Dürer reproductions have finally arrived. . . . Daily
I hold the work of this artist more precious than gold or silver. When
one realizes profoundly his truth and sublimity and even grace, one
sees that only the early Italians can equal him. But let us not say
that out loud. . . .
Henceforth keep my letters in proper order and have them bound. I
am doing the same with yours. Time passes and the little that remains to us should be guarded with due order. . . .
The Duke has had his hair cut short; 'tis the latest style of decora-
tion. I'll send you a silhouette of him for fun.

March 10, 1780

To Charlotte

Thank you for a token of your being alive and loving me. All I can
say in reply to your dear request is that I took a long walk this morning, that Knebel annoyed me terribly by causing a hell of a confusion, as though there were no rehearsal today. See you this evening.

March 21, 1780

To Charlotte

After my long walk this morning I'd like to have a good dinner at
your house. So if you're dining at home I'll come in and bring you
lilies of the valley.

March 23, 1780

To Wieland

While reading your poem "Oberon" I desired, again and again, to
bear witness to my applause and pleasure in the most lively fashion.
There is so much that I would say to you that I shall probably never
say any of it. . . . I wish that you could receive at the hands of a
friend the reward which both your contemporaries and posterity will
surely bestow upon you.

Garden House, March 26, 1780

From the Diaries

Early to Tiefurt on foot. Very varied thoughts and reflections concerning the concatenation of life and the inevitability of fate. 'Tis strange! I have done many things, which I would prefer not to have done and yet, had they not been done, indispensably good results would have been lost. It is often as though a spirit darkened our insight, in order that we might make mistakes to the advantage of ourselves and of others.

Garden House, March 29, 1780

In a mood of cleaning up and putting things in order all this day. Wrote many letters and made everything neat.

March 30, 1780

To Charlotte

Last night my old flirt, Corona Schröter, came like a comet and dragged me from my usual orbit to her house. A lot of bad temper was shown at the rehearsal, especially the author and the leading lady seemed unable to agree. I have opened Aeolus' bag of the winds halfway and sundry passions started hissing out. But I've kept the most powerful for the first night. I'll work hard this morning in order to deserve a kind word from you at dinner.

Garden House, March 31, 1780

From the Diaries

Rinsed off the twilight of sleep with fresh air and water. Nevertheless I yearn for repose and would gladly have puttered around. Pulled myself together and went on dictating the account of the Swiss journey. Council session announced. Luck seems to be on my side in that, within a few days, I'll be able to shake off a lot of horrible annoyances that have been a drag on me. *Nemo coronatur nisi qui certa-verit ante.* [*No one is crowned who has not first contended.*]

Garden House, April 1, 1780

Dined with the Duke. Have drunk no wine for three days. Must be careful to leave British beer alone. I'd be very happy, if I could give up wine entirely. . . . Duke came again in the evening and, since we're none of us in love any more and the top layer of the lava has cooled off, our talk was very cheerful and seemly. Of course one mustn't look down the cracks; in them the fire burns on.

Garden House, April 2, 1780

Sometimes I'm tempted, like the Greek Polycrates, to throw my dearest treasure into the river to placate the gods. Everything I touch seems to succeed. Read account of my Swiss journey to the Dowager Duchess. Wieland has an incredibly clear insight into one's artistic intentions, achievements, failures and successes.

April 3, 1780

To Merck

I'll answer at once your letter which came in care of the Duke yesterday, so that you may hear from me once again. I managed to recover nicely from a recent illness. I didn't feel quite well even in Frankfurt and during those chilly receptions at the Courts. . . . I'm perfectly well again. . . . Several plays and novels are more or less in a state of development. . . . I wish you would write the Duke occasionally. It entertains him.

April 8, 1780

To Charlotte

Forgive me yesterday's darkness in my soul. On such occasions I am like a somnambulist. You summon him and he falls down all the storeys of the house. You're quite right. And since we're trying to get along without each other, we may end by living on dew, like grasshoppers.

April 14, 1780

To Charlotte

I found it insufferable not to be able to see you yesterday. If I hadn't had tight shoes on, I would have walked over to your house. Dining with the Dowager Duchess today. I'm sending you three violets. Slowly the spring approaches.

Garden House, April 15, 1780

From the Diaries

I drink almost no wine. Observe a daily gain in judgment and skill in matters of the active life. Yet I seem to myself like a bird entangled in a snare; I know I have wings and may not use them. That will come, too. Meanwhile I find history refreshing and play around with a drama or a novel.

◇◇◇◇◇

Garden House, April 22, 1780

Suffered like Prometheus.

◇◇◇◇◇

Garden House, April 30, 1780

For the first time since its publication I read my *Werther* through and wondered at myself.

May 1, 1780

To Charlotte

I send you here the highest and the lowest that exists—a hymn and a pig pen. Love unites all.

Erfurt, May 2, 1780

To Charlotte

I send you this greeting by a mounted messenger on his way to Weimar. The weather is wonderful. Spring is in full bloom here and I hope to benefit in body and soul in the free air. Remain faithful to my valley and realize that I often converse with you. On this trip I am going over my entire situation: what has been done, what is to be done, the activities of my little world, my writing and my love.

Erfurt, May 5, 1780

To Charlotte

We have been riding about the land and have seen bad roads, on which much money has been spent without improving them. But in the quietude of the country have found good people and have exercised both body and soul. . . . An hundred plans are slowly coming to life within me. . . . Tomorrow I'll be dining with you.

Garden House, May 6, 1780

From the Diaries

No one except he who is willing to deny himself utterly, is worthy of ruling or can do so. . . . What a pity about Krafft. He sees his failings so clearly and can do nothing about them. If he had a job he would have the best intentions and yet create nothing but confusion. Hence his fate. I won't abandon him; he serves me in some fashion and is, after all, a noble soul. . . . I am gradually filled with great confidence. Please God that I may deserve it. I don't want what is easy, but what I truly desire. No one knows the burden that others are to me and that I am to myself. The best thing about me is that profound inner stillness in which I live and grow, despite the world, and with which I gain what that world can never take from me, though it use fire and sword.

Pentecost, 1780

To Charlotte

Would you be so kind as to send me over three chocolate cups and chocolate enough for three persons? Callers are coming. To dinner I invite myself to your house.

May 18, 1780

To Charlotte

Wouldn't it have been curious if you had been one of the two seated figures in white, whom I carefully avoided on the Esplanade night before last. First I thought it must be a pair of lovers, which ought not to be disturbed; later I thought I distinguished two women who seemed strange in that place in their white garments. By that time I had walked too far to satisfy both my curiosity and the demands of good manners.

June 4, 1780

To Charlotte

Have a happy outing. I expect you this evening. Ask Stein to send my horse this afternoon to Erfurt and to let me have another tomorrow morning on which to leave here, so that my mount there will be fresh.

Gotha, June 6, 1780

To Charlotte

I'd pay money if I could get that chapter of *Wilhelm Meister* written down. But it seems easier at this moment for me to jump into the fire. I might be able to dictate it, if I could take a secretary along. Between an hour in which things come quite alive to me and such an hour as this in which I write, the difference is as between dream and waking.

June 14, 1780

To Kestner

It's really very agreeable that we communicate with each other again. I thought of you both several days ago and wanted to ask how you were faring. . . . You must know that in addition to my seat in the Privy Council I have assumed the directorship of the War Department and the Department of Roads. . . . Thus my writing has become subordinate to life. Yet, profiting by the example of the King of Prussia, who devoted several hours daily to the playing of the flute, I likewise permit myself an occasional exercise of my talent.

June 14, 1780

To Charlotte

At my desk. 'Tis raining and the wind plays its tune in my trees. I seek you and I find you not, follow you and cannot hold you. This is the hour at which I am accustomed to see you daily and rest myself and refresh myself by talking to you from the compulsions of the day. Yesterday there arrived the ring that you sent me; I thank you for so beautiful a symbol. It is a strange ring, for now it seems too large for my finger and next moment it seems to fit perfectly. . . . All things proceed as they must. I apply myself wholly to discover and to do what is appropriate in given situations, be they high or low. . . . My greatest difficulty is that I cannot lay hold upon the vulgar in its true nature. It's incomprehensible why this enormous chasm separates me from what the meanest of human beings easily understands, regards with resignation and executes. . . .

June 15, 1780

To Charlotte

My roses will not bloom and my strawberries will not ripen. They seem to know that there is no haste. Stein tells me he is sending you a package tomorrow; so I am adding this note.

Garden House, June 22, 1780

From the Diaries

If only the fair weather would last forever and if only peoples' souls were not so poverty-stricken, and if only the rich were not so awkward, and if only . . . .

June 24, 1780

To Charlotte

My unspeakable longing for you teaches me how I love you. This longing makes to throb that old pain, which I felt that first year, when I could not see you at Kochberg. I thought it had healed; now it reminds me, like an old melody, of that period.

Garden House, June 25, 1780

From the Diaries

Attended to sundry matters. Rode to Ettersburg. There was an alarm of fire in the villages. Rode over. The wind drove the flames through the dry trees. Worked to save the church. My eyelids got singed and the water in my boots began to boil. The firemen did their work well and properly.

June 30, 1780

To Charlotte

Sometimes it seems to me as though my knees would give way under me. The cross that one bears alone is too heavy. If you don't come back soon or if you leave again for Kochberg, I must arrange my life in some other fashion. I have acquired the habit of a love and confidence that are illimitable. Since you have been gone I haven't uttered a word that has come from my deepest self.

July 24, 1780

To Lavater

I felt as though someone had given me a present, when I learned that my *Iphigenie* gave you pleasure. Our lives are close, but our opinions and imaginings are very divergent. One could compare us to two marksmen who, leaning against each other back to back, aim after wholly different targets. And so I never permit myself to hope that my writings can mean anything to you.

When you were talking about Wieland's "Oberon," you used the word talent, as though it were the contrary of genius, or, if not that, at least quite subordinate thereto. We are to consider, however, that veritable talent can be nothing but the expressive speech which genius uses. I don't mean to split hairs; I know in general what you mean to say, but I pluck you by the sleeve as a reminder.

August 10, 1780

Karl August to Charlotte

I'm going to be in the house all day, and so perhaps it wouldn't be amiss if you came over around 6 o'clock and brought our author along. The birds could be roasted in the ashes and twitter and hiss, and I would be able to obey a certain necessity the more easily, which the rhubarb the doctor prescribed imposes on me.

August 11, 1780

To Krafft

I appreciate your anxiety concerning my health. But I beg of you not to indulge in that either. Anxiety has never yet kept anyone among the living. Accustomed to try to do on each day what that day demands and what my insight, capacity and strength permit, I live on unconcerned for the duration of life, mindful of the words of that sage who said that even three truly well-employed hours would suffice.

August 15, 1780

To Charlotte

After looking for you twice at your house in vain, false rumors of your whereabouts lured me to the park, across the meadows, finally to my own garden. I'll spend a quiet evening now thinking of you and reflecting concerning the day and the morrow.

Garden House, August 26, 1780

From the Diaries

Walked in my garden early and reflected on what has come to pass and what has not come to pass in that thirty-first year of mine, which is drawing to a close. What I have accomplished, wherein I have improved.

August 26, 1780

Lavater to Charlotte

Since Goethe writes me that he is about to take a brief journey with the Duke, I address myself to you. . . . My request of you is that you take the enclosed drawing of Sir Thomas More by Holbein, have it neatly mounted and framed and hang it up in your own room. When he comes back, present it to him. He expects it. I begin with a commission! Wherewith am I to end? With all my thanks for your kind greeting which Knebel conveyed.

Ilmenau, September 6, 1780

To Charlotte

I have made my bed for the night upon the highest mountain of this region. It is called the Gickelhahn or, if you prefer, Alectruogallonax, in a more resonant language. Here I escape the confusions, the complaints, the desires, the irremediable muddle-headedness of mankind. If all the thoughts which passed through my mind today could be recorded, there would be some fine things among them.
I visited the cave of Hermannstein, where we once were together. Again and again I kissed the *S* which I carved into the porphyry. The stone exhaled its earthy fragrance and seemed to give me some kind of answer.

September 6, 1780

WANDERER'S NIGHT-SONG

(Carved on the wall of a little wooden hunting lodge.)

> O'er all the hill-tops
> Is quiet now,
> In all the tree-tops
> Hearest thou
> Hardly a breath;
> The birds are asleep in the trees:
> Wait; soon like these
> Thou too shalt rest.

Henry Wadsworth Longfellow

Gickelhahn near Ilmenau, September 7, 1780
To Charlotte

The sun has risen; the weather is bright and clear. There was a little wind in the night and it should be fine for my plans today. I am climbing higher and higher into the mountains. I send you a good morning before I start out.

Ilmenau, 7 o'clock that evening

My excursion is happily at an end. I am sitting and resting. We climbed to the highest heights and crept into the very depths of the earth. . . . Good night. I am tired. . .

Ilmenau, September 8, 1780

Well rested after a ten-hour sleep. O that it were my calling to be ever moving and living under the open sky. Gladly would I suffer all the difficulties which this kind of life entails. . . . Mankind is cursed with the curse pronounced on the serpent of old; they creep on their bellies and devour the dust. To wash and cleanse me I have been reading Greek. . . .
I have made some curious observations on the subject of the Duke's diet—what he may not eat, what he permits himself to eat and in regard to which items he follows doctor's orders. In spite of his great good sense, he has unconsciously intentional black and confused spots here and there. . . .

Ilmenau, September 9, 1780

The Duke's bowels are not yet in order. He takes care of himself and then fools himself and stops taking care of himself and so many good days of his life are wasted.
This morning we had all the murderers and thieves and receivers of stolen goods of this region brought before us for questioning and con-

frontation. At first I refused to come. For I am revolted by uncleanness. Yet it offers a great study of humanity and of physiognomies and one is tempted to be quite silent and to give God the honor, in Whom alone there are power and understanding etc. to all eternity. Amen. There was, for instance, a son who accused himself and his father of complicity in a murder, giving all the circumstances. There was a father who denied to his son's face the truth of the latter's testimony. There was a man who, at a time of famine, had to endure to see his wife perish at his side in their barn. Since there was no one else to bury her, he did so himself. Now this grievous thing is turned into an accusation against him, as though it pointed to his having murdered her. Etc. Etc.

Thereafter I went back into the mountains. We ate and saw the birds of prey soaring above us and I had the impulse to write, now to you, now on my novel, but nothing came of it. Yet I would that I could record for you a long conversation between the Duke and myself, occasioned by the delinquents we had seen, considering the measure by which one could mete the value of human deeds. In the evening Stein sat down next to me and told some anecdotes of old times rather well, of the miseries of the Court, of children and women etc.

◇◇◇◇◇

Zillbach, September 12, 1780

We arrived here very late because, as Stein correctly remarked, when boredom was creeping up on him, princes can never get away from a place on time. At the moment of leaving, our Serenity had to try new rifles and pistols. I had my Euripides and enjoyed the otherwise unpalatable delay. . . .

Whenever I awaken from my dream, I find that I still love you and long for you. Tonight as we were riding along and saw the lit windows of a house ahead, I thought: if only she were there to be our hostess. This is a rotten hole and yet if I could quietly live here all winter long with you, I'd like it very well. . . .

It was written in the stars that I was to go to the barber in Ilmenau this morning for a shave. On the way my horse took fright and stampeded; afterwards I sank into a marshy place on the meadows. Yet I managed to write some passages on the novel. Wouldn't it be nice if I could have just four continuously quiet weeks and finish the first part to show my friends?

September 20, 1780

To Lavater

The daily task which fate has assigned me and which becomes both lighter and heavier day by day, and which demands my whole being, waking or dreaming—this self-assumed duty becomes daily more precious to me. . . . Nor must I loiter or delay. The years go on and perhaps fate will break me in my middle course and my Tower of Babel will remain blunt and unfinished. At least I would have men say that its design was bold; if I live, please God that my powers suffice to complete it.

I am much aided by the talisman of that beautiful love with which Charlotte graces my existence. She has, as it were, become the heir of my mother, my sister, a sweetheart, and a bond has been established, like those woven by nature itself.

October 10, 1780

To Charlotte

The last thing you said to me this morning hurt me deeply; had the Duke not been with us, I would have wept. Evil is heaped upon evil! Oh yes, it is a sort of rage against one's own flesh when one who is unhappy seeks relief through affronting what is dearest to him. Very well, if I could be sure that these attacks are only the result of moodiness. . . . I won't be satisfied until you have given me an exact accounting of what has come to pass and the assurance that henceforth you will try to persuade yourself to assume so sisterly an attitude, that it cannot be so suddenly transformed. Otherwise I shall have to avoid you at the very times when I need you most. It's quite frightful to have to ruin the best hours of one's life, the moments we spend together and to be, as I was too, so blind and so stubborn, when all the while I would be glad to pluck out each one of my hairs separately if thereby I could please you. . . .

October 11, 1780

To Merck

Your letter reached me on a little journey. I was accompanying the Duke on a visit to certain districts which belong to him in Franconia. One of his officers has been working in those districts for six months. It gave me an immense pleasure to see something accomplished and an order carried out more precisely and swiftly and extensively than the Ducal decree required. The Duke was highly delighted, too. What has been done is that irrigation ditches have been dug and the water preserved instead of being wasted. . . .

The more you knew of the Duke in his capacity as chief of the country and of his own house, the more would you pity him. No tongue can express the hardships he has to endure. The capacity to rule is never innate. He who has inherited it, if he really means to possess it, must win it by bitterer efforts than any conqueror.

October 12, 1780

To Charlotte

It is extraordinary and yet true, that I'm as jealous and stubborn as a small boy when you are very friendly to others. For the last few days I have been restless except when I was asleep. But that's most healthy for me.

October 13, 1780, Midnight

When your note was handed me, your messenger was already gone. So soon as the sun rises you'll hear from me. From 6 o'clock on this morning I've been busy. If only one didn't need to sleep and if one interesting employment followed on the heels of another. The moon is infinitely beautiful. I walked through the new paths of the park in the exquisite night and heard the elves singing.

> At mid of night when mortals are sleeping,
> Then shines for us the moon,

Our star to us is bright;
We wander in singing
And dance our delight.

At mid of night when mortals are sleeping,
On meadows, by the alders,
Our spaces for us gleam,
And wandering and singing
We dance us our dream.

October 29, 1780

To Charlotte

I don't know why, but I have the impression that you haven't forgiven me yet. Whether I deserve forgiveness I don't know; I certainly deserve your pity. . . .

But, please, let us have no more dashes in your letters. You may be sure that I always fill them in with the worst things possible. When you get back you will, I am sure, tell me the whole story; I, too, have a rather curious and catastrophic matter to confess to you. I think that the tree of our kinship and friendship was planted long enough ago and is firmly enough rooted to resist the ill effects of season and of weather. You may believe me when I say that the people who concern themselves with our affairs would not do so, if they had better business of their own. At least they would do it in quite a different spirit.

November 7, 1780

To Charlotte

Five years ago today that I arrived in Weimar. It grieves me that we cannot commemorate the event together. Yesterday the weather was wondrously beautiful. Having been reassured of your love, I feel altogether different. We ought to get better from year to year, as Rhine wines do. In quietude I am recapitulating my life during these five years and find them full of marvelous stories. Truly, man is like a somnambulist, who climbs over the most dangerous places while asleep.

November 16, 1780

To Knebel

I do thank you most warmly for your kind words. They reach me over my play *Tasso,* at which I am working the more happily, since my immediate and, I may say, my only public, is most encouraging. I long for the hour in which I'll be able to send it to you.

November 23, 1780

To Charlotte

Tell me how you've slept and that you love me. The doctor sent me a nasty addition to my breakfast. Give the messenger who brings you this the first act of *Tasso;* I want the copying to go on. The first scene of the second act is almost done.

November 30, 1780

To Charlotte

If you would like, I'll have the saddle of venison roasted and bring it over to you, so that we may consume it together. Invite a guest, if you like. Today I wrote from dawn on.

December 12, 1780

To Charlotte

I meant to test my love for you once more today by renouncing the pleasure of seeing you. But I think it will be better to eat my lentil soup with you today out of the patty shells. So I'll be with you at noon.

December 17, 1780

To Charlotte

After I left you yesterday I took a very long walk. It was very beautiful and I was quite snug in my warm fur coat. I had a long interview with my trees and I told them how dear to me you are.

December 31, 1780
To Charlotte

Thank you, my dearest! Had this day not been so full of business from the beginning, I would have asked, whether you want me to come for dinner. But Sunday here is always like a fair. . . . I'm sorry for my Tasso. There he lies on my desk and gives me a friendly glance. But I haven't the time to bake wheaten bread, when I must furnish so much hardtack. Yesterday a man said to me: I wish I could be as young as you are once again; I'd make better use of my youth.

1781

January 1, 1781
To Charlotte

I was already awake and thinking of what I could say to you or send you for the New Year, when your package arrived. I thank you a thousand times. I cannot send you verses, for my prosaic life swallows them as the sands do running waters. Only the love of poetry cannot be taken from me. The charming receptacle you sent me I shall always keep by me. In return I send you something sweet which, alas, by its very nature, is only agreeable and perishable.

January 11, 1781
To Krafft

I think I can tell you to put all anxiety aside, since I can promise you 200 thalers for this year. I'll send you 50 thalers every quarter. But you must try to get along with that. Don't have scruples about every small detail; allocate the money as you like. Do let me know soon that your pains have left you entirely.

January 18, 1781

To Karl August

After mature reflection I decided, as was inevitable, to stay home. It is not wise to leave an unprotected realm. And I know quite well that I wouldn't get away from Gotha so soon, but would have to spend the whole week there.

Things heap up here and I would really like, though it be in the very teeth of the devil, to get my literary affairs straightened out. When, in addition, I think of the drafts in the castle of Gotha and the chill, and that one is not sure of keeping either one's coat or shoes, I am thoroughly frightened back into my badger's hole. I have a morbid preference for it anyhow. May all good spirits accompany you.

January 25, 1781

To Karl August

Tomorrow morning *Iphigenie* will be put in rehearsal. We hope you will be satisfied with the stage set. . . . Apropos of artists, that horrid girl at the Court of your mother, the Duchess, turns out to be pregnant and asserts that a quite old man is the child's father. The Duchess is furious. . . . The Duchess Louise isn't very well, for which reason the tea on Tuesday was canceled. I haven't seen her and sent her your greeting by one of the ladies. . . . Last night during the concert given by your mother, the Duchess, I sat in another room and drank a whole bottle of champagne, which seems conducive to the practice of literature. There's some hope now that my play will be finished. . . . Nothing's going on in public affairs. The Ministers of State are taking sleigh rides. . . . I'm curious to know what success you had with your hunting. My own hunting was confined to a single raven whom I shot down yesterday with my good rifle from the tall ash tree near my cottage. He dropped like a sack.

January 31, 1781

To Krafft

You have done well to confess your state of mind to me so freely. Be sure that I interpret it all justly, though I am in no position to calm

your fears entirely. My budget, within which I must keep, if I am
not to end the year with debts, which would be most unseemly in
my position, simply does not permit me to give you more than 200
thalers. . . . If you make debts, it will be most disagreeable to me.
This baleful restlessness which torments you now has been the misfortune of your whole life. You were no more content when you had
1000 thalers to spend than you are now with the 200, because
you have never accustomed yourself to accept the limitations of
necessity. I do not mean this as a reproach. I feel for you and for
the discrepancy between your present and your former condition,
which you must feel very keenly. Nevertheless, quite briefly: you'll
get your 50 thaler every quarter; for the immediate present you will
get an advance. Do your best. Every *must* is hard, but it is the test
by which a man shows what his character is. Any fool can live arbi-
trarily.

February 3, 1781

To Charlotte

I am forced to stay at home today. If you don't take pity on me, I'll
have a dreary day. It would be sweet of you to have dinner with me;
I have a pheasant ready to be roasted.

February 8, 1781

To Charlotte

I feel only so-so. I slept well but had a nosebleed this morning, which
I attribute to a roast squab and a few glasses of wine which I con-
sumed after I left you last night.

February 11, 1781

To Krafft

Look, what I chide and regret in you is precisely that hypochondriac
excess of softness and that exaggerated sensibility, which inspired
your last letter. Is it becoming of you to say to me: I am to command
the tone in which your future letters to me are to be couched? Can
you imagine anyone giving such an order to a man of sincerity and
good sense? Is it kind of you that you rub it into me on every occasion that you're living on my bounty? . . . You can't, after all,

blame me for wanting you to be reasonably contented with what I give you, little though it is.

February 20, 1781

To Charlotte

Gotthold Ephraim Lessing, 1729-1781, the truly great critic, stylist, dramatist, author of *Nathan the Wise,* who laid the foundations of German literature.

No catastrophe could have touched me more deeply than the death of Lessing. Not fifteen minutes before the news came I was planning to visit him. It is difficult to estimate the grievousness of our loss. Council meeting today. I'm dining at home. I'll see you when the play is over. I don't feel like going into the theatre today.

February 28, 1781

To Charlotte

How did my tired one sleep? I got home at 2:30 but the intemperance seems to have agreed with me. I have to be at Court both at noon and at night today. Did you manage to take any of the flowers home with you? After you had gone I still paid court to the lady you know of and waltzed with her.

March 7, 1781

To Charlotte

We jest at death, and yet it is hard to be parted for even a brief period. While I was dressing I couldn't grasp the fact that I was not doing so in order to go to you. Riding will be hard today. Goodbye, my beloved.

Neunheiligen, March 8, 1781

To Charlotte

Yesterday, during the long ride, I pondered our whole story. It is strange enough. I likened my heart to the castle of a robber knight. You have taken possession of it; the mob has been driven out; now you consider it worth guarding, and one does guard one's possessions by being jealous of them. . . . Continue your good work and bind me closer to you day by day by this bond of love, friendship, need, passion and habit. We are indeed inseparable; let us continue to believe so and to say so.

Neunheiligen, March 10, 1781

To Charlotte

I am no longer surprised that princes are so mad and stupid and silly. Few of them have such good innate qualities as the Duke; few are surrounded by so many sensible and kind people who are their friends. Nevertheless, his improvement is not in proportion. Again and again the child and the donkey peep out. I think I see the reason. He really has a passion for what is good and right, but he is less comfortable with the good than he is with the awkward. He can be so sensible and so full of insight and understanding, and yet when he wants to have a good time, it has got to be something perfectly silly, if it's only making a mess of the wax candles. It goes to show what his deepest nature is. The frog is made to swim, even if from time to time he hops around on dry land.

Neunheiligen, March 12, 1781

To Charlotte

My soul has so grown into yours that, as you know, I am inseparably tied to you and neither height nor depth can separate me from you. I would there were some vow or sacrament, which could bind me to you visibly and according to some law. How precious that would be! And surely my novitiate was long enough for me to take all due thought. . . . The Jews have cords which they bind about their arms in the act of prayer. Thus I bind about my arm your dear cord when I address my prayer to you and desire you to impart to me your goodness, wisdom, moderation and patience.

March 28, 1781

To Charlotte

The enclosure was already sealed, when your dear little note arrived. I'm quite tolerable. If we lived in a better climate, much would be different. I'm a perfect human barometer. . . . I'm send-

ing you something for your breakfast. I beg of you to write me what
your plans are for tonight.

March 31, 1781

To Fritsch

In view of the approach of the meeting of the Lodge, may I once
more draw Your Excellency's attention to my case? Assuming my
conformity to all the rules of the Order unknown to me, I would,
nevertheless, if it is conformable to those rules, take further steps to
draw nearer to the essentials. I desire this for my own sake, as well as
for the sake of the brothers of the Order, who are sometimes embarrassed by having to treat me as a stranger. If it were possible, then,
to advance me at a proper moment, to the grade of Master, I would
be most appreciative. The efforts I have lately used to acquaint myself with all necessary facts concerning the Order have perhaps rendered me worthy of attaining that grade.

April 3, 1781

To Charlotte

Good morning, dearest. The rain has caused all my buds to open.
How did you sleep and what arrangements have you for the day?
Council meeting. I am dining at home.

April 9, 1781

To Lavater

The coming weeks of spring will be beautiful to me. Each morning
a new flower or bud receives me. The tranquil, pure, forever recurrent passionlessness of the world of plants often consoles me for the
misery of man—the moral misery and even more the physical.

April 19, 1781

To Charlotte

Since kind spirits visited me at home, I did not have to go abroad
to seek them. I worked on *Tasso;* if you would like to be my hostess,
I'll come over. Since all that *Tasso* says is addressed to you, I need
not write you more today.

April 22, 1781

To Charlotte

Fritz came while I was still in bed this morning. I'm going to work on *Tasso* today, I'm sure. Tell me your plans for today. The weather is divine, but a warm rain may fall later.

April 27, 1781

To Charlotte

Here is a letter which, if you think it is fitting, I want you to send to the Duke. Talk to him, too, and do not spare him. All I want is some tranquility and I want him to know where he stands. You can add that I told you I would not go traveling with him again. Use your accustomed wisdom and gentleness.

May 20, 1781

To Charlotte

I'm dining at home and I'm afraid you will be bidden to Court. Since the wind will prevent my mounting, I'd love to have you pick me up in your carriage. I'm sending you what you asked for.

May 30, 1781

To Bürger

I cannot better respond to your confidence than by entire frankness. You desire to change your condition; you believe that I can contribute to such a change.

Before I go into the matter, I would like to ask you to tell me what it is that makes your present situation oppressive and, indeed, unbearable; what precisely have you in view; what definite talent can you name, which will entitle you to an appointment and a salary? I have every reason and occasion to be most prudent when it comes to assuming responsibility for yet another human soul. All you can ever get for anyone is a minimum of subsistence and that, after all, can be found anywhere. I feel a double responsibility in your case to be completely frank and careful.

June 1, 1781

To Charlotte

The strawberries in my garden are more nimble than the roses. I send you the first to ripen. I don't believe there will be a session of the Council today. I'd like to dine with you. Last night I strolled with the party to your very windows and said good night to you in my heart. Herder was agreeable; if only he were that way oftener. I had a very sensible conversation with the Duke. In this world no one reaps a richer harvest than the playwright, and there are sages who say: Judge no one until you have been in his place.

June 17, 1781

Elisabeth Goethe to Her Son

Prince Constantine hasn't arrived yet. I will receive him in my usual manner with friendship and graciousness and tell you all that happens later on. The president of your Weimar Chamber and Seckendorf came to see me and seemed in good spirits. But since I knew that the former is no longer much of a friend of yours, I was extremely courteous to him but very careful not to fizz up in joy at the mere mention of your name, as is my custom. On the contrary, I behaved myself with such finesse, as though the greatest Court on earth had been my nurse. . . . Last Monday which, as you know, is my club night, when I got home my maids told me that Merck had been here and would come back to see me next day. I undressed and was about to sit down at my table—it was nearly 10 o'clock—when in came Merck. The lateness of his visit rather surprised me, and I got really anxious when he asked me, what *good* news I had from Weimar. "I have no news at all from Weimar. You know, Herr Merck, that our people there don't write so very often. But if you know something, please tell me. Surely, the doctor isn't ill?"—"No," said he, "as to that I know nothing. But at all events and under all circumstances you should try to get him back here. The beastly climate there is certainly not healthy for him. He has accomplished his chief purpose; the Duke is what he ought to be. As for the rest of the filthy business there—somebody else can attend to it; Goethe is far too good, etc. etc." Now imagine how I felt. So soon as I was alone

I began to imagine all kinds of horrors. I wanted to write to the Duke, to the Duchess Amalia and to you. If I hadn't had my hands full on Tuesday, something nasty would have happened. But by now the mail day had gone by. Friday, however, I was going to send a whole flight of letters. Well, Thursday brought *your* dear letter and headed me off. And since you write that you are well, my anxieties are allayed. My dear son, I am going to be brief. You must know best what is good for you. But since my situation here is now to be mistress of all affairs and since I could see to it that you could live a good and quiet life here without any obstacles, you can easily imagine how deeply it would pain me, if I knew you were wasting your health and strength in your present service. A shallow regret after the fact would put no flesh on my bones. I am no heroine and, like the clown in the old farce, I think life should be a handsome business. On the other hand to tear you out of the circle of your activities, when there is no need, would be equally foolish. You are the master of your fate; prove all things and choose what is best. All I want is not to have to reproach myself in the future whatever be the outcome. Now you know my thoughts. *Punctum*—period! To be sure, it would be lovely if you could come here for the Fair in autumn and we could have a really good talk about all these matters. But I leave that to you, too. Your father is a poor, sick man. His physical strength is still so-so, but his mind is going. Yet he is rather cheerful, except when boredom overcomes him; then it's pretty bad. He still takes great pleasure in the repairing of our lower storey. He shows people my drawing room, which is completed now, and tells them that I designed it all myself. That's nice, isn't it? Now I'm having the kitchen done over. That amuses him very much. I thank God that this notion came to me; it helps to pass the summer. May the winter take care of itself. If the Duchess Louise has a son, I'll pretend to be wild with joy. For Heaven's sake be sure to let me know the minute the baby is born.

June 22, 1781

To Lavater

Before I leave here for a little, I must write you once again. First of all, let me thank you, O most human of men, for your printed letters. It is natural enough that they are the best of your writings. As you foresaw, many people, even good ones, were offended by the printing of these letters, but you know best what you may do and are probably right in assuming that things are permitted you, which no one else dare do. . . .

As for the secret arts practiced by Cagliostro [*the notorious alchemist and impostor*], I must tell you that I am distrustful of all those tales. In my position I come upon traces, not to say upon definite information, concerning a great mass of lies, which winds its way in the darkness, of which you can have not the slightest suspicion. I assure you that our moral and political world is undermined by subterranean passages, cellars, *cloaca,* as a great city is accustomed to be, though no one ever thinks of these nor of the conditions of those who work or dwell underground. But he who has some knowledge of these matters, is not so astonished when, from time to time, the earth caves in in one place, smoke belches from another, and mysterious voices are heard in a third.

July 2, 1781

To Charlotte

We are mounted and ready to ride into the hills. I'm glad to get away from here this time. The ghosts of old days spoil my every hour. Nor did I want to climb the mountains which, too, have been stained by unpleasant memories.

Ilmenau, July 8, 1781

To Charlotte

Knebel will give you this letter and tell you how we have fared. . . . I long for you without admitting it to myself. My mind seems to cling to littleness and takes pleasure in nothing. Now worries get the upper hand, and now irritation. An evil genius uses this perspective from home to impress upon me the troublesome aspects of my situation and bids me save myself by flight. . . . Every evening I salute Mars, the red, as he rises over the pine-clad mountains outside my window. He must be standing right above my garden; soon I will see him there with you. . . . When I get really worried I get scared about your bad foot and about your children's cough. I suppose we're married, that is to say, united by a bond, of which the bill promises love and joy, but of which the balance sheet shows a cross and grief and misery. Regards to Stein.

July 22, 1781

To Charlotte

In love and longing I send you a few flowers and these rather slight plants. I'm having Corona to dine with me. I'd like to know your plans for this evening.

August 11, 1781

To His Mother

It was a very great joy to me to read the expression, written in your own hand, of your old and well-known opinions. I beg of you to have no anxiety on my account and to let your confidence be disturbed by no one. My health is far better than I had reason to hope in former times; if it suffices to let me accomplish at least the greater part of my duties, I have good cause to be satisfied. As for my situation here: in spite of real hardships, it has very much that is desirable, of which the best proof is that I can imagine no other, for which I would care to exchange it at present. Merck and others misjudge my condition completely. They see what I sacrifice, not what I gain. They cannot understand that I grow daily richer by the daily gifts I give away. You must remember that period at home before I came here. A continuance of such conditions would have been disastrous to me. The discrepancy between the narrowness and slow tempo of middle-class existence and the wideness and swiftness of my character would have driven me mad. How much better was it to be transported into a situation, to which I was thoroughly unequal, in which it was given me to get to know myself and others through faults committed by lack of understanding and by undue haste; in which, however, left to myself and to the mastery of my own fate, I had to pass tests, which may not be necessary to hundreds of people, but which were required by my development. And even now, how could I, being what I am, desire a happier situation than one which has, at least to me, an element of the infinite? For, even if I could say that I developed new capacities daily, clarified my notions, increased my power, broadened my knowledge, rectified my discernment and grew in courage, yet I would find daily occasion to use all these qualities in great things and in little. You see how far removed I am from the sort of morbid discomfort, which afflicts so many people in their station in life, and that only the most weighty considerations and the most unexpected accidents could persuade me to leave my post. In addition, it would be irresponsible toward my own self if I were to run away at a time when the trees I planted are in growth, when I may hope to separate the chaff from the wheat at harvest time, and so cheat myself of the shade and the fruits which are bound to come. Nevertheless, I want you to know, that a great part of the good courage with which I work springs from the thought, that these sacrifices are quite voluntary and that I needed but to order postchaise and horses, in order to find not only the needful, but the agreeable, as well as tranquility, under your roof. If I had not this sense of freedom; if, in hours of irritation, I would have to look upon myself as a serf and day laborer for the sake of my necessities, much, much, would be harder to bear. So let me hear from you that your good spirits do not desert you, despite Father's present condition. Continue to get as much change as your social life affords. It is not likely that I'll be able to get off this autumn; not, at all events, before the end of September. I'll try to be with you by the time the wine is being harvested.

August 20, 1781

Elisabeth Goethe to Lavater

I, for my part, am very well, thanks be to God. I am, as I was, cheerful and in good spirits. But the poor Councillor is much changed from what he was—especially his powers of mind are fading—memory, observation, all are gone. He leads a sort of vegetative life. Providence sees fit to lead me to our goal by various paths. For I need not tell so feeling a heart as yours, that I endure much suffering, especially since I have no compensation from my children. Everything is far, far away. I had flattered myself with the hope that my son would visit me this autumn, but nothing will come of it. He is too busy, with too many different things. As a small reparation he wrote me a magnificent letter. I shall seek to have my soul exercise the needed patience.

August 25, 1781

To Charlotte

I wish you a good morning and send you a letter from my mother, in order that you may delight in the fullness of life in it.
The poems are being copied out.

September 9, 1781

To Charlotte

The harpist is coming this evening, and so is Schröter. If you want to hear the songs, come—and bring whomever you like. Perhaps your mother, too. I'm going to have both of the hares as well as the grouse roasted, so that we may all have enough to eat.

September 20, 1781

To Charlotte

Tell me how you slept. I don't seem to be able to get rid of you. Give Fritz his share of the cake. The enclosure is your own. If you like, I'll have it printed in the Tiefurt *Journal,* and call it a translation from the Greek.

NIGHT THOUGHTS

You I pity, ill-fated constellations,
Beautiful with such heroic radiance,
Gladly guiding home the hard-pressed sailor,
Unrewarded or by gods or mortals:
For ye love not nor of love have knowledge!
Irresistibly eternal hours
Lead your ranks through heaven's wide expanses!
What a circling vast have you completed
While I in the arms of my beloved
Lay of midnight and of you forgetful.

Merseburg, September 22, 1781

To Charlotte

Goethe had taken the nine-year-old Fritz von Stein along with him on this trip.

With Fritz sitting at the same table, I've rigged up an office here.
He is perfectly sweet and well behaved. Our all-day ride went off
without a single incident. The eternal stubble fields tired Fritz, the
while my brooding mind took delight in sundry poems, which I will
send from here to the *Journal* and which, in that form, will pay their
respects to you.

October 1, 1781

To Charlotte

We got back at midnight tonight. Fritz is as good as he can be. I'll
tell you more about that. . . .
I have had silent dialogues with you and given much affection to
your boy. I have held him warmly and bedded him softly. . . .

1781

THE ERLKING

This version conforms precisely to the rhythmic treatment of the poem
in Schubert's famous setting. Opus I.

Who rideth so late through nightwind wild?
It is the father who holds his child.
He guards his darling safe in his arm,
He grasps him surely, he keeps him warm.

My son, why hidest in dread thou thy face?
Seest, father, not Erlking in yon place?
The Erlking yonder with crown and plume?—
My son, it is the checkered gloom.

"Thou lovely child, come go with me!
O fair the games between me and thee;
And gay the flowers the shore doth hold,
My mother hath many garments of gold."

My father, my father, and dost thou not hear
The Erlking's promises soft at mine ear?—
Be tranquil, darling, quiet in mind,
In withered foliage rustles the wind.—

"O charming boy, wilt thou come with me,
For my graceful daughters to wait on thee,
For my daughters nightly their revels will keep,
To rock thee and dance thee and sing thee to sleep."

My father, my father, and dost thou not mark
Erlking's wan daughters in yonder dark?—
My son, my son, I see it so well,
How greyly the willows weave us their spell.—

"Enchanting boy, thy beautiful form I desire,
And coms't thou not freely the end will be dire!"
My father, my father, his touch I have felt!
A mortal wound hath the Erlking dealt.—

The father shudders, rides swiftlier on,
He hears beside him the moans of his son.
He gains the court with pain and dread;
Against his bosom the child was dead.

October 3, 1781

To Charlotte

You forbade me to bring you a present. I was looking sadly at a number of handsome objects, when good luck played into my hands a stone, such as jewelers rarely display. The carving on it represents Psyche with a butterfly against her breast. It is of yellow agate.

October 9, 1781

The only one, Lotte, whom thou canst truly love,
All thine must be, thou sayest—as is just.
And he is wholly thine.
For since I am afar,
Seems from the swiftness of living's
Rattling tumult to rise
A delicate veil through which I behold thy form:
It shines on me kindly and true,

As through the North Light's vibrating radiance
The eternal star-beams pierce.

October 19, 1781

To Charlotte

Your letter was brought to me just as I was about to write you and
send you thirty larks. I hope you and your guests will relish them.
Give my regards to the Duke.

November 14, 1781

To Charlotte

> The house he proposed to rent was the stately and reasonably spacious
> one on the Frauenplan or, perhaps, Lady's Square, which Goethe was
> to occupy for the rest of his life. It consisted of two storeys and an attic
> floor.

I have made all proper arrangements with the landlord. By Easter
the present tenant will move out. I'll have all summer to furnish
and decorate and then we can make our plans for the coming winter. Not the least agreeable feature of this house is the exit through
the garden in the rear.

November 14, 1781

To Lavater

I am more inclined than anyone to believe in a world beyond this
visible one and I have enough poetic and vital force to expand my
limited self into a Swedenborgian spirit universe. But in that case
I prefer that, by some delicate process, the silly and revolting leav-
ings of man be eliminated, so that we can feel the pure state to which
we are transferred. But what am I to say to spirits who permit themselves to be summoned by *such* people, who twaddle such inanities
and are guilty of such actions. I know why you accept these phenomena; I desire neither to contradict nor to convert you. But my
stomach turns at such follies, especially since I have seen the harm
they can do. . . . Finally, you can easily imagine that the exhibi-
tion of fragments of the true cross makes me more suspicious than
ever. . . .
By the next post I will send you the completed second act of *Tasso*.
. . . I shall be very glad to see your book on Pontius Pilate.

November 14, 1781

To Merck

This winter I shall still be confined to my little pavilion. For the future I have a house in town, pleasantly situated and roomy. I am making myself at home in the world without, however, giving up one jot of that essential being of mine which sustains me within and which makes me happy.

November 16, 1781

Elisabeth Goethe to the Duchess Anna Amalia

In this workaday world one cannot, to be sure, have everything one wishes, and each must be contented with his fate. . . . Of course what happens in Weimar influences us here mightily in both joy and sorrow. I wonder whether Your Highness would be kind enough to see to it that my son gets a dwelling in town for the winter. Whenever the weather is bad, as it is now, and it rains and rains without end, my heart is very heavy at the thought that Doctor Wolf must go and live in his garden. All kinds of evil could arise from this. And so Your Highness would put me under the greatest obligation if you would take this worry from me.

November 18, 1781

To Charlotte

The Dowager Duchess treated me to an extensive lecture yesterday, the intention of which was to prove that the Duke must and would cause me to be ennobled. I told her my opinion in the simplest terms and did not keep back anything, of which I will give you the details later.

Garden House, Late November, 1781

From the Diaries

Better order day by day, as well as decisiveness and consistency. Very happy with Charlotte. Sticking carefully to my plans. Rented town house. Pierced the thick skin of several persons.

December 3, 1781

To Knebel

The necessities of my nature compel me to engage in manifold activities. In the meanest village or on a desert island I would have to keep busy to live at all. Even if some of the things I do are not the appropriate ones, yet I manage to do them with a certain ease, because it is an article of my faith, that steadfastness and loyalty in our present condition alone entitle us to rise to a higher level, whether that be a temporal level here or an eternal level in some beyond.

Eisenach, December 10, 1781

To Charlotte

The Duke is gay and kind, but I find his escapade far too expensive. In this wilderness and in this cold weather he feeds eighty people. He has no boar yet and he plagues and annoys his own people and supports a couple of parasitic aristocrats from the neighborhood who don't even thank him for it. . . . God knows if he'll ever learn that fireworks at noon have no effect.

Wilhelmsthal, December 12, 1781

To Charlotte

Here we are and I've got to wait and see what happens. I wanted to leave this morning but it would have been too flagrantly unseemly. . . . I'll be coming home to you with an armful of moral and political secrets. The Duke's actions in connection with this hunting party are most inappropriate; yet within his framework I can't blame him. The others play their parts. Ah, Lotte, how glad I am that I need play none. I let them treat me as a guest. . . . Of course, his misfortune is that he's not comfortable at home. He would like to run the right kind of a Court etc. . . . Today the Duke of Gotha arrives, so tomorrow the hunting starts again, and I hope to be able to get away.

December 24, 1781

To Charlotte

I must say good morning to you and send you a piece of holiday cake, so as to appease in some way my desire to talk to you and so that I can think of something else during the few hours until I see you. At 10 o'clock I'm going to the theatre, but first I'll run in and see you for a moment.

1782

Gotha, January 1, 1782

To Charlotte

Dear Lotte, A mounted messenger just brings me the following letter. Please read it: "Although you sent me a refusal, I venture once more to ask you to my party on Thursday. No one knows about this invitation here except Frau von Seckendorf. Do be nice and come Thursday at noon, because we're first having dinner with the Prince." "Charlotte, Duchess of Gotha." Did you ever see such restlessness as drives these people? They can neither sit still themselves nor let their fellow men do so. I'll send her a polite letter and let it go at that.

January 3, 1782

To Charlotte

Tell me how much money your mother needs and when she can pay it back. If the loan is not for too long a period, I can give it to her myself. It has occurred to me how I can manage it. . . . I'm staying at home and being industrious. What are you doing?

Garden House, January 19, 1782

From the Diaries

Wasted the morning. Lovely conversation with Charlotte. Dined with the Duke. Talked very seriously and strictly to him on economic questions, concerning which he has a number of false notions, which it's hard to get out of his head. Stayed till 6. Then for tea to the Dowager Duchess'.

February 10, 1782

To Charlotte

It was a great pity that you weren't at Court for tea and supper last night. Things happened. Herder was quite rude to Wieland and the latter's reply was really gross. I want to live to see Wieland get older and see how his volubility develops. He babbles more emptily from day to day. The Duke by accident overturned the beautiful statue of the Vestal Virgin, and cracked one of her fingers. The Duchess took it with beautiful grace. Otherwise everybody was gay. My Mephistopheles whispered various observations in my ear and I enjoyed the punch.

February 20, 1782

To Bürger

. . . No subordinate position is fit for what we commonly call a thinking human being, nor is it apt to permit such an one to enjoy life in any higher sense. It is only the sound children of the narrow earth, who can relish their bread in the sweat of their countenance, to whom such situations are tolerable. . . . Every higher station is in its own measure more disquieting, more difficult, less desirable. I always thought that an academic job would be the best for you.

February 21, 1782

To Charlotte

The Duke has had the Council postponed, because he is tired after riding all night. As I was passing by your house I hoped to see you and beg you for a bite of dinner. As things are, I'd better stay home and work all day. Tell me when you'll get home this evening.

March 4, 1782

To Charlotte

Here are the flowers I promised you, while the world is still gaunt and harsh.

Dornburg, March 16, 1782

To Charlotte

Since the castle was burned down in 1774, there had been no regular theatre in Weimar. Soon after his arrival in 1775, Goethe arranged for amateur performances not only in Weimar but in the Ducal castles at Tiefurt and Ettersburg. The stage sets were skillfully built by the "Court cabinetmaker" Johann Martin Mieding on whose death on January 27, 1782, Goethe wrote a long and interesting elegy, of which two verses have become famous:

> O Weimar, thine was a peculiar fate!
> Like Bethlehem in Juda, small but great.

When I woke up this morning and saw the bright sunshine, I hoped that you would come, and so I spent my whole day waiting for you. Now that night is falling, my expectation ebbs and resignation takes its place. The Duke will be here within the hour and I hope he will bring me a word from you. . . .
My Elegy on Mieding is finished. I hope to read it to you tonight and so have a pleasant evening. . . .

◇◇◇◇◇

March 17, 1782
Sunday morning

The Duke did come yesterday and brought me your two letters. . . .
The half-thawed snow among the black mountains and fields gives this region a melancholy aspect. . . .
The Duke is gay enough, yet his love does not make him happy. His poor sweetheart [*a Countess von Werther-Neuenheiligen at this time*] is a poor wretched creature, married to the most arrant fool, ill and with no long expectation of life. . . .

Buttstadt, March 20, 1782

To Charlotte

I have been reading and excerpting and writing. The first day away from you is always difficult; every fibre in me yearns for you. . . .
I dare not tell you what curious and foolish emotions beset me. . . .
I hope to get at *Egmont,* but it goes slower than I thought.

Gotha, March 30, 1782

To Charlotte

The Duchess of Gotha has been unable to walk for six weeks. She insists on being carried about. No one believes in her illness; they think she's pretending and yet no one can say why or to what end. . . .

April 1, 1782

Write me once more to Eisenach and then to Meiningen. Meantime I'll write you. The Countess X will come to a bad end. Watch and see if she doesn't prostitute herself some fine day for everybody to see, so that her brainlessness will be patent beyond doubt.

Eisenach, April 2, 1782

If the affairs of our Duchy were in as good shape as my own, they would be in very good shape indeed. . . . The point is that a man can do so much for himself and so little for others. The desire to aid others is almost never satisfied. Most of what I am personally capable of I have accomplished for myself, or see it in the process of being accomplished. I work myself to the bone for others and get nowhere.

Tiefenort, April 7, 1782

Woe to him who lets the favor of the great lure him into the open without protection for his back. . . .
Let me add a word about Lavater's book on Pilate. When a fellow like myself inflicts his peculiarities and follies upon a hero, and calls that hero Werther or Egmont or Tasso or what you will, pretending that the thing be none other than it is, it's quite legitimate and the public sympathizes in proportion as the author's life is rich or poor, remarkable or shallow, and as the story is self-subsistent. Now our

friend finds this method of dramatic portrayal—for so they call it—very charming. He tricks out his figure of Christ in the same fashion and allies human birth and death, the Alpha and Omega, the weal and salvation of man to it. That seems to me both stale and unendurable. . . .

◇◇◇◇◇

Kaltennordheim, April 9, 1782

Your last letter roused many melancholy thoughts in me. One night I wept bitterly at the notion that I might lose you. My equanimity is equal to anything that could happen to me, except *that.* . . . I am putting into this letter the first violets and a bit of ancient moss. I plucked the flowers not far from the ruins, of which I made a drawing.

◇◇◇◇◇

Meiningen, April 12, 1782

O dear Lotte, most people have such a bad time in the world! Their lives are so narrow and issue in nothing. We two have treasures wherewith we could buy out kings. Let us silently cherish them. Stein's sickness will be difficult to cure. I'm so sorry. If you could get some assurance on that score, we would feel the burden of the world less. . . . I am especially sorry for our own Duchess Louise. Nor do I see any cure for her ills. If she could find some object on which to fix her affections, there might be some hope. The Countess Werther has the qualities to attract and hold a man. The Duchess has them too. The trouble is that when he goes to her he still finds the bud closed. . . .
I have just one more concert and one more supper to go through.

Ilmenau, April 17, 1782

To Knebel

The memory of the good times, not unmixed with bad hours, which we experienced together here, impels me to write you. All the more so, since I know that I'll be overwhelmed when I get back to Weimar.

Since Good Friday I have taken a long and often difficult trip through all the cities of the Thuringian Forest and have seen and learned much that gives me pleasure.

You remember how carefully and ardently I studied the mountains, eager to learn to recognize the variations in the land. I have done that now. I could draw a chart. I know every hill and every valley. I can now stand on this foundation of knowledge and can proceed to see what use nature makes of this ground and how man can make it his own.

Gotha, Ascension Day, 1782

To Charlotte

Mama sent me as a present the new Geneva edition of the works of Rousseau, including the *Confessions.* I've read only a few pages so far, but even these have a starry radiance. Think of volumes like that!

Meiningen, May 12, 1782

In my capacity as ambassador I had formal audiences granted me by both Dukes. The chamber was full of uniforms; the people of the Court were in the antechamber; the doors were opened by two pages and their gracious Lordships were waiting to receive me. Tomorrow I'm going through the same comedy in Coburg. . . . Being on the way I'll get rid of all the Thuringian Courts. . . .

I'm lodging across the street from the church—a miserable situation for one who prays neither on this hill nor on that, nor honors his God at prescribed hours. At 4 o'clock in the morning they began to ring the bells and the organ began to wheeze, so that I've got to stop. I can't command my thoughts.

Coburg, May 13, 1782

I demand no more of people than they have to give; at least, I try not to force upon them more than they desire, though, in truth, I

can't give them everything they would like. . . . But in proportion
as one treats people according to their kind and not according to
one's own nature, the soul is forced back more and more upon itself.
In the end one's attitude to men becomes that of a musician to his
instrument.

May 20, 1782

To Charlotte

I hope to be with you this evening. Around 5 o'clock I'll walk
through the yard and speak in a loud voice. If you want to see me
come to the window. Be quite calm; it will be all right. Be sure to
put Fritz to bed in the farther room.

May 25, 1782

To Charlotte

It made me uncomfortable to lose you today. So I kidnapped Fritz
and took him everywhere with me. First we went to look at the new
house, next to visit Corona, who is ill. Then we went out to the
garden and I'm keeping Fritz with me.

Garden House, June 2, 1782

From the Diaries

Except for a few paragraphs written in Venice in 1790, Goethe does not
take up the notations in his Diaries again until May, 1796.

Moved into my town house and slept there for the first time.

June 2, 1782

To Charlotte

I'm writing you for the first time from my new dwelling and send
you what you so often received from the old, a morning greeting
and the assurance of my love. I don't much care where I am, so long
as I am near you. At the same time I add a bunch of asparagus,
which I hope to consume with you at noon.

June 4, 1782

To Charlotte

I am sending you my patent of nobility, in order that you may see
how a thing like that looks. I am so curiously constituted that it
evokes no reflections in me whatsoever. How much better off I would
be if, sundered from all political matters, I could live near you and
turn my mind to those sciences and arts for which I was born.

June 11, 1782

Elisabeth Goethe to the Duchess Anna Amalia

Goethe's father, the Councillor Johann Caspar Goethe, born in 1710,
had died on May 25, 1782.

I was deeply moved by the sympathy which Your Highness gra-
ciously showed me at the demise of my husband. It is certain that
no improvement in his condition was to be hoped for, and what
happened on May 25 was anticipated from day to day. Yet I had
thought it would take longer. He is in a better estate. May God preserve us from such a life as he led during the last two years. . . .
Now I cannot help telling myself the most glorious stories of a trip
to Weimar. I hope confidently that Heaven may grant me this extraordinary joy. Of course, the thing can't be done in a hurry. But
patience! We must try to put all our affairs in good order, and thereafter on the wings of the wind hasten to that spot which contains
everything that is dear and precious to me upon this earth.

June 21, 1782

To Charlotte

The first chapters of my *Wilhelm Meister* will soon be in order; next
I hope to be inspired to go on. . . . Send me a kind word and tell
me where you are today.

July 16, 1782

To Charlotte

We'll eat the melon together. And together we will partake of an even sweeter dish, which is the most palatable both in summer and in winter.

July 19, 1782

To Charlotte

Tell me, is it something physical that is the matter with you, or is it something that hurts you spiritually? You can't imagine how your condition yesterday frightened me. The one thing I have at heart is that you are frank and open toward me. I can't endure this sullen silence.

July 23, 1782

To Charlotte

So it was, thank God, a misunderstanding that caused you to write that note. I am still dazed. It was like death; there is no word and no concept for a thing like that. Do open your heart again.

July 24, 1782

To Charlotte

While I slept the word of refreshment came from you; on awakening I received it. The day is still hot, but in a few hours I'll come and see what the meaning of this is, for I am dismayed to my very depth. It is your suffering that frightens me. If you can't feel happy in my presence again, I'll renounce the happy hour we might have had together.

July 25, 1782

To Charlotte

I feel much better. Yet a slight paralysis remains, as though the lightning had passed too close to me. That will go when the one necessary remedy is applied. But I am horror-stricken when I look back upon this incident, and I cannot be calm until I have some assurance for the future.

July 26, 1782

To F. V. L. Plessing

The son of a Churchman and theological student who, from time to time, asked Goethe's advice on problems of conscience connected with his theological studies.

It is a truth that man must shed many skins before he gains a measure of assurance concerning both himself and the world. You have experienced and reflected much, since first you wrote me. May you find both inner repose and an appropriate activity. Concerning myself, I can assure you, that in the midst of happiness I live in a continuous state of resignation and perceive daily through all the effort and work of the world that it is not my will, according to which things happen, but according to the will of a Higher Power Whose thoughts are not as ours are.

July 27, 1782

To Knebel

It will take the sacrifice of two more years before the threads of my responsibilities are all gathered up, so that I may honorably either retain my office or resign it. Meanwhile I look neither to the right nor to the left, and ever again will see to it that my old motto is inscribed over every room in which I work: *Hic est aut nusquam quod quaerimus. [What we seek is here or nowhere.]* . . .
Soon you will receive the second book of *Wilhelm Meister,* which I wrote in a state of poetic intoxication.

SONG OF THE HARP-PLAYER

Among the famous romantic characters, which occur even in this early first draft of *Wilhelm Meister,* were the harp-player and the girl Mignon. The songs placed on their lips were written between approximately this date and 1797.

> Who never stained with tears his bread,
> Nor through the sorrowful night hours,
> Weeping has sate upon his bed,
> He knows you not, ye heavenly powers.

Out into life by you being sent,
Man, luckless man, to guilt is fated,
Then left to bear his punishment,
Since guilt on earth is expiated.

Dawn paints his heaven a fiery red
With flames to the horizon flashing,
And on his guilty and defenseless head
The image of the universe comes crashing.

August 8, 1782

To Doctor Johann Jost Textor

The brother of Goethe's mother, attorney, magistrate and City Councillor at Frankfurt-on-the-Main.

My dear and honored Uncle, The privileged Jew, Elias Löb Reiss, on whom, as long ago as 1766, my Lord, His Serenity, the Duke, bestowed the title of Business Representative of the Court, has recently sought to obtain the title of Agent of the Court. He asks for mediation with the Frankfurt magistracy, in order that he may be given permission of free movement on Sundays and Christian holidays.
Now this man has deserved constantly and extremely well of the commercial communities of both Eisenach and Apolda, so that His Serenity, the Duke, would be very much pleased to have him receive the distinction and the favor he craves from your magistracy. Since, however, His Serenity would not like to intercede in contradiction to the municipal constitution, nor expose himself to a negative answer, nor yet embarrass the magistracy by forcing it to act against its will, I have been commissioned to inquire of you privately whether you believe that favorable action can be taken in the matter and also in what precise way.

August 9, 1782

To Lavater

I am no anti-Christian, no un-Christian, but very decidedly a non-Christian. Consequently your *Pontius Pilate* impressed me most disagreeably, because you rage so grossly against the God of the Old Testament and His children. I even started to write a parody of your piece; but I'm far too fond of you to have cared to spend more than an hour on it. . . .

You accept the gospel, as it stands, as the Divine truth. Well, an audible voice from Heaven would not convince me, that water burns and fire quenches, that a woman bears a child without a man and that a dead man arises from the grave. I regard all these as blasphemies against God and His revelation of Himself in nature.

You consider nothing more beautiful than the gospels. I find equally beautiful and useful to man and indispensable a thousand pages written by men who have had God's grace in old times and in new.

August 10, 1782

To Charlotte

This morning I finished the chapter of *Wilhelm,* of which I had dictated the beginning to you. It was a good hour. I was really born to be a writer. It gives me a deeper glee than ever to have written something well, according to my notions.

August 23, 1782

To Charlotte

The first time I have to say good night in writing, after the first day, alas, without you. Walking with the Duke in the square I saluted the moon between nine and ten. How many thoughts of you came to me; how much did I have to pass over in silence, which I can say to you only. Under the tent I read the second book of *Wilhelm* to the Duke and Duchess, who received it well. I hasten to finish it before your return.

August 27, 1782

To Charlotte

Dear Lotte, Do come back! . . . Tonight there was a frost. I went home at eight. The stars stood over your house, but your windows were dark. . . . The Duchess is as agreeable as one can be and the Duke a good fellow, whom one could love, if he didn't make all social occasions offensive by his misbehavior as well as force his friends to become indifferent to his weal or woe by reason of his irrepressible foolhardiness.

September 17, 1782

To Charlotte

Quite quietly I went home to read, to poke around and to think of you. I was really meant to live a private life and I don't understand how fate managed to weave me into the administration of a state and the fortunes of a princely family. . . .

I've been trying to imagine more thoroughly the first part or, rather, the beginning of a magic tale I have in mind, and verses to fit into it. Oh, it would come to me if I had the time and the domestic peace.

September 25, 1782

To Charlotte

I'm sending my messenger to you, who brings you half a dozen lemons. If you need more, write me; I'll send them Sunday. I've looked about in vain for fruit or something else that is good. But there's a dearth just now. Grapes were brought me, but they were sour and I don't want you to be reminded of me by sourness.

October 4, 1782

To Lavater

The first part of your confessions, if I may call them so, gave me great pleasure. Such things always make interesting reading, although I'm bound to observe, if I may, that the reader will have to draw up his own psychological balance sheet in order to extract the facts from these data. I can't elaborate the idea at this moment. Let me say just this, that what a man observes and feels about himself, seems to me the least part of his existence. He is more impressed by what he lacks, than by what he possesses, by what frightens him than by what delights him and enlarges his soul. It is so for the reason that the soul loses consciousness of itself under all pleasant and good conditions, as the body does too, and is reminded of itself only under the impact of the unpleasant. Thus he who describes himself and his past, will always be prone to describe the repressed and painful aspects, whence arises the impression of a shriveled personality. To this delineation of him one must add by a sort of chemical process actions of his that we have seen, writings of his that we have read. Then and then only the image of the man, as he may be or may have been, will arise before us. This is but one of a thousand possible observations.

October 20, 1782

To Charlotte

I was very busy this morning. . . . Four chapters are now in final form and in the hands of the copyist. Now I've got to put the novel aside and attend to my other business. Tell me how you are and how you passed the day, and send me back the little basket for grapes. Did I forget my wallet in your house?

October 22, 1782

Elisabeth Goethe to the Duchess Anna Amalia

Your Highness is kind enough to ask me what I'm doing. By Jupiter, as little as possible, and that little, in addition, very badly. But how can it be otherwise? I am solitary, left to my own resources. When the water is drained from the springs or they are clogged, the deepest of them will be emptied. I dig for something fresh. But either there is no water or it runs but turbidly. Either is bad enough. I could go on with this fine allegory and say that, in order not to die of thirst, I have taken to drinking mineral water. . . . All this is just patter. The pleasures I enjoy, I must now enjoy with others, instead of in my own house. For my house is silent and desolate. Once upon a time 'twas just the other way. . . . Yet who will grieve that it is not always full moon and that the sun is not as warm as it will be in July. One must use the good of the present and not reflect that things might be different. That's the way to get along in the world, and getting along is, when you think well upon it, the chief matter. . . . This week my son's *Clavigo* is being played here. All Frankfurt will be there; all the boxes have been sold. This is great fun for our imperial city. I have now obeyed Your Highness and given you a true and sincere account of my life. I commend myself to your further grace and favor.

October 28, 1782

To Charlotte

I've been prevented from saying good morning to you, finally by a visit from the Jew Ephraim. It will please me to tell you all about him. Soon I will have gathered all the significant aspects of Jewishness, and I have a great desire to delineate a Jewish character in my novel.

November 7, 1782

To Charlotte

Seven years ago since I arrived here. I would that again today there might open a new epoch of both my life and character, whereby I could become ever more pleasing to you. Ah, my beloved, how curious are our destinies.

November 17, 1782

To Charlotte

Whatever be the reason, I feel an unanswerable need to be alone. Under the pretext of not feeling well, I'm going to excuse myself from the Court and the Council meeting and stay home and pay off some old debts and put my house in order. Since Doctor Hufeland is himself ill, I can do this the more easily.

November 17, 1782

To Jacobi

Concerning my situation I dare tell you but little. Here, too, I am dedicated to my constant destiny. I suffer where others enjoy; I enjoy where others suffer. . . . Let me employ a similitude. When you see a glowing mass of iron on the smelting oven, you don't realize the amount of dross which manifests itself only when the great hammer begins to beat. Then the waste which the fire itself could not separate from the mass begins to do so and flows and flies in the form of glowing drops and sparks and the purified metal remains between the tongs of the workman. It seems as though it needed so mighty a hammer to cleanse my nature of its dross and to make my heart to be sound.

November 21, 1782

To Knebel

> Knebel had resigned the military governorship of Prince Constantine
> and had moved back to his Franconian home.

I deplore your situation. It is an ill thing to be alone, and even the
presence of your good sister hardly mitigates your loneliness. . . .
For some time past I have been very happy. I hardly leave the house;
I look after necessary tasks and in good hours write down the stories
which I have always been accustomed to telling myself. Soon I will
send you the three first books of *Wilhelm Meister's Theatrical Mis-
sion* [*the title of this first draft*]. They're now being copied. . . .
I have had by me, neatly tied up in packages, all letters received by
me since the year '72 and many manuscripts of the same period. I am
now separating this material and having the items bound. What a
spectacle that constitutes. Sometimes I flush to the very eyes. But I'm
going right on. I want this decade to lie before me like a valley,
which one has wandered through and now beholds from a hilltop.
. . . I see almost no one except people who must be interviewed on
business. I have completely sundered my political and social from
my moral and poetic life—to outward view, you understand—and it
is best for me so. Once a week I give a big tea party, from which no
one is excluded, and so I perform my social duties at small cost. My
many tasks, which I even exaggerate as far as the public is concerned, excuse me from visiting other houses. In the evening I see
Charlotte, to whom I open my heart. . . . I separate the Privy Councillor from my other self, without which a Privy Councillor can get
along very well. . . .

THE OPENING OF BOOK THREE OF WILHELM
MEISTER'S THEATRICAL MISSION

After the passage of several hours Wilhelm heard music at his door.
At first he thought the harp-player had put in appearance again; but
soon he distinguished the tones of a zither, and the voice, which was
raised in song, was Mignon's. Wilhelm opened the door; the child
entered and sang the song, which is here set down:

> Knowest thou the land where pale the citrons bloom,
> Where the gold orange breaks the leafy gloom,

Gently the wind from azure heaven blows,
And calm the myrtle, tall the laurel grows;
Knowest thou it well?
     Ah there, ah there
Would I with thee, O my belovèd, fare.

Knowest thou the house with roof on pillars tall,
Its chamber gleams, refulgent is its hall,
And marble statues stand and gaze at me:
What have men done, O my poor child, to thee?
Knowest thou it well?
     Ah there, ah there
Would I with thee, O my protector, fare.

Knowest thou the mountain bridge that fronts the peaks?
Through fog the mule its groping pathway seeks,
In caverns dwells the dragon's ancient brood,
Down plunge the crags and over them the flood;
Knowest thou it well?
     Ah there, ah there
Our path's before us! Father, let us fare!

          December 8, 1782

To Charlotte

I'm sending you the drawing crayons you asked for. After dinner I'm coming myself. The Duke insists that I take a week's trip with him. What do you say? I could almost wish to breathe a different air for a little while, and yet I hate to think of being separated from you.

        Leipzig, December 24, 1782

To Charlotte

The Duke is leaving and it is raining. I see already that I'll have no comfort here. My heart contracts and my mind narrows. Dear Lotte, if I didn't have you, I'd run away into the wide, wide world. Remember me to Stein and the children.

         ◇◇◇◇◇

Leipzig, December 27, 1782

Since I lived here in '69, I've never been back except for a couple of days. I didn't see anybody except my old acquaintances and so Leipzig always seemed to me as confined as in those early years. This time I am getting acquainted with the city in my new way and it's quite a fresh little world to me. . . . Farewell, remember me to the Duke. . . . I'm going to look around some more now and see a great number of people.

Leipzig, December 28, 1782

How wretchedly one has to climb up the ladder of life, rung by rung! I asked myself yesterday, why I didn't see people fifteen years ago the way I see them now? And yet nothing is more natural than that they are as they are. . . . I'm staying here a few days longer, partly for your sake, too, because I know how insufferable I have been recently—unable to drag things on. When I don't have new ideas to assimilate, I get sick. . . .

Leipzig, December 29, 1782

Now I have my plan, which is to stay until Wednesday and take in the concert. It will be quite a grand affair and will show Leipzig from many angles. Yesterday I gathered some very fine facts for my *Wilhelm* and filled various gaps in my knowledge. I hear and see all kinds of things. . . .
I have every reason to be satisfied with people's attitude. They show me great good will and great respect. In return, I am friendly, attentive, talkative and courteous to everyone. It is a fine thing to be a stranger and yet so necessary to have a home. Farewell.

1783

January 5, 1783

To Charlotte

Would you, my dearest, send me back the keys? I'm going to take a little walk before dinner and drop in on you and find out what plans there are for today.

January 23, 1783

To Charlotte

I lay abed long and didn't feel quite right. I am the happier to know that you're dropping in. There isn't too much snow in the garden. After the party tonight, I would like the men to come in here; I'll arrange for a little supper.

February 4, 1783

To Charlotte

This is the first moment I have to tell you how glad I am that you're well again. This evening will unfortunately be upset by the arrival of the Ducal family. We'll have to go to the picnic. At all events, I'll see you and get some refreshment, which I need, since things are pretty overwhelming again.

February 7, 1783

Elisabeth Goethe to the Duchess Anna Amalia

The long-expected hereditary prince, Karl Friedrich, had been born on February 2, 1783.

Never have I been so utterly thrilled as by the birth of the Prince of Sachsen-Weimar. Since no one told me a word of the Duchess' pregnancy, Your Highness can imagine my astonishment at so unexpected and wonderful a piece of news. . . . A prince! A prince! Thus I cried out in the privacy of my four walls. I communicated the happy event to all my friends. That evening I gave a supper for some of them. . . . Full of these ideas, it was no wonder that I dreamed I was in Weimar. Oh, all the rejoicing that I shared there! Alas, when morning came and I woke up, all the bliss was gone.

                                                    February 17, 1783
To Charlotte

I was so annoyed at myself last night that, out of a sense of haste, I
let your brother persuade me to leave with him. Sitting in the carriage, I did so want to say another word to you. Had it been earlier,
I would have come back. Today I have a great deal to do. Write
me how you are arranging your day.

                                                    March 1, 1783
Elisabeth Goethe to the Duchess Anna Amalia

So our precious prince is well—God be thanked a thousand times.
. . . I shall never forgive Wieland or my son, if they don't thoroughly exercise their Pegasus on this joyous occasion, and I shall be
extremely eager to see what they produce. To be sure, it seems to
me as though my son were not on the best terms with the Muses.
Nevertheless, old loves remain. Let him but call to them, and they
will soon respond. As for Wieland—yes, that's a different matter.
He is a very constant lover. The nine wenches may laugh or be
peeved. He yields to all their whims, and I have been told on good
authority that women like that. . . .

                                                    March 3, 1783
To Charlotte

I can't possibly invite anyone unless I am certain that you'll come.
And I would rather have you stay home and take care of yourself,
for you might get worse. Everything else aside, it's dreadfully slip-
pery underfoot, otherwise I'd get a sedan and be carried over to you.
I am going over old documents, which may make me wiser but certainly not happier.

                                                    March 3, 1783
To Knebel

The arrival of the hereditary prince is the greatest event which
could have taken place here. Its effect, though not visible, can be
distinctly felt. The people aren't changed; each is what he was before. Yet affairs have a new direction and the child in his cradle
works, if I may say so, like ballast in a ship; it lends the vessel weight

and steadiness. The Duchess is well and happy, for, needless to say, there was nothing else that could give her that enjoyment of life, which she has hitherto lacked.

As you will have seen, the Muses have taken pains to glorify this festive occasion in various ways. Wieland wrote a masque for the Court and Herder a cantata for the church. You will read them both with pleasure. I heard a rehearsal of the music for the Wieland piece; it was very happily done. . . . It is only the copyist who is so horribly delaying the sending of *Wilhelm Meister*.

March 20, 1783

To Herder

Thank you for your confidence in sending me your sermon. I am returning it with a very few observations. . . . When I heard you preach the sermon, I wished that you could have added and had wanted to add a kind and consoling word for the Duke. You led your hearers to the broadest part of that abyss which separates our present from the future beyond the grave. Each hearer sought a bridge or else some little spot at which he could probably slip across. You gave no one any hope, except that he have wings and could use them. But since you did not choose to give your discourse that turn, I hold it inadvisable to add anything now.

April 6, 1783

To Charlotte

I'll go into my garden and think of you in the lovely sunshine. When you come from church you can speak a word to me. You must have your hair dressed and come to Court tonight. I am looking forward to supper. I feel very well. During the night I saw the Northern Lights. I hope it was no sign of an earthquake somewhere.

April 13, 1783

To Charlotte

I've got to go to Ilmenau tomorrow. Hard to be separated. I feel as though I must take you along. Let Fritz come as your image. Let

him come over early and sleep with me, and let your man pack what
he needs to take with him. I'll see you soon.

April 24, 1783

To Charlotte

'Tis a bitter way of earning one's bread to have to try to establish
harmony among the discords of the world. All year long there isn't
really a pleasant piece of business for me to attend to, and the
misery and awkwardness of people tugs one hither and yon.

April, 1783

From the Reminiscences of Friedrich von Matthisson

Matthisson, 1761-1831, director of the theatre and librarian in Stuttgart, a minor elegiac poet, several of whose pieces Longfellow translated.

I made Goethe's personal acquaintance on an occasion on which his
humanity was purely and exquisitely revealed. In a garden on the
outskirts of Weimar he was giving a party for children. It was Easter
and there was an egg hunt. The gay boys and girls, among whom
were the offspring of both Herder and Wieland, fought their way
through the garden. It came now and then to fisticuffs among them
at the discovery of the skillfully hidden treasures.
I see Goethe before me. His rather stately figure in a brown riding
habit edged with gold appeared in the midst of this volatile and
wanton group like that of a benevolent but serious father, who engages both the reverence and the affection of the children. He kept
them with him till after sunset, when he regaled them with a pyra-
mid of sweets.

May 4, 1783

To Charlotte

The way you said to me last night that you had a story to tell me
frightened me for an instant. I feared that it had something to do
with our relationship. And for some reason, which I don't understand, I have been in a state of anxiety for some time. Curious, how
so weighty a thing as a man's happiness should hang by one slender
thread.

May 5, 1783

To Kestner

I want to thank you for your forbearance in both old and recent days and for your kind attitude toward me. I have been guilty of rather mad carryings on on several occasions in my life. Don't think I didn't pay for them. Your letter pleased me rather specially at this moment. In calm hours I have recently gone over my *Werther* and, without really revising what was so sensational a success, I hope to advance it all to a somewhat higher level. . . .

Fate, I must say, seems to have been very kind to you. First so many boys, that one would think it was enough of a good thing, and then the little girl so long desired at the right moment. God preserve you both.

May 19, 1783

To Knebel

At last *Wilhelm* goes off to you by today's post. I commend it to your and your sister's kindness. When you have read it, send it on to my mother. I have had the little case made in order to make packing easier. . . .

I quite understand what you say about wanting a little place in the country. But I'm not going to advise anyone not born on the soil to meddle with it. It is hard to wring anything from the soil and foolish to let it wring gifts from you. Yet that is what happens to anyone who approaches the cultivation of the earth with any imagination. My poor friend Stein is a melancholy instance.

June 2, 1783

To Charlotte

More than half of my day is gone and I haven't yet finished reading the official documents for tomorrow. This lovely occupation will still take several hours and I must renounce the pleasure of seeing you. Nevertheless, I hope to be able to get to you by 6 o'clock. . . . I'm planning different quarters for Fritz. Don't tell him about it. The air was not pure enough in the small room. He'll be nicely situated now.

Spring, 1783

Charlotte to Her Sister-in-Law

Goethe has taken Fritz to live with him. He is so sensible and kind in educational matters, that one can really learn from him. He is one of the few who grasps the inner meaning of Rousseau's educational theory, and because Fritz was really born with a harmonious nature, it gives Goethe pleasure to supervise him.

Gotha, Pentecost, 1783

To Charlotte

The English garden here is lovely and calm. The monument that marks the grave of a prince on an island is quite charming. Instead of doing the way our Duke did by having the gates and bridges of his gardens and parterres opened, the various parts of the gardens here are self-contained and represent outer courts and temples and sanctuaries. The difference is very characteristic.

Wilhelmsthal, June 15, 1783

The Duke is developing well enough. We had a long talk about many things. He sees more clearly and is certain to be easier in his own mind and more benevolent toward others. . . .
I'm longing to be with you; I seem to have nothing of my own any more. Sometimes I wish it were not so and that I could give my thoughts a different direction. It seems to be impossible.

Wilhelmsthal, June 17, 1783

The Duke of Meiningen arrived unexpectedly yesterday. . . . I want very much to go home and the Duke wants to go on to Meiningen. I did do some drawing and wrote another chapter on *Wilhelm*. It's far from pleasant here. Fog and dampness penetrate hill and forest and the place where we're staying.

June 24, 1783

To Charlotte

Here, dear Lotte, at last the copy of *Werther* about that Lotte who foreshadowed you. I like the English translation very well. So far as I have read it has good feeling, good sense and good taste. Had it been translated from the original instead of from the French, it would have taught me more. It was charming to read my thoughts in that language.

July 3, 1783

To Knebel

I'm so very happy that you received my *Wilhelm* so kindly and that you communicate your reflections. The things you praise I did, indeed, strive after, but I have not at all, alas, realized my ideas. I myself can't relish this composition. It was never written in tranquil moods, nor have I had a chance to view it as a whole. It is rare, too, that a reader can tell what precisely has pleased him. Book Four is half done. But send the three books which are in your hands to my mother, who wants very much to see them. You can have them again some other time.

July 21, 1783

To Charlotte

I'd like to know whether you're going to Court today or whether I can have you. I've got a lot to read and to straighten out. I found it hard to be even tolerable yesterday. I am sending you cherries, which came by messenger from the country. How is your headache?

August 2, 1783

To Charlotte

I am sending my beloved beautiful fruit. Keep some of it for me, since it tastes best in your presence.

August 29, 1783

To Charlotte

In delightful recollection of yesterday's kindness, I send you tasty remnants of our festive day. Return to me the manuscript of *Iphigenie* and send me a loving word.

Langenstein, September 9, 1783

To Charlotte

> Goethe took with him on this journey Fritz von Stein, who was now eleven. They stopped at the estate of Langenstein near Halberstad, which belonged to a well-known beauty, the Marquise Branconi, formerly the mistress of the Duke of Brunswick, the Duchess Anna Amalia's brother. Goethe had made the lady's acquaintance in Switzerland in 1779.

This is the first chance I have to write to my Lotte, though she has been in my mind the whole while. I wish you were here all day, though invisible and at night, when I go to bed you could suddenly enter through a wall. . . .

Everything is very pleasant here and everyone very gracious and Fritz extremely well behaved and pulls himself together quickly when anything untoward occurs.

I'll have a lot to tell you about. It's doing me good to breathe another air and to survey my situation in perspective. The lives of strange people are the best mirrors in which to get the right images of our own.

Blankenburg, September 11, 1783

This is the first fair day of this entire journey. As long as I was with the beautiful lady, 'twas you, no doubt, who caused storm and bad weather. On the contrary, you bless my pilgrimage up the mountain with a magnificent day. After we had surveyed the land from its peak, we descended into the valley, where Fritz and I had our dinner on a great, flat block of granite, which had aforetime plunged into the river. I can't tell you how well he behaves and how delicate is his attitude toward me.

September, 1783

Charlotte to Fritz

I am so glad that you don't forget me out in the beautiful wide world and that you write me this in tolerably though not very well-formed letters. Since you're staying so much longer than I expected, I'm afraid that your clothes won't be looking very well. If they get soiled and you, too, tell the Privy Councillor Goethe just to throw my dear little Fritz into the water. I posted your little letter and gave your regards to your fellow pupils. The kittens want to be remembered to you; they leap and fight, as the Stein boys used to do. Murz, the mother cat, has become quite as serious as your own old mother. Try to appreciate your good luck and do your best to please the Privy Councillor by your behavior. Your father wishes to be remembered to you.

Klausthal, September 20, 1783

To Charlotte

The journey is going very well and the weather is very beautiful. Tomorrow morning early we'll climb the Brocken. Fritz is sweet and good and a source of great pleasure to me. We didn't arrive here till late on the 18th. I'll tell you a lot about the beautiful lady. She didn't know where she stood with me. I was tempted to say to her: I am in love and am loved in return and scarcely have enough left for friendship. . . .

Klausthal, September 21, 1783

I'll say good morning to you before we start on our way up the Brocken. The sky is overcast, which may be of advantage tomorrow morning, since we're spending the night on top. . . .

Zellerfeld, September 24, 1783

Our mountain climbing is now over. From the peak I turned my eyes to where you dwell to make me happy. Fritz was cheerful and brave. He rode his little horse, as though he had never done anything else. He is very happy and has only the tiniest streaks of whimsiness and misbehavior.

Kassel, October 2, 1783

Now we're here and very gay. Forgive me that we stay away so long. If Fritz had his way, we would go on to Frankfurt. He nags me and does his best to persuade me. When I tell him that we shouldn't leave his mother alone so long, he assures me that *my* mother would be so very happy to see us. Etc. . . .
On Sunday, the 5th, we're leaving here and will hasten home by way of Eisenach.

October 7, 1783

To Charlotte

How happy I am that I can send you something for breakfast again and wish you a good morning. I'm adding a letter about *Iphigenie* which I received from the Kestners in Hannover. It will please you. I don't know whether I'll be over this morning.

November 9, 1783

To Charlotte

Your delightful encouragement last night persuaded me to go on writing at *Wilhelm* this morning. I hope to complete Book Four today and to start the fifth one at once. The fourth one has taken me exactly one year, as I marked down in my diary.

November 12, 1783

To Jacobi

I have long wanted to answer your very dear letter, all the more since I don't remember your having sent back the manuscript copy of *Iphigenie*. I do remember that your letter said you were returning it, but I don't recall its arrival, nor do I find that copy among my papers. Don't let it trouble you, however; it's no great matter. . . . The pleasantest thing that has happened to me in a long time is this, that the wretched clouds which so long separated Herder from myself have finally been dispelled and, I am convinced, forever. You would feel very happy among us now.

November 22, 1783

To Charlotte

I wish you good morning, dear Lotte, on the occasion of the first frost. Perhaps I'll soon be skating. Yet I take little pleasure in that, since you refuse to join me. Write to tell me how you are and that you love me.

December 2, 1783

To Charlotte

Since the Council meets today and since I have never missed a session except through utmost necessity, I have decided to attend. I feel just so-so. You'll hear from me when it's over.

December 7, 1783

To His Mother

From your letter, dear Mother, I saw with great joy that you are well and that you try to enjoy life as much as one can. Quite soon you will receive Book Four of *Wilhelm Meister* which, in view of your fondness for plays and for the theatre, I can commend to you warmly. Don't raise an alarm over that copy of *Iphigenie;* it does little good. Follow up the matter calmly and have the package traced. It certainly didn't arrive. . . .
The woman you speak of offended against all good manners and certainly offended your maternal feeling by trying to spoil even one

moment of your life by the gossip which she retailed to you. You never saw me with a fat face and a fat belly. Naturally, grave affairs have made me graver, especially since I am thoughtful by nature and strive after what is good and right in the world. . . .

Let us take these goodly years as a gift from above, even as we must take all our lives and accept with gratitude each of these years as it passes.

Considering my constitution, I am well; I manage my affairs; I enjoy the society of good friends; I retain enough time and strength for a few of my favorite preoccupations. I can't imagine a better place for myself than the one I have, especially now that I know the world and that the fields behind the mountains have no secrets for me.

As for you, take what pleasure you can in my life and work and continue to do so, even if I should leave the world before you. I have brought no shame upon you; I would leave behind good friends and a good name and it would be your best consolation that what I have done will not wholly perish. Meanwhile, live tranquilly. Perhaps fate will grant us to spend a pleasant old age together which we should then gratefully accept. . . .

I don't know whether I wrote you that I have taken the son of Frau Charlotte von Stein, my closest friend, to live with me. He is a very good child and a very handsome one. He is 11 years old. I take much pleasure in him; he cheers my silent and my serious hours. . . .

December 11, 1783

To Charlotte

My outing yesterday left me with an inflamed tooth and swollen cheeks; it seems that there are all kinds of things in the body which cannot find a vent. I hope you'll come to see me today. Or, perhaps, it might be better if I wrapped myself up well and came over this evening. We're more tranquil at your house and I feel better there.

Late December, 1783

To Lavater

The New Year looks upon me in friendly fashion, while I calmly leave the old one behind me with both its sunshine and its clouds.

One of the chief satisfactions of my life is that the things which separated Herder and myself have vanished. Were it not for his iron silence, harmony would have been established long before. In compensation, it is now permanent and promises much delight. For I know no one of a nobler heart or a more liberal spirit. . . .

Do the balloonists who sail through the air delight you as much as they do me? I would love to see mankind achieve this thing.

1784

January 1, 1784

To Charlotte

All my thanks, dear Lotte. Yes, as you prophesied, I shall be ever happier. Happiest through you. I'll see you after dinner. This morning I must do a little drawing to give a friendly beginning to the year.

January 9, 1784

Elisabeth Goethe to Friedrich (Fritz) von Stein

Your letter gave me great delight. So you are having a fine time at my son's house. Oh, I can well imagine that. Goethe was ever a friend of fine young people. . . . The dearer he is to you and the less you would care to miss him, the more certainly will you believe me, when I tell you that separation from him causes me many darkened hours. And so, my little friend, you could accomplish something quite wonderful, which will not be too troublesome, since you seem to be fond of me too. This is my plan. Since you are constantly with my son, and thus know more about him than anyone else, how would it be if you kept a little diary and if you sent it to me at the end of every month. Only little notations, something like this: "Yesterday Goethe went to the play; this evening he dined out; today we had guests. Etc." In this way I would be living, as it were, in your midst; I would rejoice in your joys; absence would lose much of its discomfort. . . . When some day my son comes to Frankfurt, I want you to come along. We shall not lack for pleasures. . . . Well, it may happen one of these days.

January 16, 1784
To Charlotte

I know I didn't behave well last night and I'm afraid you could hardly love me. So tell me the contrary early today. Surely we'll spend this evening together.

Ilmenau, February 24, 1784
To Charlotte

> Goethe had gone to the mountain town to deliver an address at the re-opening of the mines.

The affairs go well. On Tuesday, at 10 o'clock in the morning, send the enclosed copy of my speech to Herder. Tell him that I will be delivering it at that very hour. He is to show it to no one until I get back. Remember me to the Duke and tell him of our happy arrival here. The tranquility of this place does me good. If you were here, I'd gladly settle down for the rest of the winter. What studying one could do.

Jena, March 1, 1784
To Charlotte

Let us stick together, for the things of this world are all too fragile. The Duke is carrying on a military discussion with a cavalry officer beside the oven. I'm going to sleep. Good night.

March 2, 1784
Elisabeth Goethe to the Duchess Anna Amalia

I can truly say that the ribbon of no order has ever been worn with more joy and pride and the feeling of undeserved grace, than I have received the striking likeness of Your Gracious Highness. . . . May God give His blessing to the undertaking of the new mines and grant my son the health and strength to perform all fruitful services to your house. We've had a great flood here. Even as I write my cellar is full of water. We cross the streets in boats. In the lower parts of the city even the first storeys were flooded. The wretchedness was much greater than during the flood of '64.

Jena, March 3, 1784

To Jacobi

> Jacobi had just lost his wife.

I have not yet dared to write you, for what is there to say. Any word of sympathy, consolation or reflection sticks in one's throat. The thought of you has been with me on this otherwise agreeable trip, which I took on the occasion of the reopening of the old mines at Ilmenau. The thought follows me here, too, where, if I may say so, I am surrounded by floods and ice and human misery and am required and have occasion to ruminate on the fate of mankind. Herder will invite you to visit Weimar this coming summer. I wish I were certain to be at home. I'll do my best. . . . I am a poor slave of that duty to which destiny has bound me. Therefore, forgive me if I seem dry and slothful.

Jena, March 27, 1784

To Herder

> Goethe's dealings with science, though supported by a good deal of observation and, in his later life by simple experimentation, were largely intuitive and deductive in character. The discovery he announces in this letter was accepted by scientists as a genuine contribution to comparative anatomy. The bone in question is between the maxillae or jaws.

Following the admonition of the gospel I must hasten to announce to you a piece of great good fortune that has come to me. I have discovered—nay, neither gold nor silver—but something that gives me more joy than I can say, namely, the *os intermaxillare,* the intermaxillary bone, in man. I came upon it by comparing human skulls and animal skulls. Suddenly—there it was! Now I beg you for complete discretion. The matter must be treated as a secret. It should delight you, too, for it is, as it were, the final stone in the structure of man. It is not lacking; it, too, is there!

April 3, 1784

To Charlotte

I thank you, dear Lotte, for calling my attention for a moment to the dear object that lurks behind this mass of accounts and documents and figures. How precious you are to me, and how I hated to see you leave me yesterday. I don't know when I'll be able to come today.

April 19, 1784

To Ernst II, Duke of Sachsen-Gotha

Your Serenity's confidential letter bids me answer it with the utmost promptness. What Your Serenity says about the work of the young painter in question agrees, upon the whole, with my own opinion. I am, however, less sharply critical and inclined to more hope for his future.

The painting representing two figures has quality, although I admit that I, too, find it lacking in charm. May I venture to make the observation that this fact may proceed from our artist's moral innocence. Had he enjoyed the charms of the female body both physically and spiritually; had he been irresistibly drawn to the fairer half of creation, assuredly his painting would have had more life and sensual power. . . . I do wholly agree with Your Serenity that he has the makings of an excellent portrait painter. And that happy talent is rare enough in our time. . . . The request then which, hitherto, I have hesitated to address to Your Serenity is that you will have the kindness to allocate to the young artist a modest sum of money, which he is to use to hire living models and to buy good colors and thus to have a chance to perfect himself.

April 29, 1784

To Charlotte

It was very clever of me to wrap you round about me; I could almost wish I had not done so. Something quite new seems to penetrate my being and a not disagreeable restlessness draws me toward you.

May 5, 1784

To Charlotte

I must beg of you rather earnestly to increase my love for you by sweetness of behavior. Why do I have to tell you that? Since the days of Dejanira a more dangerous garment has not been given to a lover. . . . If I do have to go to Eisenach, let me go with peace of mind.

May 29, 1784

To Charlotte

Tell me, dear Lotte, whether the Counts Stolberg and their wives are staying in Tiefurt this evening. I'm not going down there and I hope to see you in my garden. I am so happy over the couple of free days that have been given me.

June 3, 1784

To Charlotte

My packing is done and I need merely say farewell to you.
The Stolbergs gave us a gaily memoried day. It was lovely that before my departure I could be bathed once more through recollection in those waters of youth.

June 2, 1784

Count F. L. zu Stolberg to J. H. Voss

Johann Heinrich Voss, 1751-1826, the well-known poet, author of the popular idyll in hexameters "Louisa," which inspired Longfellow's "Evangeline," and author of perhaps the best translation of Homer into any modern language.

We reached Weimar on May 27. . . . We were at the supper table when Goethe came in, pale with emotion and with joy. He has been the same old Goethe from that moment to this morning, when he had to leave, because he had to go with the Duke to a meeting of the Diet. He is less effervescent (only that's not the right word), less easily inflammable, but certainly not less fiery, than he used to be. His heart is as loving as ever and still yearns after more freedom than human life affords.

June 11, 1784

Count F. L. zu Stolberg to His Sister Katharina

. . . Goethe is not yet old, halfway between my brother and me; yet eight years of wearing business preoccupations do tell on a man. He has a little garden house near the city in a grove by a river and a crag. Here he lived for three years, winter and summer. Often he would walk on foot out of the noisy town by moonlight over the up-land paths; in winter he would cross the deep snow by the light of a torch. Then would the confusions of the day leave him and high imaginary visions come to him. But the press of affairs forced him to leave this charming hermitage.

Gotha, June 5, 1784

To Charlotte

Once more Goethe took Fritz Stein with him on this journey, while Charlotte stayed at Kochberg.

This is the first quiet hour I have in which to write you. . . . Fritz is very cheerful. I have sent him to various places alone, in order that he may learn a courtly behavior; as I both hear and observe, he has done very well. . . . I have been shown all kinds of fine things, which entertained me greatly. Last night the Mistress of Ceremonies of the Court here confided to me under a solemn pledge of secrecy the *Mémoires pour servir a l'Histoire de M. de Voltaire, écrits par lui-même* [*memoirs meant to contribute to the story of M. de Voltaire, written by himself*]. Rumor has it that the book will be published. It will create a great scandal and I am looking forward with delight to your reading it. It is as distinguished and as full of exquisite humor as anything he has written. He writes about the King of Prussia quite as Suetonius revealed the scandalous lives of the Roman emperors. If the eyes of the world could and should be opened about kings and potentates, then these pages would be as a precious ointment. The trouble is the book will be read as men read a satire on women. They lay it aside and continue to commit the follies of love.

Eisenach, June 7, 1784

To the horror of the so-called decent people the book of Voltaire will be printed. I'll get hold of one of the first copies and send it to you at once. You will find that he writes as though a god, say, Momus, that is, a god but a vulgarian, were to write about a king and about the great affairs of the world. But that is indeed that character of all of the productions of Voltaire's wit. There is no drop of human blood, no spark of sympathy or human warmth. There is an ease, an intellectual superiority, a sureness of touch, which are enchanting.

I say superiority, *not* elevation. He may be compared to a balloon which, floating far above earth sees plains below it, where we see hills.

Eisenach, June 9, 1784

Our business proceeds not too badly; unluckily nothing can come of emptiness. I know perfectly well what should be done in place of all this running about and the making of these propositions and the passing of these resolutions. It's like sprinkling a garden, when there is no way of persuading the rain to come down. How narrowly limited is man, now in understanding, now in capacity, now in power, now in will.

Eisenach, June 11, 1784

They tell me that I could get to Frankfurt from here in thirty-one hours. The thought of going to Frankfurt doesn't even skim the surface of my mind. You have so absorbed me that I have no sensibility left for the other duties of the heart.

Eisenach, June 28, 1784

The order for the ending of my committee work is signed. Now this can't last much longer, and I'll be able to get off within a week. . . . It's perfectly clear to me that you have become and must remain my other half. I am no single independent creature. You support all my weaknesses; you protect my softer qualities; you fill my gaps. When I am away from you my condition is most curious. On one side of me I am armored as with steel; on the other side I am like a raw egg, because I neglected to protect myself, seeing that you are my shield and protection.

Eisenach, July 4, 1784

To Charlotte

Four days in succession I was obliged to dine and sup at Court. The result is a badly upset stomach and the consequent depression. It's coming to an end and I'll be so glad when I can get rid of all the business and go to the mountains and then home to you.

Eisenach, July 7, 1784

Your last letter saddened me. Do you believe that distance can destroy or diminish my longing for you? Where is anything equal to your love? The elegance, charm, agreeableness of the women whom I see here, even their apparent liking for me—does it not all bear the mark of transitoriness on its front? You only are permanent for me and I for you upon this fleeting earth.

Eisenach, July 9, 1784

I am sending you one more letter through the people of our Chancellory who are leaving. I'll follow them soon. Tomorrow I go to the mountains, taking Fritz with me. . . . I used a few quiet moments to read in a volume of Rousseau which happened to lie about. How wonderful and fitting to see the soul of one who has gone and the innermost secrets of his heart on a table somewhere.

July 21, 1784

To Charlotte

I hope this very restless day will be followed by a good night. I find documents stacked up on all sides; they must be gradually attended to. I had to make visits and sort of find myself again. Knebel is going to spend the night with me; he's very agreeable to be with. . . . I've got to close. I am sending you various things. Remember me to Fritz.

Dingelstadt, August 8, 1784

To the Herders

Early in August Goethe set out on another journey to Brunswick and the Harz Mountains.

Between Mühlhausen and this place the axle of our heavily loaded carriage broke. So we had to stop over here and I immediately attempted to go on working at the promised poem [*the never completed philosophic epic* The Mysteries]. What I am sending here is a proem to serve instead of the traditional invocation of the Muse and similar matters. It is not yet all as it should be; I scarcely had time to copy the verses. . . . Send them with this letter as soon as possible to Frau von Stein.

Zellerfeld, August 11, 1784

To Charlotte

The stanzas in question, eliminating several too intimate ones to Charlotte, were to serve thereafter as the dedicatory poem of all subsequent collections of Goethe's verse. The poem bears the title "Zueignung," i.e., "Dedication."

I hope that by this time you have the opening of the poem which I asked the Herders to pass on to you. You will select from the poem the stanzas addressed to you. I am happy to be able to tell you in this way how much I love you.

Zellerfeld, August 13, 1784

I am thinking intently of the plan of the poem. It grows clearer and clearer. If we have rainy weather or any kind of accident, I'll certainly continue to write on it. I can assure you that except for yourself and the Herders and Knebel, I have no public whatsoever. . . . All I need is a letter from you.

Brunswick, August 18, 1784

For about two weeks from this date on Goethe's letters to Charlotte are
written in French, fluent and correct, but almost devoid of accent marks.

. . . I'm very well and I amuse myself because I live without pretense
and without desires and because so many new objects stir me to a
thousand reflections.
Our good Duke on his side is frightfully bored. He's trying to find
an interest in life. The dignified tempo of Court life embarrasses
him. He has had to give up his dear pipe. A good fairy couldn't please
him better than by changing this palace into a charcoal burner's hut.

Brunswick, August 19, 1784

There's another reflection that I want to communicate to you. I've
known this for a long time and again I see how true it is. It's so
easy to exist in this world incognito. Everybody forms his own idea
of you and doesn't care much whether it be true or false. Everybody
is preoccupied with himself and if you tread just a little softly you
can do as you like and no one takes notice. And that's the reason why
rogues succeed better than honest people.

Brunswick, August 22, 1784

I can't help telling you that at the Fair here I saw a beautiful zebra
or striped ass. It gave me so much pleasure. Its shape is that of a true
donkey, but the design on its hide whence comes its name, is so
charming that one can neither describe nor imagine it.

Brunswick, August 24, 1784

Ah, my dear, what ill-luck! The Duke has changed his plans and we
won't be leaving for a week. I wouldn't mind, for there are all kinds

of things to see here, if it weren't for the six hours a day that you
have got to spend at table. . . .

I'll end up with a stanza in German. It will be placed in the poem
which I have so much at heart, because in it I can speak of you and
of my love in a thousand forms which no one but yourself will understand.

> Ah surely, long ago to some far distance
> I would have fared of the wide world before me,
> If stars omnipotent would brook resistance
> And from that strict entwinement would restore me
> Which finds in thee the meaning of existence.
> My hope, desire, aspiring, in and o'er me
> Toward thee alone and toward thy being yearns,
> And my whole life about thy breathing turns.

Brunswick, August 24, 1784

I started my birthday at the ball where I danced a lot without taking
any interest in it. I slept late this morning. When I woke my heart
was saddened at finding itself so far from all it holds most dear. This
day won't be as festive as my birthday was last year. I'll spend it
at the Court and at the gaming table, when I would so love to have
celebrated it amid fields and rocks and woods. . . .

Brunswick, August 31, 1784

My heart which speaks to you day and night, will not be silent. I
am persuaded that yours does the same and that softens the pain of
absence. I would be even happier if I knew that you were well and
that the toothache had left you. I've been very well the whole time,
except that the irregularity of the diet has caused me a good deal
of discomfort.

Elbingerode, September 6, 1784

At last I am free of the fetters of the Court and am in the freedom
of the hills. The weather is magnificent and I am sending you this
word.
The Duke had an irresistible impulse to go to Dessau. . . . The days
have been magnificent and I climbed the Brocken once again. . . . I
can hardly say how close the sense of your love is to me. I wrote you
from here seven years ago, too. . . . I hope to be in Weimar by the
15th and to see you there.

September 9, 1784

Elisabeth Goethe to Fritz von Stein

. . . It is a true sign of your affection and friendship that you ask
for an exact description of my person. I'm sending you two silhouettes. On the big one the nose is too large; the small one is too young
looking; yet there is some truth in both. I am rather big and fairly
corpulent; I have brown eyes and hair. If I were an actress I might
act the part of Hamlet's mother not ill. Many people assert that it is
unmistakable that Goethe is my son. I do not see the resemblance myself, but it must be so, since it has been said so often.

September 19, 1784

To Charlotte

Jacobi and his sister arrived yesterday; I'm very pleased to have them
here. I wish, dear Lotte, that you would escape from your solitude at
Kochberg and come here for a few days. Jacobi is a very interesting
man—more so than ever. . . . I was in Jena today and I took Fritz
with me. I feel that you wish he were mine. He was good and sweet
and I am very fond of him.

◇◇◇◇◇

September 20, 1784

You and I are so attentive to our duties that in the end people might doubt of our love. Business and friendship keep me here, the management of your estate keeps you in Kochberg. I can't possibly come to see you and I quite appreciate the reasons that keep you from coming here. Nevertheless, I am annoyed at both you and myself for being so reasonable. . . . Destiny is going to reward us for the privations we have suffered during this period. I'm not going to follow the Duke on the journey he wants to undertake. I'll make a short stay in Ilmenau; then I'll come back and we'll be together the whole winter without anything to separate us. I'll attend to my business and the rest of the time I will live for you alone, and so the harsh season will be the most agreeable, because I will pass it at your side.

October 12, 1784

To Charlotte

Fritz and I took a long drive yesterday and yearned to eat the duck which you meant us to have. We were punished by hunger for our carelessness. Fritz was very nice. I explained to him the two earliest periods of human culture according to my new system. He understood well and I found to my delight that, explaining the matter to him, it increased in clarity and decisiveness in my own mind.

October 28, 1784

To Charlotte

It is not well that you stay away so long. For your sake I have pushed into the background my mother and the city that was my home and now I must spend my days alone. No good can come of that.

Jena, November 19, 1784

To Charlotte

I'm sending you the Duke's letter. You will see that the trip is doing
him good. I am very well here. I would like to spend some time here
in tranquility, provided that you could share it. I am bringing with
me the original Latin version of Spinoza's *Ethics,* in which everything is much clearer and better expressed, as well as a life of Marcus
Antoninus and an easy treatise on astronomy. . . .
I'll be back tomorrow night and we will continue our life.

November 26, 1784

To Karl August

I trust that this letter will still reach you in my father's house and
be a welcome for your return journey. I got your letter from Zürich
and was happy to know how agreeable it was there. I am curious to
know how you found Lavater nowadays and from what new and
changed points of view you were able to see the people and the
country. Among us at home there is peace or, at least, outer quietude. . . .
I myself live, so far as circumstances permit, according to the dictates
of my mind and temper and not only feel well but better than usual
at this period of the year.

November 29, 1784

To Charlotte

I want very much to sup with my beloved, and so I am sending for
this purpose the rest of the pig, in order that it may be roasted.

December 6, 1784

To Karl August

I dislike writing this letter instead of coming myself, for I see that
it would please you to find me in Frankfurt. But so many inner as
well as outer circumstances hold me back, that I am unable to follow

your summons. . . . My heart bids me pass the final weeks of this year in concentration. I am completing various activities and acquisitions; I am trying to prepare myself for the quiet pursuit of these during the coming year and I fear the impact of new ideas on all within which my present vocation seems to lie.

December 8, 1784

To Charlotte

The Duke writes me from Frankfurt. He asks me to join him there and return with him. I'm really embarrassed. The bad weather and my state of health and the unpleasant recollections of the journey of '79 are in my bones.

December 12, 1784

To Karl August

Your kind letter relieved me from the anxiety, that you might take my refusal in ill part. . . .

I don't, please understand, grudge you the delight you take in hunting. But I do hope that upon your return you will relieve those about you from their fears concerning an evil which threatens. I mean, of course, the wild boars of the Ettersberg who ruin the arable land. I dislike mentioning this matter. I protested in the beginning against bringing these animals there, and I don't want to seem to be saying: I told you so. But I am asked on all sides to break a silence which I had determined to preserve. And I'd rather write you than confront you with this matter on your return. I omit the damage done and the disproportion of the herd to our area. I limit myself to the impression made on the inhabitants. I never saw such wide disapproval of any matter. The owners of estates, the lessors of farms, your subjects and officials, even the guardians of your hunting preserves, all unite in desiring these intruders to be eliminated. . . .

I've been reflecting on the nine years which I have passed here and the various epochs of my way of thinking in that period; I'm trying to grasp the past very clearly, in order to have a sharp conception of the present. After some meditation I determined to try to imagine that I had but just arrived and just now entered service with some knowledge of people and circumstances but with my own energy and desire to be effective quite fresh. . . .

The attention of our society here is at the moment fixed upon Frau
von der Recke. People differ about her according to the various
points of view from which the aspects of a beautiful object may be
regarded. I can say very little, because I have seen her just once.
Everybody else is certain that, upon your return, you will, to use a
trivial expression, pay court to her and that the lady would not be
averse from reciprocating your gallant attention. For though she is
a very model of virtue—despite the fact that in evening dress she
exhibits more of her person than even Wieland approves—and a
model of propriety, yet has she confessed that her heart has played
her odd tricks on previous occasions and that she has a special admiration for princely persons who have not forgotten their common
humanity.

December 30, 1784

From the Diaries of Sophie Becker

Sophie Becker was the otherwise unknown companion of the Baroness
Elise von der Recke, 1754-1833, a member of the German nobility in
Kourland who was divorced from her husband and had published in
1780 a volume called *Spiritual Lyrics by a Noblewoman of Kourland*.

I mustn't forget to set down that yesterday we had dinner at Frau
von Stein's. Toward the end of the meal the Privy Councillor
Goethe came in. He is an intimate of the house of Herr von Stein.
There is something horribly unbending in his behavior and he says
very little. I had the impression that he was embarrassed by his own
eminence. I am told, nevertheless, by all who know him well that he
is conscientious and honest in office and does much charity in secret.
But these same people say that his rapid advancement has introduced
an alienating element into his character, which some consider pride
and others weakness.

December 31, 1784

Goethe called for fifteen minutes this afternoon. He talked a little
more today. Anyhow, everyone is rather interested in Goethe, reserved as he tries to be. Frau von Stein's father also came to call, and
at the sight of him Goethe rushed out at once. The old gentleman is

the very caricature of the type of the superannuated, old-fashioned hanger-on of Courts, whose very existence is dependent on the princely smile.

1785

January 3, 1785

To Charlotte

I have but two divinities at present—yourself and sleep. You two heal everything within me that can be healed and are my alternate talismans against the evil spirits.

January 6, 1785

To Charlotte

Last night after I got home I wished that you were with me or that I were back with you. Here are some sweets. I am inviting the Herders for this evening. If they accept, I'll let you know and you will arrange about your young woman [*Charlotte von Lengefeld, the future wife of Schiller*].

January 12, 1785

To Jacobi

I enjoyed the wine you sent and didn't even thank you for it. Forgive my paralysis as a letter writer. So many things press upon me that it is difficult to work my way through. . . .
I exercise my mind on Spinoza, reading him over and over. . . . I reserve judgment entirely, but I confess to you that in these matters I am thoroughly at one with Herder.

February 2, 1785

To Charlotte

The wine I imbibed last night had its usual beneficent effect. I slept well and got up feeling well. I've refused a dinner invitation from the Dowager Duchess in order to do some work. I'll see you this evening.

February 17, 1785

To Charlotte

The wind awakened me again and again during the night and brought to me the image of my beloved, the remembrance of my friend.

1785

FOR EVER

For all that man in mortal limitation
Of happiness to source diviner owes:
The deep harmonious faith which no gradation,
The friendship which no care or sorrow knows;
The light which is the sage's inspiration
And in the poet's plastic vision glows—
All that, all that in our best hours abounded
In her wise heart where for myself I found it.

February 20, 1785

To Herder

I saved your manuscript for this morning, in order to spend profitably the early hours of the Sabbath day and to read it with pure eyes. It is admirable and will have a good effect upon the public. . . . It is also delightfully written and the things you could not say nor wanted yet to say are well prepared for. . . .

March 3, 1785

To Charlotte

I have said it before and will say it again and again that the *Causa finalis,* the first great cause of the world and of all human action is dramatic poetry. For the stuff is absolutely no good for any other purpose. I got what will be one of my best scenes out of the Conference last night.

March 1785
Charlotte to Knebel

Goethe was deeply troubled by the fact that Karl August, tired even of his wild hunting and bored by the civil administration of his Duchy, was thirsting for a chance at military activity on some world scene. Two years later, immediately after the death of Frederick the Great, he caused himself to be appointed a major-general in the Prussian army and thus attached his country to the Prussian war machine.

It is strange that just as I received your letter, I was myself reflecting silently and sadly on the subject, of which you speak. Unfortunately our friend Goethe has had to abandon hope in this matter. There is nothing to hope where there is nothing to be changed, because the rhythm and the tone now predominant here are both morally false.

April 2, 1785
To Charlotte

After I had undressed and made myself thoroughly comfortable, it came all over me again that I am condemned to solitariness because I lack the presence of the one heart with whom alone I can communicate happily. I think of all the things about today I would like to discuss with you. It was not a significant day, yet it had quite a bit of significance and even a moral for me. I'll try to write a few stanzas before going to bed.

April 24, 1785
To Charlotte

I am well enough but not exactly gay. The spring still hesitates and we must wait for it. Fritz sends a note too. He didn't cough at all last night. If you like, I'll invite the Herders for this evening. I've refused an invitation to Court.

April 30, 1785
To Knebel

Goethe had consulted Knebel on the Duke's predicament and plans for the future.

It does one so much good to discuss a certain condition with friends. I left you with a much lighter heart; I've gone back to work at my tasks with a quite permanent impulse.

I was grateful to you too for making me feel that my life is so deeply intertwined with yours. . . . Seckendorf's death will have been as unexpected a shock to you as it was to us all. There is much food for thought in the event.

May 10, 1785

To Charlotte

You don't ever write me any more unless I ask you to. How are you? . . . The balloon is going up between 4 and 5.

May 16, 1785

Elisabeth Goethe to Fritz von Stein

. . . On the 16th of April the delight and joy of our city came near to being changed into mourning and lamentation. After midnight a fire broke out in our magnificent new playhouse; had help been delayed but fifteen more minutes, all would have been lost. The owner-manager is completely ruined. He saved nothing but his own life and the lives of his six children. But in such cases our Frankfurt people are worthy of all honor. Three different collections were at once taken up—one among the nobility, one among the merchants and one among the masons. A goodly sum was soon raised. . . .

I wrote to give my son a detailed account of my illness. It was a very bad cold, but I am quite well again. Farewell and greet my son from me.

May 24, 1785

To Charlotte

The Duke who, as you know, is fond of cleansings of conscience, took occasion prior to his departure to give me an increase of salary of 200 thaler a year, as well as 40 louis d'or toward my trip to Karlsbad.

June 9, 1785

To Jacobi

The book by Jacobi, which Goethe acknowledges, bore the title: *Concerning the Teachings of Spinoza in Letters to Moses Mendelssohn.*

It is now some time since we received your book and read it. I have reproached both Herder and myself that we put off answering so long. Try to forgive us. I, at least, am far from fond of expressing myself on such matters in writing. Indeed, I find it very nearly impossible. On one thing Herder and I agreed at once, namely, that the explanation you give of the teachings of Spinoza is far closer to our interpretation than we had expected from our conversations with you. I believe that a discussion might bridge the gaps that remain.

You acknowledge the existence of that highest reality on which all else is based, from which all proceeds, and which is the foundation of Spinozism in its entirety. Spinoza does not demonstrate the existence of God; he demonstrates that existence *is* God. Let others call him an atheist on this account; I am inclined to call him and praise him as most godly and even most Christian. . . . Forgive me that I prefer silence when people talk about that Divine Being, whom I know only within and from those *rebus singularibus,* the concrete phenomena, to the closer and deeper contemplation of which no one has encouraged men more than Spinoza himself, although to his personal vision all particular things seem to have vanished.

I cannot assert that I have ever read the writings of this remarkable man in the proper order, or that I ever had a clear intellectual vision of the entire structure of his thought. Neither the operations of my mind nor my way of life have permitted that. But when I look into his books I seem to understand him, that is, he seems never to contradict himself and I receive from him the most wholesome influences upon my own thinking and acting.

Therefore I find it difficult to compare his own words with what you say of him. In him expression and thought are so deeply interfused that it seems, at least to me, that if one does not employ his own words, one says something quite different from what he says. . . . Forgive me that, after so long an interval, this is the best I have to say. But I never pretended to any ability in matters metaphysical.

June 20, 1785

To Charlotte

This note is to bid you welcome on your arrival in Karlsbad, where you probably do not expect to hear from me. When you open it you will feel me nearer to you and it is long since I have had so delightful an expectation as to meet you in the Bohemian hills. See to it that our lodgings are not far and that we can take our meals together. I am enclosing a song of Mignon from the sixth book of *Wilhelm Meister*.

MIGNON'S SONG

Bid me not speak, speech is forbidden,
My secret is a duty laid on me;
I would pour forth what in my heart is hidden,
But silence is my destiny.

At the due hour the sunrise in its might
Expels the dark so that the craggy mountains
Open their bosoms to the new-born light,
Yet grudge not unto earth her subterranean fountains.

In some friend's arm each mortal seeks repose
Where he his griefs may utter and reveal them;
Alas, a vow commands my lips to close,
And other than a god dare not unseal them.

June 24, 1785

From Knebel's Diary

We left Jena yesterday at 11 in the forenoon, Goethe and myself. My traveling companion was in a quieter and calmer mood than I. What he did say was intimate and confidential and I responded. On the way, while our carriage stopped he made a drawing of a gateway and a driveway.

That evening when we arrived at our destination he elaborated the drawing charmingly with pen and ink. A little while thereafter, when

I was going to light my pipe, he begged me not to do so. He said that tobacco fumes made him feverish. I didn't smoke, of course, but I was surprised that his nerves could be irritated by so minute a cause. In fact, his discomfort increased. He had to go to bed with chills and a painful sort of convulsions. He had not quite recovered by morning and we will probably have to spend the day here.

I could not but observe that Goethe's nature was in the habit of holding out unchanged up to a certain last moment, at which it uses the slightest circumstance for a complete collapse. This is characteristic of him in many respects.

Neustadt an der Orla, June 27, 1785

To Charlotte

I am writing you at once in order to relieve the anxiety you must feel on my account. Unfortunately we are still here and are wasting the goodly days. . . .

My indisposition was very much like last winter's, but neither so violent nor so painful. . . .

These days can be counted as almost lost, except that I have been studying *Hamlet*. Today is the finest weather imaginable. I do not permit myself to grumble. Since the sun will shine as brightly when we lie in our graves, why should it annoy us that he does his duty, when we are confined to our room and our bed?

Zwota, July 4, 1785

To Charlotte

Only six hours away from you now, but a mounted courier will give you this letter when you get up. We'll start off early again tomorrow morning and be with you by noon.

Karlsbad, August 7, 1785

To Charlotte

Goethe had arrived in Karlsbad on July 5. Assembled there were the Duchess Louise, Charlotte von Stein, the Herders and, among others, the lovely Countess Christine Brühl who, as Goethe remarked, "seemed in the end to pay more attention to me than I deserved of her." Charlotte's watchful jealousy was aroused and the common stay in Karlsbad was not as happy as had been anticipated.

I can't begin to describe to you, nor need I do so, how empty everything seemed to me after your departure. In my thoughts I have gone up the stairs of the Three Roses many times. I continue to exist and drink the waters and take the baths every other day. Tomorrow the Countess Brühl is leaving. I'm sticking it out here. . . . I love you deeply and you only.

August 17, 1785

To Karl August

Before I leave Karlsbad I want to thank you for your affectionate letter. It gave me much pleasure and I had a feeling that it would come. . . .
During my stay here I have been indescribably lazy. The waters agree with me and the necessity of being constantly among people has done me good, too. Many rusty places induced by stubborn isolation are whetted away by this process. Everything from the granite formations on and up the spiral of created things even unto women has contributed to make my stay agreeable and interesting. . . . I must thank you, too, for your sympathy with the illness which kept me back for a week in Neustadt. . . . I wish you much luck with your new acquaintance, the beautiful English woman, if that can be called luck which casts one out again upon so dangerous a sea.

August 31, 1785

To Charlotte

Charlotte withdrew to Kochberg on September 1; Fritz was sent to Frankfurt to visit Goethe's mother.

Since it appears that we no longer succeed in communicating with each other face to face, I say this farewell in writing, in order not to become wholly estranged from you. I trust that the journey will do Fritz good.

September 1, 1785

To Kestner

Your letter, dear Kestner, followed me about in vain. I did not travel with the Court but was far away from you, namely in Karlsbad.
It would have been a great joy to see you both again, to share your happiness and your grief and to recall old times. The death of your little daughter grieves me much. But since you are such fruitful trees, you must seek to make up for this loss. Remember me warmly to Lotte. I think she still feels kindly toward me and my sentiments toward her will always be the same.

September 5, 1785

To Friedrich von Stein

I am so glad that you arrived safely and were well received. Just keep thinking of the maxims of Polonius and all will go well with you. Write us a little every day, so that we may know what happens. Your mother is in Kochberg and your father here. Give my love to my mother and tell her about everything. Since she is not as deadly serious as I am, you will be the happier with her.

September 5, 1785

To Charlotte

The messenger I send is bringing Fritz's letters, too. I can hardly wait until you see how well he is getting along and how much at home he feels. . . . Last night I performed what you might call a bit of psychological sleight of hand. Karoline Herder was still in a state of hypochondriac tension about her varied unpleasant experiences in Karlsbad. I let her tell me everything and confess everything: the misbehavior of others as well as her own mistakes, down to the minutest details and consequences and finally I gave her absolution and tried jestingly to make her understand by this formula that these things were now all dead and done with and sunk in the depths of the sea. It amused her immensely and she is really cured. . . .
The Duke is happy with his new pack of hunting dogs. I don't grudge it to him. He gets rid of his courtiers and buys dogs. It comes to the same thing. All this tumult to hunt a hare to the death.

September 11, 1785

To Jacobi

Everyone is kind and friendly to everyone else here, although Frau von Stein has gone to her estate again. I have sent Fritz to Frankfurt in order that he may see the famous balloon rise and watch the Fair as a little image of the varieties of mankind. I have a good idea! I'll bring him up to marry your little daughter. She'll never get a handsomer or a better man, seeing that I can never be your son-in-law.

September 22, 1785

To Charlotte

It's raining very hard and I think of you in that old castle where I called on you ten years ago and where you attached me to you through your love. I wish I were with you and were following my intimate inclinations and were happy in your being there. If you stay away much longer it will go badly with me. . . . I am slowly continuing on *Meister*. . . . Here are letters from and about Fritz which are sure to please you.

October 1, 1785
Four o'clock in the morning

To Charlotte

I was awakened by a fire alarm and I don't want to lie down again without a good morning to you, my dearest. The fire was on the Swine Market; it was the corner house of a smith on the way to the gate to Erfurt. . . . Our fire department proved its worth and the pumps worked well. . . . I am writing you from Jena where I went yesterday in a kind of desperation. . . . From there I intended to ride out to you but could find no horse. All the horses were at the Fair. Finally I meant to go on foot, but it began to rain and the wind blew up harsh and cold. . . .

October 3, 1785

To His Mother

You have shown me so many kindnesses this year, dear Mother, that I must thank you from the very heart. Your hospitality to little Fritz and the care you lavished on him is of course something that you do out of your love of me, although you did find, I am sure, that he is a precious child and now his stories about you are a source of great delight to me. If in the manner of the ghosts of Swedenborg one might desire to see through others' eyes, it would be well to use the eyes of children for this purpose.

October 24, 1785

To Charlotte

It will all depend upon you how and where I spend today. If you're staying at home I'll come over and bring my work with me as well as food for dinner and supper. If you're going to dedicate yourself to the world, I'll stay home and work hard and enjoy the happiness of being with you when you can get away from the Court.

Ilmenau, November 9, 1785

To Charlotte

I wrote a chapter of *Meister* today; one more and this part will be done. I look forward to reading it to you. We must have tea and a fire in the chimney, so that we have the right décor and atmosphere.

◇◇◇◇◇

Ilmenau, November 11, 1785

Today at last I finished the sixth book. I hope it will give people as much pleasure as it has given me anxiety and trouble. The point is that when one knows what one is aiming at precisely, one is never satisfied with the execution. . . .

I did keep my word of the 12th of November of last year about doing another book, but at this pace we'll grow old together before the work is finished.

Gotha, November 13, 1785

Don't regret my staying away a few days longer. I will hasten home to you with a fuller soul. . . . Barring accidents I'll be with you by Tuesday night.

November 14, 1785

Elisabeth Goethe to Charlotte

I was very happy to see from your letter that your son's visit here was so satisfactory to him. I did all in my power to make my native city agreeable to him, and it pleases me to have succeeded. To be sure, God has granted me the grace that no human soul has ever left me in ill humor, of whatever station, age or sex the individual may have been. I am fond of people—old and young feel that; I make my way through the world without pretense, and that is comfortable to all the sons and daughters of Eve. I get on no high moral horse and try to appreciate people's good qualities, leaving the evil to Him who made man and who knows best how to smooth the sharp edges. Using this method I keep well and contented and gay.

November 18, 1785

To Knebel

I continue my quiet life and go occasionally to Jena, where I always miss you. I'm just back from Ilmenau and from spending a few very friendly days in Gotha.

The sixth book of *Meister* is done. I read it to Frau von Stein and the Herders. If you had been there my little public would have been complete. Their approbation made me very happy. But I won't send it to you. I want to have something to regale you with when you come back.

Jena, December 12, 1785

To Charlotte

Thank you for your dear letter. I expected it. Tell the Duke I've found so much to do that I can't come back till Wednesday or Thursday. If you could be with me in this tranquil place, it would be a very happy sojourn.

December 18, 1785

Elisabeth Goethe to Fritz von Stein

Dear Fritz, In order that I may be remembered by my dear son and he not forget his good mother, I am sending him a little present. I am adding your two favorite songs and since I don't know whether it is fashionable in Weimar to sing *Figaro* in German I'm sending a song from it too. You remember, dear Fritz, how you and I sang it together and what a lovely time we had. "Gaiety is the mother of all virtues," says Götz in my son's play—and he was right. . . . Everything is very quiet here now and so I can't write much that is amusing. I do better to transcribe the song from *Figaro*.

December 30, 1785

To Knebel

What will become of me next year, I have no idea. I don't want to turn my vision upon great and far prospects. Whatever happens, I'm going to Karlsbad; I can't tell you what improvement I owe to those waters. For the rest, I am busy; my affairs go their accustomed way; they serve to form me while I execute them. The sixth book of *Meister* is done. I've started the libretto of a musical play. But I'm afraid it won't do for Munich. Here is a letter to you from the Duke. I took it out of the envelope without looking at it, in order to reduce the postage.

1786

January 4, 1786

To Charlotte

I can't tell you how glad I was to possess you again yesterday, seeing that I have been so disquieted about you.
Here is a calendar. Farewell.

January 6, 1786

To Herder

Since I am told that a Ducal order concerning the improvement of the school system according to your proposals has gone off to the Consistory [*the religious and educational council of the Duchy, of which Herder was chairman by virtue of his office*], I would, following the excellent example of your wife, no longer hide from you my pedagogical desires for this year.

1) I would request that your plan be extended to include the military school and applied there according to your pleasure.

2) I would like you to direct the education of the orphans of the late Lieutenant von M. First they were in the orphanage where they were treated like swine, next they were in a boarding school where they were treated like sheep. I want those boys to have a chance to become human.

3) I'd like to commend to your attention Charlotte's oldest, Ernst; I would also like you to pay some attention to Fritz. I want some intelligent preparation for their future. I'll tell you my ideas about both boys, but since I'm an ignoramus myself, I have no expert knowledge as to what other people, and especially children, ought to know.

January 14, 1786

To Charlotte

I am sending my dear one candy and flowers, in order that she may have an image of how sweet and beautiful my love for her is. Are you going to your brother's house today? He invited me.

Gotha, January 26, 1786

To Charlotte

. . . The Duchess looks ill and is hoarse. I read to them in the evening. . . . The wind blows madly about the castle and the drafts penetrate my room; I hug the stove, roasting on one side, freezing on the other. . . .

February 20, 1786

To Charlotte

Moses Mendelssohn had died on January 4 of this year. Just before that he had published a small work *To the Friends of Lessing,* which was a reply to Jacobi's interpretation of Spinoza. The Berlin papers had printed ironic notices and verses. For instance:

> God is. Thus Moses taught us long ago,
> But Moses Mendelssohn did prove it so.

I hope you'll have a better time with the Jew's last testament than I had. I couldn't finish reading it. I'm sending you the latest Berlin documents. How picayunish and how poverty stricken! They can't even let a poor Jew leave the world without being jeered at. . . .

February 28, 1786

To Charlotte

My mother writes me as follows: "As long ago as January 1 of this year I sent the jewels and the lace to Frau von Stein by the regular post. I have been hoping from day to day to have receipt acknowledged—in vain. Since the guarantee of the post office is near its expiration, I beg if only for a line."
I'd like to have you for tea today. Can't keep you for supper.

March 20, 1786

To Charlotte

I beg of you to come over to me at 3:30. I am dining with the Duke and thereafter the musicians and the Herders are arriving here at that hour. I have been tempted to act a part in a play again, but I've happily resisted the temptation.

April 9, 1786

To Charlotte

In my mind I have been with you. Never have I wanted more to be under one roof with you than I do now.

Ilmenau, May 5, 1786

To Jacobi

I have read your little book with sympathy, not with pleasure. It is
and remains a philosophical polemic and I have such a distaste for
all literary quarrels, that Raphael could paint me one and Shakespeare dramatize it and I would scarcely take joy in it, whatever it
may express. . . .
Whenever heightened self-consciousness expresses itself in the contempt of others, even the humblest, it becomes revolting. A frivolous
man may jest at others and humiliate them and spurn them, because
he ends by exhibiting his own nature. But he who truly respects
himself thereby renounces the right to value others below their
worth. And what are we all that we should dare to be arrogant?

Jena, May 23, 1786

To Charlotte

I have been writing on *Meister*. Soon I hope to finish the book on
which I'm working. But it is a curious matter with things like this.
Thought and creative planning do little good. The best comes quite
spontaneously.

May, 1786

Charlotte to Knebel

I would like to tell you what Goethe thinks about Lavater's theory of
magnetism. But he seems to have entered a stage of silence. Neither
do I know anything about Jacobi's visit here. Goethe told me not the
least detail. You know his present way. He thinks a great deal and
says nothing. I am sorry for the poor man. Those who feel happy
speak out.

June 13, 1786

Herder to a Friend

In his researches into nature Goethe's is the freest, most thorough
and purest mind, observations of which I have ever followed. In this

respect he sets an example of the highest kind. My association with him is my highest consolation and his discourse never fails to enlarge my soul.

June 25, 1786

To Charlotte

Do exactly as seems well to you and it will seem so to me, too. Keep me in your heart, so that we may at least preserve a possession, which we shall never find again, even if moments come, during which we cannot enjoy it. I am correcting *Werther* for a new edition and find that the author made a mistake when, having finished the book, he did not put a bullet through his head.

July 9, 1786

To Charlotte

Charlotte had left for Karlsbad on July 1, where Goethe planned to follow her. He was asked however not to leave until the expected confinement of the Duchess Louise had taken place.

I am almost as overripe as the fruit of the princely womb, and I am awaiting my release. My business here is accomplished and I must go if I am not to start all over again. . . .
The thing can't last more than another week. I beg of you, when you receive this letter, to bespeak lodgings for me in your house from the 16th on. If it can't be there, look about elsewhere.

July 14, 1786

To Charlotte

One day passes after another and everything is at a standstill. . . .
I have many, many thoughts, but they are rather dark ones, and I can say no more today.

July 17, 1786

To Charlotte

No one knows any longer what to do. The period of your cure is going by and I must pass the days in this humiliating fashion. I haven't anything more to say. All thought and action are fused in a mere sense of waiting.

July 21, 1786

To Charlotte

At last the child arrived. It is a girl. . . . I expect to leave here on
Monday and Jena on Tuesday. . . . On Thursday evening I ought
to be with you.

Jena, July 24, 1786

To Karl August

I was disappointed in my hope of passing the day with you today. So
I cannot bid you farewell either. I was just about to write you at
length when the military messenger came. All I can do is to thank
you for your friendly consent to my leave of absence.

Karlsbad, August 22, 1786

To Charlotte

> Goethe did arrive in Karlsbad on July 27. Charlotte left on August 14
> and Goethe accompanied her as far as Schneeberg, a small mountain
> town on the frontier between what was then Bohemia and the Kingdom
> of Saxony.

Now I must write to my dearest. . . . I read to our little group
every evening; enough of it has remained. Last night I read my version of *The Birds* of Aristophanes with enormous effectiveness. Tonight I'm reading *Iphigenie;* tomorrow it will be something else.

◇◇◇◇◇

August 23, 1786

I did read *Iphigenie* last night; it was well received and gave the
Duke a curious sensation. Now that the play is rewritten in verse it
gives me a new pleasure. I am working at the recasting and expect
to finish tomorrow. At all events I must stay another week. Then my
stay here will come to a gentle ending and the ripe fruits will fall.
And then I will live with you in a free world in happy solitariness,
without name or station and so draw nearer to the earth from
whence we came. . . . The rumor goes that the old King of Prussia
is dead. If it's true, you should know it in Weimar by now.

August 30, 1786

To Charlotte

Now things draw toward an end for me here. On Sunday the 3rd of September I'm planning to leave. The others will stay on until the 11th. They celebrated my birthday. . . . I am sending the poems and presents. Keep them for me against my return.

September 1, 1786

To Charlotte

Now a final farewell from Karlsbad. I want to repeat to you that I love you dearly and that our last journey to Schneeberg made me very happy and that your assurance that you are again taking pleasure in my love renews the joy of my life. I have borne much in silence hitherto, but I have desired nothing more intensely than that our relationship might take a form, over which no circumstance can have power. If that cannot be, I would not dwell where you are, but rather be alone in that world, into which I now go forth.

September 2, 1786

To Charlotte

I am leaving here tomorrow, Sunday, September 3. No one knows of it nor even suspects that my departure is so near. But I must hasten away, otherwise the year will be too far advanced. . . . If you receive a package or scroll, do not open it in the presence of others but lock it carefully away.

Karlsbad, September 2, 1786

To Karl August

Forgive me for speaking of my travels and my absence so indefinitely at the moment of our farewell. I don't myself yet know what's going to become of me.

You are fortunate in following a course you have desired and chosen; your domestic affairs are in good order and I know that you will now permit me to think a little of myself. You have yourself often asked me to do so. In general I think you can do without me at this moment. The specific affairs which lie within my province I have ordered in such a manner that for a period they can proceed without me. Even if I were to die, there would be no jolt. I pass over many other circumstances dictated, as it were, by the stars, and I beg you merely for an indefinite leave of absence. The repeated use of the baths here has greatly improved my health; I hope for an equal improvement in the elasticity of my mind if, for a period, left wholly to myself, I can enjoy the freedom of the world. The four first volumes of my collected works which Göschen [*the well-known Leipzig publishing house*] has agreed to publish are in order. Herder has been tireless in helping me. . . .

May you be fortunate in all your undertakings and enjoy a happy event for each. If I were to let my pen run on, there would be much else to say. But I must end with a farewell and with a request to remember me warmly to the Duchess.

Karlsbad, September 2, 1786

To the Herders

I leave behind me my best thanks and wishes and blessings for you both. I am leaving very quietly. I must hurry on account of the weather and other circumstances. Wherever I go the memory of your affection and loyalty will remain with me. I shall be happy when I see you again. . . . Tell the friends at home whatever is handsome and, if possible, whatever makes sense in my name, that they may forgive this secret leavetaking.

Book Four

FLIGHT AND REBIRTH

1776-1788

ITALY

(September, 1786 to June, 1788)

1786
(Continued)

The Italian Journals

At 3 o'clock in the morning of September 3 I stole away from Karlsbad. In no other way could I have escaped. It was observed that I wanted to flee; I let nothing hinder me, for the time had come.

Regensburg, September 5, 1786

All that I took with me from Karlsbad was a carpetbag and a badger-skin bag, more than enough for my clothes, but I have so many books and papers. . . . Now I've bought me a little trunk, which pleases me. I enjoy being alone, too. Being constantly surrounded by servants makes one old and feeble before one's time. . . .
I must hasten away! A clerk in a book shop here, who used to work in Weimar, recognized me. Nothing good ever comes to an author from the booksellers. . . . I've assumed the name of Möller, and I'll stick to it. . . .
I suppose Herder is right when he says that I'm a great child and continue to be one. It's wonderful to be able, as I am doing now, to follow my childish impulses, without fear of punishment.

South Tyrol, September 10, 1786

When evening comes and a few clouds rest on the peaks in the mild air and stand in the heaven rather than travel across it, and when right after sunset the crickets raise their loud chirping, it seems to

me as though I were born here and had been brought up here and
had just returned from a whaling expedition to Greenland.

September 13, 1786

I am in Malcesine, the first town of the Venetian state, on the south
shore of the Lago di Garda. I stayed overnight at Torbole, the little
harbor town. The inn has no locks on the doors, and the innkeeper
said I needn't worry, though my luggage consisted of diamonds.
There is no glass in the windows. Oil paper is stretched in the
frames and yet it is most agreeable in the rooms. Finally, there is
no privy. On my arrival I inquired of the porter where the necessary
convenience was. He pointed to the yard: *"Qui abasso! Puo servirsi."*
[*"Right down there! Help yourself."*] I asked: *"Dove?"* [*"Where?"*]
He answered: *"Per tutto, dove vuol."* [*"Anywhere you like at all."*]
This freedom from care, accompanied by lively activity is characteristic. . . .

(Verona), September 17, 1786

To Charlotte

Yes, my beloved, I have at last arrived where I should have been
long ago. Perhaps, in that case, much of my fate would have been
milder. Yet who can predicate such things? Frankly, I really had no
right to wish this thing for myself even six months earlier.

(Verona), September 18, 1786

To Charlotte

I want to show you that I'm still alive without telling you where I
am. I am well and I do wish that I could share my enjoyment with
you. . . . I am keeping a journal; I am recording the most interesting things I have seen and thought. According to my reckoning the
journal will reach you by the middle of October.

(Verona), September 18, 1786

To the Herders

Wherever I am, I think of you both, and now that everything is so wonderful I could almost wish not to be as alone as I am. I am working at *Iphigenie;* it should be done by the end of October. . . .
I must use the utmost restraint not to say more. Among the best that I hope for myself is a happy reunion with you. I hope to return a newborn person.

(Verona), September 18, 1786

To Karl August

Out of the solitary distance I send a kind greeting. I am well and desire that you, too, may have arrived at your goal. . . .
For a little while I am still concealing my whereabouts. Life is so kind to me that it often saddens me not to be able to share its goodness. I already feel both in my soul and in my notions a very marked difference. I hope to bring back a thoroughly cleansed and far better equipped human being.

Vicenza, September 24, 1786

The Italian Journals

I keep to my schedule. Every morning I work at *Iphigenie.* The play should show that it ripened under this heaven, where one does not think of one's body all day long, by reason of one's well being.

Padua, September 26, 1786

I drove over from Vicenza in four hours today. As usual it was in a one-seater, packed with all my belongings. Usually the trip takes only two hours, but since I enjoyed the magnificent day under this pure sky, I was glad that the driver did not do his duty.

◇◇◇◇◇

Venice

And so it was written on my page of the Book of Fate that on the evening of September 28, emerging from the Brenta River into the lagoon, I was to have my first vision of Venice and soon thereafter to enter that marvelous island city. Now, thank God, Venice is no longer a mere word to me. . . . When the first gondola came to meet my ship, I suddenly remembered a toy of my childhood, which I had not thought of for twenty years. My father had brought with him from Venice a beautiful model of a gondola. He treasured it extremely; it was a great privilege when I was permitted to play with it. . . . I am well lodged at the Queen of England, which has the great advantage of being not far from the Piazza di San Marco.

❖❖❖❖❖

Venice, October 4, 1786

I have a manservant now, an excellent old fellow. He is a German and saves me what he costs me day by day. He has traveled with people through all Italy and knows his way about. He is able to curb the Italians, as they need to be. He makes me pose as a merchant and manages to reduce tipping to a minimum.

❖❖❖❖❖

Venice, October 5, 1786

How Roman history rises before me! Alas, alas, my beloved, that it all comes to me a little late. O that my father had been a clever Englishman! I have had to acquire and conquer everything for myself and must do so still. . . . You remember that I promised you coffee from Alexandria; you probably didn't think that I would fetch it myself in Venice. I have made various inquiries and asked of people who know, but I want to be perfectly certain. The coffee I have seen sells at seven pounds a ducat; that wouldn't be much. To be sure, one would have to add the cost of transportation to Thuringia. Never mind, you shall have some.

❖❖❖❖❖

Venice, October 7, 1786

Tonight I summoned the famous singing gondoliers, who sing Tasso and Ariosto to their own melodies. By moonlight I entered a gondola, one singer in the prow, the other in the stern and they raised their voices and sang the stanzas in alternation—something between a choral and recitative.

(Venice), October 13, 1786

I have put pages from the journal and drawings in the box with the coffee. It is the choicest Alexandrian coffee to be had here. I am sending you 25 pounds; give five pounds to the Duchess Louise with my kind regards and five pounds to the Herders. Keep the rest. If you like it, I can get you more.

(Venice), October 14, 1786

To Karl August

A happy greeting from afar, still without place and date. Soon I will be able to be frank and to tell you how well off I am. My health is good; I hope all that is best for you and your family; how delighted I will be to hear from you again.

I can't tell you how strange the vision of our stay in Karlsbad seems to me—how in your presence I was impelled to give an accounting as it were, of a great part of my past, and how one thing led to another, and how my Hegira coincided with the date of your birthday. You know how superstitious I am and how significant these things seem to me. The connections which God decrees, let not man put asunder.

Ferrara, October 16, 1786

The Italian Journals

I have passed two nights on the deck of a ship wrapped in my cloak. The chill rose only toward morning. I am now in the South and I repeat that I would leave these people everything they have, if only, like Dido of old, I could take with me as much of their climate as

may be contained in the hide of a cow and bring it to my northern
dwelling. It is a different life.

◇◇◇◇◇

Bologna, October 19, 1786

The world seems to be spinning under my feet and an inexpressible
passion drives me on and on. . . . An evening walk in the direction
of the hills calmed me a little.

◇◇◇◇◇

October 26, 1786

I am in Fuligno in the midst of an Homeric household. In a great
hall everybody is assembled about a huge fireplace. There is crying
and shouting. Food is taken at long tables, as in the painting of
the wedding of Cana.

Rome, November 1, 1786

The Italian Journey

> *The Italian Journey,* the more formal work which was elaborated from
> the Journals or Diaries sent to Charlotte.

At last my lips are unsealed and I can communicate with my friends
in the right mood. May they forgive me my secretiveness and my subterranean journey hither. I dared hardly say to myself what my goal
was; even on the way here I was still full of fear; not until I entered
by the Porta del Popolo was I certain that Rome was mine at last.

Rome, November 3, 1786

To Karl August

Only when I came to realize that you were fettered to the North by
the deepest political involvements and when it was clear that you
had given up all plans of Southern travel, did I decide to take this
long and lonely path and to seek to see the objects toward which I
was drawn by an irresistible inner necessity. During recent years
this longing assumed the form of a sickness. Only the present vision
of what I needed could heal me. I may confess it to you now: it got

to the point where I dared not look at a Latin book or the delineation in art of an Italian landscape. The desire to see this country was ripe and overripe; through the satisfaction of it I find at last my friends and my country become dear to me again and the thought of my return a desirable one.

Rome, November 4, 1786

To His Mother

First of all I must tell you, dear Mother, that I arrived here happy and well. My journey, which I undertook in secret, gave me much pleasure. I am alone and unknown and observe a kind of incognito. I can hardly express to you my sense of well being in that so many dreams and desires of my whole life are realized, and that I see in their reality those objects which from childhood on I had seen in pictorial representations and of which I heard my father speak so often. To be sure, I see all this a little late; perhaps, for that reason, with greater profit. I don't know how long my stay will be. It will depend upon the aspect of things at home. In any event I shall return by way of Switzerland and come to see you. Then we'll have a truly good time together. But let this remain between us.

Rome, November 7, 1786

To Charlotte

Let it not vex you, my very dear, that your lover has gone far away; he will be given back to you a better and a happier man. I hope that the journals from my departure through my stay in Venice will reach you safely. Between Venice and here I added a good deal which will be sent together with *Iphigenie*. . . .
The weather is what the Romans call *brutto*, brutal; a wind from the south brings daily showers. But I find this weather pleasant, for it is warm all the while, as rainy summer days in the North are not.

Rome, November 10, 1786

To the Herders

After a brief stay at an inn Goethe had taken lodgings with the well-known painter J. H. Tischbein who had resided in Rome since 1782.

Tischbein did a portrait of "Goethe in the Campagna" which has been reproduced many times.

When you look at a civilization more than 2000 years old, transformed in every aspect and in its very foundations by the mutability of the ages—and yet the same, the same earth, the same hill, often enough the same pillar and the same wall and in the people traces of that permanent character—one becomes a comrade and intimate of the great decisions of human destiny. . . .

Farewell and write me soon and forgive my haste. Do write me at length and circumstantially and put the letter in a wrapping to be addressed: *a Mr. Tischbein, Peintre Allemand al Corso incontro al Palazzo Rondanini [to Mr. Tischbein, German painter, on Corso Street opposite the Rondanini Palace].*

May 14, (1821)

Tischbein to Goethe

Never did I feel a livelier pleasure than that day when I saw you for the first time on the way to St. Peter's in the Locanda. You were dressed in a green coat and you came toward me and you said: I am Goethe.

November 17, 1786

Elisabeth Goethe to Her Son

Dear Son, No vision arising from the land of the shades could have astonished me more than your letter from Rome. I was jubilant that the wish which was in your soul from your earliest youth on has now at last been fulfilled. To a man like you, with your knowledge, with that pure, great vision which you have for everything that is noble and beautiful, with the very eye of an eagle, a journey like this must have an effect on your contentment and happiness for the rest of life—and not alone for you, but for all who are lucky enough to come within the circle of your influence. Eternally shall I remember the words of my dear and blessed friend Klettenberg. She said to me: "When your Wolfgang goes as far as Mainz he brings back more knowledge than another would from Paris and London." Ah, I would like to have seen you when first you stood beside St. Peter's Church! But you promised to visit me on your return journey. Then **you** must tell me every smallest detail. . . .

You must be sure to let me hear from you before you come here, otherwise I will expect every postchaise to bring me the only one I love—and hope deferred is not in my line.

Rome, November 24, 1786

To Charlotte

I must write to my dearest. Tomorrow is mail day which I must not miss. You ought to hear from me about every week. I'm sure you will also be writing, so that I get a series of letters. The first one ought soon to reach me.

Rome, December 2, 1786

To Charlotte

I can't begin to tell you how much I shall have to communicate to you face to face. Descriptions do one little good when it comes to convey the quality of sensuous or moral perceptions. I do immensely want to have a word from home. Here I will have been gone three months tomorrow and no syllable has come to me from those who are nearest to me.

Rome, December 2, 1786

To the Herders

Every morning when I get up I work on *Iphigenie*. Daily I conquer some difficulty and the whole is progressing well. It is approaching the end. So it occurs to me that after the two first volumes of the Göschen edition have appeared, one might print the fourth volume next. But do about that as you think best. . . . It's rather wonderful how so many things have been concentrated in this year. It is wholesome and, indeed, blessed that my long inner stagnancy has begun to stir and flow. I am a very different man and feel so much better.

Rome, December 8, 1786

To Charlotte

Goethe had left Fritz von Stein in his house under the care of his trusted servant and secretary, Philip Seidel. Charlotte promptly took Fritz back home. When Seidel came to her to get a letter to forward to his master she handed him a brief note to the effect that she did not intend to correspond with Goethe any more and that she desired the return of all the letters she had written him in the course of the years.

I have Seidel's letter enclosing the note written by you. So that was all that you had to say to a friend, to a lover who has so long yearned for one kind word from you, who has neglected on no day, no hour since he left you to think of you! I trust that my package from Venice will soon reach you and bear witness to my love. . . . I shall not tell you how your note lacerated my heart. Farewell, my only one, and do not harden your heart against me.

Rome, December 9, 1786

Tischbein to Lavater

You are right in all you said of Goethe. . . . I found him to be quite what I expected. The one thing that surprised me was the gravity and tranquility of one of such vivid sensibility and also that he is able to be at ease and at home in all circumstances. What pleases me still more is the simplicity of his life. All he asked me to provide him was a little room where he could sleep and work without interruption and the very simplest fare. I could get him what he wanted since he is so easily contented. Now he sits in that little room and works at his *Iphigenie* early in the morning until 9 o'clock. Then he goes out to study the great works of art that may be seen here.

Rome, December 13, 1786

To Charlotte

Your note hurt me, but most on account of the hurt that I caused you. You are going to be silent? You are going to retract every evidence of your love? You can't do that without suffering keenly. And I am the cause of it. But perhaps a letter from you is even now on the way to me which will raise me up and console me. Or perhaps my diaries have arrived and created a pleasant hour for you. I, at least, will continue to write to you and to record whatever is remarkable in my experience and to assure you of my love. . . .
Consider that at this moment I am forced to think of my other writings, to meditate on how they are to be arranged and that, in consequence, I must retrace a thousand situations in my past; consider

further that there rush in upon me in a few days the impressions of the most remarkable city in the whole world, calculated to confuse the new arrival—thus will you get a picture of my situation. I scarcely think of the coming hour. I will continue thus and do what is most necessary and bear what is to be borne and await the developments that will arise.

Rome, December 13, 1786

To the Herders

I am deeply delighted that you took my disappearance quite as I would have you do. Try to reconcile Frau von Stein and the Duke. Since I meant not to hurt anyone, I am prevented from saying anything in my own justification. . . . I am recovering gradually from the great leap I took; I am more given to study than enjoyment. Rome is a world and it would take years to become aware of one's self within that world.

December 20, 1786

The Italian Journey

The rebirth which is transforming me from within continues to be active. I thought to learn something quite solid here; I did not think that I would have to go so far toward the origin of my schooling, to seek to forget so much, to relearn so thoroughly. But now I am convinced of these necessities. I have yielded myself to them utterly and I am glad in the measure in which I am able to deny myself.

Rome, December 20, 1786

To Charlotte

No letter from you yet. Most likely, then, your silence is intentional. I'll try to bear that, too, and consider that I set the example, that I taught you silence. It is not the first time that I have taught something to my own hurt.

Rome, December 23, 1786

To Charlotte

Let me thank you for your letter. Let me forget for a moment all that is painful in it. My dear, my dear, I implore you to ease my return to you and not to force me to be banished in the wide world. . . . I cannot express to you how it pierces my heart to know that you are ill and ill through my fault. Forgive me. I myself fought with death and life and no tongue can speak the things that went on within me. . . .

December 25, 1786

Charlotte von Stein to Lotte Schiller

I have many agreeable letters from Goethe in Rome. I'm sure he means to come back to us, but Heaven often disposes of us mortals according to its will. It was rather rude the way he left his friends. . . .

1787

Rome, January 4, 1787

To Friedrich von Stein

I write to you, dear Fritz, wrapped in a voluminous cloak with my charcoal brazier beside me. In my room there is neither stove nor fireplace and since yesterday a cold north wind has been blowing. But the weather is bright and it is pleasant to take walks on the dry streets. . . .

I can tell you all kinds of stories. . . . The other day we saw or, rather, we heard a thousand swine being slaughtered in a narrow space. This happens during the winter on every Friday on a square where once upon a time there stood the Temple of Minerva. . . . Then, too, I saw my first performance at the Opera, where the people in the stalls made a louder noise than even the thousand swine. . . . Look, this is a bad smear, and I still have much to write. Don't imitate my handwriting. . . . Remember me to the Herders and read them this letter.

Rome, January 6, 1787

To Charlotte

Karl Philip Moritz, 1757-1793, a philologist and archaeologist, had broken his arm in a fall from a horse. Goethe nursed him through a long convalescence.

I have just returned from seeing Moritz whose broken arm was relieved of splints today. I learned a great deal in the forty days of his
illness, while I was his father confessor and confidant and financial
agent and private secretary. I shall profit by it and I hope that you
will, too. This morning I got your bitter-sweet letter dated December 18. Our letters come and go regularly now. I hope there will be
no other interruption while we live. . . . My heart is not stubborn;
I am ready to make every sacrifice to become sound again for my own
sake and the sake of those who are closest to me. . . . Since yesterday I have a colossal cast of a head of Juno in my room or, rather,
only the fore part, the mask. It was the first thing I fell in love with
in Rome. I wish we were looking at it together. I will have it sent
home and we will all be glad of its presence with us. No words can
give an inkling of what it is—like a passage of Homer.
I am dismayed to hear that the Duke had such a bad fall. I am
afraid that that will some day be his end.

Rome, January 20, 1787

To Charlotte

I have your letter of January 1; it gave me both joy and pain. All I
can say is this: I have but one life and I have risked all of it on this
throw of the dice. If I come out of this alive and sane, if my mind,
my constitution and my good luck get the better of this crisis, I will
be able to make up everything to you a thousandfold.—If I perish,
I perish! Without this experience I was of no use any more.
Moritz is like a mirror held before me. Imagine my situation when,
in the midst of his pain, he told me and confessed to me that he had
left a beloved woman behind him, that he had torn asunder what
was no common relationship, full of deep sympathy and the play of
the mind—that he had fled without farewell, giving up his liveli-
hood and position. He handed me a letter of hers; he asked me to
open it; he dared not read it himself in his fevered condition. I had
to write to her and tell the story of the accident.

Rome, January 20, 1787

Moritz to J. H. Campe

J. H. Campe, 1746-1818, pedagogical expert and writer of children's
books.

For forty days I was immobilized and in uninterrupted pain. There
are no words with which to thank the noble, the benevolent Goethe
for what he did for me. At least I'll never forget it. In this frightful
situation . . . he was everything to me that one man can be to
another. He came to me several times a day and watched with me
many nights. . . . And very often when I was ready to despair I
drew new courage from his presence and because I wanted to be
brave in his eyes I succeeded in being so.

Rome, January 25, 1787

To Charlotte

I have a letter from the Duke from Mainz, a letter so gentle and
kind and indulgent, so encouraging and warm that, from this angle
too, my situation seems an entirely happy one. . . . He doesn't ask
me to return before the end of this year. . . .
You anticipate a request I meant to address to you, namely, to let my
mother share in everything that I write to you.

Rome, February 1, 1787

To Charlotte

Now I can go to my work in a happier mood, since I have a letter
from you in which you tell me that you love me and that you take
delight in my letters and the news from me. If only I could give you
a great deal.

Rome, February 3, 1787

To Karl August

Angelika Kauffmann, 1741-1807, the celebrated painter, married to an
Italian colleague and resident in Rome.

Your merry little note from Gotha and your kind and congenial
letter from Mainz arrived almost simultaneously and gave me a
truly good hour. They brought new light and joy into both my
career and my travels. Without the understanding sympathy of those
to whom fate has so closely allied me, without their satisfaction, I
can relish nothing and all notions of voluntary separateness are but

the phantoms of self-deception. . . . I have met quite a few interesting men; of women only one, Angelika Kauffmann. Here, as everywhere, one cannot become involved with the fair sex without loss of time.

The girls or, rather, the young women who are to be found as models in the studios are occasionally very charming and very willing to be both admired and enjoyed. One could in this way indulge one's passions very comfortably, were not certain "French" influences a menace in this paradise. I shall bring with me a portrait of one of these little creatures. You cannot imagine anything daintier.

Rome, February 10, 1787

To Karl August

I'm especially pleased at the understanding with which you are reading *Wilhelm Meister*. Since the time when you first read the book, I have turned it over and over in my mind. The great labor still requisite, if it is to be made into a whole and completed, seems to me tolerable only in view of such sympathetic encouragement as your own. My intention has a mystical element. I would like to make the completion of the book coincide with the beginning of my fortieth year. By that time it ought to have been written.

Rome, February 21, 1787

To Charlotte

I am using a moment while packing to write you a few words. . . . I cling to you with every fibre of my being. Memories horrify me and lacerate me. Dear Lotte, you do not know what violence I have done to myself and still do and that the thought that I do not possess you does, at bottom, though I may turn and twist as I will, exhaust and consume me. I may lend my love to you what form I will, ever and ever—forgive me for uttering once again what has so long stagnated in silence. If only I could tell you my true attitudes, the thoughts of my days and of my loneliest hours. I am confused and almost weak today. . . . I am going on from here now and you will hear from me soon.

Tischbein's Recollections

On February 22, 1787, Goethe and I set out together from Rome to
Naples. It was easy for me to call all remarkable sights to his attention. I had traversed this way once before and all that was beautiful
upon it was vivid in my memory. . . .
I cannot but record an interesting incident. At a certain place on
the road Goethe, being thirsty, asked for water. Since I was careful
of what he ate and drank and since I noticed that the water in the
glass was turbid I warned him and ordered another glass. The answer was, this was the only water available. It came from the cistern
and was good and healthful and everybody drank it daily. We exam-
ined it carefully and found it full of minute living creatures like
tiny crabs, with or without claws or like little eels. Goethe was of
the opinion that the water need not be bad, since oysters and crabs
and other products of the sea not only have an agreeable taste but
are wholesome. He drank the water. We asked the people to show
us the cistern. With a glass we dipped water from the bottom and
brought up creatures of the most exquisite forms and could not but
observe the creative productivity of nature in these warm regions.

Naples, March 10, 1787

To Fritz von Stein

This is a land as merry and gay as you usually are. Sea and land provide so much that the people are easily fed. The markets are full of
fish. Donkeys loaded high with cauliflowers are driven into the cities;
the street vendors offer a great plenty of raisins, almonds, figs, nuts,
small oranges etc. The bread is good nor is meat lacking. No one
need take thought of the morrow, for all days are alike and there is
no need to prepare for dearth or winter.

March 10, 1787

Elisabeth Goethe to the Duchess Anna Amalia

Your Highness' wishes are as an eleventh commandment to me. I
shall send the two letters from my son—for that is all I have received

—to our friend Merck, though I doubt whether his avidity for knowledge will be greatly nourished by them. Needless to say, they gave me infinite pleasure because they showed that his deepest and warmest wish had been fulfilled. . . . May God bring him back well and safe.

Your Highness may be sure that I was delighted by the unexpected visit of our Lord, the Duke.

Naples, March 17, 1787

The Italian Journey

Concerning my Sicilian journey the scales are still in the hands of the gods; the balances rise and fall.

◇◇◇◇◇

At Sea, March 29, 1787

Today, unlike the other day when the packet boat left, there did not blow a good northeaster to help the ship onward in its course, but from the opposite direction a tepid southwest wind, the worst for our course, which gave us occasion to experience how dependent the seafarer is on the whims of wind and weather.

◇◇◇◇◇

March 30, 1787

I could enjoy the noble sights about us for only a few moments. Soon seasickness overcame me. I retired to my cabin and stretched myself out and by abstaining from all food and drink except white bread and red wine I did not feel too uncomfortable. Shut off from the outer world, I let the world within prevail, and since a slow voyage was to be foreseen, I set myself a serious task. The only manuscript I had with me consisted of the first two acts of *Tasso*. These two acts, structurally very much like those in the final version, but written ten years ago, had a softish and misty quality, which soon disappeared when I reworked them in the stricter rhythms according to my newer insights into poetic form.

Palermo, April 13, 1787

Italy without Sicily casts but an imperfect image on the mind. The key is here.

The beauty of the climate cannot be exaggerated. . . . I must say something of food and drink in this land. . . . The fruits are marvelous; the lettuce is of a remarkable tenderness with a flavor as of milk; one understands why the ancients called it *lactuca,* the milky plant. Oil and wine are good and could be even better if more care were used in their preparation. The fishes are the best and most delicate.

Palermo, April 17, 1787

It's really miserable to be pursued and tempted by such varied spirits. Early today I went to the public gardens, quietly and firmly determined to pursue my creative meditations. Before I was aware of it another spirit, by which I had been haunted for days, overcame me. Here under the open sky stand the various plants which we are accustomed to see only in tubs and pots and, in fact, for the greater part of the year only within glass enclosures. Here in their natural habitat they are far more vivid. And in view of these many new and renewed botanical forms my old whimsical reflection overcame me again: whether the primordial prototype of all plant life were not discoverable.

Palermo, April 18, 1787

To Charlotte

A word of farewell from Palermo. . . . My journey is assuming its specific form. It would have been blunted by not going beyond Naples. . . . This is an inexpressibly beautiful land, although I know only one small strip of coast. . . . My heart is with you, and now that distance and absence have cleansed of dross all that which recently stagnated between us, the flame of love and fate and memory can burn and gleam once again in my heart.

The Italian Journey

Girgenti, April 24, 1787

Since there are no inns here a friendly family has put us up in a raised alcove behind their largest room. Green hangings separate us and our belongings from the members of the household who manufacture noodles in the large room adjoining. Those which they make are of the whitest and smallest kind which fetch the highest price. They are first made in straight, needle-like forms; these are then twisted by the tapering fingers of girls into shapes resembling seashells. We sat down among the pretty girls who explained their methods to us and told us that their noodles were made of the best and heaviest wheat which is called *grano forte*.

Catania, May 2, 1787

In our inn here we are badly off. The muleteer is cook and he is not a very good one. A hen boiled in rice might not have been despicable, had it not been ruined by the excessive addition of saffron.

Taormina, May 7, 1787

In a weedy, neglected garden I sat down on the branches of an orange tree and yielded to my fancies. . . . I sat there meditating the plan for a Nausikaa—a dramatic concentration of the *Odyssey*. It is a not impossible project, provided that the writer lays firm hold upon the distinction between the dramatic and the epic mood.

At Sea, May 11, 1787

Once again I had the unpleasant sensation of seasickness which was not mitigated this time by privacy. The central cabin was big enough, however, to hold several people and there were some good mattresses. I lay down again and was fed with red wine and good bread. Yet in this situation the whole Sicilian episode appeared in a less pleasant light. For in reality we had seen nothing but the vain

endeavors of the race of man to sustain itself against the violence of
nature, the treachery of time and the contentions caused by its own
angry passions. Carthaginians, Greeks, Romans and many other peoples had built here and destroyed. . . . These rather seasick reflections of one tossed on the waves of both life and the sea did not long
obtain mastery over me.

Naples, May 15, 1787

To Philip Friedrich Seidel

I landed here yesterday and got your letter of March 7 and your
good, faithful words were most welcome to me. . . .
What you tell me concerning various matters at home I'll keep
discreetly to myself and let it bear fruit. Since I seem to have imitated the grotesque whim of the Emperor Charles V, that is, to witness my own funeral within my lifetime, I mustn't be surprised if
the pallbearers and gravediggers act after the ways of their kind and
if the priests intone the funeral hymns. . . .
I can't let Herr von Knebel have my garden. I gave the keys and
ceded the occupancy for the period of my absence to Frau von Stein.
Try to arrange it so that Herr von Knebel does not ask her for it;
in order to please him she might consent against her real inclination.
I know you'll manage this matter properly.

Naples, May 17, 1787

To Herder

I do want to thank you a thousand times for your most kind supervision of the publication of my writings. I would like to write something much better just to give you pleasure. . . . I must tell you
how, as it were, veils between Homer and myself have been torn
asunder. His descriptions and similitudes seem poetic to us; yet they
are of an inexpressible naturalness, though delineated, of course,
with a purity and intimacy never equaled. Even the strangest and
most fantastic of the described occurrences have an inevitable naturalness which I never felt as I did in the very presence of the objects
which Homer described. Let me express my thoughts briefly: the
ancients represent life itself; we commonly describe its effects; they
represented the terrifying, we delineate terrifyingly; they exhibit the

agreeable, we write agreeably. Etc. Thence arises the exaggerated, the mannerized, the falsely graceful, the bombastic. For when one labors to express the effect of things and the effect only, it is easy to feel that one cannot render it too intensely. If what I say here is not original, yet I may assert that I have had occasion to feel it with a new vividness. These coasts and promontories, these gulfs and bights, these cliffs and beaches, these green hills, soft meadows, fruitful fields, well-cultivated gardens and orchards, these heavy grapes and mounting clouds and ever serene plains, these crags and sandbanks and the all-surrounding ocean with its everlasting multiformity—to have had these present to my spirit has at last made of the *Odyssey* a living word to me.

Naples, May 25, 1787

To Charlotte

Your dear letters—five of them—were all forwarded to me from Rome yesterday. . . .
Whatever bears witness to your love of me is most precious to me; so are, as things are now, your melancholy little notes. . . . I do feel entirely different here and all that I fear is that the Northern climate will rob me of the enjoyment of life. We'll wait and see. . . .
I'll try to get along with Göschen. I know people of his kind and I also know that everybody must try to succeed in his trade. I am eager to hear that the four volumes have been issued. . . . One other thing. If it should come to your ears that the Duke is making changes in my departments, don't let it disturb you. I know all about it and desire it to be done. . . .

Naples, May 29, 1787

To Karl August

C. F. Schmidt, a high-ranking member of the Privy Council.

Your three dear and valued letters were forwarded from Rome several days ago. . . .
Your plan to give Schmidt supervision of the business of the Chamber is one that I fully approve. He is in every respect the right man. Only I beg of you to remember that if, as you plan, you make him vice-president of the Council and leave a directive function in my hands, it would subordinate one member of the Council to another,

which is not at all a good thing. I would suggest that you release me in a perfectly friendly fashion from my incumbency, using the common formula: "at his request." . . . I hope to be in Frankfurt by early September. If I can then spend some time with my mother, prepare the last four volumes for publication, elaborate my travel notes, perhaps even work at *Meister* and some new ideas, I would feel much easier in my mind. For the time must come when these tasks lie behind me. In view of all this, I want to thank you for your kind and wise intention of relieving me of other duties. As matters stand now, you can do it without any hurt to the affairs in question. In fact I can be of more value to you than I have hitherto been, if you will let me do only what no one else can do and assign the rest to others. . . .

Rome, June 8, 1787

To Charlotte

I write you once again from this ancient capital. I arrived day before yesterday in the afternoon. . . .
I am in a mood of great doubt, but I will let things resolve themselves, as they have done so well recently. I must use every effort to complete those last four volumes. As I wrote you before, they must be put in order before my return. New subjects, too, press for execution, and life is brief. Whether I sit and do these things here or in Frankfurt is no matter. Yet Rome is the one place in the world for an artist and that is what I am. . . .
Moreover I have made the acquaintance of happy people who are so because they are *whole*. The humblest human being, if he be whole, can be happy and attain perfection in his own way. That is what I will and must strive after; and I can do it, for at least I know wherein it consists and how it works. I have come to know myself better than I can well say. . . .
Tell Herder that I have come very close to the secret of how plants are reproduced and organized. It is the simplest thing in the world. . . . I'm sorry that you lost the little lion I sent you. It will be hard to find another carved jewel that is so pretty. But I'll try. Maybe you will still find it. I am addressing this letter to you in Karlsbad. Think of me. Hope dwells among the living; it is the dead who lack it.

Rome, July 5, 1787

The Italian Journey

All my present life resembles a dream of youth. It remains to be seen whether I am destined to enjoy it or to discover that this thing, like so many others, is vanity. . . .

I am working at *Egmont* and I hope it goes well. While writing it I have come upon symptoms which have never yet deceived me. It is very strange that I have been so often deterred from finishing the play and that now I do so in Rome. . . .

Wilhelm Meister is constantly expanding. The old things must be gotten out of the way. I am old enough now and if I am to continue to be productive I must not put it off.

Rome, July 14, 1787

To Kayser

> Philip C. Kayser, a composer, who collaborated with Goethe on many undertakings.

Instead of meeting you, my dear Kayser, I'm obliged to write once more. I hardly know when I will be able to bear to leave Rome. I find here the fulfillment of every wish and dream. How shall I leave a place which alone on earth can be a paradise to me? Daily my bodily and spiritual health improve and I have no wish left except that this condition may endure.

I often think of you when I hear a comic opera. Cimarosa still entertains us and lures us into the playhouse, despite the heat.

Rome, July 20, 1787

The Italian Journey

I have recently discerned clearly the two chief failings that have pursued and tormented me all my life. One is this, that I never really wanted to acquire the craftsmanship of any matter that I needed or had to accomplish. That is why, in spite of much natural talent, I have created and done so little. I have either forced things by energy of mind, letting them succeed or fail as luck and chance dictated; or, else, when I tried to carry out something well and thoughtfully, I got frightened and never completed it. The second fault, closely akin to the first, is that I never felt like giving as much time to a piece of work or a piece of business as it required. Since I am lucky enough to be able to think and plan and work things out very swiftly, I always found a deliberate execution a great bore. The time and the hour have arrived in which I must correct those two failings.

Rome, Early August, 1787

The Italian Journey

At the very beginning of this month I came to the deliberate decision to spend the coming winter in Rome. What finally decided me was the feeling and the insight that I was not yet ripe for a break with my present situation; also that nowhere else would I find either equal space or tranquility for the completion of my works. And now, that I have announced this decision at home, a period of a new kind sets in.

Rome, August 4, 1787

To Herder

. . . On my return by way of Switzerland I will pay some attention to this matter of magnetism. It is not quite empty and not all charlatanism. The trouble is that the people who have hitherto practiced it are suspicious characters—noisy promoters, gentlemen of high rank, so-called prophets, all people who like to accomplish a great deal at small expense and want somehow to be on top.

Consider the famous witch trials at certain periods of history. I never thought the matter psychologically explained; it made me attentive to and at the same time made me suspicious of all so-called wonders. Now the connection between magnetism and witches is one of those intricate associations of ideas which I can't elaborate on this small sheet of paper.

Rome, August 11, 1787

To Karl August

I thank you warmly for your dear and valued letter. . . . You give me the opportunity of becoming my true self and yet you do not separate our destinies. . . . I expect another letter to contain a

definite decision concerning my extended leave of absence. I believe
that I make no mistake if I request you to let me remain here until
next Easter. . . . By Easter I expect to have closed a certain epoch,
my first or, in another sense, my second period of authorship. *Egmont* is done. By the New Year I hope to have *Tasso* done and by
Easter *Faust*. That is possible only in this isolation. At the same
time I hope to complete the smaller things which are to fill the fifth,
sixth, and seventh volumes. . . . The completion of my older works
is marvelously useful to me. It represents a recapitulation of life and
art; it forces me to fuse my present way of thinking and writing
with an earlier one while, at the same time, I proceed to the execution of what I have recently conceived. Thus I gain an intimate
knowledge of myself, both of my narrower and my broader qualities.

Rome, September 3, 1787

The Italian Journey

Today a year ago I left Karlsbad. What a year! And what a strange
period opened for me upon this day which is the Duke's birthday
and which marked for me the birth of a new life. At this moment
I can give an accounting of my use of this year neither to myself
nor to others. But the time for that will come.

September 4, 1787

Charlotte to Her Sister-in-Law

I dreamed most strangely of him last night; I fear that some catastrophe will befall him and just at some moment when he remembers
us. It is thus that I am bound to interpret my dream. If only I could
get over this feeling of never seeing him again.

Rome, September 5, 1787

The Italian Journey

This morning's writings will be festive to me, for *Egmont* is really
being completed. . . .
Meanwhile I am so well in body and in soul that I almost believe a

radical cure is being accomplished. I do everything with great ease
and sometimes it is as though a breath of youth blows upon me.

◇◇◇◇◇

Rome, September 22, 1787

Strange fate that these four slender volumes, the fruits of half a lifetime, should find me here in Rome. I can truly say: there is no letter
that has not been lived and felt, enjoyed, suffered, meditated upon
and so it all speaks to me with a living tongue.

Frascati, September 28, 1787

To Karl August

> For several weeks in September and October Goethe withdrew from
> Rome to Frascati and Castel Gandolfo. In the latter place he was often
> the guest of the English banker and art dealer Thomas Jenkins. It is
> here, too, that he made the acquaintance of the "beautiful lady of
> Milano," Maddelena Riggi, 1765-1825, of whom more will be heard.

Although we are so far apart I often converse with you and tell you
how well I am faring and I have the intuition, too, that you are
feeling well and that you are glad to be alive and active in your new
position in the armies of Prussia and that you are enjoying your life.
My place is among the peaceful aspects in the world, yours among
the warlike. These are the two opposite poles of existence. In this
country powder is used only for fireworks and celebrations on festive
days and the soldiers avoid rain as much as they do fire. . . . That
I am half mad with drawing and all kinds of writing Frau von Stein
will have told you. No one can live more simply and at the same
time more variously than I do now. Art, if one is at all strict in one's
notion of it, is a most serious matter and any intimate knowledge of
it is a business of unbelievable difficulty.

Rome, October 23, 1787

The Italian Journey

A lady of Milan interested me during the brief period of her stay.
Through her naturalness and common sense and agreeable ways she

contrasted favorably with the ladies of Rome. . . . She was introduced to me by the sister of one of the employes of Herr Jenkins, a young man who was highly esteemed by his employer. The two young women seemed to be great friends. . . . I sat at a game, similar to the game of Lotto, between these two lovely girls. At first the Roman lady was my partner; later I tried my luck in the partnership of the lady of Milan. . . . In my ignorance of the manners of the country I did not at once perceive that this change of partners was not well thought of here. When the game was over the mother courteously but seriously told me in private that, having been her daughter's partner, it was not seemly to transfer my partnership to another lady. . . . While I offered my excuses, it was borne in upon me most strangely that my inclination for the lady of Milan was a decisive one and that it had developed with such speed and intensity as is likely to happen in an idle heart. . . . Next morning the three of us met again and my preference for the lady of Milan was but intensified. . . . In the course of the forenoon the company increased; Angelika Kauffmann, too, had arrived. A great table had been spread and she had been assigned the place at my right. The girl from Milan, who had been placed on the opposite side, did not hesitate for a minute to make the tour of the table and sit down at my other side. Angelika observed this with some surprise. Her experienced glance taught her that something must have taken place and that her friend who had hitherto withdrawn from female society to the point of harshness, had been tamed and overcome. . . .

As I kept listening to the conversation of the Italian ladies I could not but perceive that they were discussing the question of a trousseau. . . . Finally, too, the conversation turned to the merits of the prospective bridegroom; a favorable view was taken of him, though his faults were not concealed. . . . Rather shyly I asked who the young man's fiancée was. With surprise they replied that everyone knew, and only then realized that I was no intimate of that circle, but a stranger. It is hardly necessary to describe the horror which overcame me when I understood the prospective bride to be the girl whom I had just taken into my heart. Upon a slight pretext I left the company. . . .

It is not uncommon and well known that inclinations thoughtlessly indulged for a period are transformed into intense pain when one is rudely awakened from the dream. The case I am describing has this peculiarity: that a vivid and mutual kindness was here destroyed at the very moment of its germination and therewith the presage of happiness which an emotion of this character arouses. I returned home late; next morning I took my drawing utensils and set out on a long excursion, in order to have an excuse for absenting myself from the common meals.

I was old and experienced enough to regain my self-control at once, painful as it was to do so. How strange would it have been, I cried out to myself, if a fate similar to that of Werther had overtaken me in Rome and ruined my whole situation, which meant so much to me and which I had hitherto guarded so well.

◇◇◇◇◇

Rome, November 10, 1787

Kayser is here now and we have a threefold life to which music is added. He is a good and excellent man and is falling in with the simple natural life that one can lead only on this soil. Tischbein is returning from Naples. Our living quarters must be readjusted, but since we are all good-natured, it will not take more than a week to do so. . . .

I am so happy that *Egmont* is being well received. There is nothing that I have written with greater freedom of spirit as well as with conscientiousness of execution. Yet one never knows, provided one has written at all, what will satisfy the reader who always demands that one imitate one's former work.

Rome, November 17, 1787

To Karl August

You have been urging me to write you more often. I shall be happy to do so if I may set down on paper whatever the day and the hour supply. It cannot always be highly significant. Great results are few in number and the longer that one contemplates the objects in this world, the less one is apt to venture on generalizations. . . . *Egmont* is now in Weimar and its reception by our friends gives me intense pleasure. I hope it will make a good impression on you, too, for I would write nothing further except what will appeal to those who, like yourself, lead lives that have greatness and variety. . . .

I want to add a word about your mother's project for a journey to

Italy. The matter troubles me. She was planning to arrive still this year. It seemed to me an overbold undertaking, to say the least, to traverse these regions with the people who have been named to me. They are good fellows but uninstructed and wholly unacquainted with the country. As a matter of both private and official obligation I explained to her why it seemed necessary to me to put off the journey for another year. Happily other circumstances also persuaded her to wait. I have now been in this country for over a year and I know how hard it is for distinguished strangers to combine in some measure enjoyment, reasonable economy and personal dignity.

Rome, December 1, 1787

The Italian Journey

This much I am sure of: I have attained certainty concerning the most important points, and although this knowledge could be extended into infinitude, I have already a clear and communicable conception of the finite aspects.

◇◇◇◇◇

Rome, December 15, 1787

This week has been a very gay one. Last week nothing seemed to go right, and since the weather was fair and since my knowledge of the sky taught me that bright days were coming, I picked myself up and in Kayser's company made a tour of all the spots which I knew already and penetrated corners I had not yet seen. We reached Frascati on Tuesday. Wednesday we visited the loveliest villas and saw the exquisite statue of Antinous. . . . Today we returned from Castel Gandolfo to Rome. . . .

Rome, December 16, 1787

To Karl August

Just one more word about our official affairs, which I don't want to put off until my return. I wish you would persuade Schmidt that he put Philip Seidel, who has been in your service quietly and in small matters, to some intimate test and find out for himself in what manner and to what purpose the young man may be useful. I'm not in a position to recommend him unconditionally, because he is, in the best sense of the word, the product of my training. But I do wish him to be known. . . . He is young and has the most promising aspects. Have him put to some test; do so yourself; unless I am badly deceived, you will hardly find his equal within his class and sphere.

Rome, December 20, 1787

To Charlotte

I am sending you another little carved lion. It is not as charming as the first, yet it has its own quality and may make the loss of the first more bearable.

Rome, December 29, 1787

To Karl August

I hear on all sides that you are well and gay at The Hague and that the clouds of war are leaving the sky. The luck that you have always had with women is not likely to desert you in Holland either and will somehow compensate you for having missed seeing the lovely Emilie Gore on her home ground.

The god of love has relegated me to an unhappy corner of the world. The public votaries of love are dangerous as they are everywhere. Unmarried girls are of an appalling virtue; there is no chance of so much as touching them. If you are but polite, they ask: *e che concluderemo?* [*What bargain do you propose?*]. They either want you to marry them or get them a husband out of hand. Once they have a husband, the fat is in the fire. For though it is true that all married women are at one's disposal, it is on condition that one support the whole family. . . .

1787

COPHTIC SONG

Perhaps despite himself Goethe had become interested in the notorious impostor Cagliostro and in the affair of the "Diamond Necklace" which stirred all Europe. He suspected the existence of secret and cynical associations of swindlers and wrote a comedy, *The Grand Cophta*, on these matters which was hardly worthy of him. The following two poems composed in Rome express what he felt to be the possibly valid elements at the bottom of this matter. He seems to have invented the words

Cophta and Cophtic, though there may have been in his mind the word Coptic, the name of post-hieroglyphic Egyptian writing.

Come, let the learned contend in their rages,
Stiff, starched and strict the professors let be!
All who were wisest throughout all ages
Smiling and winking did fully agree:
Foolish to dream that the fools will grow better!
Children of wisdom, in spirit and letter,
Treat them as fools—as is fitting to do.

Merlin the mage at his sepulchre's gateway
Where in my youth he once spoke to me straightway,
Taught me a similar doctrine as true:
Foolish to dream that the fools will grow better!
Children of wisdom, in spirit and letter,
Treat them as fools—as is fitting to do.

And on the highest East-Indian altars,
Deep in Egyptian tombs where man falters,
Holy the word from of old that they knew:
Foolish to dream that the fools will grow better!
Children of wisdom, in spirit and letter,
Treat them as fools—as is fitting to do.

1787

ANOTHER COPHTIC SONG

Take my council, make no blunder,
In thy days of youth be ready
Life's last wisdom clear to see:
Fortune's wheel is never steady,
Never stops to wait for thee;
Thou must progress or go under,
Thou must ruler be and winner,
Or the servant and the loser,
Suffering's or triumph's chooser,
Anvil or else hammer be.

1788

Rome, January 19, 1788

To Charlotte

When I think of the ills you suffer and hear about your toothache, a kind of desperation overcomes me that you must drag out a painful life under that inclement sky. All the time that I have been here I haven't suffered any of the ills that tormented me in the North and with my same old constitution have been constantly well and thoroughly alive. Signs multiply, alas, that this well-being, as well as many other good things, will have to be left behind me in Italy.

Rome, January 25, 1788

To Karl August

The chief purpose of my journey was to cure myself of those physical and moral ills which plagued me in Germany and finally made me quite useless. Next I wanted to quench my fevered thirst for art in its true aspects. The first purpose has been measurably attained, the second completely. . . .

I convey to you the following accounting of my expenditures. I have continued to draw against the sum which your kind foresight allocated to me. After deducting from it what was needed for my household at home, I have spent the rest on living expenses plus the 1000 thaler from the publisher for the first four volumes of my works. Considering the simplicity of my life I ought to have been able to do on less. But my existence has resembled that of my Wilhelm Meister. In spite of that, I am well contented, having attained all my chief objects. I have also had to be careful to render my incognito respectable by a modest but appropriate generosity. By always sharing what I had with several artists, I succeeded in gaining teachers, friends and aids. . . .

Coming to your affairs, I think you have an excellent councillor in Schmidt. He has an inborn talent for economics; I would not have had a quiet moment, had I not known your finances to be in his hands. . . . I am infinitely delighted that the success of the mines is now assured and that we can really proceed toward serious exploitation. . . . Finally, I repeat: if, on your return home, you find that you need me, I am ready to come at a word from you.

Rome, Carnival, 1788

The Italian Journey

. . . Now the masks begin to increase. At first appear young men, dressed in the festive garments of women of the lowest class with naked bosom and impudent bearing. They caress the men whom they meet, indulge with the women in such vulgar familiarities as though *they* were men and carry on as whim or wit or mischievousness impel them to do. . . . The women are as fond of donning men's clothes as are the men to do the opposite. Thus wenches have adopted the favorite costume of Pulcinello, and it is not to be denied that their equivocal appearance succeeds in being intensely provocative.

◇◇◇◇◇

Rome, February 1, 1788

I have now made a survey of my lyrical poems for the eighth volume, which I may bring out before the seventh. It is a curious thing, this summation of a life. How slight the traces left by any existence!

Rome, February 16, 1788

To Karl August

I have been busily puttering around with my former works. . . . Now what I face is the hill called *Tasso* and the mountain called *Faust*. I won't rest day or night till the two are done. I am strangely drawn to both and have recently had marvelous insights and hopes.

Rome, February 16, 1788

To Karl August

When I saw your dear handwriting in Frau von Stein's envelope, I thought it a message from you in Weimar. It was still from Mainz and gave me real pleasure by its assurance of your recovery. When I read your other letter which your messenger brought me I was good-natured enough to think the trouble was haemorrhoids. Now, of course, I see it was adjacent parts that suffered. I do hope that the disagreeable inoculation will serve to drive all the evil from the body at once. I shall not fail to defy the spirits of ill with the proper secret symbols. [*Here follow the traditional symbols of sundry signs of the Zodiac: Sagittarius, The Scales, The Ram, Leo, Scorpio.*] You write so convincingly that a man must be a *cervello tosto* in order not to be seduced into that sweet garden of flowers. It would seem that the good idea in your letter of January 22 was immediately effective in Rome, for I could tell you the story of several charming excursions of my own. So much is certain and you, in your character of a doctor *longe experientissimus,* are perfectly right that moderate exercise of this kind refreshes the soul and creates in the body a delicious equilibrium. I have experienced this fact several times in my life. I have also, on the contrary, felt the discomfort of leaving the broad path and entering upon the narrow one of continency and safety.

Rome, February 16, 1788

The Italian Journey

The other day the Prussian courier brought me a letter from the Duke as kind and friendly and delightful as ever I received. Since he could be quite unreserved he described to me the entire political situation as well as his own. His words to me personally were most affectionate.

◇◇◇◇◇

Rome, March 1, 1788

This past week was so rich in content that it seemed like a month to me. First of all I made an outline of *Faust;* I trust that it was a happy one. Of course, it's quite a different thing—writing the piece now or having written it fifteen years ago. It is not likely to lose by the postponement, especially because I believe I have now gathered up all the threads. I am reassured, too, in regard to the tone of the whole. I have already executed a new scene; if the paper had the color of the old manuscript, I venture to say that no one would

pick it out as new. Since this period of tranquility and separation
has brought me back to the level of my own existence, I see with
some amazement how like to myself I remain and how little the
inner man has lost through the years and their events. I often brood
over the old manuscript when I see it before me. It is still the very
first, with the chief scenes written quite extempore. Now time has
yellowed it and tattered it. The sheets were never bound. It is so
brittle and ragged at the edges, that it really looks like the fragment
of some antique codex, so that, even as in the years when I wrote
it I was transported into an earlier world, so it transports me now
into a period of autobiographical antiquity.

◇◇◇◇◇

Rome, March 14, 1788

It is odd that external causes forced me to take measures adjusted
to a new situation whereby my residence in Rome became ever love-
lier, happier, more profitable. I can truly say that I have enjoyed the
highest measure of contentment I have ever known during these
past eight weeks, and if no more I have gained a norm according to
which I will be able ever hereafter to measure the degree of happiness that is given me. . . . My departure will deeply sadden three
persons. Perhaps they will never find again what they found in me
and I leave them with deep grief. Here in Rome did I first discover
my true self; in profound harmony with my own soul I have become
both happy and sane, and it is this sane and happy man whom these
three that I leave behind me have known, possessed, enjoyed, each in
a different sense and degree.

Rome, March 17, 1788

To Karl August

All things considered, I believe that I will be in Florence by the end
of April. I will not linger too long over what that city offers; I shall
proceed to Milan and from there find my way home. I have already
had to rob my mother of the hope of seeing me on my return journey
and have sought to console her with the promise of a later visit. . . .
According to these plans I will reach home during the first half of
June, and I have one more request to make of you, namely, that you
will let me continue to be on that leave of absence already granted

me, although I shall be present. My strange and undisciplined nature, which has made me suffer so much even in complete freedom and in the full enjoyment of every desire, will make it necessary for me to find my way back gradually even to you, even to our friends, even into the domain of your affairs. . . .

What I may say above all is this: in these eighteen months of solitariness I have found my true self again, and that self is the self of an artist. . . .

Now all that I have said and requested takes it for granted that you have no immediate need of me in the mechanics of the administration. Had I not been certain that he who took my place would be most satisfactory to you, I might have gone, but I would not have stayed nearly as long. . . .

The status in the Council which you want to continue to have me occupy is so honorable that I am ashamed to accept it and equally embarrassed to decline it. I have given you my reasons for being inclined to the latter. I would repeat these reasons, were I not convinced that it is almost as immodest to refuse a high distinction as stubbornly to strive to attain it.

Rome, March 28, 1788

To Karl August

I am now reading a very well-written life of Tasso. I am trying to fill my mind with the character and the fate of this poet in order to preoccupy myself with them on my trip. Before I come back I would like to advance this play considerably, even if I can't finish it. . . . What would then remain for me to do next winter is the execution of *Faust,* to which I feel a very special inclination. If it only turns out to be half as good as I desire and hope.

Rome, April 10, 1788

The Italian Journey

My body is still in Rome, not so my soul. As soon as it was decided that I must go, my interest died, and I could have wished to have left two weeks ago.

◇◇◇◇◇

Rome, April 11, 1788

The days go by and I am incapable of doing anything. . . .

◇◇◇◇◇

Rome, April 14, 1788

Confusion cannot be greater. . . . It was clear to me that I must get at *Tasso* at once. So my thoughts did turn in that direction. . . . In the meantime I am packing and it is, of course, at such moments that one sees how much has been accumulated and brought together about one.

◇◇◇◇◇

Rome, Late April, 1788

My departure from Rome was to have an element of solemnity. For three nights the full moon stood in the faultless sky and that magic which radiates from this enormous city, so often felt by me, penetrated me profoundly. . . .

After distracted and painful days I traversed the city once more alone. After I had measured the length of the Corso for the last time, I mounted to the Capitol. . . . Dark and throwing a dark shadow the arch of Septimius Severus arose before me; in the deserted Via Sacra the familiar objects seemed strange and ghostly. . . . All that is massive produces an impression at once sublime and concrete. Under its impact I drew up a final accounting of my entire stay. From it my soul, stirred to its depth, produced a mood in which the heroic and the elegiac were blended and whence an elegy in poetic form was about to arise.

But what actually came to my mind—and why should it not at such a moment?—was the elegy in which Ovid spoke of his banishment from Rome, which was also marked by a moonlit night. *Cum repeto noctem!* How that night comes back to me! His recollection in his exile by the Black Sea, his mournful and lamentable condition, did not leave my mind. I repeated his whole poem to myself as it arose in my memory and disturbed my own productivity, so that the elegiac verses which had begun to float into my mind, were never to be written.

Milan, May 23, 1788

To Karl August

The precision of my schedule shows you that I am trying to imitate our Chancellor Schmidt and that I am trying from at least one aspect to return to discipline and order. For in all other matters I am frightfully demoralized. To be sure, I never was good for much anyhow, and so my one consolation is that you won't find me very greatly changed.

The farewell from Rome cost me rather more than is fair and proper at my age. But I wasn't able to subdue my temperament and I gave it free rein on this final trip. This meant that I was in seven different humors every hour, and all I am glad of is that this smear of a letter coincides with one of the merry sevenths. . . . Please remember me to your wife and let me find the happiness of old in having a kind master and a sympathetic friend.

Book Five

THE HOME AND THE WORLD

1788-1805

WEIMAR

1788
(Continued)

Addenda to the Metamorphosis of Plants

Goethe drove into Weimar, after a two years' absence, on the moonlit night of June 18.

From the plastic beauty of Italy I returned to the formlessness of Germany. I exchanged a serene sky for one dark with clouds. My friends, instead of consoling me and seeking to draw near to me again, brought me close to despair. My delight in far and almost unheard-of objects, my suffering, my lamentation over all I had lost, seemed to affront them. All sympathy was lacking; no one understood my language.

Late June, 1788

Charlotte to Charlotte von Lengefeld

Everybody around here seems to want to go to Italy. I myself prefer my own home. People who are not happy at home will not be happy anywhere, and these journeys considered as cures are mere palliatives.

Late June, 1788

Charlotte to Her Sister-in-Law

I did very wrong to give up these lovely days in Kochberg on Goethe's account. For I did put off my departure. But our meeting was utterly false in tone and nothing but boredom was exchanged between us. The presentiment that our lovely circle would be destroyed and its members scattered is very vivid in my heart. Goethe has it on his conscience for having taken the first step toward this end.

353

Early July, 1788

To Charlotte

I'll try to leave Court early this afternoon and come over to you.
This morning, too, I'll try to come in for a moment. I'll be glad to
hear whatever you have to say. Only I beg of you not to hold me too
responsible. I am distracted, to say the least. I can afford to tell you
that the inner man does not correspond to the outer appearance.

July 22, 1788

To Charlotte

I hope you will be contented and above all well in the tranquility
of Kochberg. I'll go on living as best I can, although it is a curious
task that lies ahead of me.

July 23, 1788

To Jacobi

Yes, my dear man, I'm back and sit in my garden behind my hedge
of roses and under the branches of my trees and am gradually coming to myself again. I was very happy in Italy. So many things within
me returned to life that had long been stagnant, and joy and hope
took up their dwelling with me again. My stay in this place will be
very useful to me. For since I have recovered my true self again I
will now be able to be creative from within and to extend that
knowledge and to cultivate it. . . .
I am hard at *Tasso. Faust* is to be the occupation of my winter. As
soon as the eight volumes are out, I shall also get to *Meister*.

August 12, 1788

To Charlotte

It was very pleasant to see Fritz again. I think he'll stick to me when
everybody else deserts me. Herder has left for Italy; the Dowager
Duchess is going on Friday; the Duke has a bad foot, otherwise he
would have gone to the Gores' [*the English parents of Karl August's
current mistress*] on Saturday. He wants me to accompany him to
Dresden next month; I shall decline, if at all possible.

Karoline Herder to Her Husband

> Goethe had been interested for some time in a young man, Christian August Vulpius, 1762-1827, a writer of what we would now call mystery and horror stories. Sometime in July the latter had sent his twenty-three-year-old sister Christiane, 1764-1816, who worked in an artificial flower factory, with a written petition to Goethe's garden. Further meetings followed and within a few weeks Goethe took the girl to his house to live with him.

Goethe came to call. He said things about his domestic and human situation that amused me but at the same time rather stunned me. But in everything he said there was so much that was clear and straight that I recovered. His theory now is that happiness and well-being depend on right measure and proportion and that unhappiness is merely the contrary of these. He is thoroughly comfortable now that he has a house and food and drink and similar things. . . . This is of course a mere excerpt from the conversation which we carried on in a very pleasant mood.

August 15, 1788
Karoline Herder to Her Husband

Goethe keeps on visiting me. I told you something about our last conversation in the letter which the Dowager Duchess enclosed in hers. By and large I'm not comfortable in his presence. He is keeping his heart out of his life. Charlotte Stein is of the opinion that he has become a sensualist, and there's a good deal to that. He even likes to go to Court and share the meals there. He says that this winter he's going to stick to the Duchess; she is the only person who has remained true to him. He wants me to come to tea sometime. I said I would, if Charlotte Stein came too. "Oh," he said, "you can't do anything with her; she is ill-humored and seems not to improve at all." I defended her as best I could, but I don't believe that he is willing to meet her even halfway.

August 18, 1788

Karoline Herder to Her Husband

Goethe drops in nearly every other day. He was here yesterday afternoon. He is very much like a chameleon. Sometimes I like him,
sometimes only half. He doesn't want to show his hand and avoids
saying anything from which inferences could be drawn. That's the
reason too, I believe, why he jumps from subject to subject.

August 24, 1788

To Charlotte

The Duke's foot has forced him to return. He won't join his regiment nor probably go to Dresden. . . . Pretty soon I'll send you
copies of the poems. Wieland has them now. Fritz is a very good
boy. But I can do little for him, as indeed I seem to be perfectly
useless. Enjoy your solitariness. It won't be long before, by God's
help, I will have recovered my own, never to give it up again.

August 29, 1788

Karoline Herder to Her Husband

. . . Goethe was very pleasant. I complimented him for coming at
an appropriate hour, since he hadn't been here all week. "Yes," he
said, "I was on the way to my garden and had to turn back. What
drove me here was not love but perhaps despair."

August 31, 1788

To Charlotte

Forgive me for the confusion of my last letter. Everything will improve and be resolved; one must give both oneself and circumstances
a little time.
I am so frightened under this sky and on this earth that I'll hardly
be able to come to you. The weather here makes me quite miserable,
and I feel well nowhere except in my little room beside a hearth
fire. Then it may rain all it will. . . .
Be so kind as to let me have the letters I wrote you during my jour-

ney, if you have them by you. Or let me know where I can get hold of them. I want gradually to use them as a basis for a piece of writing. . . .

September 4, 1788

To Herder

The Duke's bad foot keeps him on a sofa against his will. Now that he sees that it can't be helped, he does pull himself together and lets no one notice how desperately he is annoyed. But his inner man is in a bad way. He let himself go completely in his passion for the Gore girl as well as in political matters. Both proved futile. How can he have any satisfaction? His wife keeps him company faithfully with good humor and patience. I eat dinner with them every day and spend many hours with them, when there is no one else. So time dribbles away. One is neither aware of life nor glad of it.

September 9, 1788

To Jacobi

You ask me to recommend a young man to act as your secretary and to tutor your children. Well, I have one whom I would like to see settled; I trust that he will suit you. . . . He has had a taste for letters from his youth on. He began to write and publish early, partly through inclination, partly because he was poor. His name is Vulpius. You may have read his name somewhere and not in a context to recommend him to you. We are frightened at our own sins when we see them in others. It was hard enough work to support himself and his brothers and sisters in this way. . . .
I always had great hopes of your son Georg, and I was annoyed with you and your wife, because you were never satisfied with the child. A little leaf in the process of growth is full of wrinkles and folds before it has a chance to develop. If you have no patience with it and want it at once to be as smooth as a willow leaf, it's a bad business. I congratulate you that I was right.

September 12, 1788

Karoline Herder to Her Husband

Goethe said the other day: "You don't travel in order to reach your goal but to be on the way." Before I go on I want to tell you something about our excursion to Kochberg. It was on the 5th and we started at 6 in the morning—Goethe, Charlotte's little sister-in-law, Fritz and myself. . . . At half past ten we had come to the end of that bad road. Lotte Lengefeld came out first to bid us welcome. Frau von Stein followed her and received us all very sweetly but her attitude to Goethe was stiff. That spoiled the day for him. He showed us drawings that he had made. In the afternoon he slept and that night read us passages from your letters. . . . The next day, Sunday, we went to Rudolstadt to see the Lengefeld family, very pleasant people. Schiller was there. Goethe behaved very well toward him and the moral atmosphere was good. In the evening under a bright moon we walked back to Kochberg. Goethe recited passages from his unfinished poem, *The Mysteries,* and talked about his play *Tasso.*

September 12, 1788

Schiller to Christian Gottfried Körner

Körner, 1756-1831, Saxon official and a close friend of Schiller's, whom he had often generously entertained in Dresden. Schiller was secretly engaged at this time to one of the daughters of the Lengefeld family.

At last I can tell you about Goethe, and I know how eagerly you will listen. I spent nearly the whole of last Sunday in his company. He came to call on us with Frau Herder and Frau von Stein. At first glance the general opinion concerning his attractive and handsome figure is very much diminished. He is of medium height and carries himself very stiffly, even when he walks. His countenance is reserved, but his eyes are impressive and lively and one looks at them with pleasure. Although he is very serious, his expression has much benevolence and goodness. He is very dark and struck me as older than, according to my calculation, he can possibly be. His voice is exceedingly pleasant and his manner of narration fluid and witty and spirited. . . . He is fond of speaking quite passionately of his Italian experiences. . . . All the vices and virtues of the Italians are the natural results of their burning sensuality. . . . In Rome it is not customary to have relations with single women; the tradition is to use married ones. The contrary is true in Naples. Upon the whole, the treatment of the other sex in Italy betrays the nearness of the Orient. . . . Upon the whole, the very great idea I had of him has not been diminished by this personal acquaintanceship, but I doubt whether we will ever be able to be close to each other. Much that still interests me extremely, that I desire and hope for, lies in a past epoch of his life. He is so far ahead of me, less in years than in experience and development, that we'll never be able to meet at any point of our path. His whole character, moreover, is fundamentally different from my own; his world is not my world; our ways of thought are far apart. However, no final or certain inference can be drawn from a single meeting. Time will teach us.

October 10, 1788

To Herder

Herder, a cleric of Episcopal rank, was accompanied to Rome by the youthful Canon Dalberg who brought with him his friend, the widow of the late Chamberlain von Seckendorf.

Let me bid you welcome in Rome; let me welcome you to every spot on which you will set your foot. For there is no noteworthy one where I had not thought of you. . . . Forgive your wife if she has confided more to me than you desired; forgive me if my criticism of certain people was violent. . . .
The Seckendorf woman is a caution and you are far too much of a gentleman. But since that is your nature, I want you to abide by it and not let her cut up too rough. Dalberg, like all weaklings, is very glad when you make things easy for him, when you should make life hard for him. The woman, on the other hand, who should brighten his life, ends by boring him. Nevertheless I commend her, as the Lord did the unjust householder. The whores always come out on top. No honest man or woman or girl can prevail against them.

Late October, 1788

Karoline Herder to Her Husband

I talked to Goethe about that promissory note. I have now 150 Reichsthaler in cash, that is, the Duke's semi-annual supplement. I was going to borrow another 150 and so send you a note to the amount of 300. He advised against my taking up the loan and told me to send you immediately the 150 thaler or, rather, 100 scudi, there being an advantage in the exchange. So he did that for me on the last day on which mail went to Italy.

Late October, 1788

Schiller to Charlotte von Lengefeld

Do enjoy the last beautiful days at Kochberg. You are in very good hands. I have grown very fond of Charlotte Stein, since I have watched the workings of her mind. I love her beautiful earnestness of character and her interest in everything she holds to be true and noble.

Jena, November 16, 1788

To Fritz von Stein

I send you back a corrected version of your translation. Now you can copy it and it will be finished. . . . I am having a very gay time. There was a ball at which I danced; day before yesterday there was a festive supper and last night a concert. And so it goes. Jena seems to inspire a merry life.

Tell your mother that I am learning a lot and thinking a lot. I have much conversation with Knebel and he encourages me to write things down. As for my virtue, the only expression that will fit is an Italian one: *Crescono le mie virtù, ma la mia virtù cala.* My virtues increase but my virtue vanishes. Farewell. Remember me to your father. I'll be back soon.

Jena, November 16, 1788

To Karl August

August Friedrich, Baron von Zigesar, 1746-1813, Vice-Chancellor of the Duchy had a handsome estate near Jena and several beautiful daughters.

I want to announce to you that we were on the Zigesar estate to view the progeny. The tall grown girls nearly put our eyes out. The youngest is being prepared for confirmation and has difficulty memorizing the Prophets; the middle one is a real treasure; the oldest begins to resemble her mother. . . . Mother, daughters and sons will soon visit us two old bachelors. I need not be ashamed to display to you the old student spirit which begins to throb again.

December 9, 1788

Memorandum to the Private Session of the Privy Council

Herr Friedrich Schiller whom some years ago His Serenity created a titular councillor, has recently taken up residence either here or in the vicinity. He has earned a considerable reputation through his writings, especially through his recent *History of the Revolt of the Netherlands against Spanish Domination,* which shows his mastery of historic studies. Since he holds no office and has no security of any kind, the thought arose whether one could not attach him to Jena to the considerable advantage of the university there. People who know him well describe him as of excellent character and ways of life. His demeanor is serious and pleasing; there is no reason to doubt that he would have a good influence on young people.

He has been sounded out on this matter and declared that he would be not disinclined to accept an associate professorship at the University of Jena, even though at first no honorarium were to be attached to the position. He would seek to continue his historic studies and to render himself useful to the university.

The undersigned, having occasion to discuss academic matters both with His Serenity of this Duchy and with His Serenity of Gotha, broached the subject in question and the plan was thoroughly approved, especially since it involves no immediate expenditure.

His Serenity thereupon commanded the undersigned to bring the matter to the attention of the Privy Council, commending the plan to the favorable judgment and early decision of the Council, in order that the aforesaid Councillor Schiller may be able to make the necessary arrangements prior to Easter and may be able to proceed to qualify himself as a Magister Artium.

Respectfully submitted:

(signed)   J. W. v. Goethe

December 27, 1788

To Herder

I am with you and converse with you in spirit both independently and through your letters to your wife. I thank you for addressing a

word or two to me from Rome. Ah, how often do I repeat to myself
the verses of Ovid:

> Cum subit illius tristissima noctis imago,
> Quae mihi supremum tempus in urbe fuit.

[*How often the saddest image arises before me of that night which
was my ultimate moment in the city.*] Only too keenly do I feel what
I lost by exchanging that atmosphere for this. I do not seek to hide it
from myself, yet do the best I can to settle down here again. I continue my studies which in some respects may supplement your
own. . . .
Tasso isn't quite finished yet. I'm ashamed to say so. The eighth
volume will soon be printed. I'll send a copy at once to Angelika, in
order that you may both have it.
Deep snow here and bitter continuous cold and now and then dreadful storms. I cower in my little room, while you move about in that
free and beautiful world. Well, each one must have his chance.

1789

From the Supplementary Confessions

Scarcely had I settled down again to my life and situation in Weimar
and taken up my affairs, my studies and my literary pursuits, than
the French Revolution reached a climax and arrested the attention
of the entire world. As far back as 1785 the scandal of the Diamond
Necklace episode had made an ineffaceable impression on me. An
abyss opened in the immorality of cities, courts and states. From it
arose like ghosts the most detestable phenomena. For a long time I
could not rid myself of these horrors. I took them so strangely that
friends with whom I was then staying confessed to me only much
later, when the Revolution had already broken out, that I had
seemed to them quite mad on that earlier occasion.

February 2, 1789

To Count Friedrich Stolberg

I view with much more understanding than you may think the consoling experience which your letter communicates, namely, that your

dear, departed Agnes has recently appeared to you in a guise purer and more saintly than in her life, and that thus her departure has given you a foretaste and a premonition of a blessed and perfected permanence. Though, for my own part, I cling more or less to the teachings of Lucretius and confine myself and all my hopes to this life, yet I am always glad and deeply refreshed when I see that our Mother Nature reserves within the undulation of her harmonies more delicate tones and echoes for her tender children and thus grants finite man a feeling of community with the Eternal and the Infinite.

February 2, 1789

Schiller to Karoline von Beulwitz

Frau von Beulwitz was Schiller's sister-in-law.

It would make me very unhappy to have to be with Goethe a great deal. I don't like his character; I wouldn't wish to have it, and I would not be at ease around a man like that. But disregard this judgment; the future may cause it to develop or even, what would be better, contradict it.

February 20, 1789

To Charlotte

I'll expect you this evening. Let us be friends and combine our sorrow and our joy, so that the brief days of life may be enjoyed.

February 25, 1789

To Charlotte

If you want to hear it, I don't mind telling you that your reproaches, though I feel them keenly at the moment, leave neither annoyance nor anger in my heart. I can interpret them. Since I make you suffer, it is but fair that you should do the same to me. It's much better, too, that a friendly accounting be drawn up than that a vain attempt at identification be made. If that doesn't succeed, we shun each other. I am least of all inclined to a strict reckoning. Whatever comes or goes, I remain your debtor. When you consider how troublesome most people are, we two ought to have some indulgence for each other. One of these days I'll tell you a little more about my mysterious adventures in Italy.

March 2, 1789

To Herder

I rejoice in your life in Naples; the bright and luminous image of it will remain with you forever. Like a badger I've dug myself into my hole and am quite merry after my fashion. Despite snow and gray skies I relish what is best in art and nature and have concentrated on the interior life.

March 3, 1789

Karoline Herder to Her Husband

Charlotte Stein has now herself revealed the secret to me, why she can't be on good terms with Goethe any more. The Vulpius girl is his sweetheart and she visits him all the time; Charlotte is shocked and bitter. A man of his eminence, 40 years old—he shouldn't do things that reduce him to a vulgar level. What is your opinion?

Late March, 1789

Herder to His Wife

What you write me about Goethe and his girl displeases me more than it surprises me. A poor girl of the people—I couldn't permit myself a thing like that under any circumstances. But people have different ways of thinking and the life he lived here among quite good but certainly crude people was not calculated to lead to anything better.

March 20, 1789

Karoline Herder to Her Husband

I have copied the latter part of *Tasso.* Goethe dropped in while I was doing so. He sends his regards. Confidentially he told me the inner meaning of this play. It deals with the inadequacy of talent in the face of reality. He is much pleased that I felt this so keenly.

March 29, 1789

Charlotte to Charlotte von Lengefeld

I wasn't very well all winter and so inclined to thoughtfulness, which doesn't make life any happier. It's hard for me to grasp the situation concerning him who was once my friend and remained so for fourteen years. It weighs upon me like an illness. Once there was a beautiful star; it fell from the sky. . . .

Early April, 1789

Knebel to Charlotte

The Duke has about him men as disinterested and kind and noble as any prince in Germany. Yet an evil genius has driven him to transfer his attention from his own people to a Prussian regiment of cuirassiers. Thus he has transferred the center of his life to a foreign land, whereby everybody at home loses courage, force, vitality, especially in view of the narrow circumstances and the small salaries here.

May 8, 1789

Karoline Herder to Her Husband

> On May 5 Charlotte had left to take the cure at Ems. On her way she visited Goethe's mother in Frankfurt. She left behind her a letter to be given him.

I can't praise Charlotte Stein enough on this occasion. Since the Duke is with his regiment, she wrote him about us in the Duchess's name and in her own, and I really believe that he came home for two days on that account. . . .
As soon as you can, do drop her a few lines. She's worth it. Console her, too. She's very unhappy and Goethe's behavior is certainly not nice. I honestly believe her grief will shorten her life. She left on Tuesday to take the cure at Ems. She believes that he has turned away from her entirely and has given his heart to this girl who was a common whore before he met her.—"I looked forward so much to seeing Herder again," she said to me; "if he doesn't come back, nothing is left me here."

May 9, 1789

Karoline Herder to Her Husband

I haven't told you much about Goethe recently because I hardly ever
see him alone. He read all of *Tasso,* except three scenes, to the
Duchess. . . . He called on me last night. When we had finished
discussing *Tasso*—and I'm sure it will charm you—we talked about
you. He has informed the Duke that our debts amount to between
1800 and 2000 thaler. The Duke had already determined to pay
them. But our financial arrangements must be changed and improved, if we are to stay here.

May 10, 1789

To Herder

I would like this letter to meet you somewhere on your way home,
because your wife tells me that you are thinking more strongly than
is well for you of leaving here and accepting a call to Göttingen. If
it means your happiness and pecuniary advantage, I won't grudge
it to you; indeed, I would advise it. But to make a profitable exchange it is necessary not to undervalue what one has. Decide nothing until you are back home. Then let us weigh the issue of your
and your children's welfare. Meanwhile, be calm. . . . This matter
is one for objective consideration, not for emotion. . . .
Your and your wife's present state of mind makes me afraid for you
both. . . . I repeat: I'm not concerned over Weimar or Göttingen,
but exclusively over the welfare of yourself and your family. Remember, you're not a young man gambling with your single fate
which, after all, can improve again, even though it is momentarily
in a mess. You are of mature years with a large family and neither
you nor your wife would be able to stand it, if conditions in Göttingen were not to answer your expectations or even become oppressive.

May 12, 1789

To Karl August

Tasso seems to have pleased your wife. I would be very happy, if it
were quite completed. I have been reading my erotic poems [*The
Roman Elegies*] to Wieland again and I have taken much joy in

the sound and antique spirit which dictated his attitude. I nurse the
hope that this small collection will anticipate the work of my successors in both poetical substance and in craftsmanship. . . .

One of my principal worries just now is the fate of the Herder
family. Sometime soon you must permit me to say a frank word to
you about this case and similar cases.

A prince who commands means of all kinds can easily come to the
help of many, especially those who are close to him, if he treats the
matter like a tree nursery—doing a little at a time, but doing that
little at the right time. Thus the people who need help will aid their
own growth. . . .

1788

FROM THE ROMAN ELEGIES

I

Speak, eloquent stones and lofty palaces!
O ways, give voice! Genius, dost thou not stir?
For animated are thy sacred walls,
Eternal Rome, though silent yet to me.
Ah, at some casement shall I one day behold
A being all grace who whispering will sear
And quicken me at once? No presage yet
Have I of the recurrent paths by which
I'll seek her door and sacrifice my days.
Palace and church, pillar and ruin are
Still but cool visions and contemplative.
Soon will this pass. Soon will a single shrine,
The shrine of love receive the neophyte.
Thou art a world, O Rome, but without love
Rome were not Rome, nor yet the world the world.

II

Spirit and joy rise from this classic ground;
Clear and more resonant the ages speak,
And I make the Horatian counsel mine
To turn with busy hand and relish new
The pages of the ancients. Only my nights
Are other in the busy toils of love,

And though in lore I lose, in joy I gain.
Yet is it studious too with sensitive hand
To mark her bosom's lovely curves and let
Wise fingers glide down the smooth thigh, for thus
I master the antique sculptor's craft, reflect,
Compare and apprehend and come to see
With feeling eye and feel with seeing hand.
Some daylight hours the girl takes from me, too,
But high is the nocturnal recompense.
Nor are the kisses ceaseless. Talk will rise;
Next sleep o'er comes her; wakeful I reflect,
Often compose new verses in her arms
And with light fingers tapping on her back
Scan me the rhythmic numbers. In her sleep
Her glowing breath my bosom penetrates,
The while a god trims the low lamp, remembering
His equal service to Rome's triumvir.

III

Autumnal fire glows on the pastoral hearth,
The dry twigs crackle, upward roars the flame.
Exquisite evening fire—before it dies,
Before the crumbling charcoal turns to ash
My lovely one will come. Then will the logs
Flame and the warmèd night all festive be.
Dawn will behold her leave the couch of love
And deftly from the ashes lure new fire,
Seeing the god of love gave her the gift
To reawaken ecstasy scarce quenched.

May 15, 1789

Charlotte to Her Son Fritz

I am faithful to you in my love and I am tempted to add: love me!
But this manner of ending a letter has a bitter taste on my tongue.
Goethe's picture no longer hangs in my room. It is too deeply im-
bedded in my heart for me to need it against my wall.

June 1, 1789

To Charlotte

I thank you for the letter which you left behind for me, even though it grieved me in more ways than one. I delayed answering, because in such cases it is difficult to be frank and not to wound. My return from Italy sufficiently proves how much I love you and how aware I was of my duty toward you and Fritz. So far as the Duke is concerned I might have stayed on. I shall not mention again what I left behind me in Italy; you treated my confidence in that matter in no friendly fashion.

Unfortunately when I came home you were in a strange enough mood and I am bound to say that your reception of me, as well as the reception of others, annoyed me not a little. Herder left; the Dowager Duchess offered me a seat in her coach before she left. I stayed here for the sake of my friends, even as I had returned for their sakes and yet all I heard persistently was that I might as well have stayed away, that I sympathized with no one etc. And all this happened before the particular personal relationship which seems to wound you so was thought upon.

And what kind of a relationship is it? Whom does it rob of anything? Who has a claim upon the feelings which I give to this poor creature? Who has a right to the hours I spend with her?

Ask Fritz or Herder or anyone who is close to me, whether I am less sympathetic, less communicative, less active for my friends than before. And it is a very strange circumstance indeed that I should forfeit my best and most intimate friendship, that with you.

But I don't mind telling you that I cannot endure your recent treatment of me. When I was talkative, you closed my lips; when I was eager, you accused me of indifference, and when I sought to help my friends, of coldness and neglect. You criticized every expression, every gesture; you found fault with my every way and always made me feel ill at ease. How were confidence and sincerity to flourish between us, when you had made up your mind to repel me by your mood?

There is much else that I might add if I did not fear that in your present state of mind it might tend rather to affront than to conciliate you.

Unhappily you have for a long time now ignored my advice in respect
of coffee. You have used a diet most harmful to your health. . . .
I do not wholly abandon the hope that some day you will see me
again as I am.

June 8, 1789

To Charlotte

I never wrote a page at bitterer cost than my last letter to you, and
it was probably as disagreeable for you to read as for me to write.
Nevertheless it did re-establish openness between us and I trust that
it will never be withdrawn again. I have known no higher happiness
than was brought me by my boundless confidence in you.
When I can no longer exercise it, I become a different human being,
and this change in me is bound to increase.
I do not complain of my situation here. I have readjusted myself to
it and hope to be steadfast in it, although I suffer from the climate,
which interferes with any capactiy I may have for good. When I
consider the cold damp summer here and the severe winter; when I
consider further that the Duke's foreign adventures as well as other
circumstances have rendered everything here inconsistent and hope-
less and when, finally, I add the fact that almost no one here is happy
or comfortable in his situation—well, you will admit that it takes
some energy to remain erect and cheerful and active and not to
consider some method of liberating oneself by and by. To crown it
all, there comes this evil discord with those nearest to me. It is hard
to know what to do. I say this from your angle as well as from my
own; given all these circumstances, it grieves me profoundly to add
to your dismay.
I shall say nothing in my own defense. I would ask you to help me
see to it that this relationship which repels you so remains at this
point and does not overstep all bounds. . . . You gave my mother
much pleasure by your visit and also Sophie de la Roche. May your
return be a kindly thing to me too. . . .
Farewell. Think of me lovingly. *Tasso* is nearly done. Otherwise I've
done little. Regards from Fritz.

Ruhla, August 10, 1789

To Herder

I've thought of you an hundred times these last few days and I am annoyed on your account that the Duke likes it so much here. I beg you to be calm. Everything will be arranged, for the Duke's attitude is the best possible. Saturday we're going to Gotha. We'll stay there a very few days and then come back to Weimar, where the Duke will certainly attend to everything at once. So don't worry and enjoy being together after your long absence. On this trip the Duke took a real fancy to your August and I hope the boy will thus fall into a job which suits him.

October, 1789

Charlotte to Knebel

It's sweet of you to tell me about things. Alas, you must always be the giver, because you are rich and I am poor. Fortunately you find your happiness in giving, as few people do. . . . Your last letter was so very charming that I blame myself for not being sufficiently fond of you. But the love of an old woman is nothing very desirable. In exchange, I promise you a double measure, if ever I grow young again.

Late October, 1789

The Duchess Louise to Charlotte

Am I so neglectful or inconstant that you think me capable of a change of feeling toward you? Rid your heart of this notion; I do not deserve it. You regard me, I know, with as much affection as I have always had for you. Goethe accompanied me exclusively because the Duke desired it.

December, 1789

Charlotte von Lengefeld to Schiller

Charlotte von Stein was the only confidant of the young couple. She was partly instrumental in obtaining from the Duke an annual stipend of 200 thaler, so that, over the objections of Frau von Lengefeld, Schiller and his Lotte could be married on the subsequent February 22, 1790.

Don't ever believe that Frau von Stein is indiscreet or that her knowledge of our engagement will be detrimental. She is sure to keep her council. Her interest in my happiness is so deep and so true that it hurts me to practice the slightest deception. She would use her utmost endeavors to contribute, however slightly, to our happiness. She loves you too and knows your value and esteems you. I was so touched the other night and I felt her affection so keenly as we sat talking of your future life and mine.

December, 1789

Karl von Stein to Fritz von Stein

Karl, Charlotte's oldest son, 1765-1837, was at this time a student in . Göttingen.

I find that our mother, when she argues about anything, not only never yields a point, but also by accusations, reproaches, and remarks which have nothing to do with the matter, knows how to put her adversaries out of countenance. I am cautious about entering into a dispute with her because she never discusses, but at once becomes aggressive.

1790

From the Supplementary Confessions

In November, 1789, Christiane Vulpius took up her permanent residence in Goethe's house, where on Christmas Day their son August was born. The Duke was the child's godfather and Herder baptized him. Christiane bore Goethe three other children. Two died in early infancy, the other was stillborn.

Agreeable domestic and social conditions gave me new courage and put me in a better mood, so that I was able to write the *Roman Elegies* and to perfect them.

February 28, 1790

To Johann Friedrich Reichardt

Reichardt, 1752-1814, composer and orchestral director in Berlin. Set many of Goethe's lyrics to music.

Don't be surprised if I don't consider the letter of your theatrical manager as mad as you do. I knew beforehand what his answer would be, for I know his situation. A German theatrical director would be a fool if he took a different attitude. Since the public has no notion of art and since plays find favor which can be tolerably played by mediocre actors, why should a director not want the credit of a moral group of actors, seeing that he does not need that conspicuous talent which would excuse all other qualities?

On an average, the Germans are law-abiding, decent people, but they haven't the slightest suspicion of what constitutes the originality, invention, character, unity and execution of a work of art. That means, in brief, that they have no taste. And this is generally understood. You fool the mob by variety and exaggeration; you take in the so-called cultivated by a kind of decency. You stick to knights, robbers, benefactors, grateful recipients, an honest, respectable third estate and an infamous nobility, and if you sustain a thorough mediocrity, from which you may drop to the completely trivial or venture to surpass by a few flights into sheer nonsense—all goes well. Such have been the ingredients and the character of our novels and plays these ten years.

March 3, 1790

To Jacobi

I haven't written to you in so long and even today I don't know whether you'll hear anything that makes sense. My situation is as happy as any man could wish. I have worked my way through much this year and you'll get the two last volumes of my collected writings, such as they are, by Easter. At that time, too, I will make my first appearance as a natural scientist. I am curious to know how the public, both learned and lay, will receive a little book of mine which constitutes an essay on the Metamorphosis of Plants. . . . You can readily imagine that the French Revolution is a revolution to me, too. But I continue to study the ancients and seek to follow their example, as well as one can in a place like this.

I am preparing to take a little journey. I shall probably go to meet the Dowager Duchess who returns from Italy and thus take a look at the other side of the Alps while spring is still beautiful.

March 4, 1790

Elisabeth Goethe to Fritz von Stein

The first thing I want you to do is to thank my son for his sixth volume. *Tasso* is new to me and I hope to derive much pleasure from it. Tell him, too, that his description of the Roman carnival was magnificently executed at the Court Ball in Mainz. 'Tis Mama La Roche who sends him this piece of news with warmest greetings. The death of the Emperor [*Joseph II of the Holy Roman Empire*] has turned our city into a living grave. The chiming of the bells which takes place twice daily for four weeks—from 11 to 12 by day and 5 to 6 in the evening—has so lugubrious a tone that one weeps, whether one would or no.

Jena, March 12, 1790

To Herder

I am still in Jena and if this place could ever grow hateful to me, it would have done so these last few days. You can't imagine and no words can express the horror of mismanagement into which I had to introduce some sort of balance.

I hate to leave home this time. But I must start for Italy tomorrow. As one gets older one gets to be soft-hearted and anxious. So it suddenly occurred to me that, after my departure, my girl and my little one will be utterly deserted if anything untoward happened, which the girl could not manage alone. I told her to turn to you in any extremity. Forgive me.

Venice, April 3, 1790

To Karl August

I arrived here happily on March 31. The journey was agreeable and the weather unusually beautiful, especially crossing the Tyrol. . . . I am bound to tell you in confidence that my love for Italy has received a rather deadly blow on this occasion. Not that anything at all untoward has happened; indeed, how should it? But the first bloom of love and curiosity is gone and, perhaps, in one way or another, I've become a bit of a fogy. Add to that my affection for my abandoned sweetheart and for the little creature in diapers, both of whom

I commend, as I do all that is mine, to your kindness. I rather fear
that I have done all that I can with the Elegies; the little book may
be considered complete. On the other hand, I am bringing back with
me a *Libellum Epigrammatum* or Little Book of Epigrams which,
I dare to hope, will win your applause.

1790

FROM THE VENETIAN EPIGRAMS

I

This is the Italy I left. Still whirls
Dust on the roads. The traveler must beware
Of being cheated. Vainly doth one seek
Strictness or order. This abundant life
Seethes with distrust, self-seeking, vanity,
And they who rule seek only their own gain.
Fair land, so fair! Yet since Faustina's lost
No more the land I left with aching heart.

II

Yes, I've designed, engraved, painted in oils,
Molded in clay, inconstant evermore,
Learning, achieving naught. One gift alone
I brought near mastery: writing my tongue,
And so, ill-fated poet, I corrupt
In an imperfect medium life and art.

III

Of France's ill fate let the great beware,
But let the humble have an equal care!
Yes, the great fell. But who protects the mass
Against the mass, which its own tyrant was?

IV

So poor, so stripped my girl at that first thrill;
She pleased me naked then; she does so still.

Venice, May 4, 1790

To Karoline Herder

Dear Frau Karoline, I got your letter of April 19 yesterday. It was my first word from you. Meanwhile my sheaf of Epigrams will have arrived and you will see therefrom that I have not been quite idle. . . . I regret that your husband is neither well nor comfortable; a few lines from his hand would have pleased me greatly. I cannot deny that sometimes during this past month a great impatience took hold of me, but I have seen, read, reflected, created as I do not usually in a whole year when the presence of friends and of my sweetheart contributes to my comfort and my gaiety. . . . I am expecting the Duchess here in a few days. She can see whatever is likely to interest her quickly enough, and after Naples Venice will seem flat. I hope we'll get away from here before Pentecost and be home by the middle of June. My sentiments are far more domestic than you imagine. . . .

I'm so grateful for the enclosure you sent. It contained the news that my little one is better. He was quite ill for a couple of weeks. It worried me frightfully, and I'm not used to such things.

Mantua, May 28, 1790

To Herder

I got your letter sent *poste restante* in Venice. I thank you for it and the pleasure it gave me. If only it had not contained an account of your illness! I hope to find you recovered, and I do thank you from the heart for your attitude toward those I left behind me. They are very near and dear to me and I gladly confess to you that I love the girl passionately. It took this journey to teach me how deeply my feelings are committed to her.

Augsburg, June 9, 1790

To Herder

I am doubly and trebly glad to find a letter of yours here. We had a frightful scare in Innsbruck; for at the Court of the Archduchess there a stranger came with the news that Herder had died, to the

grief of all who knew him, as the man had pretended to have read
in the Augsburg newspaper. We didn't believe it and yet we were
miserable. Luckily one of our party ran through the file of the
Augsburg papers and found that a man named Heinicke in Leipzig
had died. We wished him eternal joy and were at peace.

I'm intensely eager to get home. Farewell, thou rearisen one! It
was the damnedest thing to have to imagine even for a moment that
you were gone.

July 9, 1790

To Knebel

Goethe reached home on June 18. The Duke, however, summoned to
Silesia as a Prussian general for the mobilization against Austria, soon
requested Goethe to join him.

My *Faust* [Faust: A Fragment, *the earliest printed version*] as well
as my little work on botany you will have received. With the first
item I closed this edition of my writings, which gave me as much
trouble as it required talent. With the latter I begin a new career
which will have its own manifold difficulties. Yet more than ever my
mind is impelled toward the natural sciences, and what surprises
me is that in this prosaic country any cloudlet of poetry remains
afloat above my head. My little book of Epigrams got itself written.
Some day you'll see it; I cannot spare the manuscript yet.

Scarcely had I recovered from my Venetian journey, when there
came the summons to another from which I promise myself many
burdens but also some pleasure and profit. The Duke has called me
to Silesia, where I will find the fields sewn with warriors instead of
stones and plants.

July, 1790

Charlotte to Fritz

Do write to Goethe. There are occasions other than this when the
living write letters to the dead. Compassion for him overcomes me
from time to time, so that I could weep over him.

From the Supplementary Confessions

Hardly had I reached home when my presence was demanded in Silesia where the armed forces of two great powers led to the Congress of Reichenbach [*at which Great Britain, Prussia, Austria, Poland and Holland guaranteed the integrity of Turkey*]. The headquarters inspired me to sundry epigrams which were incorporated in the little book. In Breslau, on the contrary, where there was the glitter of the Court and the nobility of one of the dominant provinces of Prussia, my mind was continuously busy, odd as it may seem, with the problems of comparative anatomy, so that I lived the life of an intellectual hermit within the stir and movement of the world.

                                                Breslau, September 11, 1790
To Herder

I'm back in Breslau after a journey over Tarnowitz, Cracau, Wilitzka, Czenstochowa. I've seen much that is remarkable, though in a negative way. . . . Now we're back here in this noisy, dirty, stinking Breslau, from which I hope soon to be saved. . . .
I want to tell you that the centripetal impulse is much stronger in me now than the centrifugal one. The world is full of trumpery and lousiness, and I certainly will not have a pleasant hour until I have supped with you two and gone to bed with my girl. If you continue to be fond of me and a few friends stick to me and my girl remains faithful and my baby lives and my big stove works well—why, I have nothing left to wish for. The Duke has been very nice to me and is, of course, in his element. None of your letters tells me whether the circle of your family has been increased by one or by twins. I thought the new arrival had been expected before now.

                                                        October 17, 1790
To Knebel

Back safe and sound from Silesia. . . . I saw much that was interesting and was, above all, delighted with Dresden. . . .
I write you today on a matter which I want you to consider well. For

the present, however, it must be treated with the utmost discretion.
No breath of it must be blown hither.

The Dowager Duchess has quarreled hopelessly with the chief of
her ladies-in-waiting. The breach cannot be healed. The Duchess
wants to get rid of her at the earliest moment. . . . She is thinking
strongly of your sister. That's what I wanted to tell you. I want you
people to consider if this would not be a good way of rendering your
relationship to us and to this country both pleasanter and firmer.
. . . I needn't tell you how much I would like this thing to come
about. But I'll say no more till I have a word from you.

October 21, 1790

To Christian Gottfried Körner

Goethe had made the acquaintance of Schiller's friend during his visit
in Dresden.

At the very beginning of an acquaintanceship it is just as well that
one's new friends are taught to be indulgent to one's inveterate faults
and learn to forgive them. Nothing comes harder to me than writing
letters and over and over again I commit every possible breach of
duty and decency. And so without further excuse I send you my
belated thanks for your friendship and kindness. . . . Your beautiful and interesting city and your family will remain a single memory
in my mind. . . .

I am sending you some epigrams. They are more in the manner of
Martial than in the better Greek manner. I send my greetings to you
both; kiss the little girl and remember me to all friends.

From the Supplementary Confessions

Late in 1790 plans were made for the establishment of the Court Theatre. Goethe was made both dramaturgic director and business manager.
He kept the post for twenty-six years.

The theatre is an enterprise for which no plans can ever be made.
At every moment it is dependent upon the period and upon one's
contemporaries. What the playwrights write, the players play, the
public wants to see and hear—these are the circumstances which
tyrannize the director and reduce his own will and intention to a
minimum.

From the Memoirs of Anton Genast

Genast, 1765-1831, for many years actor and assistant stage manager in Weimar.

When he was directing, Goethe never found fault harshly. His criticism, especially of the older members of the company, was never calculated to hurt. He would say: "Well, that's not half bad, although I had a different idea of how it should be done. Suppose we think about it until the next rehearsal; we may find ourselves in agreement then." He wasn't quite as considerate of the younger people. To them he often said: "Look, *this* is the way I want it. Then we'll get the proper effect."

                                                        November 1, 1790
Schiller to Körner

Goethe told us a great deal about you and spoke most handsomely of you personally. He himself raised the subject and spoke with great warmth of his visit to you and of the city of Dresden. I had the same experience with him as you had. He called on us yesterday and the conversation soon turned to the Kantian philosophy. It's interesting to observe how he dresses up everything in his own way and manner and gives back what he reads in this surprising form. But I wasn't going to argue with him concerning matters that are so close to my heart. He is totally devoid of the impulse of adhering warmly to anything. Philosophy is to him a purely subjective matter, and that forbids both conviction and argument. Nor do I care for his personal philosophy: it derives too much from the world of the senses, whereas mine derives from the soul. His whole way of thinking depends too much on a sensory approach. Yet his mind is forever engaged in research in all directions and strives to build itself a *universe*, which shows that he is a great man.

His personal situation is comical enough. He's beginning to get old and the love of women, against which he has so often blasphemed, is taking its revenge upon him. I'm afraid that he is about to commit a great folly and bring down upon himself the usual destiny of an old bachelor. His girl is a Ma'mselle Vulpius; she has a child by him and is as good as established in his house. In all likelihood he will marry her a few years from now. I am told that he is extremely fond of the child. He will persuade himself that he marries the girl for the child's sake and will thus try to diminish the absurdity of the whole business.

1791

To Knebel

After my return from Silesia and all that unquiet time, I managed to pull myself together during the past three months. . . . The little book of elegies and epigrams is complete and put aside. I was not disinclined to publish the former. Herder advised against it and I followed his advice rather blindly. Encouraged by the Dowager Duchess I have taken out the manuscript of *Wilhelm Meister* once again. Perhaps the new year will bring this old work to completion. . . .
I have settled down for the winter in my downstairs rooms. It has taken much time to make the arrangements and all is not yet in order.

March 20, 1791

To Jacobi

The fourth report of the progress of the mines at Ilmenau occasions this letter. I wish that in the course of your work you might have an opportunity to visit our mountains. It seems to me as though I had not written you for a whole year. . . .
I have embarked on an occupation of possible public effectiveness. . . . I have undertaken to manage and direct the theatre which is being established here. I am treading very softly to begin with. Some profit both for the public and for myself may result. At least I have assumed the duty to study this matter closely and to write every year a couple of plays that can be played.
My life, upon the whole, is one of contentment and comfort. I have every reason to be satisfied with my condition and nothing to desire but that it may endure.

May 30, 1791

To J. F. Reichardt

I get a lot of fun out of our theatre; it is already much better than anything we ever had here. My chief aim must be to have the actors work together harmoniously, pay attention to certain mechanical advantages and gradually abandon the horrible traditional routine, according to which most German actors turn out their tunes. I'm going to write some plays myself, trying in some measure to meet the taste of the hour and then see if it is possible gradually to get people accustomed to a better integrated and more artistic type of performance.

June 1, 1791

To Jacobi

I have both the mood and the occasion to write to you about many things. If I am not disturbed and distracted by various circumstances, you'll receive several communications between now and Easter. . . . I think I will publish the genealogy of Cagliostro and the facts about his family which I learned in Palermo, in order that no doubt may remain as to the nature of this scoundrel. I don't know whether you read the excerpts from the account of his trial which were printed in Rome. They contain almost nothing that was not known before; but there were many people who didn't want to know. It is pitiful to see how people are avid after miracles, in order to be the more stubborn about the nonsense and follies they believe and in order to resist the dominance of the human understanding.

July 1, 1791

To Karl August

J. F. A. Göttling, 1755-1809, professor of chemistry at the University of Jena. The chemists of this period still believed that during the process of combustion a substance called phlogiston was given off.

I should long ago have given an accounting of conditions here and recalled myself to your mind. Here, then, is a multicolored story— petitions, posters that have been put up, above all, Göttling's experiment with de-phlogistonized hydrochloric acid. He took paper that had been turned into printed matter and reduced it to the original pap. He steeped the pap in his acid which drew out the printer's ink. Paper was manufactured of the pap once more and is —like the specimen I enclose—almost a purer white than the original was. What a consolation for the world of living authors and what a threat, as of a last judgment, for those who have passed away. It is a very fine discovery and can have a remarkable effect.

This matter revives an old idea of mine, namely, to found a learned society here, quite unpretentious, of course, to begin with. The talents we have here combined with those at Jena may accomplish much, once they work together. . . .

Our pretty women keep dying here under rather peculiar circumstances. One lady died of an indigestion after a meal of which she had not partaken. Another was assisted in her labor, which was long and difficult, by a young fellow. At the end of three hours the midwife found out that the fellow was not the woman's husband. Beside herself over the indecency of it, she threw the man out, summoned the husband and, as the child was born, the woman died. . . .

July 4, 1791

To G. J. Göschen

G. J. Göschen, 1752-1828, founder of the Leipzig publishing house.

I am obliged to you for the books you sent me and for the courtesy of your letter. I wish that I could oblige you in some way. But I was sorry that you refused my essay on the Metamorphosis of Plants. Your refusal made it necessary for me to look for another publisher and to enter upon agreements with him which cannot be easily dissolved. It is probable that in the future I shall be as productive on the side of science as on that of imaginative literature. I have by me manuscripts of both kinds which, when completed, should be published at the right time. At Michaelmas there will appear my new venture in respect of the theory of colors. I am sincere when I say that I would have wished all my things to appear over the same imprint.

I am working at a long novel and shall have occasion to write more for the theatre than I have hitherto done. The account of my Italian journey is not in final form. A little book of elegies as well as one of epigrams which I wrote in Venice are still here and await the proper moment of publication.

Since, as you say yourself, my things don't sell as well as those of others whom the public finds more to its taste, I see clearly that I have to be guided by circumstances and that, unfortunately, the publication of my future writings will have to be scattered among several publishers.

I have not lost sight of your collected edition. I have a copy here and correct and improve as time permits me to do, in order that I may be prepared, should a second edition be necessary or advisable.

October 8, 1791

From Böttiger's Anecdotes

After supper at Wieland's there was discussed the reason why there were so few even halfway comely faces among the peasant girls of the region. Wieland thought it was because they were always stuffing cake. There were at least eight festivals a year on which they gorged on cake. Goethe made the observation that it was the habit of dragging all loads on the human back which produced stunted bodies and flat faces. Among the ancient Greeks and in Italy the girls carry everything on their heads. He had often observed the charming outline of a slender girl walking at ease with a well-shaped amphora balanced on her head. In Italy there were, too, except in the harbor cities, few burden bearers among the men. The poorest grower of cabbages owns a donkey whom he loads with the produce of his patch of earth and drives into town.

November 17, 1791

To Reichardt

Johann Heinrich Meyer, 1759-1832, the Swiss painter and art historian, whom Goethe met in Rome. He persuaded him to move to Weimar where he taught art, becoming director of the Art Institute in 1807. One of the closest friends of the second half of Goethe's life.

My well-known dislike of writing letters has recently had many circumstances to justify itself. That is why my friends have heard so little from me. I pull myself together today to answer your letter.

I shall be most happy to see you here even though I can't offer you a lodging because my Swiss friend Meyer, whom you remember to have seen in Venice, lives in the second storey of my house. In all other ways a most friendly reception awaits you. I hope there will be time enough to discuss all matters that have to do with the five senses of man. . . . I shall commend my optical experimentation to your lasting attention. . . . Let us also make a common effort in the realm of acoustics. . . . Let us confer and each of us make his contribution. I have already formed an intimate association with a painter and a mathematician. . . . Let me know the date of your arrival.

November, 1791

From the Memoirs of Anton Genast

The reference is to Shakespeare's *King John*, Act IV, I. Christiane Neumann, 1778-1797, a young actress trained by Goethe and celebrated by him in the poem *Euphrosyne*.

At the dress rehearsal of *King John*, in which Christiane Neumann played the part of little Prince Arthur, she did not show enough horror when the irons with which the little prince's eyes were threatened were brought forth. Impatiently Goethe snatched the iron from the hand of the actor who took the part of Hubert and bounded toward the girl with a look so grim that she trembled with horror and fell to the floor in a faint. Thoroughly frightened Goethe kneeled down beside her and took her in his arms and commanded water to be brought. When she opened her eyes again she smiled at him and kissed his hand. Then she offered him her lips.

From the Supplementary Confessions

1791 was a tranquil year spent in my home and in town. . . . In order not to neglect the poetic and aesthetic side of life it gave me pleasure to assume the management of the Court Theatre. . . . We did not try to put on new pieces but worked through the older ones intensively, so that the company started the season in October with fresh courage. . . . Toward the end of the year we also put on charming operas by Cimarosa and Mozart. Our highest achievement was the presentation of Shakespeare's *King John*. Christiane Neu-

mann in the part of Prince Arthur, trained by me personally, was
marvelously effective. I took great care to raise the others harmoniously to her level. This was my method from the beginning: to note
the most excellent performance in each play and to seek to raise the
other actors to the same quality.

1792

March 14, 1792

To a Member of the Court Theatre Company

In your letter which I consider extremely proper in tone and sentiment, you express the desire to resign from the company at Michaelmas and your intention to renounce the acting profession. You give as
your reason your state of health, with which I am acquainted and
which I deplore. I cannot avoid confessing to you that I would be
very glad if you could summon the courage and the impulse to hold
out until Easter.

I would try to make life as easy for you as possible; I would assign
no new parts to you unless you specifically desire them; I would relieve you of those parts which please you least. You would then act
merely such parts as are wholly suitable to you and as you know
thoroughly.

I am glad to take this responsibility on your account toward both
the Court and the public; I am sure no one will blame me if in this
way I seek to keep a much admired artist for a little longer and to
render his withdrawal from the theatre more convenient and honorable. If, however, your situation is such that you would find it a
burden to remain even under these conditions, I will certainly, however regretfully, release you from your contract.

April 18, 1792

To Karl August

Even as the ancients used to begin their letters with a set formula:
si vales bene est, ego valeo [*if you are well, 'tis well; I am well*], so it
would be suitable for me to set a solemn formula at the beginning of
every letter to express an excuse for my silence. For instance: *ignoscas
tarde scribendi* [*you are not ignorant of my always writing late*] or,

simply i.t.s., which abbreviation could then be variously interpreted. . . .

Meyer is very industrious. He is painting a portrait of my little
family (which can hardly be called a holy family) in order to practice this department of painting. His students are gaining confidence
in him, a thing not always to be expected in a world full of vain
people.

July 17, 1792

Johann Daniel Falk to His Brother

> J. D. Falk, 1768-1826, pedagogue and satirist. He moved to Weimar in
> 1798 and later founded there an Institute for the education of neglected
> and delinquent children.

On the second day of my stay in Weimar I called on the Privy
Councillor Goethe. He is of medium height; his countenance is
bronzed and manly, his eyes dark and lustrous, his glance penetrating, his features significant but regular. He was unpretentiously
dressed in a simple, long, blue coat. His courtesy was unaffected. A
seriousness inborn rather than assumed awakens in those with whom
he converses a certain feeling of respect, I had almost said of reverence. But one is not at all repelled or awed. I would rather have
taken him for an honest and not unkindly magistrate than for a
great writer.

July 19, 1792

To Karl Theodor von Dalberg

> Dalberg, 1744-1817, was the emissary at Erfurt of the Electoral Prince
> Bishop of Mainz, to which office he succeeded in 1802. In the autumn
> of 1791 a powerful movement against duelling and especially against
> the brutal methods used by certain fraternities, had arisen among the
> students of Jena. Goethe supported this revolt. He condemned the ac-
> cepted code of honor. He submitted a proposal and plan of the simplest
> kind: verbal insults were to be expiated by a personal apology; assaults
> real or feigned were to be punished by brief imprisonment; a serious
> blow would entail the expulsion of the guilty student. The rowdier
> fraternity men were of course opposed to these innovations. Four hun-
> dred and fifty withdrew to a nearby village belonging to the electoral
> domain of Mainz and threatened to register at Erfurt.

It is common knowledge that a number of students who are not satisfied with the regulations which it has been necessary to impose for the maintenance of public order, have conceived the plan of withdrawing for the time being from the university and of betaking themselves to Erfurt and other places, in order that, like the plebeans of old, they may, as from another *monte sacro* or sacred hill, treat with the fathers of the city and enforce their own conditions.

We by no means intend to restrain those who are unwilling to submit to the regulations considered advisable for the public good. We are inclined to let them go in peace, all the more as the university cannot fail to profit by the withdrawal of these rough and unruly elements and thus, in the end, be advantaged by this unpleasant event.

The Privy Councillors have suggested that I convey this information to Your Archepiscopal Grace. I myself consider the act a duty, since I cannot but suppose that it will be agreeable to you to be warned in time of the arrival of these emigrants, of whom the rumor may already have come to you.

It would appear that in our regions we are not to lack an image of those greater evils which infest the world. It is well, however, that we are probably dealing only with a kind of infantilism, from which the greater number of the patients are likely to recover.

Gotha, August 9

To Christiane

The coalition of various states against revolutionary France had provoked the French to declare war against Austria on April 20, 1792. Prussia was now allied with Austria and so Karl August had to take part in the campaign. He insisted that Goethe accompany him. Reluctantly leaving his family, his work, his house which the Duke had just bought and presented to him, he proceeded by way of Frankfurt, Trier, and Luxemburg and met the Duke on French territory on August 27.

It's not a bit of good to be parted from those whom we love. The time drags on and there is no substitute. We are now as far as Gotha and I hope to get away as soon as possible. I am very restless. Meyer will tell you how even in Erfurt I was plagued by bedbugs; I'm actually afraid of going to bed. . . . From here all I send you is my warmest greeting and the assurance that I love you very much. From Frankfurt, however, a most dainty little bargain will reach you. Farewell and love me. Keep the house in good order and kiss the little one.

Frankfurt, August 12, 1792

To Christiane

I announce to you, my dear, that I arrived here this afternoon. Everything is calm in my house and all I wish is that you were with me. You would like it very much. My mother has gone to a social gathering. She asked me to go too. But here as elsewhere I prefer to stay at home. Now the first thing I shall do is to attend to your little orders and look for your bargain. Farewell and kiss the little one and write me how he is and when you two will return home from Jena.

My mother has given me very handsome material to send you. I do so at once, because I can't keep anything from you, as you know. I will enclose the ribbons which you asked for. The other things will be added gradually. Farewell, my dearest.

P.S. How would it be if you have the material made up for your next pregnancy? There's enough; you can always have it taken in again. In addition I'll send you a great big shawl and you'll be dressed up fit to kill.

Frankfurt, August 17, 1792

To Christiane

Today I got your letter, dear little girl, and I'm writing to tell you once again how very fond of you I am and that I miss you wherever I go, whatever I do.

I found my mother contented and in good health; all my friends gave me the kindest reception. There are many things worth seeing here and I have been on my feet all these days. My first care was to get the little bargain for you which is to be packed tomorrow and sent off next week. When it arrives you will certainly celebrate, for you have never seen anything like this. Take good care of it; one doesn't find anything so lovely every day.

Farewell. Remember me to Herr Meyer and kiss the little fellow. Tell him Father will be back soon. Think of me. Keep the house nicely in order and write me from time to time.

Frankfurt, August 18, 1792

To Jacobi

Monday the 20th I am off for Mainz and thence to join the army.
Tents and the service of camp-followers will seem horrible after my
mother's house, bed, cuisine and cellar, especially since I am utterly
indifferent to the deaths of both the aristocratic and the democratic
sinners. I am seeing with joy my old friends and the growth of my
native city. Unfortunately, all social meetings are a bore; wherever
two or three assemble one hears the same old song concerning the
Revolution, the same *pro* and *contra*—not a single variation but the
same crude theme. For that reason I wish I were back among my
Thuringian hills, where I can lock my house and garden against the
world. . . . Unfortunately the newspapers now penetrate everywhere; they are my most dangerous enemies. I hoped to stay in this
vicinity for at least a month. In that case I would so gladly have
come to meet you as far as Mainz or even Coblenz. My return will
fall in the time of bad weather. I would have been so glad to see you
in order to give you an accounting of my household and attach your
interest to it.

Frankfurt, August 21, 1792

To Christiane

Today, my dear little girl, I am leaving to go to Mainz. I must tell
you that everything went very well with me, except that I had to eat
and drink too much. Yet everything will taste better to me when my
own treasure prepares the dishes in our kitchen. The little bargain
is being sent off today, too, and should arrive not much later than
this letter. I wish I were a little mouse and could be present when
you unpack. I had such a good time wrapping it up. Take good care
of everything. Adieu, my dear child. I haven't done a bit of flirting.
Love me as I do you. Regards to Herr Meyer. Kiss the baby and
write soon.

Trier, August 25, 1792

To Christiane

There's no way of your knowing or imagining where in the world Trier is situated. The worst of it is that it's far from Weimar and so from you. . . . My only desire is to see you and the little one again. When we are together, we don't know how lucky we are. I miss you badly and love you very much. I'm sure the present has come and pleased you. On my way home I'll bring along much else. I hope it will be soon. Regards to Meyer, my dear domestic treasure.

Military Camp at Longwy, August 28, 1792

To Christiane

Yesterday I joined the Duke in this camp. He is well and cheerful and I am writing you in his tent amid the tumult of people who are felling trees on one side in order to burn them up on the other. It rains uninterruptedly; people are soaked day and night; I am lucky that I have been given a place in the Duke's sleeping coach where I pass the night. All food is scarce and dear. . . . Write me at once after receiving this letter. Herr Meyer will see that it is forwarded. I can hear from you within a week. . . . Don't worry about me. I love you dearly and will hurry home as soon as possible. Kiss the little one, of whom I think often.

Late August, 1792

From the Diary of a Prussian Artillery Officer

Before I met him I had been told that this Goethe was a famous author. . . . When I first heard it and that I would be often in this gentleman's company and even share the same quarters, since I, too, had been commanded to join the suite of the Duke of Sachsen-Weimar, I felt quite a prejudice.—I had always before pictured these people whom they called poets as shabby and morally corrupt fellows. . . . Imagine my surprise when I made the personal acquaintance of this Herr Goethe. He was an uncommonly impressive and good-looking man, elegantly attired and in his best years. His demeanor was so distinguished that one would have thought him a prince, rather than a mere commoner and secretary. His assurance was complete, and the words flowed so beautifully and skillfully from his lips that the hearer thought he were being read to from a printed book. . . . Naturally he was fond of hearing himself talk and occasionally he pronounced discourses which sounded very beautifully but were empty of any real content, because they concerned things about which he could not possibly have any knowledge.

Near Verdun, September 8, 1792

To Christiane

I have no time to be hypochondriac. If you were here with me, I'd ask for nothing better. I keep thinking of you and the little one and visit you in the house and garden and dream of how nice everything will be when I get back. But you must keep on being fond of me and not do any flirting.

Before we leave here I'll send a little basket of liqueurs and sweets. Taste of these things and offer some to Herr Meyer. Keep the rest. I will be sending you various things for the household. By the time you get this letter you may already have moved into the front rooms. Arrange everything neatly and prepare yourself to become a dear little cook. . . .

Verdun, September 10, 1792

To Christiane

I want to tell you again that I am well and that I love you dearly. The beds we use here are good and broad; if you were here you would not complain, as you sometimes do at home. Ah, my sweet, there is nothing better than to be together. And everything will be better at our house when once my sweetheart supervises the kitchen and the cellar. Be a good domestic treasure and arrange our interior nicely. Take care of the little fellow and continue to be fond of me. I am sometimes jealous of you in my thoughts and imagine that some other man might please you better, because I know there are many men better looking and more agreeable than myself. But you must not look at them; you must think that I am the finest because I love you so intensely and take pleasure in no one but yourself. . . .

While I was at my mother's I ordered two featherbeds, as well as pillows and all kinds of good things. You just see to it that our little house is kept in good order; I'll provide us with everything . . . In Frankfurt I'll pick up a second bargain. . . .

Verdun, September 10, 1792

To Christian Gottlob Voigt

C. G. Voigt, 1743-1819, Ducal Minister of State.

You have probably heard that this army, after its leap from Longwy to Verdun, is at a standstill, perhaps like a grasshopper, to prepare to leap again. Perhaps before this letter reaches you, the second leap will have been taken. It is most interesting to be present where nothing indifferent can possibly take place. . . . I would like to ask your friendly assistance in a private matter. In Frankfurt I found that I was in a position to draw a certain sum of money and invest it in Weimar. I have long had an itch to buy a little country estate, especially the one you know of near Lobeda. It was once offered for sale. . . . Could you find out for me how the matter stands and whether the place can be acquired at a reasonable figure . . . Since revisiting my native city I have been more than ever impressed by the fact that it can never become my place of habitation again. Have the kindness to say nothing to anyone of this matter or these observations.

Verdun, September 27, 1792

To Christiane

Your little letter with the big ink blot came at last. I am so glad that you and the little one are well and that you are quietly enjoying the comfort and plenty amid which I left you. I can just imagine you cutting up the cloth from Frankfurt and busily sewing at it. But don't cut up the beautiful length of lace. It is just right for a beautiful collar. If you're a busy domestic treasure you'll have much joy when I return just loaded with handsome things. . . . The hardships here are plenty, especially the wretched weather. But I will soon recover from it all in your arms. . . . Kiss the little one and see to it that everything is in good order when you move into the front rooms.

Verdun, October 10, 1792

To Christiane

Now I have all your letters, my dear heart. . . . I can well imagine
your delight when you unpacked the presents. I blame myself that I
sent no toys and forgot my son in my concern for his mother. But
I'll get him some now and either bring them or send them.

You will have been told by now that instead of going to Paris this
army is retreating. By the time you get this letter I may be back in
Germany. . . .

You did well not to tell me of the baby's indisposition until it was
all over. . . . You must forgive me if I wrote you anything that made
you sad. Your love is very precious to me and you must forgive me
a little jealousy and worry. . . .

Luxemburg, October 15, 1792

To Christiane

I can't tell you how glad I am to be on my way back. The misery we
have had to undergo is indescribable. The army still lags, the roads
are ruined, the weather is frightful; I hardly know how the men and
the baggage wagons will be extricated from France.

We'll have a wonderful time when we're together again. . . .

Düsseldorf, November 14, 1792

To Christiane

From Coblenz I hastened to Düsseldorf, to visit my old friend Jacobi.
. . . I am quite embarrassed as to how to return. I am so eager to
see you and yet I am, as it were, cut off from you. Frankfurt is still
occupied by the French and the way through Hessen is far from safe.
If things don't change within a week I'll go on through Westphalia.
I shall not let the bad roads deter me. . . .

Have a good time, my dear child, and enjoy your quiet life. Think of
the thousands of people who have been driven from house and home
and wander about in the world and know not where to turn. Kiss
the little one and love me. My only desire is to possess you once
again.

December, 1792

Jacobi

The sketch of a projected letter to Goethe which was never sent.

How clear the image of our reunion stands before me. You had come in order to give me an accounting of your domestic arrangements. I was to question you without reserve concerning whatever I would know about you and you were to answer me fully and freely. . . . I cannot but remember that visit of yours in the winter of 1792 and that confession from the depth of your soul which you made to me at parting. We experienced hours which neither one of us will ever forget.

Winter, 1792

Helene Jacobi to the Countess Sophie Stolberg

Helene was Fritz Jacobi's sister and Sophie Stolberg the second wife of Goethe's old friend Fritz Stolberg.

. . Goethe is and remains a true magician and you, too, will love and admire him so soon as you know him. The odd and silly gossip you hear comes from people who see only the wrong side of him, and a sort of madness makes him prone to display that wrong side. . . . Veracity is most precious to him when he recognizes it as such. Its feigned image is equally hateful to him. . . . In order not to be deceived by what he detests, he often cheats himself of what he loves. When beauty comes to meet him with all its bloom he feels that he must be doubly careful to detect a possible trace of artifice upon its countenance. I enjoyed his presence infinitely but also felt many a deep pang. The more I came to love him, the more eager I was to protect him, lest he do himself some hurt.

December 14, 1792

Elisabeth Goethe to Her Son

Goethe had been offered a Councillorship in the governing body of the city of Frankfurt.

Dear Son, This moment comes a letter from Fritz Jacobi informing me that by the middle of this month you hope to be back in your tranquil Weimar. When you get there you will find a letter forwarded by me in which the Duke, who thought you still in Düsseldorf, invites you to join him here. In my accompanying note I gave you a hint that it's no joke to be here now. . . . I thought you had better send what excuses you could.

In this city we live in daily terror and danger, and if I were one grain more fearful than, thank God, I am—why I'd run out into the wide, wide world. As it is, I'm sticking it out. . . . I have been asked the old question, of course, whether I have not heard about your making a decision one way or another. I told them that you intended to come back here, but that the tumult of war was the cause of your absence, etc. I wrote you a letter with my opinion both for and against and, of course, I know that if you had meant to accept you would have answered earlier. I'm inclined to believe that you're much better off in body and in soul than you would be in some new career, because in the real sense of the word you are your own master. However, the respect which your friends paid you deserves an answer in any event—and I don't want these questions addressed to me all the time. . . . An officer and two privates are billeted in my house—Hessians, good enough people but, between us, very poor—and I've got to feed them while the French have plenty of everything, and you can imagine what a nuisance feeding them is.

December 19, 1792

Elisabeth Goethe to Her Son

> Goethe did go home by way of Westphalia. At Münster he was the guest of the Princess Amalia Gallitzin, 1748-1806, whose piety Goethe respected, though he could not share it. He reached home on December 16.

Dear Son, I am sending some Christmas bonbons with the request that they be given to the Herder child named August in my name. Here we live in terror and await the things to come. The very top people assure us that all will be well. They mean that the French will not return. But so long as Mainz is still in their hands we can hardly pretend that we are victorious. You will be recovering from your hardships in your beautiful new house and among your friends. It is very sensible of you to do so. Her Highness, the Duchess Amalia, has been kind enough to invite me to escape the tumults of war and

come to Weimar. Thank Her Highness in my name and tell her that
I have firm faith that my God Who has protected me hitherto will
continue to do so. His Serenity the Duke is well and gay; so is His
Majesty of Prussia. God give you a Happy New Year.

December 24, 1792

To His Mother

The hope of seeing you soon again, dearest Mother, as well as my
Frankfurt friends, has vanished for the present, since circumstances
obliged me to return home by a different route.

I have suffered great anxiety on your account and deeply deplored
the situation of our fellow citizens. I have equally admired their
fortitude in these critical circumstances. Assuredly, nothing could
have been more flattering to me than the question, whether I could
decide to accept a position in their Council—above all since this
question was addressed to me at a moment when it was an honorable
thing in the face of Europe and of the whole world, to be a citizen
of Frankfurt. . . . It had been my intention to thank them in person
for the distinguished honor conferred upon me and at the same time
to give them a circumstantial and sincere delineation of my present
position.

In view of the irresistible preference felt by all men of good will for
their native city, it is indeed a grievous thing to refuse an offer which
every citizen would accept with joy. . . . But His Serenity, the Duke,
has treated me for so many years with such extreme graciousness and
I am so deeply in his debt, that it would be the grossest ingratitude
to abandon my post at a moment in history when the state has sorest
need of its faithful servants.

From the Supplementary Confessions

During the winter of 1792 the performances at our playhouse gained
more and more consistency. . . . Most significant were our productions of Mozart's *Don Giovanni* and of Schiller's *Don Carlos*. . . .
In the middle of the summer I was once more summoned to the field
and this time to more serious scenes of war. . . . Amid the movement of martial events I made various significant observations of

natural objects. . . . Visiting Mainz, Düsseldorf and Münster, I could not but remark that my old friends were hardly able to recognize me again.

1793

New Year's Day, 1793

Elisabeth Goethe to Her Son

Dear Son, Many thanks for your splendid letter which is just what it should have been, so that I can make use of it among our friends. . . . In a week at the latest I shall forward the things you left behind you—perhaps even earlier, that is to say, on the Friday of this week. You have no idea how the molestation of the billeting puts everything out of one's mind. So forgive me for not having forwarded the things at once after your first letter came. The lamp with the three burners has been ordered; as soon as it is done it will be well packed. Many such lamps have been sent and have all arrived unharmed. . . . My health, thank God, is quite good; I keep up my spirits and bear with patience what cannot be helped. I hope for better times and try not to be frightened of the present. Quite between ourselves, billeting these Germans is a misery. When the French were here, if you had privates you had privates and no officers or the other way around. Now I have to put up two officers and two privates, which means that I have to heat two rooms, which is a horrible expense at the present price of wood. Moreover, even the French privates had their own meat and rice and bread in great plenty from the commissariat. These people have nothing but some very wretched bread. The French officers would have died of hunger before they would have asked for anything. I've got to send these people food even when they're on sentinel duty. *Summa summarum* —add it up and it's a great burden. Mine are Hessians. How it is with the Prussians I wouldn't know. There you have my situation.

January 22, 1793

Elisabeth Goethe to Her Son

The Duchess Louise had joined her husband in Frankfurt at this time.

Dear Son, I was favored by being invited to dinner last Sunday by Her Serenity, the Duchess Louise. Mama La Roche was there and sundry Prussian officers. We were very merry—stayed on till 5 o'clock—and then all of us together went to the play. . . . No change in our situation. I feed two Hessian officers and ditto privates. If these creatures would only not smoke tobacco the livelong day! My rooms look like guard rooms!!

February 1, 1793

To Jacobi

I am happy that my little poem gave such pleasure to you and your circle. We can but do what we *can* do, and applause is a gift from Heaven.

During the last few days I read Plato for the first time in my life, namely, *The Banquet, The Phaedrus,* and *The Apology.* How strange this admirable man seems to me. I'd like to tell you about it. I made Herder laugh. It seems that I acted like that housewife who had once been a cat and who exchanged what was on her husband's table for a mouse. I have undertaken a piece of work which attracts me immensely, but of which I dare to say nothing until I can send on a small specimen. . . . I am well and happy. My little woman manages her house carefully and busily; my boy thrives and is full of life. . . . Meyer is doing some excellent illustrations for the new quarto edition of Wieland's works. . . .

FROM WILHELM MEISTER. BOOK VIII

It happened that the birthday of the twin sisters was approaching. They had always been very well behaved and I promised them that this time an angel would bring them the little presents which they had so well deserved. They looked forward with great eagerness to this apparition. I had chosen Mignon for the part, and on the day appointed she was clad in a long, light, white garment. Nor was there lacking a golden girdle for her waist or a diadem for her hair. . . . When the curiosity of our little company had been satisfied and the impression of the angelic figure began to fade, it was planned to take these garments from her. She warded off her friends and took her zither. She sat down on a tall desk and with indescribable grace sang this song:

Oh, let me stay bright, let me stay light,
Nor yet the angel's robe forego!
I hasten from the lovely daylight
Into that earthen house below.

Brief is the darkness that will bind me,
The heavenly vistas will prevail,
And I will only leave behind me
The wreath, the girdle and the veil.

And those high forms beyond the portals
Ask not if man or woman died,
No flowing garments worn of mortals
The incorruptible will hide.

In care and toil I paid not dearly,
Yet deeply felt our earthly pain.
The griefs that touched me aged me early—
Make me forever young again!

March 15, 1793

Elisabeth Goethe to Her Son

My dear Son, There is more than space enough in your mother's little
house. You just come! It's true, you'll have to be satisfied with the
second storey. But a man who has gone through a military campaign
with the earth as his bed and the sky for a tent, won't mind a little
thing like that. Moreover, there shall be nothing lacking that is
needed for the body's nourishment. The people I am billeting now
are good and decent. I reckon it a misfortune that they will leave in
a couple of days. What I get next I shall await in patience. . . . In
another month, I suppose, the poor venerable city of Maintz will be
besieged. Never can we be grateful enough to God that we have been
spared these French sons of freedom! If only we need never see them
again! . . . All else that need be said, let us say it to each other
when we meet. I am much fonder of chattering than of writing, as
you know.

April 26, 1793

Elisabeth Goethe to Her Son

Dear Son, I am looking forward to seeing you with so much joy. Though the theatre of war is so near us, 'tis as calm in our town as though the war were at the other end of the world. . . . Although our city is not occupied, I have my share of the few strangers, the gayest part of it being, that he is a Frenchman of the French and doesn't know a syllable of German. He is one of the *émigrés* and serves as engineer in the Prussian army. . . . P.S. Considering the fact that your intentions often undergo the strangest changes, and that unforeseen circumstances may prevent your present plans, do not, whatever happens, let me expect you in vain. That's the one thing I can't stand.

April 28, 1793

David Veit to Rahel Levin

Doctor David Veit, 1771-1814, son of Frederick the Great's Court jeweler, a patron of Jewish learning. Rahel Levin, 1771-1833, married in 1814 to the writer Varnhagen von Ense, reputed the most brilliant woman of her time. She presided over the first of those Jewish salons in Berlin in which arose the intimate cult of Goethe's greatness.

My brother and I arrived in Weimar at 11 in the morning. We changed our clothes with lightning speed and repaired to Goethe's house. His manservant said, there was now a Count with him who would scarcely leave before 2 o'clock; would we not please return around 2. I was not to be put off, but told the man he was to announce us as coming from Berlin with a letter of introduction from the Councillor Moritz. Hereupon we were led up two flights of stairs. From the stairs we entered an anteroom and from it a small and dainty room, in which we arrived simultaneously with Goethe whom, even from that antechamber, we had seen approaching through a flight of several connecting rooms. He had not made us wait quite two minutes.

He received us with extreme courtesy. He approached us with a very friendly mien. His glance is said to be serious, as a rule, but quite without arrogance. When he does not face his interlocutor, he looks toward the floor, keeps his hands folded behind his back and thus

speaks on. He asked us after the purpose of our journey and told us
that there was a great commotion in Frankfurt and that he hoped
peace would soon come. After he had read our letter of introduction
he inquired coolly but very attentively after Moritz. As soon as I mentioned the flight of Moritz's wife, he said in a very serious tone: "He
must be sure to keep busy, he must go to work; he is really a very
dear man. . . ." He chatted again about our journey as well as
about the war, but seemed to be a partisan of neither of the contend-
ing parties. He spoke most naturally and as though he were not
interested in words but in things. . . . The room in which we stood
—for he did not bid us be seated—was papered with green wallpaper
in the modern manner. He kept us slightly more than a quarter of an
hour. Then he smiled significantly and we were not so stupid as not
to take the hint. . . . He accompanied us as far as the antechamber
and bade us a courteous farewell.

                                          At the siege of Mainz, May 29, 1793
To Christiane

> The execution of the French King, Louis XVI, on January 21, 1793,
> intensified the military activities of the counter-revolutionary forces in
> Europe. Mainz was invested by a considerable army. Goethe left home
> on May 12 and, after spending ten days at his mother's house in Frank-
> furt, once more joined the Duke in his camp at Marienborn.

Once more I have arrived in a military camp. It looks quite a little
better than last year's. One must simply forget all the pleasures and
comforts of home for a while and do the best one can. There is
enough variety here and much to see and hear. The Duke feels fine.
The army surrounds this great city, separated from it by a couple of
rivers, and the shooting goes on day and night. If you were with me,
I could stand the rest. I was well billeted in a village, if only, as usual,
the bedbugs had not driven me forth. Now I sleep in a tent fully
dressed on a heap of straw and covered by my own blanket which
will, I hope, soon cover the two of us again. I think of you a lot and
kiss you and the little one in my thoughts.
You will have received the second package and enjoyed it. The flatiron for you is still in Frankfurt; the shoes and bedroom slippers
weren't ready yet. But I'll soon get back there and pack a little box
for you.

Last night we were quite rudely awakened. The French attacked headquarters in a village half an hour's distance from here. The firing was quite lively but the attack was repulsed. . . .
I'm not running any dangers—for your sake, who are dearest to me in the world. Kiss the little one.

Before Mainz, May 31, 1793

To Voigt

. . . His Serenity is well and cheerful and everything is nicely arranged here. The tents have been enlarged by adding arbors to them; a dining room has been built; kitchens and cellars have been constructed underground and the whole military household established admirably and, it would seem, with an air of permanence. Then, last night, the French attacked the headquarters at Marienborn and thus offered me the spectacle of a military surprise and a very vigorous nocturnal combat. . . . Our batteries and small arms were active for almost an hour and many a good fellow lost his life. Finally the French were driven back to the city. . . . The Duke came out of the engagement safe and sound. It was a curious sensation to ride down to the scene of the fray at dawn and to be wondering *whom* I would find among the dead and wounded.

Before Mainz, May 31, 1793

To Christiane

So glad to get your letter and the news that you're both well. I believe you that the frock pleased you. Now you have also the big silk shawl with which to hide the (fy fy) growing belly. When I get back to Frankfurt I'll buy you something all white, too. Kiss the little one. Regards to Meyer. So sorry he's not feeling well. Love me and write soon.

Marienborn, June 14, 1793

To Christiane

When Goethe visited his mother in August, 1792, he had revealed his domestic situation to her.

You did well to write to my mother. I hope she'll be able to read it.

She's very fond of you, because I told her how good you are and how happy you make me.

I hope your sore foot will soon be better. It saddens me to have you suffer. Kiss the little one and take good care of him. Write me something about the gardens, too; I like to think of the work being done consecutively. Life is very unquiet here and yet, in the end, a bore.

Marienborn, June 15, 1793

To Herder

. . . I haven't crossed the river except on one beautiful excursion up the Rhineland. We went by water to Rüdesheim and tasted the wine in the cellars. . . . We returned to the camp by land. Just as we arrived the French made a sortie from the city and took the Convent of the Holy Cross and burned it to the ground.

I see many people who mean nothing to me. I wish I were home with my instruments. I envy you your tranquility behind the church. . . .

June 20, 1793

Elisabeth Goethe to Christiane

It was very agreeable to me to learn that the things I sent you gave you pleasure. Wear them as a souvenir of the mother of him whom you love and esteem and who, in truth, merits both love and esteem. He was with me and his friends for but ten brief days, which we passed splendidly and happily and now we console ourselves with the thought of his return and hope that we will be able to enjoy his presence longer. . . . And now I turn to inquire after the welfare of dear little August. I trust he is well and thrives. Tell him that if he is a clever child and learns his A.B.C. well, I'll send him the finest sweets and lovely playthings to boot.

Marienborn, June 22, 1793

To Christiane

Your letter of the 14th has just arrived. It is well that we can say a word to each other, even though it's miserable that the days and nights pass and we're not together. . . . I do hope to see you soon

again. Have the house in the best order and adorn everything, that I
may rejoice upon my return and forget the disconsolate things which
I must witness here day and night.

I am calm and safe. Don't believe people who exaggerate and love to
bear ill news. I am not likely to incur danger foolishly. No one gives
you credit for it and the hurt is yours. . . .

Tell your brother I wouldn't mind news of our theatre from time to
time. Kiss the little one and tell him about his father, so that he
keeps on loving me.

Marienborn, July 3, 1793

To Voigt

How happy are my friends who at least do not witness this accursed
thing with their own eyes. . . .

In my present situation a sort of stupor overcomes me and I find the
trivial expression, that I am dumbfounded, exactly applicable to my
state of mind. . . . Since the beginning of the actual investment our
men on their regular posts knew little danger. This did not please
sundry of them at all. One who had fought bravely, by the name of
Blumenstein, requested yesterday that a marriage certificate be
issued to him. He has long been living with a girl named Günther.
His Serenity is inclined to grant his request. Would you have the
kindness to see to it that the girl, whom he left behind him in a
pregnant condition, be not harassed by the magistracy before his
return? So many dwellers on this earth are now meeting their death
that one should facilitate the arrival of those who would enter upon
our mortal scene. . . .

Marienborn, July 7, 1793

To Jacobi

If Mama la Roche will not grasp what has happened here, despite
my faithful narration, it does her honor. It proves that she will not
let her reason be imprisoned by a belief in history. When first I came
here I started to note down many things. I soon stopped, for my
natural laziness found many good excuses. . . . Maintz is still holding out as best it can, although the siege is being carried on with
great violence. . . . I suppose I should visit Schlosser on my way
back, but I am too frightened. One of his daughters is mortally ill

and I could not bear to see my sister die a second time. My mother showed me letters from the child which were most touching.

July 10, 1793

Elisabeth Goethe to Her Son

Dear Son, The unexpected arrival of your serving man pleased me greatly. By him I am sending you nankeen for short-clothes and a waistcoat of a quality you can't usually buy by the yard. You mustn't be offended by the circumstance that it was once a skirt of mine. When it is made up it will not show that it was once something else. I am getting the material for the featherbed and two pillows and will send these together with the tablecloth and napkins to Weimar with the earliest conveyance. By all means drink your mineral waters and be careful not to catch cold in the evening. For the north wind, refreshing as it is, causes bellyaches. The heat here is unbearable.

July 11, 1793

Elisabeth Goethe to Christiane

I am forwarding to you an entire bolt of ticking. That will suffice for the nether featherbed and a pillow. I add 2¾ ells for a second pillow. Use them in health. There will also arrive a table set of one cloth and twelve napkins. I hope it will please you well; I find it very pleasing.

Middle of July, 1793

Christiane to Goethe

That my letters give you pleasure makes me very happy, and so I will write you real often. And you are very good to write me so often. I thank you from the heart for your dear letters; they console me a lot. I can imagine that it looks very sad where you are. . . . Everything is ready in the house. The big room will be finished by the end of the week; the man is working at the chairs. Now the stables are being cleaned out and I keep everything in as good order as possible. I've bought a lot of geese and chickens and I love to watch them. . . . I'm very well, too, and I got nine bottles of seltzer water from the doctor and drink it with milk and it agreed with me. He wants me to go on drinking it for a whole month. Herr Meyer wants to seal this letter, so I must close.

Frankfurt, August 9

To Christiane

I didn't get your dear letter of the 25th until I arrived here. It followed me about. Now I can hope to be with you soon and enjoy you. Your shoes and the flatiron and other minor things I'm bringing with me, as well as the toy sword for the little one. Kiss him for me and let him have all kinds of pets. . . . Love me and see to it that I find the household in neatness and order.

September 6, 1793

Elisabeth Goethe to Her Son

While Goethe visited his mother between August 9-19, they had discussed the dissolution of the household in the great house of Goethe's father and the question of Frau Goethe moving into rented apartments.

Dear Son, I have attended to the letters and commissions you wrote about the other day. The Fair here is more brilliant than it has been for years. The theatre profits greatly thereby. The performance of *The Magic Flute* was sold out. Otherwise everything is as usual. I have discussed the matter you and I planned with the agent in question who wishes to be remembered to you. He will help me carry out the plan. But we won't be too hasty in regard to the chief matters. We will not have a catalogue of the library made until after the Fair. I hope all will go well. I pray God to preserve my health, for these are all nerve-wracking matters.

September 26, 1793

To Wieland

During the distractions of this year, even in the camps of war, Goethe took refuge in the reworking of the mediaeval Low-German beast epic *Reynard the Fox*. Between February and May he recast it into twelve cantos written in hexameters. He interpolated several passages of original political comment.

I meant to have the enclosed three cantos of *Reynard the Fox* more neatly copied before submitting them to your critical attention. But since, as you know, one always lags a few paces behind one's good intentions, I am sending them in their present imperfect condition. I know you will have the goodness to go through the manuscript, critical pencil in hand, giving me hints on additional corrections and telling me whether to publish at once or to let the work ripen another summer. Forgive me for using an old privilege which I should hate to renounce. You know how highly I value your observations and your approval.

FROM REYNARD THE FOX

(A Political Credo)

Worst of all do I find the conceit of that arrant delusion,
Which lays hold upon all men, that each of them can in the frenzy
Of his violent will rule over the world and correct it.
Would each man but keep his wife and his children in order—
Would he but check his arrogant servants, he might at his leisure,
While fools squander, enjoy himself in moderate living.
How can the world, however, improve? Self-loving in all things,
Each would forcibly bring all others into subjection.
And thus deeper and ever more deep we sink into evil.

Translated by Alexander Rogers

November 9, 1783

Elisabeth Goethe to Her Son

Hercules cleaned out the Augean stables and was made a god. I have cleaned out stables, but there's no sign of my being made a god. I have gone through three hundredweights of papers. Of the few not useless items I have enclosed some in the case I sent you. The rest I sold to the paper mill. The two attics and the third floor have now been emptied of all useless furnishings. . . . As for the actual sale of the house: I must first await Schlosser's arrival in order to discuss it with him. Secondly, I must, above all things, find a dwelling appropriate to my station and dignity, so that I may not be reduced to humiliation in my later years. When the fifth act comes, there should be applause and not hissing. . . .
Nothing new here except that Mozart's *Magic Flute* has been performed eighteen times to overflowing audiences. Nobody wants it

said of himself that he hasn't heard it, neither the workers nor the gardeners. . . .

December 23, 1793

Elisabeth Goethe to Her Son

Dear Son, I'll do anything to please you and do it with great pleasure, but to buy a miniature model of the infamous guillotine as a plaything for the baby—no, I won't do that at any price. If I had a say in the government, the manufacturers of this toy would themselves be put under the guillotine and I would have had the machine itself publicly burned. What!—Let children play with anything so revolting and make them think of murder and bloodshed as a game? Oh no, not as far as I am concerned.

1794

My First Acquaintance with Schiller

Surpassing any hope or wish was the sudden development of the relationship with Schiller. I account this as one of the highest favors of fortune during my later years. Oddly enough, this favorable turn of events was due to my interest in botany. Through it a situation was created which eliminated the disharmony that had so long put a distance between us.

After my return from Italy . . . I found certain creative works enjoying great respect and popularity which, alas, repelled me in the extreme. . . . Among these was Schiller's *The Robbers*. . . . It seemed to me that in this play a powerful but crude talent had embraced the ethical and dramatic paradoxes from which I had been seeking to cleanse myself and had poured them out over the land like a violent river. . . . The reputation acquired by these strange extravagances and the applause accorded them by everyone, from undisciplined students to cultivated ladies of the Court, dismayed me. I was forced to believe that all my efforts had been wasted. The style according to which I had sought to develop my own culture and the very objects I had used for this purpose seemed brushed aside or else paralyzed. . . . Had it been possible, I would have been tempted to give up the contemplation of the plastic arts and the exercise of my poetic talent; for what prospect was there of being heard above this tumult of temperamental outbursts and extravagant form? . . .

Thus, though he was living quite near me in Weimar, I had avoided Schiller. The appearance of his *Don Carlos* was hardly calculated to reconcile me. . . .

His "Essay on Charm and Dignity in Literature" only widened the breach. . . . Certain harsh passages in the Essay could have been interpreted as definitely directed against me; they exhibited my convictions in a false light. I felt, in addition, that the matter was even worse if I had not been personally meant; for in that case the chasm between our ways of thought would be seen to be all the deeper. . . . By and by, Schiller moved to Jena, where I did not see him either. At that time, however, a society for the cultivation of the natural sciences was called into existence. I usually frequented its sessions. At one of these I found Schiller. We happened to leave the building together. A conversation developed. He had followed the proceedings with true interest, but he made an observation, a very sensible one and one very welcome to me, that this fragmentary method of regarding nature could not fail to displease the layman who was not averse from studies of this kind. I therefore replied that the initiate, too, was perhaps estranged by this method and that there must be another way. . . . He desired this matter to be clarified. . . . Walking along together we reached his house. The interest of our conversation persuaded me to enter. I gave him a vivid exposition of my theory of the metamorphosis of plants and drew for him with a few strokes of the pen a symbolical plant. . . . But when I was through he shook his head and said: "You are not describing an empiric experience but an idea." I was startled and rather dismayed. He had stringently defined the very center of our divergence. . . . Schiller who had much more worldly wisdom than I, and who was much suaver; who, too, planning to publish his magazine *The Hours,* desired to attract rather than repel me, replied in his character of a trained Kantian. My stubborn realism gave rise to a lively contradiction. The controversy was not resolved. Neither could consider himself the victor, yet each held himself to be invincible. . . . Nevertheless the first step had been taken and Schiller's personal power of attraction was great. He welded to himself all who approached him. I sympathized with his plans and promised to contribute to *The Hours* sundry manuscripts hidden in my desk. His wife, of whom I had been fond and whom I had valued since her childhood, contributed her share to a lasting understanding. All our mutual friends were happy and so, despite the great and perhaps never adjudicated contest between object and subject, we sealed a bond which lasted uninterruptedly and brought forth much good for us and for others. To me especially it was the beginning of a new springtime marked by a happy germination during which many things sprang forth from expanding seeds and branches.

January 7, 1794

Elisabeth Goethe to Her Son

Dear Son, In all my life I never so passionately desired to get rid of things—wine cellar—house—library. How can I get away with all these things still on my back? And in all these tumults nobody dreams of buying and selling. If God will deliver us from the enemy and nothing more is to be feared, I will not stop or rest until I am rid of this worry. Now listen to my plan. All the proceeds of the sale of the house, the cellar, the library, I'll divide into two parts. I'll transfer one half to you for you to invest as may seem wise and profitable. But you must let me have the interest, since I will have no house and must pay rent, and no wines, for even the small wines must be sold, nor will I have the usual harvest in my garden but will sell the grapes on the vines, so that I will even have to buy my beverages. On the same conditions the other half of the proceeds will go to Schlosser. If I die, each one of you will already have a share of your inheritance. The capital that is invested here will stay here for the present and can be divided in good time. Be sure that, though the burden is grievous, I will proceed neither too hastily nor without due consideration. I will report to you and Schlosser and do nothing final without your advice. There are on hand five vats of old wines, two vats of 1706, one of 1719, two of 1726. The three first are the finest, but everything must be sold together. There are three vats from the vines in our garden of the year '47, but they're bad; one of '88 and '89, which are so-so and one of various years. . . . If I had an offer of 10,000 florins for the entire contents of the cellar, I would be tempted to accept. . . . I do thank you for your kind invitation to live with you. But I can't leave everything at sixes and

sevens. How would the military act, if an empty house were found?
I am still of good courage, nor do I believe for a moment that the
enemy will return. And finally I have faith in God Who has something to say in the matter, too.

January 13, 1794

Elisabeth Goethe to Her Son

. . . I thank you from the heart for your dear letter of the 8th in
which you offer me your help to get away from here with so much
loving-kindness. I do not yet entertain the slightest fear and do not
dream of fleeing. It is true that Frankfurt is in a state of panic and
it would be no wonder if one were infected by it. Terror is as infec-
tious as a cold in the head. I take good care to avoid the cowards—
so as not to have my brains addled too. It's hard enough to do. You
know how it is when a fire breaks out. Every goose and every ass
babbles out his opinion. And as a child, to whom its nurse has told
a tale of ghosts, thinks every white cloth is one—so it is among us.
If it only sounds frightful enough, they believe it, whether it's likely
or not. No one regards anything in cold blood. If it's mad enough,
it's credible. . . . But all this business and confusion has, thank
God, not yet caused me a melancholy hour. I get my eight hours'
sleep, eat and drink as is seemly, have my friends over every Monday and every third Sunday, as has been my custom and, what is
best of all, I feel very well.

February 6, 1794

Elisabeth Goethe to Her Son

. . . Now we're having mass billeting again for the winter—three
battalions of the Prussian Guards and so many wounded and ill that
the government has been forced to double the billeting since last
week. We'll have to see how we get by. The worst is the high price
of wood. . . . The sick colonel whom I have doesn't go out, of
course. So I have to keep the house hot all day. . . . But be things
as they may, let us not be prematurely frightened and let us pass our
days as contentedly as we may. We cannot grasp the spokes of the
turning wheel of fate without being ground under.

April 1, 1794

Elisabeth Goethe to Her Son

The "friends of your youth" mentioned refer to Goethe's favorite volumes in his father's library which had now been catalogued.

. . . What kind of foolishness causes your indecision? You're a queer child! Let me send you these friends of your youth which you hate to have sold. Pick out whatever might give you pleasure. What does it matter about a hundred florins more or less? You have the first and the best right to the books. Only see to it that I get the catalogue back before or at the beginning of the Fair. Early in summer another great library is going to be sold here and ours can be joined with it; that's more profitable. Remember that Schlosser has to see the catalogue and that it has to be printed and the copies sent out. So don't hesitate and delay. Take what you like and let it go at that. Then I can send you everything you selected at one time; I don't want to pack and forward more than once. Don't think that there's any chance of my being overhasty, though I'm not inactive either. I pursue the matter calmly, for he who seeks not, will not find.

May 25, 1794

Elisabeth Goethe to Her Son

Although the books will, I hope, be packed this week and then turned over to the drover at the earliest moment, I didn't want to wait any longer to forward the enclosed Holland cloth and the batiste. Don't be surprised that the batiste consists of remnants. Your bed treasure will know how to manage, so that it will suffice for cuffs and front insets for twelve shirts. A friend of mine always buys remnants for her husband. And why didn't I buy a bolt? Answer: Because this is just as serviceable and because batiste, the war having cut off imports from France, is enormously dear. I'm saving at least half. Use everything in health. My internal revolution is in full blast. What will be must be decided soon. Concerning the wines I have consulted sensible people among my acquaintance. One of them, who was recently faced by a similar situation, was good enough to give me the specifications according to years as well as the valuations and finally what his wines fetched. From which I can see, in view of the proportion between the two lots, that I can sell mine for 8000 florins. . . . One man did offer me 7500 florins. So I asked another merchant yesterday who offers 8000. In God's name he shall have them. . . .

The matter of the house is moving along. The agent has approached three or four probable buyers. . . . The agent is asking 30,000 florins. I hardly expect to get that much. We shall see. Meanwhile I seem to be finding what I need. If only I can get that apartment, I would be more than happy. It is situated on the Horse Market with a fine full-time view and the morning sun. I would have: in the basement one room with two windows for my maidservants, a kitchen, a court, a wood shed, a cistern and rain pump, and a cellar. On the first floor I would have a front living room with three windows and a lovely view and adjoining it a bedroom with two windows on the courtyard. On the same floor there are two more rooms with two windows each which give on the court. In addition there is a foyer, a privy and closets. It would be just wonderful for me. I would have a bell pull in my bedroom which would ring a bell in the maid's room if I needed anything, and so I would have all my accustomed comforts.

Jena, June 13, 1794

Schiller to Goethe

The enclosed prospectus expresses the desire of a group of men who hold you in the highest esteem that you honor the periodical which they expect to publish with contributions from your pen, concerning the rank and value of which there can be but a single opinion. . . . Since it is necessary to arrange to submit all manuscripts offered to the judgment of an editorial committee, we would be infinitely obligated to you, if you would permit us to submit to your judgment manuscripts that are sent in from time to time.

June 24, 1794

To Schiller

You offer me a doubly pleasant prospect, both concerning the periodical which you plan to publish and the collaboration to which

you invite me. I shall be happy to join your group wholeheartedly.
. . . An interesting discussion should arise concerning the fixing of
principles according to which contributions are to be judged. The
vigilance concerning content and form which will distinguish this
periodical from others should, at least for some years, give it a clear
advantage.

July 25, 1794

To Schiller

Be good enough to remember my friendly interest and be assured
that I look forward with the liveliest pleasure to a frequent exchange
of ideas with you. Do give my regards to your colleagues. An unexpected call of duty compels me to leave for Dessau and thus I shall
miss an early reunion with my friends in Jena.

July 26, 1794

Elisabeth Goethe to Her Son

. . . Everything is more madly topsy-turvy here than ever. Everybody
is packing and preparing for flight. Whence this crazy confusion
arose I cannot tell you with any assurance. Rumors arise which I
would not put down on paper. Never was it as miserable as it is now.
In order not to be wholly inactive and to anticipate whatever reproaches may some day be addressed to me, I have had my most
precious movables packed in three great boxes by our agent and sent
for safe keeping to Langensaltza. Why not to you? I'll tell you—'tis
the complete lack of any drovers on the road from here to Weimar.

J. D. Falk to His Brother

On the morning of July 17, 1794, I called on the Privy Councillor
Goethe. . . . He told me among other things that when Schiller
works he works with inexpressible intensity. When he still lived in
Weimar he would lock himself in for a week at a time and not permit
a soul to approach him. When evening came the food that had been
brought him at noon would be untouched on the desk at which he
sat. Yet he was never satisfied that he had met his own stringent
artistic demands. . . . After that Goethe spoke at length of Italy
where he had spent nearly two years.

August 14, 1794

To Friedrich von Stein

You deserve great praise, my dear boy, for never having imitated the faults and bad habits of your former foster father. You not only think of your friends in absence; you even like to hear from them and take pleasure in writing to them. . . . In the Rhineland everyone is worried and terrorized. My mother, too, has packed up her best things and sent them out of the city. If things get worse she can come to me. Schlosser has gone to Bayreuth. Germany is divided into people who are afraid or indifferent or those who welcome disaster. I would like you to tell me how things are in England. There the great activity of life probably devours everything else. For myself, I find nothing more advisable than to play the rôle of Diogenes and continue trundling my barrel. I continue the studies with which you are familiar; I would that I could be instructed and edified by seeing those things which you are now seeing. . . . Farewell and think of me.

August 15, 1794

Elisabeth Goethe to Her Son

I must give you an accounting in the matter of the house. I'll tell you how it stands and I request of you a prompt and decisive answer. Nothing is more dreadful than not to know what one should or should not do. . . . Yesterday there turned up a buyer who offered 22,000 florins. I suppose that 30,000 is too much to expect and this offer is not too bad. It can probably be raised—so at least I think—to 24,000. The utmost would be 25,000. I'm in no great hurry, but I want to know for how much I am to hold out. I'll sell or not as you and Schlosser desire it to be. Just now a little bit of omniscience wouldn't come amiss! If we have peace it might be well to wait. But if the French were to overwhelm the Empire and continue their victories—then I wouldn't mind watching the spectacle untroubled by responsibilities and possessions from a little corner of my native city. You men ought to have a better insight into this matter than a woman who understands nothing of it. I need your advice. I want to be free of this burden. I am quite resigned to sell or to let it be.

Schiller to Goethe

August 23, 1794

In the rightness of your intuition you grasp everything and grasp it more perfectly than any analysis can trouble to seek it out, and only because you grasp it in its wholeness is your inner wealth hidden from yourself. Minds of your kind consequently rarely know how far they have penetrated and how little reason they have to borrow of philosophy which can itself be schooled by them. For philosophy can only analyze its data; productive giving, however, is not the business of the analyst but of genius, which makes its constructions under the dark but unerring influence of the pure reason according to objective laws. . . . Although at some distance, I have long watched the path of your spirit and observed with ever renewed admiration the way which you determined to tread. . . . What, however, you are hardly likely to know, seeing that genius is always a mystery to itself, is the harmonious agreement of your philosophical instinct with the purest results of the speculative reason.

To Schiller

Ettersburg, August 27, 1794

No one could have sent me a more agreeable present for my birthday which takes place this week than the letter in which with so friendly a hand you cast up the sum of my existence and by your sympathetic understanding encourage me to a busier and livelier use of my abilities. . . .

How advantageous your understanding sympathy will be to me you will soon see for yourself. For, as you get to know me better, you will discover in me a certain darkness and hesitatingness which I have never been able to master, though I am always fully aware of it. Phenomena of that kind are inherent in one's original temper by which one is gladly ruled so long as it does not become too tyrannical. . . . Unfortunately I gave my novel to a publisher several weeks before you invited me to contribute to your magazine. Proof-sheets are already in my hands. I thought several times recently that it might have been suitable for you; it's the only thing I have that is at all massive and the sort of problematical composition such as our German public loves.

August 31, 1794

Schiller to Goethe

Our acquaintanceship which, though it came late, arouses such fair hopes, proves to me once again how much better it is to let chance have its way than to anticipate the course of life by busy intrusion. . . . Now I venture to hope that we may wander together down as much of the way as remains to us and do so with the greater profit since the last comrades of a long journey always have most to say to each other.

September 1, 1794

Schiller to Körner

On my return from my recent trip I found a cordial letter from Goethe who at last seems ready to meet me trustfully.

September 3, 1794

To Baron H. C. E. von Gagern

An eminent politican of the period, 1766-1852.

You do me the honor, Sir, which I would like to deserve, of naming me in the presence of our country in a manner which proves your equal confidence in my gifts and in my character. Not without painful sympathy have I followed the contemporary course of affairs. I have done what little I could as a writer and my very best as a private citizen to decrease the spirit of faction by clarity and moderation in at least a small circle and to re-establish its equilibrium.

Nothing would be more desirable for a writer, if he could flatter himself that the nation gave him a hearing, than to appear as the expressive organ of the active, leading, saving part of that nation, especially since there are so many who misuse their talent to increase dangerous excesses and to favor the trivial stubborn obstacle of mere party spirit. . . .

But if I am to be honest with you, I must confess that it might be more conceivable to persuade the ruling classes of Germany to unite in an effective plan for the defense of the country than to inspire them with confidence in their writers. The causes which work against this confidence on both sides must be sufficiently known to you. My few personal experiences tend only to confirm those melancholy truths. I assure you that there has been during this time no admixture of anything in my opinion and intentions, of which a decent German need be ashamed. Alas, one is generally forced into silence lest, like Cassandra, one be considered mad for prophesying that which is already at our gates.

September 4, 1794

To Schiller

I have a proposal to make to you: next week the Court is going to Eisenach and for about two weeks I am going to be as alone and as independent as I am not likely to be again for some time. Why don't you visit me during this period? You'll live in my house, of course. You could calmly go on with your own work. We could converse at convenient hours and see the friends who are most congenial and would certainly profit by this companionship. I would want you to live exactly as you are accustomed to do and to guide yourself quite as though you were at home.

September 20, 1794

Schiller to His Wife

I pass the greater part of the day with Goethe so that, since I need so much sleep, I hardly have time left for the most necessary letters. A few days ago we were together uninterruptedly from the moment I was dressed at 11:30 on until 11 o'clock that night. He read me his Elegies which, to be sure, are scabrous and not very decent but certainly among the best things he has written. We talked a lot about his things and my things, of the tragedies I have started or am planning etc. . . . He asked me to correct his *Egmont* for production here. He himself doesn't dare to do it and I think I will. He advises me to do some rewriting on my own *Fiesco* and my *Cabals and Love,* in order that these plays may become part of the permanent repertory. When it comes to his contributing to the magazine, he has zeal enough but not very much to give us. He will give us the Elegies for the very first issue. Next he proposed to me that we exchange letters concerning certain matters of interest to us both and then print these letters in the magazine.

October 19, 1794

To Schiller

You would not, I think, have been too dissatisfied with our production of *Don Carlos,* if we had had the pleasure of seeing you here. . . . By the end of the week I'll probably send you the Elegies. Most of the manuscript is copied and only one or two recalcitrant verses are holding me up. I am also sending some pages in answer to your first letter. The dictation is done, but some passages must be rewritten. I seem very odd to myself when I set out to theorize.

October 19, 1794

David Veit to Rahel Levin

> The subject of the discussion was Solomon Maimon, 1754-1800, a Polish Jew who made his way to Germany under incredible hardships, mastered the language and culture of that country and made significant contributions to philosophy and to the foundations of modern psychology. Half genius and half rogue, he is best remembered today by his pungent autobiography, the publication of which was made possible by Karl Philip Moritz, Goethe's old friend of Roman days.

Now to my pleasant incidents with Goethe. This morning I went to his house on purpose at an hour when he is always there but sees no one and sent in a note by his servant saying that I would return at 3 o'clock to ask whether the Privy Councillor would honor me with an interview. I did go at 3 and the man ushered me into the reception room.

GOETHE (from another room): You've brought me a letter from Herr Maimon?

VEIT: At your service.

GOETHE: And your name is?

VEIT: Veit.

GOETHE: Delighted.

VEIT: I had the honor of seeing you 18 months ago; I had an introduction to you from the late Councillor Moritz.

GOETHE: Ah, yes! I recognize you now. Well, how is Herr Maimon?

I explained Maimon's situation and the fact that he had to live on the little brought him by his writings.

GOETHE: Well, well, and yet he writes such powerful and such graceful things.

VEIT: True, but philosophy is a very hard matter.

GOETHE: You are right, it is very difficult. He is not well known and his public is very restricted. I wish he would come here.

VEIT: Did you see the outline of his new theory, Councilor?

GOETHE: Indeed I did. He also sent me the synopsis of another theory; I wish he would elaborate it.

VEIT: He would like to work together with other scholars.

GOETHE: Why should he? You see, in scientific matters collaboration is not necessary. When an idea occurs to me I tell everyone about it, indeed I must do so, and when the outline is seen, people know what to expect. In aesthetic matters it's the other way around: when a poem comes to me I cannot tell anyone about it until the poem is finished, otherwise I am confused, and that is true of all art.

October 26, 1794

To Schiller

Here are the Elegies at last. Please don't let them leave your hands but read them to those who must judge of their fitness. Next I ask you to send them back; I may want to improve them here and there. If you have any criticism to make, please let me know.

October 31, 1794

To Jacobi

We, too, are much disturbed about conditions in Frankfurt. I have invited my mother to come here, but she insists on staying.

November 1, 1794

To Schiller

Tomorrow morning at 10 o'clock I hope to arrive in Jena with Meyer and to pass some agreeable days in your immediate proximity. I trust that we will find you very well.

December 2, 1794

To Schiller

I can't tell you anything about *Faust*. I dare not unwrap the package which contains the manuscript. I could not copy it without adding to it and I haven't the courage to do that. If ever in the future I can bring myself to go on, it will certainly be due to your sympathy.

December 6, 1794

To Schiller

Johann Friedrich, Baron Cotta von Cottendorf, 1764-1832, head of the famous publishing firm of Stuttgart.

Cotta may be right to demand signed contributions in the magazine. He knows the public which is more impressed by a trademark than by quality. As far as the other contributors go, they can do exactly as they please in the matter. I must request that my contributions continue to be anonymous. Considering all my involvements, this is the only way in which I can write for your magazine in freedom and as my mood dictates.

December 23, 1794

Schiller to Goethe

I have not only read, I have devoured the first book of *Wilhelm Meister* with a kind of rapture. . . . I would be truly dismayed if I were forced to attribute the distrust with which you speak of this admirable product of your genius to any cause other than the magnitude of the demands which your spirit always makes upon itself. For I find not a single detail which does not wholly harmonize with the exquisiteness of the volume. Anything more detailed I cannot tell you today.

December 10, 1794

Elisabeth Goethe to Her Son

. . . I hope that the fabric I send will be comfortable for little August; it keeps you warm but is lightweight. Our fine Frankfurt candy will be available during Christmas week. . . . I'm not too unhappy

over the billeting this time. I have the head auditor and his wife.
. . . To be sure they cook in my kitchen. But we manage. You want
to know what I think of these 20,000 Prussians flooding our town
again? Well, I'll say what the Cardinal said to the Pope. This particular Pope had lived very tranquilly in a monastery. When he saw
the great crowds on the day of his elevation, he asked the Cardinal:
What do all these people live on? Your Holiness, they shit on each
other—each defrauds the other.

December 23, 1794

To Schiller

I am sending back the printed sheets of the magazine. The print and
paper are very pleasing. . . .
We had better put off our demands in the matter of honoraria until
the first number is out. Then we'll calculate and make our conditions, because we're certainly not going to let Herr Cotta measure
these fruits of our fields with his ordinary bushel measures. That
wouldn't serve the future of the enterprise very well.

December 25, 1794

To Schiller

I'm writing you a word in reference to the old gentleman in question.
He seems to be in great destitution. I have 20 thaler for him which
I am sending on Saturday. Meantime help him out and later keep
the money I send for him, giving it to him as he needs it, for it is
certain that he will never learn to manage money himself.

From the Supplementary Confessions

How could one recover any equanimity in 1794 during which the
monstrous events in France grew daily to be more terrifying and
threatening? The horrors committed by Robespierre had shocked
the world so deeply that no one was capable of joy even over his
downfall. . . . The unhappy division among the Germans in respect of defense and counter-action was clear from all the political
developments. Prussia refusing to announce its intentions demanded
the provisioning of its troops. . . . The Austrians crossed the

Rhine; the English retired to the Netherlands, the enemy occupied more and more territory and had more effective means. The news of refugees multiplied everywhere; there was no family, no group which did not sustain injuries. . . . On more than one occasion I offered my mother a tranquil dwelling in my house. She felt no anxiety for herself, however, and fortified herself through her Old Testamentary faith (quoting at the right time from the Psalms and Prophets) in her affection for her natal city, with which she had become so tightly integrated that she refused even to visit me. . . .

Nature in her accustomed way took no notice of these disasters. The fruits of her fields throve; harvests were anticipated by a month; all fruit, apricots, peaches, melons as well as chestnuts ripened to perfection and the year 1794 is even reckoned among the years of excellent vintages.

1795

January 3, 1795

To Schiller

Wilhelm von Humboldt, 1767-1835, Prussian statesman and distinguished philologist.

Much luck for the New Year! Let us pass this year, as we ended the last, in mutual sympathy with all we love and do. . . . Herewith I send the first volume of *Meister*. The second copy is for Humboldt. I hope that the second book will please you as much as the first. I'm bringing the third along in manuscript.

January 4, 1795

Schiller to Wilhelm von Humboldt

Goethe is visiting us and he is far too noisy for my taste. Since he has been here, however, we have been writing epigrams of one distich a piece after the manner of Martial's in that kind [*The Xenia in the XIII book of Martial*]. . . . We've done twenty of them in these few days; when we have several hundred we'll sort them out and keep about an hundred to be printed in the almanach.

January 19, 1795

Elisabeth Goethe to Her Son

Dear Son, My best and heartiest thanks for your *Wilhelm!* Ah, that was once again a time of joy for me! I felt myself 30 years younger and saw you and the other boys clambering up the three flights of stairs to prepare the Puppet Theatre. If I could clearly convey to you the feelings that overcame me, you would be glad, very glad, to have given your mother so happy a day. . . . I forwarded Schlosser's copy at once; I'm sure it did him good, too. And as for the appearance—such wonderful paper and such clear print!! You read it with pleasure. . . . Kiss little August—your bed treasure, too.

January 27, 1795

To Schiller

Thank you for the copies of *The Hours*. Their appearance is very pleasing. I gave one copy to the Duke in your name and I wish that you would write him a word on this occasion.
I don't doubt but what the magazine will do well.
The third book of *Meister* is off to the printer's. I went through it once more with your observations in mind.

February 18, 1795

To Schiller

. . . Inspired by the courage which arose from our conversation the other day I have worked out the outline of the fifth and sixth books. How much more profitable it is to see one's image in the mirror of another's mind than in that of one's own.

February 21, 1795

To Schiller

How very glad I am that you prefer to stay in Jena and are not yielding to the attractions of your former Saxon homeland. I do hope that we will work out and accomplish many things together.
Do let me have back the manuscript of the fourth volume of *Meister*.

March 1, 1795

Schiller to Goethe

I was not in the least surprised by Jacobi's criticism of *Meister*. A man like that was bound to be as much offended by the unsparing truth of your delineations of man and nature as you were bound to occasion that feeling in him. Jacobi is one of those people who seek only their own ideas in creative work, who want the poet to describe what, according to them, should be rather than that which is. . . . So soon as I suspect that a man is more intent in a work of art on anything except its inner truth and necessity, I give him up. If he could prove that the immorality in your portraits does not proceed from objective nature and that your treatment was subjective in character—then, to be sure, the responsibility would be yours, but not because you had erred according to a moral but rather according to an aesthetic criterion.

March 11, 1795

To Schiller

In spite of my intense desire to see you and talk to you I simply couldn't stir this week. I had to give auditions to several actors and I caught a cold on account of the bad weather which led to rheumatism—these were the successive hindrances and I don't see yet when I can get away.

Jena, April 10, 1795

To Christiane

Herewith, sweetheart, I am sending back the five empty bottles and even the stoppers that go with them, so as to set you a good example in careful housekeeping. I'm so pleased that you're all having a good time. I was afraid the weather might interfere with your amusement. . . . When you come here arrange it so that you can stay a few days. Love to the little fellow. Even if you're not quite well yet, I hope your condition is tolerable.

April 10, 1795

Elisabeth Goethe to Her Son

Dear Son, Coming Monday, which is April 13, I am forwarding two boxes to you. One of the boxes contains the Turkish grain, two pounds of Turkish yarn and some lettuce plants. I've had these latter dug up with the roots. If they're replanted at once they should thrive. Hereabouts they grow wild and are not cultivated and I've had a hard time getting them from the farmers. All the artichoke plants were frozen last winter. I can't get you any.

May 12, 1795

To Schiller

After the pleasant days in Jena the spell of harsh weather here gave me an unpleasant reception. For some hours I was exposed to a draft which induced a fever. The right half of my head was very painful and the left was of no use. I'm sufficiently recovered to stay indoors without pain and continue my neglected work.

I'm afraid that the best you can do will be to omit the second and sixteenth Elegies. Any mutilation or any attempt to substitute something else for the offensive passages would be conspicuous, nor have I any skill in such matters. . . . The second volume of *Meister* seems to be stuck in the jobber's warehouse. I ought to have received the copies and be able to send you one today. I'm now working on Book Five and hope to have not much left to do by Pentecost.

May 16, 1795

Elisabeth Goethe to Her Son

Thank you heartily for the power of attorney. Nothing could depress me today nor pour water into my wine except your catarrh, since one thing I can't stand is for you to suffer any physical discomfort— because I immediately have all kinds of anxieties. Otherwise these past two weeks have been just wonderful! The reason? Because everything seemed to combine to ease for me the trouble of moving out of the house and into my new dwelling. . . . The contract for the sale of the house was signed two weeks ago, and one of the provisions is that I could stay in the house until the right occasion arose and until I found a dwelling to my taste. . . . My heart is grateful for everything, and since I made you a present of 1000 florins from the proceeds of the sale of the meadows, so I'm going to make you another present of 1000 florins from the proceeds of the sale of the wines. You can begin to draw these sums at your convenience from the beginning of August on. . . . I'm also sending you 12 bottles of the oldest wine. . . . One more thing. I have a number of objects which would make moving difficult and for which there is no place in my new quarters. First of all, your famous Puppet Theatre; next the family portraits, next still other big frames, as well as—3 busts of Stein—1 of His Serenity, the Duke—2 of the Duchess Amalia— finally 1 of yourself. I'll have to deny myself all these in my new house. Either I have them packed up and send them to you by a drover or else I'll give them away.

May 17, 1795

To Schiller

Friedrich August Wolf, 1759-1824, professor at the University of Halle who in his famous essay of 1794 advanced the theory of the multiple authorship of the Homeric poems.

I have read Wolf's preface to the *Iliad*. It's interesting enough but I can't say that I was edified. There may be something to the idea and the scholarly effort is worthy of respect. The trouble with these gentlemen is that, in order to protect their weak flanks, they are apt to lay waste the most fruitful gardens in the realms of beauty and to transform them into fortifications. And in the end there is a much more powerful subjective element in this business than is usually supposed. . . .
The rest of the Elegies will follow and so, please God, will I.

June 8, 1795

Lotte Schiller to Goethe

Since the completion of his poem has utterly cut Schiller off from the world today and since he would like you to have a message from him, he asks me to give you his kind regards and to say that his health is tolerable. The attack of fever was not followed by another.

He wishes you were here now and that he could talk himself out to you. We were in hopes that you would carry out the good idea you had and visit us once more before you depart for your dark fir-forests. I dare say you know without further assurance how welcome you are.

June 11, 1795

To Schiller

Since I am not patient under physical suffering, I'm probably going to Karlsbad which, some years ago, did cure me of a similar indisposition for a long period.

June 18, 1795

To Schiller

The satisfaction you expressed with the fifth book of the novel pleased me greatly and encouraged me to go on with the work. I am especially gratified that my curious and not unhumorous secrets have had their right effect and that, according to your testimony, the execution of the scenes planned is a happy one. Hence I was glad to make use of your observations on certain passages of theoretico-practical chatter and have made good use of my scissors. Vestiges of an earlier treatment are always hard to get rid of, though I have shortened the original draft by one-third.

Karlsbad, July 8, 1795

To Schiller

So far I have only looked around and talked to people. What else will develop must be awaited. To provide for eventualities I have started a little improvised romance, very necessary to lure a man out of his bed at 5 o'clock in the morning. It is to be hoped that the sentiments can be moderated and the events guided in such a fashion that the affair will last only the necessary two weeks.

My reception here as a famous writer was most satisfactory, though the usual humiliations were not lacking. For instance, a most charming little female told me with how much pleasure she had read my recent writings and had been perfectly fascinated especially by Giaffar, the Barmecide. You can imagine how I modestly wrapped myself in our friend Klinger's cast-off Arabic garments and so made a most favorable impression on the lady.

Karlsbad, July 9, 1795

To Christiane

Over some tolerable and some bad roads I arrived in Karlsbad. The first days were very rainy; now the weather is improving. I've started drinking the waters and making many acquaintances. Quite a few chances to flirt, yet all the time I wish that I could show you the crags and the landscape. There are some wonderful promenades here. I'm sending you a box of dried fruit. Love to the little one. I look forward with pleasure to our well-ordered house.

Karlsbad, July 15, 1795

To Christiane

I am sending this letter by a returning drover. I have been feeling quite well. The waters agree with me and get rid of the evil elements. I expect to come back to you nicely rinsed out. The company here is numerous and agreeable; there is much opportunity for amusement and flirtations, all of which serves to convince me that:

> Go east or go west,
> At home it is best.

I am sending you, my little treasure, some beautiful taffeta. The taffetas are so fine here that it hurts one to choose among them. I'm adding something else that you will like.

Kiss Gus for me. In the last analysis I see nothing better in life than to love you and to live with you.

Karlsbad, July 25, 1795

To Lotte Schiller

Your letter arrived on one of the few sunny hours we have been able to boast of and would have rendered that hour even more enjoyable, had the news of Schiller's illness not clouded it again. . . . There are many agreeable and amiable people here and since I usually live alone it does me good to see so great and varied a company. . . . At first I picked up many acquaintances; at the end of one's stay this impulse decreases. I've done no work at all but have let these distractions do for me what they can. A week from today I hope to be on my way home.

Karlsbad, July 29, 1795

To Schiller

In a place like this where nobody is at home, everybody is more accessible and shows himself from his best side. . . . Everybody asks after you and I adjust my reply to the character of him who asks. For in general the public has only the obscurest notion of what a writer is. People use a traditional approach; of his true way of life and development almost no one takes any notice. Yet I must be fair and add that I have found a few noteworthy exceptions.

Karlsbad, July, 1795

From the Diaries of Friederike Brun

> Friederike Brun, 1765-1835, an otherwise obscure writer who was introduced to Goethe by common friends in Karlsbad.

One evening my friend brought Goethe to see me. No one can be less pretentious in his speech and silence or in his demeanor. His countenance is nobly formed but a bitter apathy clouds his brow. His excellent figure lacks elegance and his behavior poise. Is this, I asked myself, the darling of the Muses and the Graces—the creator of Tasso, Egmont, Iphigenie, Werther, Götz, Faust and, above all, the singer of those songs which make the heart rebel and tranquilize it again, which lull it to sleep and stir it with terror? All I saw on that first evening was the author of *Wilhelm Meister* who, doubtless, is worthy of all honor, too. Then, suddenly, at the flaming of his eye I saw the poet of *Faust*. . . .

◇◆◇◆◇

At first his glances, which I found hovering over me whenever I did not look at him, disturbed me; for they were the glances of an acute observer, of an observer without hope or faith in pure human values who is merely seeking for new models for some of his vivid portraits and peers into the world as into a peep-show. . . .
Fortune and the favor of women have spoiled him. He has reveled without enjoyment; he has taken without giving. Has his heart ever given forth one pure tone of love? . . .

◇◇◇◇◇

Today he talked to me at length about his domestic situation, his friends, his boy. He told me how, though shy of an exacting union he had nevertheless glided into such an one. . . . He also spoke of poetry, of the fact that it was subject to no law but the law of beauty and, impatient of any fetters, lived its free life between heaven and earth. . . .

◇◇◇◇◇

The other evening he was here again with little Rahel Levin and a young actress friend of hers who is very sensible and who has a great simplicity and sincerity in her glance. But the tone Goethe takes with women who are not strict with themselves is far from delicate. He has no grace or tenderness at all. . . .

◇◇◇◇◇

There was another evening on which Goethe was Faust-like and quite wild, as he is apt to be toward women who are mere things of beauty to him. Yet he said magnificent things about Voss, about Homer, about the art of writing letters.

August 14, 1795

David Veit to Rahel Levin

At a ball in Karlsbad Goethe addressed me spontaneously and amiably and asked me where I had recently been. I said that I had been in Teplitz and observed quite in passing that I had seen you, because I had known you for long and had really gone to Teplitz to see you. . . . He said: "You did well to do so. That Levin girl has done a lot of thinking; she has both sensibilities and good understanding. I must say that she is a rare person. Where will we find her like? She and I established a real intimacy; we were together constantly. Yes, that is very certain! If you hadn't seen her for long you did well indeed to seek her out." . . .

Ilmenau, August 29, 1795

To Christiane

We're not coming back right away, as you expected. There's so much business here that I'll have to stay another week. But I'm keeping

Gus with me. He is as well behaved as possible. He has taken in everything: the mine, the porcelain factory, the glass factory, and the mill which makes toy marbles. He got presents everywhere and talks about them very nicely. He takes to people well and everybody around here knows him. He sends you a big, white spice cake which he would have preferred eating himself.

Ilmenau, August 29, 1795

To Schiller

You can imagine no greater contrast than between the social idleness of Karlsbad and this busy little town. . . . I always liked it here and do still. . . . There is here a quiet, moderate activity of a practical character and everywhere observable nowadays the transition from handiwork to machine production.

Ilmenau, September 2, 1795

To Christiane

Well, darling, I'll soon be with you. I am leaving here Sunday morning. Both the little one and I have had a good time. The weather has been fair and sometimes even beautiful. Today is magnificent. Gus is well behaved and is charmed with everything he sees; he remembers things and asks sensible questions. He makes friends with everybody. I have had a miner's garment made for him; tomorrow the miners are having a procession and he will march with them. That amuses him immensely, but he refuses to enter the church with them. He's bringing you a cup and saucer which have been given him. He eats extremely well. I hope to find you well and the house in good order. I'm bringing along a roast of venison and intend to invite guests to eat it with us next week.

September 14, 1795

To Schiller

I haven't written you for several days because I intended to come to see you, but it wasn't possible. Meyer is preparing to leave for Italy. . . . As far as I'm concerned you must have felt how I was, as it were, poised to cross the Alps as well. . . . The magazine is daily in

my thoughts. I hope to do something for it. I do hope that you are
enjoying the beautiful weather under the open sky.

September 24, 1795

Elisabeth Goethe to Her Son

I congratulate you on the expected addition to the family. It does
annoy me that I can't insert a notice of the birth of my grandchild
in the local paper nor give a party to celebrate the event. Yet, since
nothing under the moon is perfect, I console myself with the reflection that my Cuddly Johnny is merrier and happier than in some
oppressive marriage. Kiss the bed treasure and little Gus and tell the
latter that grandmother will send him lovely things for Christmas.

Eisenach, October 13, 1795

To Schiller

I'm still here awaiting the development of things before I continue
on my journey. The Austrians have crossed the Main again and
surrounded Frankfurt; a battle between them and the French may
be in progress now. Well, I have no desire to risk my skin by being
drawn into such confusion; I happen to know how delightful such
situations can be.

October 16, 1795

Elisabeth Goethe to Her Son

I've been expecting you for five days. Now, instead of yourself, there
comes a letter in which you speak of a change in circumstances and,
to my sorrow, intimate a longer absence. . . . Whatever be the reason of your delay in coming, there are two things which I beg of
you: one, to tell me the precise day of your departure from Eisenach,
so that I may not sit by the window all day long and strain my eyes
watching every postchaise, as I did last Sunday. Secondly, that you
arrive by daylight. This is no longer my own house, and it is difficult to make the necessary preparations by night. . . . I am well and
gay enough, though somewhat morose over your delay. . . . Your
trunk arrived. Do come soon. And don't pass the beautiful autumnal
days in Eisenach.

October 16, 1795

Lotte Schiller to Goethe

We would like to know how you are and how you found things at home. Since Schiller is frightfully busy with the magazine he himself couldn't write. We were so grieved that you had to leave us so soon. Do come back, so that we may be as merry once more as we were.

October 25, 1795

To Schiller

I can't come today, but I hope to do so soon. Daily we are expecting the new arrival in our family, to whom I would like to give a friendly reception.

October 26, 1795

Schiller to Goethe

Let me congratulate you by anticipation. May it be a girl, so that our two families can be united by an intermarriage.

October 30, 1795

To Karoline Herder

In 1788 when Herder received a call from Göttingen Goethe had persuaded Karl August to assure the Herders help in educating and placing their children. The Herder boys had grown up; an extravagant bill was presented to the Duke. When he hesitated to pay it Karoline wrote Goethe a furious letter.

. . . It would not be advisable for me to talk to you in your present passion. Neither would convince the other. You have written me what I should never have had to read; I should fear to hear from you things that I dare not hear. . . .

At the end of a number of years you demand suddenly an indeterminate but apparently large sum from the Duke to supply the shortages in your budget caused by the study and travel abroad of your sons and insist that the Duke owes you whatever you have spent.

His promise to pay for your children's education and help them toward a career could not be interpreted as saying: do as you will about your sons, spend what you like, present me at the end of several years with a total bill and I will pay the expense of every step they took beyond the paternal door, for every extravagance and then, in addition, provide for them. Such an interpretation would not be admitted before any tribunal of honor or of conscience. . . . If you are willing to approach the Duke once more in the matter of the support and careers of your sons; if you are willing to make some fair proposal concerning both past and future expenditures, let me know through Knebel. I know very well that one is never grateful for what is possible to him, of whom one has asked the impossible. But that will not prevent me from doing what I can still do for you and yours.

November 1, 1795

To Schiller

Instead of a pretty little girl a delicate boy arrived, and so now one of my worries lies safely in the cradle. Now, if you want our families to be allied, it is for you to increase the number of poets by producing a girl.

Jena, November 9, 1795

To Christiane

I am all right and very busy. I wish I were sure that you and the baby were equally so. See to it that someone writes me at the earliest moment. I may stay to the end of the week, for I can think well and work well in my rooms in the tranquil castle. I spend the evenings with Schiller and we talk until late into the night. I hope the baby is drinking and eating and putting on weight.

November 9, 1795

Schiller to Wilhelm von Humboldt

Goethe has been here since the fifth of the month and remains for several more days in order to celebrate my birthday with me. We sit together and talk from 5 o'clock in the afternoon until midnight or even 1 o'clock.

November 20, 1795

Schiller to Goethe

Both of us lament from the heart the loss of the child. Perhaps it will console you that it happened so early and inflicts a wound only upon your hopes. I do not know how I would bear the loss of one of my children at their present age.

November 21, 1795

To Schiller

. . . I wish you would persuade Cotta to pay at once for the manuscript I send you. It will be easy enough to estimate how many pages of print it will be. There is no immediate occasion for this, but I think it looks much better and encourages people to contribute and helps to bring the magazine into good repute. Since every publisher has to pay advances, why can't he pay for a manuscript on acceptance? . . .

Did you read Stolberg's abominable introduction to the *Dialogues of Plato?* . . .

I got your letter this moment. Thank you for your sympathy, of which I felt quite sure. In cases like this one never knows which is better: to yield to grief in a natural fashion or to master it through those means which human culture offers us. If one decides on the latter course, as I am prone to do, one's condition is momentarily improved, but I have observed that nature will not be flouted and substitutes other crises to try us.

November 23, 1795

Schiller to Goethe

. . . I quite share your annoyance at Stolberg and company. . . . But it was never different and it never will be. You may be sure that if you have once written a novel or a comedy, they will want you eternally to repeat writing that novel, that comedy. Nothing else is expected of you, nothing else will be acknowledged. . . .

November 29, 1795

To Schiller

I return your treatise on poetry with many thanks. Since I am so
well treated as a poet according to your theory, nothing is more
natural than that I should applaud your principles and approve your
inferences. Nevertheless, I would have regarded what you say with
more distrust, if I had not initially been quite opposed to your opinions. For it is not unknown to you that, out of an excessive preference
for the poetry of the ancients, I tend to be unjust to that of the
moderns.

December 15, 1795

To Schiller

As far as time permits I shall try to make use of various criticisms
of the Elegies. In so curious a language as the German some point of
imperfection tends always to remain.

December 17, 1795

To Schiller

I have recently found a genuine treasure in the *novellas* of Cervantes,
both for entertainment and for instruction. How delightful it is to
be able to appreciate the good things which the world has appreciated and how improving it is to oneself to see works of that character
created according to the same principles which we use in the measure
in which we can among ourselves.

December 23, 1795

To Schiller

I am eagerly awaiting the New Year, trying to get rid of various
small business matters in order to be able to come over and visit you
for some time. What I most hope is that I may then find you not only
well but poetically productive, that being in truth the best condition
that God has granted man to enjoy. I'm hard at work on my novel; I
will not tire till it is done. . . .
The notion of epigrams, each in a single distich, like the Xenia of

Martial, we must continue to cultivate and print a collection of them in your *Muses' Almanach* next year. We must write many and pick out the best. Here are a few specimens:

> The century begot an epoch great,
> But a small race was the high moment's fate.

◇◇◇◇◇

> They speak, I know it well, in alternation—
> Successive monologues do not make conversation.

◇◇◇◇◇

> "Improve our morals, poet!"
>   So your back
> Dare not one hour the copper's night-stick lack.

◇◇◇◇◇

> *Publisher's Advertisement*
> "Mankind must know its destiny!"
>   How true!
> I have it at three "bucks" on sale for you.

1796

January 3, 1796

To Heinrich Meyer

Meyer had gone to Rome for two years, whence he returned in 1797 to take up his permanent residence in Weimar.

The argumentativeness of the Germans certainly sounds more repulsive in Rome than it does at home. And yet conversation is everywhere nothing but the exchange of fallacies and a circulation of the peculiarities of second-rate people. Let us therefore follow our own path quietly but very stubbornly. Let us not betray our hypotheses or theories or intentions, if we want the mob to retain any sort of good opinion of us.

January 22, 1796

Schiller to Goethe

. . . May I trouble you with a small commission? I would like 63 ells of wallpaper of a beautiful green color and 62 ells of border. I leave the choice entirely to your taste and according to your theories of color. . . . Here is a distich:

> *To a Moralizing Poet:*
> Man is a wretched creature—that I knew,
> And trying to forget it—came on you.

January 23, 1796

To Schiller

The coming week is going to be one of great variety for me. Their Lordships of Darmstadt arrive today, which means that tomorrow there will be a Court reception, dinner, concert, supper, and ball. Monday Mozart's *Don Giovanni* will be performed. The rest of the week I'll work at rehearsals. . . .

The wallpaper you want is not to be bought here. I'm sending you samples of both paper and border from Frankfurt. The paper comes in rolls of which each contains 20 ells and is 1 ell wide. Therefore you must have 4 rolls and have a considerable remnant. A year ago the paper cost 1 gulden and 20 kreuzer per roll. The border that goes with it comes in rolls of 40 ells and costs 3½ gulden. So you need 2 rolls. You may match green with green, but a livelier effect can be obtained by using a very fine rose colored border of the same breadth. If you will send me back the samples at once, I'll write to Frankfurt Monday evening and you should get the paper quite soon.

January 27, 1796

To Schiller

I'm not yet ready with the entire collection of our little epigrams. Meanwhile I'm sending you my contribution for this week. If we are to do the number we proposed to ourselves, we'll have to treat certain matters that are very close to us, for out of the abundance of the heart the mouth speaketh. Also it is a gorgeous chance to take these things out of the study and the world of reviewers and spread them abroad among the public. . . .

February 2, 1796

Elisabeth Goethe to Her Son

It grieves me that so brief a mortal sojourn was granted to that dear little son of yours. Truly, not all the blossoms can become fruits— and it hurts—but if, when the harvest is ripe, and a hail storm comes and crushes to the earth what seemed ready to store in the barns— that hurts much worse. And so, if but the tree remains, hope is not lost.

May God preserve you and dear Gus and your companion—this is the deepest wish of my heart. I am so glad that the nice bargain I sent proved its usefulness. The ladies of Weimar seem more skillful and seem to be better managers than here. . . .

February 7, 1796

Schiller to Goethe

> Abraham Abramson, 1754-1811, a distinguished seal cutter and designer of medals. 250 specimens of his art were once in museums and private collections.

Do you happen to know a designer of medals in Berlin by the name of Abramson, and have you seen specimens of his work? He wrote me in connection with a design on the magazine in order to use it for a medal. I'd like to know what he amounts to.

February 15, 1796

To Schiller

Abramson in Berlin is a skillful designer of medals. If you would like him to execute the medal, I would advise you to let our Klauer [*Martin Klauer, ?-1803, a local sculptor*] make a clay model in relief and send a plaster of Paris impression of it to Berlin. Abramson can work better according to it than according to a drawing. And who is here now to make an adequate drawing? A pity that Meyer is away. . . .

February 16, 1796

To the Actress Henrietta Beck

Since the member of our company, Herr Becker, has undergone the deserved punishment for the excess committed by him during a certain performance by being arrested and taken to police headquarters, therefore, now, it is decided that the actress, Madame Beck, whose confessedly abusive speech undoubtedly led to the outbreak of violence on Becker's part, shall be fined one week's salary, whereby, as far as the management of the theatre is concerned, the matter is settled.

Copy to the actor Heinrich Becker

Jena, March 3, 1796

To J. H. Meyer

The first half of last month I spent on theatrical matters; during the second half I came here and have now been here for more than two weeks. In addition to proceeding to the end of my novel, I have also translated a long piece of the autobiography of Benvenuto Cellini, in order to have the first part appear in the April number of *The Hours.*

I have the same experience in translating a book that you have in copying a picture: it teaches you to know the work through refashioning it. . . . The life of a single man may make us in a vivid though limited fashion the contemporary of a perished age. And it is extremely charming how his dealing with his art and the description of his life each points up the other.

Jena, March 7, 1796

To Christiane

Since the weather is quite good and I want to stay here a while longer I want you and the child to come over. You can bring along your brother and your sister Ernestine; I'll order a warm room for you at the inn At The Sign Of The Bear. You can come over to see me while the rest can eat at the inn. See to it that you have clothes enough to wrap up Gus during the cold nights.

I have worked so hard that I am saturated with it, and I'd like to

have a good time once again with you and the little one. I'm looking forward to it. Bring along money. Break the seal on the wrap-
pings of the key and bring me the silver which you will find in the
small drawer on the left side of my desk.

March 7, 1796

To Friedrich Gottlob Unger

F. G. Unger, 1753-1804, publisher and bookseller in Berlin.

I was very pleased, dear Herr Unger, to hear from you again. I quite
understand that you would like soon to have the manuscript of the
last volume of the novel. I can assure you that the hour at which I
send it to you will be a pleasant one to me. Your expectation and
that of the public is no keener than my desire to spare no effort toward excellence in this case. Among all that I've written this book
is in more than one sense the most necessary and the hardest, yet if it
is to be what it ought to be, the execution should have the marks of
freedom and of ease. So time and the right mood are needed. Add the
circumstance that various persons, excellent and exacting friends,
swear and wager that the work requires more than a single volume. . . .
A French *émigré* here has translated the first volume into French.
. . . If you were inclined to publish this translation, I would ex-
amine it more carefully. But you must tell me frankly the amount of
the honorarium you would be willing to pay.

March 17, 1796

Charlotte von Stein to Goethe

Thank you for sending me the letter. As for myself, I have received
six letters from Fritz on two successive delivery days. They are very
sensible and very cordial. He closes with a verse which he memorized:

—home is the resort
of love, of joy, of peace and plenty.

It saddens me greatly that the Duke is minded to send him abroad
again for several years. I was looking forward to a few years of domestic existence, and who knows how many years will still be granted
me?

March 18, 1796

Schiller to Goethe

The preparations for so intricate a matter as the composition of a
drama always create a strange stirring in my soul. . . . I would like
to know how you react to this situation. With me the initial feeling
is devoid of a clear and definite content; this content develops later.
First there arises in me the mood of a certain musicality which is
later followed by the poetical idea itself.

Jena, May 1, 1796

To Christiane

I do beg of you, my dear child, to enjoy the good and beautiful days,
such as not many people enjoy and not let anything annoy you and
spoil your pleasure. You know very well that I haven't the proper
concentration at home to complete my difficult task; I may not find
it here either, in which case I'll have to go to Ilmenau after all. Kiss
the little fellow. I want you both to visit me soon.

Jena, May 5, 1796

To Christiane

That's what I like to see, that you are gay in good company and then
again industrious and careful at home.
Herr Cotta sent various currencies as he promised; so I'm sending
you some money herewith. I'm well enough, except that the novel
refuses to move on.

Jena, May 20, 1796

To Schiller

A messenger summons me to Weimar and I must leave at once. But
I'll be back tonight and see you tomorrow. . . . Do send the manuscript with this note to the little woman. . . . Herewith some epigrams and a thousand thanks for all your kindness. Regards to your
wife. August looks forward so much to seeing your Karl.

Jena, May 27, 1796

To Wilhelm von Humboldt

. . . I am obliged to you for the sympathetic attention which you
continue to pay to my writings. . . .
Schiller visited us for three weeks. Now he has returned to his habitual life and does not leave his room even during the finest weather.
Perhaps I need not commend my Cellini to you. If you don't know
the original I hope you'll enjoy the story of this curious person in
my translation.

June 13, 1796

To J. H. Meyer

This letter may no longer find you in Rome. . . . What tragedy has
befallen that beautiful land. . . . We don't even know yet whether
the French have occupied Bologna. . . . Luck attends their arms.
From Düsseldorf to the Lahn the country is again in their hands. . . .

June 14, 1796

To Schiller

There are some excellent details in Herder's volume of criticism but
the total impression is unpleasant and you can see that the writing
gave no pleasure to the author. A certain reserve and prudence, a
twisting and turning, a tendency to ignore things, a parsimonious
dealing out of praise and blame renders especially what he says of
German literature thin and meagre. It may be my momentary mood.
But I have come to believe more and more that if you don't discuss
books as well as actions with an affectionate sympathy, even with a
measure of enthusiastic partiality, there is so little left that it isn't
worth talking about. Delight, joy, sympathy with things—such is the
only genuine attitude which leads to a genuine result. All else is
vain and brings forth vanity.

June 18, 1796

Jean Paul F. Richter to a Friend

Jean Paul, 1763-1825, the eccentric and romantic novelist whose reputation was furthered in the English-speaking world by Carlyle.

I was quite shy about meeting Goethe. He was described to me as cold
toward all men and all things on this earth. It was said to me: he admires nothing any more, not even himself. His every word is icy,
especially toward strangers whom he seldom consents to see. . . .
So I went without warmth, just as a matter of curiosity. His house is
striking. It is the only interior in Weimar in the Italian taste, with a
noble stairway, with a Pantheon full of pictures and statues. A chill
of terror contracts the heart. Finally the divinity enters, cold, mono-
syllabic, toneless. For instance, Knebel says: "The French have taken
Rome."—"H'm!" says the divinity.—His figure is compact and gives
out heat; his eye radiates, but no agreeable color. Finally not only
the champagne but the conversation began to kindle him and one
recognized—Goethe. His eloquence does not bloom and stream like
Herder's; it has more decisiveness and tranquility. At last he read us
or, rather, performed for us a magnificent unpublished poem which
act caused his heart to flame through the icy crust, so that he pressed
my enthusiastic hand. He did so once more at the moment of farewell
and bade me come again. He said that his poetical career was at an
end.

June 26, 1796

To Schiller

Here at last I am sending the magnum opus. I can't say that I am
able to rejoice, because at the end of a road so long one is always
weary. . . .

June 28, 1796

Schiller to Goethe

. . . Out of the mass of my impressions there emerges at this moment
most luminously the image of Mignon. . . . It may be an accident
because the pages opened on one of her songs and it moved me so
deeply that I could not later temper the impression. . . .

June 29, 1796

To Schiller

Business matters will absorb me for another week, which is not too bad, for else the tales one tells would turn one into a fable. Thereafter more epigrams and Cellini and work on the novel will take up the month of July. I am imitating your way of life and scarcely leave the house.

July 5, 1796

To Schiller

So soon as I received your first letter about *Meister* I reflected on a tentative answer. Now, in the midst of my rather earthy preoccupations, your two other letters come to me truly like voices from another world. All I can do is listen. Continue to refresh and encourage me! Your observations will make it possible for me to complete the eighth book so soon as my hands are free.

July 7, 1796

To Schiller

How rare it is that one finds any understanding amid the business and activities of common life. Such understanding is more than one hopes for on the higher aesthetic level, for how many people fix their eye upon a work of art in its own nature? . . .
Certain observations which Knebel communicated to me as well as what you tell me, convince me once more that what our hearers and readers lack is the power of *attention*. . . . They're willing to accept whatever strikes them immediately; anything that is an obstacle to them they condemn. They look neither forward nor backward; they regard neither the general sense nor its continuity. It never occurs to them that it is their duty to ask of the poet, why he wrote thus and not otherwise.

July 9, 1796

To Schiller

The fault which you remark upon quite justly comes from my innermost nature, from a certain realistic tic which leads me to withdraw my existence, my actions, my writings from the eyes of men. By the same token I like to travel incognito; I prefer the plainer garment to the handsomer; in talking to strangers or mere acquaintances it makes me prefer the insignificant subject matter and the less eloquent expression as well as to behave more frivolously and thus, so to speak, to interpose myself between myself and the impression I would naturally make.

July 9, 1796

To Schiller

Do remember me to your dear wife. In case you would like to send Karl over to us, while the addition to your family arrives, it would be very welcome to August and he'd have a good time among the many children who gather in my house and my garden.

July 11, 1796

Schiller to Goethe

. . . My wife is very near her time; the doctor thinks it may be today. Thank you cordially for your kind offer to take Karl off our hands. But he is no trouble. We have engaged extra servants and disposed differently of the rooms.

July 13, 1796

To Schiller

Good luck in all that pertains to the new arrival. Remember me to your dear wife and to the dear godmother. I would have invited myself to the baptism, did not ceremonies of that kind exasperate me so. . . . Today marks an epoch in my own life, being the eighth anniversary of my marital union and the seventh of the French Revolution.

July 22, 1796

Elisabeth Goethe to Her Son

. . . I felt not the slightest fear of the French and their occupation of the city. I was convinced that there would be no plundering. So why pack up? I left everything in its place and was quite calm. No one

believed that the Imperial troops would try to hold the city, and
the result showed how foolish it was. But they did it anyhow. . . .
So on the evening of the 12th the bombardment started. We all
gathered in the room of the landlord downstairs. When it decreased
I went to bed. But at 2 o'clock in the morning it started again and we
got out of our beds and I began to rescue my things, not from the
French but from the danger of fire, and in a couple of hours everything was in the cellar except the iron chest. . . . Up to this time
I was still calm. But now dreadful news began to arrive of people
whom I knew being hit by cannon-balls and having their arms and
legs shot away from their bodies and I began to get scared at last
and decided to go away—not too far—to avoid the bombardment.
But there was no conveyance to be hired for any money. Finally I
heard that a family in my neighborhood was driving to Offenbach. I
begged them to take me along and they consented very courteously
to do so. I am no timorous soul, but the night which I passed comfortably at the house of Mama la Roche might easily have cost me
my life or health. I stayed with her the 12th, 13th, and 14th. On the
15th the capitulation took place and there was no further danger to
life or limb. It was necessary, however, to get back on the 16th for the
French, upon occupying the city, insisted on closing the gates. I
would not have stayed in Offenbach at any cost, firstly, because I
wasn't going to have anyone consider me a refugee and, secondly, because I didn't want my beautiful rooms to be empty and so subject
to seizure, because I had taken my maids with me to Offenbach.

July 23, 1796

To Schiller

. . . The bombardment cost Frankfurt 174 houses. The French demand that the city pay 8,000,000 livres in cash and furnish the
French army with 1½ million ells of cloth and a great quantity of
victuals. In return the inhabitants are not to be annoyed without a
proper trial. . . . I have no news as yet of my mother. She lives on
the great square, where the garrison is stationed and has a view from
her windows of that whole semicircle which was under bombardment.

August 17, 1796

To Schiller

Although I happen to be at present quite dependent on outer circumstances from moment to moment, yet I hope that nothing will prevent me from spending tomorrow evening with you. I'll bring back the "votive tablets" which you have written. The verses are extremely fine and will certainly be very effective. If the Germans can be gotten to understand that a man may be good and able without being either a Philistine or a milksop, your fine epigrams will certainly accomplish it.

September 4, 1796

Charlotte von Stein to Goethe

Fritz von Stein had been studying at Karl August's expense. The young man now proposed to enter the service of Prussia which, of course, annoyed the Duke. He finally gave his consent at Goethe's request. Fritz wrote at the time: "The Duke says that both my mother and I are egoists and have Goethe to thank for this trait in our character."

I hate to burden you with a request about Fritz and thus withdraw you from the realm of the Muses to a more earthly one. . . . It seems to me from Fritz's letters that in the Prussian service, too, he would have to draw on his capital. But since the Duke expressly told me that he would get only the 300 thaler a year which he used to have, this is no very lucrative prospect either.

Jena, September 6, 1796

To Christiane

I can't tell you today when I'll get home. I'll be able to decide on Saturday. Things don't go as quickly as one imagines. . . . Be sure to put the household in good order and arrange things so that we can spend a good part of October here. Get yourself a riding habit and all that goes with it. Since the master of the stables is altogether obliging, I would under no circumstances rob you of the fun. . . . Send me some chocolate. Give my love to the boy and see to it that he visits Frau von Stein often.

September 7, 1796

To Charlotte

I am sending you, dear friend, a page meant to be shown to the Duchess. . . . I don't know how much can be done. The Duke has a natural and not unreasonable prejudice against such plans. However, I'll see to it that the matter is discussed and that some proposal is made to counteract the other offer. . . . Don't think that I blame Fritz in the least. . . . He is bound to be horrified by the prospect of such narrow circumstances. . . . I am enclosing a letter to him. . . . Do continue to let my poor child enjoy your society and cultivate himself by observing you. I cannot but be moved by the thought that you are fond of him.

September 10, 1796

Charlotte to Goethe

. . . Unless you come before Monday you'll find me gone. After Michaelmas I'll return from Kochberg and count on your good advice in the matter of packing Fritz's books. August is always very sweet when he is with me. It hurts me to be away from him for so long. You cannot but find it natural that my heart goes out to your child with so much fondness.

Jena, September 11, 1796

To Voigt

. . . I am very much obliged to you for the political information. If you do hear anything from Frankfurt, let me know at once. I am very anxious about my mother and I'm not at all sure whether, when this storm blows over, I should not insist on her coming to Weimar. As things are now, those unhappy regions may continue to change hands. . . .

September 17, 1796

Elisabeth Goethe to Her Son

. . . We are once more in the hands of the Imperial army. God grant that we remain so until peace is made. For the last seven weeks were like breathing with the hangman's noose about one's neck. We lived in terror of what was to come. . . . But when I got up at 5 o'clock in the morning on the 8th and to my inexpressible joy saw our Frankfurt civic guards on the square—I dared not trust my eyes but fetched my lorgnette. The poor boys have nothing but sticks, because the Frenchmen had taken their rifles. Thus they marched up and down. I cannot describe my feelings, except that, naturally, I thanked God with all my heart and when they blew taps that night it sounded better to me than an opera of Mozart.

October 1, 1796

Elisabeth Goethe to Her Son

. . . I am still in Frankfurt. No need to tell you that. If you were in Jena when my letter of the 17th arrived, it need not have been lost but may be lying in Weimar. I am looking forward with joy to the next volume of the novel. . . . Remember me for a change to Your Serenity and to our gossip Wieland and to Herder and his wife. We all had many good times together and are all still alive, praise be to God, and we shouldn't act as though any of us had departed to the land of shades.

October 15, 1796

Elisabeth Goethe to August Goethe

Dear Gus, It is splendid for your grandmother to get such a fine little letter written by yourself. I didn't know you were so clever at your age. If only I knew what would please you most this coming Christmas! Do you know, I think it will be best that you tell your father what you would prefer to have and he will let me know. Think it over, for you have a lot of time. As a reward for your lovely letter I send you some bonbons.

October 26, 1796

To Schiller

I am sending back the zwieback box. I have filled the empty box with duplicate copies of the philosophical journal. . . . I have thought of the next number of *The Hours*. . . . But nobody could edit the diary of my journey to Rome or my letters from there except myself. And then everything written at that period shows the character of a man who is escaping from undue pressure, rather than that

of one who lives and strives in freedom. . . . Rewritten with complete awareness these documents might attain a certain value; as they
stand, they are far too naïve.

Jena, November 12, 1796

To Schiller

Your two letters, my dear friend, arrived quite late in Ilmenau,
whither as to the Cimmerian regions, messengers go slowly and the
sun seldom penetrates at this season. . . . I have not so much as
caught a glimpse of the hem of a Muse's garment; I wasn't able even
to write prose nor capable of any impulse either productive or
reproductive.

November 15, 1796

To Schiller

> The poem that Goethe refers to is the epical idyll *Hermann and Doro-
> thea* in nine cantos which proved to be the most widely popular of his
> works since *The Sorrows of Young Werther.*

I have carefully revised and recopied the three first cantos of my narrative poem. I am looking forward to reading it to the Humboldts.

November 18, 1796

Schiller to Goethe

. . . People will never forgive you your veracity nor the depth of
your nature, nor will they forgive me, if I dare speak of myself, the
powerful opposition of my character to the age and to the mass
which constitutes the public. . . .

November 19, 1796

To Schiller

. . . The other day someone wrote me that a certain passage in the
second volume of *Meister* should have been made the central point
of the whole work. . . . Somebody else assured me in person that
my idyll might be a good poem but he rather thought that it had better be divided into two or three poems.
It is a wonder that at such remarks the fountain of Hippocrene does

not freeze over and that Pegasus does not shed his coat! Well, it was
so twenty-five years ago when I began writing; it is so today and it
will be so long after I have quit. . . .

Schiller to Cotta

Goethe has still a great deal of work to do before *Faust* is done. I
nag him all I can to finish and it is his intention to do so by summer.
The undertaking is unquestionably a most precious one. The book
will be a longish one of 20 to 30 sheets [*a sheet equals 16 pages*] and
he wants engravings, too. He counts on a considerable honorarium.
I am quite sure that he will let you publish the work if you meet
his terms, for his attitude to you is a friendly one.

December 2, 1796

Wieland to a Friend

Goethe, who was away in Jena for about five months, has been back
home for several weeks and continues to sustain an agreeable relationship to me. . . . He is a strangely and wonderfully made mortal,
yet withal so of one piece, so bona fide in all he is, so devoid of
malice despite his egoism or, rather, at bottom so kindly and with all
his anomalies of productivity a person of such mighty intellect and
inexhaustible talent, that I find it impossible not to love him, though
I often wish that he were different in one way or another. You are
right as to his share in those epigrams. But the world is not very
indulgent and our two epigrammatists, by pouring out their whims
and also their bitterness, have done themselves an infinitely greater
harm than all their literary adversaries together could have done
them in a lifetime.

December 7, 1796

To Schiller

To be brutally frank, I don't mind the way the mob acts at all. It is
not well enough understood nor often enough practiced that one who
has a claim on posthumous fame, should force his contemporaries to
come out freely with every grudge they nurse against him. For he

can obliterate such impressions by his presence, his life, his influence. What did it avail many a clever and meritorious man whom I have outlived that, through incredible indulgence, abstention from action, flattery and adaptability, he preserved a tolerable reputation during his lifetime? No sooner was he dead than the Devil's Advocate sat himself down beside the corpse and the Angel who was to take the poor fellow's part contented himself with a pitiful gesture.

December 8, 1796

To Körner

. . . I cannot refrain from thanking you for what you wrote to Schiller about the last volume of the novel. . . . Even though a man were capable of knowing what station a piece of work which he has just completed and which must be what it is, since thus it came to be, deserves to occupy in the realm of literature, a thing quite impossible, yet would the harmonious and penetrating opinions of others be most welcome. But since a man (I ought really to say *I*) is never more uncertain than about a piece of work which he has just completed at the expense of all that was in him and of his purest will and of which a certain stealthy judgment of his own believes that still other demands could be made—under these circumstances a sympathetic understanding, not of this detail or that, but of the whole work is infinitely refreshing.
Like a mariner who, though he has returned from a fortunate voyage, will nevertheless not stay in the harbor but fares forth again at the earliest moment, I, too, have set out on the sea anew. A narrative poem which may extend to 6 cantos and 2000 hexameters is now the object of all my solicitude. But the more my friends applaud what is already written, the more I am in dread that I may not be able to end as I have begun.

December 21, 1796

To Schiller

Two days after Christmas I shall accompany the Duke to Leipzig. Tell no one except Humboldt. Ask him whom he wants me to see there. Since we shall probably go on to Dessau, I won't be back for twelve days or two weeks. . . .

Late December, 1796

Reminiscences of Karoline von Wolzogen

Lotte Schiller's sister who had divorced Beulwitz and married a Baron von Wolzogen.

I cannot but remember with what profound emotion, the tears running from his eyes, Goethe read to us almost as soon as it had been written the canto in which Hermann talks to his mother under the pear tree. Drying his eyes he said: "Look, thus one melts in the fire that one oneself has kindled."